with best wishes.

PEACE
WITHOUT
JUSTICE

Margaret Popkin

PEACE
WITHOUT
JUSTICE

*Obstacles to Building
the Rule of Law
in El Salvador*

The Pennsylvania State University Press
University Park, Pennsylvania

Library of Congress Cataloging-in-Publication Data

Popkin, Margaret.
    Peace without justice : obstacles to building the rule of law
in El Salvador / Margaret L. Popkin.
          p.   cm.
    Includes bibliographical references and index.
    ISBN 0-271-01997-2 (cloth : alk. paper)
    ISBN 0-271-01998-0 (pbk. : alk. paper)
    1. Criminal justice, Administration of—El Salvador. 2. Rule of
law—El Salvador. 3. El Salvador—Politics and
government—1979–1992. I. Title.
    KGC5404 .P67 2000
    364.97284—dc21
                                                    99-34791
                                                    CIP

Copyright © 2000 The Pennsylvania State University
All rights reserved
Printed in the United States of America
Published by The Pennsylvania State University Press
University Park, PA 16802-1003

CONTENTS

        Purging the Military   106
        The Truth Commission's Work   109
        The Truth Commission's "Binding" Recommendations   125
        The Commission's Report, the Role of the Courts, and the
            Amnesty Law   140
        The Truth Commission: An Overall Perspective   159

5.   Institutionalizing the Safeguards Included in the Peace Accords   165
        The National Counsel for the Defense of Human Rights   166
        The National Civilian Police (PNC)   175
        The Role of Salvadoran Nongovernmental Organizations
            (NGOs)   192

6.   Justice Reform in the Postwar Years   197
        The Supreme Court and Judicial Governance   201
        The Role of the Attorney General's Office   217
        Protecting Individual Rights: Criminal Justice Reform   218

7.   Lessons from the Salvadoran Experience: The Role of International
     Actors and Civil Society in Building the Rule of Law and Establishing
     Accountability   243

     Bibliography   265
     Index   277

PREFACE

Working as an immigration lawyer in Los Angeles in the early 1980s, I represented many Salvadoran refugees who recounted stories of unfathomable repression. After meeting many of the brave individuals in El Salvador who carried out human rights work in the midst of this repression, I decided to find a way to work with them in El Salvador.

I first visited El Salvador in January 1984 when the Salvadoran military and its U.S. allies were shaken by audacious guerrilla actions that had blown up the principal bridge linking the eastern and western parts of the country and overrun a military garrison in northern Chalatenango department. Later in 1984, I returned to El Salvador with a delegation of lawyers. We interviewed a number of people about the treatment of political prisoners, the justice system, and U.S. efforts to promote judicial reform. After a week in the country, we prepared a report on justice in El Salvador, making sweeping assertions based on our limited knowledge of the country. Much of what we said then was accurate; but we could not comprehend the depth of the problems, their complexity, or the many subtleties I was to become aware of over the years.

I went to El Salvador to work in January 1985, and to my surprise, I was still there seven years later when the peace accords were signed. My years in El Salvador taught me many hard lessons as people I knew were imprisoned, tortured, and even murdered. I spent four years (1985–89) working with Father Segundo Montes, the first director of the Central American University's Human Rights Institute. In November 1989 Salvadoran army troops came on campus in the middle of the night and executed Father Montes and five of his fellow Jesuit priests, as well as their cook and her daughter, on the grounds of their new residence, just across from our building.

Throughout the 1980s I had struggled to understand the Salvadoran legal system and its relation—or lack of relation—to the violence going on around me. Naively, I had thought my public interest law training from the United States could be of some relevance: I had clung to the notion that law could be used as a tool to protect people. But over and over again, I had learned first hand of the irrelevance of law in El Salvador's wartime reality. And I came to wonder how much relevance the law had ever had for so many of the people I knew there, the *campesinos* and workers. What use was the law if ranking officers could order the murder of the Jesuits and expect that they would face no consequences?

Freeing political prisoners, of whom there were thousands during the 1980s, did not require finding the best lawyer to make creative legal arguments, but finding the lawyer most adept at negotiating with the appropriate judge or with the judge's secretary. When I asked a lawyer who had won the freedom of many political prisoners if he could help in the case of a community leader imprisoned on charges of collaborating with the guerrillas, he took me along to "talk to" the military instruction judge. The judge, a colonel, sat at his desk taking apart and cleaning his revolver; no papers were anywhere in sight. Neither the lawyer nor the "judge" addressed the issues of the case. Days later the accused was released from prison.

In high-profile cases, the law seemed equally irrelevant. When the Farabundo Martí National Liberation Front (FMLN) could not win the release of prisoners through discreet payments to corrupt officials, it exchanged them for military officers and other individuals, including a president's daughter abducted by guerrilla forces.

High-profile prosecutions of the military likewise had little to do with the role of law. On the very rare occasions when these prosecutions moved forward, enormous international pressure had been exerted. Even in those cases, the military never offered up more than the minimum: triggermen or midlevel officers. Prosecutions never reached those with the power to give orders for killings that would have powerful repercussions.

The bizarre verdict in the murder case of Father Montes and his fellow Jesuits shattered any illusions I had about progress in holding the military accountable for its crimes. The judicial investigation and trial were carefully conducted under the watchful direction of the president of the Supreme Court. In fact, the jury deliberated in his chambers. Out of nine defendants, and despite confessions from the triggermen, the jury convicted only the colonel in charge of the military zone and a lieutenant under his command.

The jury inexplicably convicted the lieutenant only for killing the cook's teenage daughter. No evidence linked him to this particular murder more than any other, and it could in no way be separated from the others. A verdict so utterly contrary to the facts and the law seemed to acknowledge the need to respond to international pressure by convicting a colonel, while at the same time demonstrating that the outcome had nothing to do with a functional legal system.

A year later, after the end of the war, a young man allegedly linked to the FMLN was tried before another jury for the 1989 murders of two spokesmen for the far right. Prosecutors argued for his conviction on the grounds that the jury in the Jesuit case had convicted two military officers. The only evidence against the accused was an "extrajudicial confession" that contradicted known facts to such an extent that the original prosecutor had himself called for dismissal of the case. The judge on the case had indicated that his boss, the president of the Supreme Court, insisted on a prosecution—and conviction—despite the lack of evidence. Before the trial, I discussed this baseless prosecution with an FMLN lawyer, who insisted that in any case the law was irrelevant—whoever pressured the hardest would win.

Over the years I followed the U.S.-funded judicial reform efforts intended to revamp El Salvador's criminal justice system. The failure of this program during the 1980s was not hard to understand, given the nature of the armed conflict and the enormous U.S. involvement in counterinsurgency efforts. Harder to understand was the inability or unwillingness of U.S. officials to recognize the failure of their program.

Even before the peace accords were signed, however, the U.S. program drastically changed its course, tacitly recognizing the failure of its earlier efforts. The peace accords and the international attention devoted to their implementation would seem to have provided an ideal scenario for true reform of the judicial system—as they did for military reform and the establishment of a new police force. But six years after the peace accords were signed, any such hopes had been largely dispelled.

The Salvadoran peace accords are generally considered successful: the FMLN was fully demobilized and incorporated into the political system as the leading opposition party; the military has been reduced in size and mandate, and it appears to have accepted civilian control; and the new police force, though flawed and inadequate to cope with the realities of a postwar crime wave, is universally recognized as a significant improvement over its predecessors. Yet certain critical issues have not been adequately addressed: the socioeconomic situation of the majority of people in the country remains as bad as, or worse than, it was before the war; and progress toward achieving a reliable, independent justice system remains painfully slow. Justice for those who suffered human rights violations during the war or lost relatives to violence has never seemed a possibility. Given the extent of international involvement in, and support for, El Salvador's much-heralded peace process, it is reasonable to ask why overcoming impunity and establishing the rule of law have proven so challenging.

After I left El Salvador in 1993, I was able to study these issues in comparative perspective—thanks to the support of grants from the John D. and Catherine T. MacArthur Foundation and the United States Institute of Peace. This book seeks to combine my empirical observations of the Salvadoran criminal justice system between 1984 and 1993 with historical and comparative research carried out mostly in the United States. Since 1993 I have continued to follow these issues through regular visits to El Salvador and ongoing contacts with Salvadorans and others working there. My goal in writing this book has been to analyze the complex process of reforming a criminal justice system in the particular context of El Salvador in the 1980s and 1990s. Although I recognize the unique nature of the Salvadoran experience, I am convinced that it can offer valuable lessons—many relating to pitfalls or assumptions that international actors should avoid. The ways in which international actors can and cannot move a process forward, and the role of domestic civil society are both critical questions that I have sought to address.

Trained as a lawyer and working in the field of international human rights, I have the perspective of an advocate who has worked closely with people whose lives are affected by these issues and who is seeking to understand how criminal justice functioned and how changes come about. Despite the hard lessons of my years in El Salvador, I firmly believe that evolving international human rights standards can contribute to improving respect for human rights in a country such as El Salvador.

Progress, however, depends on a mobilized civil society and appropriate international involvement. By following the Salvadoran peace process, I have also observed the effects of ignoring the dictates of international human rights standards in a transition process. Although not easy to assess, the long-term consequences of failing to establish accountability for human rights abuses may undermine efforts to establish the rule of law and may leave both victims and society embittered and without recourse. On the other hand, recent developments in Chile and Argentina suggest that persistence, coupled with the creative use of international law and societal pressure, can belatedly open cracks in the wall of impunity.

ACKNOWLEDGMENTS

The research for what would eventually become this book began in the 1980s while I was working at the Central American University's Human Rights Institute. The Jesuits at the UCA took the risk of hiring me in 1985 and gave me the opportunity to observe and, at times, be part of efforts to achieve justice in El Salvador during the following eight years.

In 1993 the John D. and Catherine T. MacArthur Foundation and the United States Institute of Peace generously provided me with grants that allowed me to carry out research in El Salvador and the United States and write the original draft of this book. I carried out much of the actual research and writing while I was a Senior Schell Fellow at Yale University Law School's Orville H. Schell Jr. Center for International Human Rights. The Schell Center provided a travel grant for additional research in El Salvador in 1994. An early version of the manuscript was included in the Schell Center's working paper series. I am grateful to Harold Koh and Ron Slye for the Schell Center's assistance.

I finished the original draft of this book while I was a fellow at the Washington Office on Latin America in 1995. While serving as Program Director for Latin America at the Robert F. Kennedy Memorial Center for Human Rights, I was able to revise and update my manuscript. I am particularly thankful for the constant support and encouragement of former RFK Center Director Jim Silk. Of course, the conclusions and opinions are those of the author and do not necessarily reflect those of the institutions that provided support.

Over the years, many people in El Salvador and the United States provided me with documents not easily obtainable, allowed me to interview them, and otherwise provided valuable information. Unfortunately, I could not possibly name them all.

I am grateful to the many Salvadorans who have patiently answered my questions and provided information as I carried out research for this book: friends and colleagues in the human rights and legal community, government officials, legislators from across the political spectrum, justice sector officials, members of the government and FMLN negotiating teams, and victims of human rights abuses. Salvadorans who provided assistance in this effort include Benjamín Cuéllar, Francisco Díaz Rodríguez, David Escobar Galindo, René Hernández Valiente, Ricardo Iglesias, Jaime Martínez, Florentín Melendez, José María Méndez, Mirna Perla de Anaya, José Albino Tinetti, Félix Ulloa, and Rubén Zamora.

I would also like to thank the many UN staff and representatives who shared their insights about the justice system, the civilian police, the truth commission, and the negotiating process. These included Blanca Antonini, Gino Costa, Pedro Nikken, Felipe Villavicencio, and Teresa Whitfield.

Likewise, many people who worked with AID's judicial reform effort were generous in sharing information or insights they had gleaned from their work. I am particularly grateful to Alberto Binder, Linn Hammergren, Deborah Kennedy, and Jorge Obando.

During the lengthy process of writing this book, many colleagues have reviewed part or all of the manuscript and offered helpful suggestions and encouragement. Martha Doggett and William Stanley went over my original manuscript in great detail and gave me many useful comments. Others who read all or part of the manuscript, offered helpful comments, or provided useful information include Carolyn Patty Blum, Reed Brody, Hugh Byrne, Charles Call, Margaret Crahan, Alejandro Garro, Robert Goldman, David Holiday, Juan Méndez, Rachel Neild, Diane Orentlicher, Denis Racicot, Naomi Roht-Arriaza, Keith Rosenn, Geoff Thale, George Vickers, Robert Weiner, and Richard Wilson. Of course, the errors that remain are my responsibility.

I am also grateful to Penn State Press for deciding to publish this book. I would particularly like to thank Sandy Thatcher for his enthusiasm about my manuscript and for his patience while I revised and updated it; Cherene Holland for overseeing the production of the book; the production and design staff; and Elizabeth Yoder for fixing so many of my citations as she copyedited the manuscript.

My parents, Richard and Julie Popkin, gave me their unflagging support throughout this long process. My mother, a literary agent, was determined that this book would be published and made the original contact with Penn State Press. Finally, my son Damian helped me through the struggle of writing and rewriting this book with his cheerful disposition.

As this book goes to press, important new initiatives have been undertaken to try to establish the truth and seek justice in El Salvador and strengthen the justice system, reinforcing the conclusion that this is very much an ongoing process. To those who continue to seek justice in El Salvador, I dedicate this book.

Abbreviations

AID – U.S. Agency for International Development
AIFLD – American Institute for Free Labor Development
ANC – African National Congress
ANEP – *Asociación Nacional de la Empresa Privada* – National Association of Private Enterprise (El Salvador)
ANSESAL – Salvadoran National Security Agency
AOJ – Administration of Justice (AID program)
ARENA – *Alianza Repúblicana Nacionalista* – Nationalist Republican Alliance (El Salvador)
ATJ – *Dirección General de Asistencia Técnico Jurídica* – law reform unit of the Salvadoran Ministry of Justice
CACIF – Guatemala's private enterprise coordination
CDHES – *Comisión de Derechos Humanos de El Salvador* – nongovernmental Human Rights Commission
CEPES – *Centro de Estudios Penales de El Salvador* – Salvadoran Center for the Study of Criminal Law
CESPAD – *Centro de Estudios para la Aplicación de Derecho* – Center for the Study of Applied Law (El Salvador)
CNJ – *Consejo Nacional de la Judicatura* – National Judiciary Council (El Salvador)
CONADEP – Argentine National Commission for Disappeared Persons
COPAZ – *Comisión Nacional para la Consolidación de la Paz* – National Commission for the Consolidation of Peace (El Salvador)
CORELESAL – *Comisión Revisora de la Legislación Salvadoreña* – Revisory Commission on Salvadoran Legislation

DAN – *División Antinarcotráfico* – Anti-Drug Trafficking Division of the National Civilian Police

DIC – *División de Investigación Criminal* – Division of Criminal Investigation of the National Civilian Police

DICO – *Departamento de Investigación del Crimen Organizado* – Organized Crime Investigation Department of the National Civilian Police

*ERP – *Ejército Revolucionario del Pueblo* – People's Revolutionary Army

FDR – *Frente Democrático Revolucionario* – Democratic Revolutionary Front

FENASTRAS – *Federación Nacional de Trabajadores Salvadoreños* – National Federation of Salvadoran Workers

FESPAD – *Fundación para el Estudio de la Aplicación del Derecho* – Foundation for the Study of Applied Law

FMLN – *Frente Farabundo Martí para la Liberación Nacional* – Farabundo Martí National Liberation Front

*FPL – *Fuerzas Populares de Liberación* – Popular Liberation Forces

FUNDAPAZ – *Fundación para la Paz* – Salvadoran foundation for the promotion of peace and democracy

FUSADES – *Fundación Salvadoreña para el Desarrollo Económico y Social* – Salvadoran Foundation for Economic and Social Development

GAO – General Accounting Office

HCC – Guatemalan Historical Clarification Commission

IACHR – Inter-American Commission on Human Rights of the OAS

ICC – International Criminal Court

ICITAP – U.S. Justice Department's International Criminal Investigative Training Assistance Program

ICRC – International Committee of the Red Cross

IDB – Inter-American Development Bank

IDHUCA – *Instituto de Derechos Humanos de la Universidad Centroamericana José Simeón Cañas* — Human Rights Institute of the Central American University José Simeón Cañas (El Salvador)

IEJES – *Instituto de Estudios Jurídicos de El Salvador* – Salvadoran Institute for Legal Studies

IIDH – Inter-American Institute of Human Rights

ILANUD – *Instituto Latinoamericano de Naciones Unidas para la Prevención del Delito y el Tratamiento del Delincuente* – United Nations Latin American Institute for the Prevention of Crime and the Treatment of Offenders

ISTA – *Instituto Salvadoreño de Transformación Agraria* – Salvadoran agrarian reform agency

IUDOP – *Instituto Universitario de Opinión Pública* – the Central American University's polling institute

JRII – Judicial Reform II (U.S. AID, El Salvador)

MINUGUA – *Misión de Naciones Unidas en Guatemala* – United Nations Mission in Guatemala

MINUSAL – *Misión de Naciones Unidas en El Salvador* – United Nations Mission in El Salvador

OAS – Organization of American States

ONUSAL – *Misión de Observadores de las Naciones Unidas en El Salvador* – United Nations Observer Mission in El Salvador

ONUV – *Oficina de Naciones Unidas para la Verificación* – United Nations Verification Office in El Salvador

ORDEN – *Organización Democrática Nacionalista* – Democratic Nationalist Organization (El Salvador)

PCN – *Partido de Conciliación Nacional* – National Conciliation Party (El Salvador)

*PCS – *Partido Comunista de El Salvador* – Communist Party of El Salvador

PDDH – *Procuraduría para la Defensa de los Derechos Humanos* – National Counsel for the Defense of Human Rights, or human rights ombudsman's office

PNC – *Policía Nacional Civil* – Salvadoran National Civilian Police

*PRTC – *Partido Revolucionario de los Trabajadores Centroamericanos* – Central American Workers Revolutionary Party

REMHI – *Recuperación de la Memoria Histórica* – Guatemalan Catholic Church's Recovery of Historical Memory project

*RN – *Resistencia Nacional* – National Resistance

SIU – Special Investigative Unit of the Commission to Investigate Criminal Acts (El Salvador)

TRC – Truth and Reconciliation Commission (South Africa)

UEA – *Unidad Ejecutiva Antinarcotráfico* – Executive Anti-Drug Trafficking Unit (El Salvador)

UNDP – United Nations Development Program

UNICEF – United Nations International Children's Emergency Fund

URNG – *Unidad Revolucionaria Nacional Guatemalteca* – Guatemalan National Revolutionary Union

USG – United States Government

USIA – United States Information Agency

UTE – *Unidad Técnica Ejecutiva* – Technical Implementing Unit of the National Coordinating Committee of the Justice Sector (El Salvador)

*Constituent organization of the FMLN during the war years.

INTRODUCTION

Six years after the historic Salvadoran peace accords were signed and twelve years of bloody civil conflict ended, Salvadorans were well aware that peace did not bring them justice. The justice system, so frequently cited as key in the postwar period, has struggled to establish itself as a fully independent and credible institution, capable of imparting justice to all, regardless of social or political position. Those who were excluded from judicial protection at the beginning of the war still found themselves essentially without recourse, both for what happened to them and their families during the war and for cases that have arisen in the postwar period. A postwar crime wave reached epic proportions: by some counts, El Salvador surpassed Colombia and rivaled South Africa as the homicide capital of the world. Violence threatened efforts to build the rule of law. In 1996 a Salvadoran public opinion survey found that almost half of those polled believed that "people have the right to take justice in their own hands because the government does not provide justice and security." Two years later more than half of those polled supported this view.

Long one of the least democratic countries in the hemisphere, with a tremendous imbalance in the distribution of land, El Salvador headed toward full-scale civil war in the 1970s as electoral fraud prevented broad

In the absence of any official or cited translation, translations from the original Spanish are the author's.

sectors of society from participation in the political process. An increasingly militant popular movement encountered heightened repression and had no effective avenues of legal recourse. Following the example of other Latin American countries, the Salvadoran government invoked the "national security doctrine" and resorted to forced disappearances of political opponents, forced exile, torture, and political murder. Instead of holding the military accountable for its actions, civilian leaders enacted, and the judiciary endorsed, draconian antiterrorist legislation.

Both domestic and international factors fueled the descent into civil war. The closing political space and growing repression swelled the ranks of an incipient guerrilla movement. Following the 1979 Sandinista victory in neighboring Nicaragua, Cuba's Fidel Castro urged the five Salvadoran guerrilla groups to form a united front. In October 1980, they formed the Farabundo Martí National Liberation Front (FMLN).[1] The (Christian Democrat) civilian-military junta that governed starting in 1980, following the October 1979 coup carried out by reformist military officers, decreed a major land-reform program and nationalized the banks and the coffee industry.[2] Still, the failure to establish the rule of law has been termed the "Achilles heel" of the Christian Democrats.[3] The junta declared a state of siege as the country descended into civil war.

The 1980 election of Ronald Reagan as president of the United States and the anticipated hardening of U.S. policy led the newly formed FMLN to launch its first nationwide offensive in January 1981. Keenly aware of the Sandinista victory in Nicaragua, the Reagan administration placed great strategic importance on El Salvador. It justified a huge and disproportionate outlay of military and economic aid as necessary to prevent a communist takeover.[4] Years later the end of the Cold War would prove to be a critical factor in facilitating a negotiated end to the war.

---

1. These were the Communist Party of El Salvador (PCS); the Popular Liberation Forces (FPL), an offshoot of the Communist Party; the People's Revolutionary Army (ERP); the National Resistance (RN), which had split from the ERP following that organization's 1975 execution of revolutionary poet Roque Dalton; and the Central American Workers Revolutionary Party (PRTC).

2. See, e.g., Enrique Baloyra, *El Salvador in Transition* (Chapel Hill: University of North Carolina Press, 1982).

3. Ibid., 106.

4. Military aid went from 6 million dollars in 1980 to 196.6 million dollars in 1984, totaling over one billion dollars in 1990. Economic aid went from 58.2 million dollars in 1980 to a high of 462.9 million dollars in 1987 and reached close to three billion dollars in 1990 (Americas Watch, *El Salvador's Decade of Terror* [New Haven: Yale University Press, 1991], app. 1). For a comprehensive account of U.S. policy in El Salvador and Central America in recent years, see Cynthia Arnson, *Crossroads: Congress, the President, and Central America*

In 1982, with the election of a Constituent Assembly and a provisional president, El Salvador ended almost fifty years of direct military participation in government. In 1984 Christian Democrat José Napoleón Duarte was elected president with strong support from the United States. Elections were held seven times between 1982 and 1992, with the eventual participation of a broader spectrum of political parties. In addition, the country experienced a gradual liberalization and reduction of restrictions on freedom of the press throughout the 1980s.

Despite these initiatives, the armed forces, bloated by massive aid from the United States, remained the real power in the country as they carried out counterinsurgency warfare. Human rights violations continued at alarming levels, and those responsible were not held accountable. The judiciary lacked independence and failed to investigate cases of serious human rights violations. Large sectors of the population found themselves excluded from the political process: the left and the popular sectors it represented were not included in the democratic opening. The outbreak of war led to increasing militarization and restrictions on individual liberties, precluding the consolidation of democracy. A former U.S. ambassador to El Salvador characterizes failures of the justice system in the 1980s as having been "the most ominous threat to maintaining U.S. assistance, to the American Government's ability to continue pursuit of a policy involving an investment of ten years, and over five billion dollars."[5]

At the outset of the UN-mediated peace negotiations, the goals set by the negotiators were to end the armed conflict by political means, to promote the democratization of the country, to guarantee unrestricted respect for human rights, and to reunify Salvadoran society.[6] While two of these goals

---

1976–1993, 2d ed. (University Park: Pennsylvania State University Press, 1993); Thomas Carothers, *In the Name of Democracy: U.S. Policy Toward Latin America in the Reagan Years* (Berkeley and Los Angeles: University of California Press, 1991).

5. William Graham Walker, *Justice and Development: A Study* (USAID, January 1995). Walker served as ambassador from 1988 until 1992.

6. These goals were established in the Geneva Agreement of April 4, 1990. See Report of the Secretary-General on the Situation in Central America; UN Doc. A/45/706-S/21931, November 8, 1990, Annex I, reprinted in *The United Nations and El Salvador 1990–1995*, UN Blue Book Series, vol. 4 (hereafter cited as *The UN and El Salvador*). For background on the negotiations, see George Vickers, "The Political Reality After Eleven Years of War," in *Is There a Transition to Democracy in El Salvador?* ed. Joseph S. Tulchin (Boulder and London: Lynne Rienner Publishers, 1992), 25 (hereafter *Is There a Transition?*); Terry Lynn Karl, "El Salvador's Negotiated Revolution," *Foreign Affairs* 71 (1992): 147; George Vickers, "El Salvador: A Negotiated Revolution," *NACLA Report on the Americas* 25, no. 5 (May 1992); Hugh Byrne, *El Salvador's Civil War: A Study of Revolution* (Boulder: Lynne Reinner Publishers, 1996); William M. LeoGrande, *Our Own Backyard: The United States in Central America, 1997–1992* (Chapel Hill and London: University of North Carolina Press, 1998).

related to the armed conflict itself, the other two—democratization and respect for human rights—were meant to address causes of the war that continued to hamper its resolution. The parties explicitly recognized that a meaningful end to the civil conflict required more than an end to armed combat.

The peace accords brokered by the United Nations and signed by the government of El Salvador and the FMLN on January 16, 1992, gave new impetus to efforts to consolidate democracy in El Salvador. The Salvadoran peace process was the first in which the United Nations successfully mediated the resolution of an internal armed conflict and assisted in "peace-building" after an agreement had been reached.[7] Unlike the more common Latin American "transition to democracy" heralded by the end of a dictatorship or authoritarian rule,[8] the Salvadoran peace process did not call for a change of government. Instead, it was the product of a negotiated agreement between an elected government with an undefeated military, and an undefeated insurgency. Because the FMLN had not been defeated and enjoyed substantial support inside El Salvador as well as international recognition, it was able to negotiate a far-reaching peace agreement as the price for ending the war. On the other hand, the first "transition" government consisted of the same authorities that were in power during the war.

President Alfredo Cristiani of the right-wing Republican Nationalist Alliance (ARENA) was elected to a five-year term in March 1989, succeeding Christian Democrat José Napoleón Duarte. ARENA, while not in control of the presidency during most of the 1980s, was heavily implicated

7. The Salvadoran government and the insurgent FMLN signed the formal agreement to enter into UN-mediated peace talks in Geneva on April 4, 1990. See UN Secretary-General Boutros Boutros-Ghali, *Agenda for Peace*, UN Doc. A/47/277, June 17, 1992. In the Esquipulas II Agreement signed on August 7, 1987, spearheaded by Costa Rican President Oscar Arias in 1987, the Central American presidents undertook to launch a process of democratization in their countries, to promote a national dialogue, to decree a general amnesty, to bring about a genuine cease-fire and to promote the holding of free, pluralistic, and fair elections. *The United Nations and El Salvador*, 9–10.

For a critical discussion of the UN role, see David Holiday and William Stanley, "Building the Peace: Preliminary Lessons from El Salvador," *Journal of International Affairs* 46 (1993): 415.

8. For analyses of various transitions to democracy in Latin America, see, e.g., Guillermo O'Donnell, Philippe C. Schmitter, and Laurence Whitehead, *Transitions from Authoritarian Rule* (1986); Larry Diamond et al., eds., *Democracy in Developing Countries: Latin America* (1989). These studies focus on large South American countries such as Peru, Argentina, Brazil, Chile, and Paraguay. Some of these countries had experience with democratic politics, and all were emerging from bureaucratic authoritarian regimes. Similar scholarly attention has not been focused on El Salvador. See Tulchin, *Is There a Transition?*

in death-squad activities and repression throughout the war years. Until mid-1994, all three branches of government remained under the control of ARENA. After the March 1994 elections, ARENA retained the presidency and effective control of the legislature, although the FMLN won the second largest parliamentary delegation. Until June 1994, the Supreme Court was led by an ARENA hard-liner. Military leaders were replaced, but the new leaders represented continuity rather than a break with the past.

The remarkable resolution of the armed conflict, including a highly successful demobilization of guerrilla forces and political reconciliation, has been rightly admired; but the obstacles to building the rule of law, an essential element for democratization and respect for human rights, have proven far less tractable.

The FMLN had placed human rights and the judicial system on the negotiating agenda.[9] In its effort to ensure a durable solution in El Salvador, the United Nations turned to international experts in the human rights field to assist in the negotiation and implementation processes. Yet the negotiators' efforts in this area were limited by a number of practical and political constraints. Unlike the negotiations about the armed forces and the creation of a new civilian police force, no blueprint for reform of the judiciary emerged.

Nonetheless, several mechanisms were ultimately established to overcome impunity and guarantee human rights. These included a commission to purge the military of human rights violators (the "Ad Hoc Commission"), a commission to examine the most serious acts of violence that occurred

---

9. The Caracas Agreement of May 21, 1990, established the negotiating agenda. A cease-fire was to follow political agreements in the areas of armed forces, human rights, judicial system, electoral system, constitutional reform, socioeconomic problems, and UN verification. Then further political agreements were to be negotiated after a cease-fire. This two-step negotiating plan was later changed by agreement of the parties to a one-stage process (New York Agreement of September 25, 1991, UN Doc. A/46/502-S/23082, September 26, 1991, and addendum, A/46/502/Add.1-S/23082/Add.1, October 7, 1991). A final peace agreement was negotiated in New York at the end of 1991 and formally signed at Mexico's Chapúltepec Palace on January 16, 1992. For reports on progress and setbacks in the implementation of the different agreements reached, see George Vickers and Jack Spence et al., *Endgame: A Progress Report on Implementation of the Salvadoran Peace Accords* (December 3, 1992); Jack Spence and George Vickers et al., *A Negotiated Revolution? A Two Year Progress Report on the Salvadoran Peace Accords* (March 1994); Jack Spence, David R. Dye, and George Vickers, *El Salvador: Elections of the Century*; Kevin Murray et al., *Rescuing Reconstruction: The Debate on Post-War Economic Recovery in El Salvador* (May 1994); Jack Spence, George Vickers, and David Dye, *The Salvadoran Peace Accords and Democratization: A Three-Year Progress Report and Recommendations* (March 1995); Jack Spence and David Dye et al., *Chapúltepec: Five Years Later, El Salvador's Political Reality and Uncertain Future* (January 1997).

during the war (the "Truth Commission"), a temporary UN human rights verification mission, a new National Counsel for the Defense of Human Rights, the replacement of military security forces with a civilian police force, and constitutional reforms to enhance the independence of the judiciary.

Those involved in negotiating transitions often portray as inevitable—or as a necessary compromise for the sake of a peaceful transition—the inclusion of agreements not to establish accountability for war crimes, crimes against humanity, and serious violations of human rights. The effects of foreclosing the possibility of establishing accountability remain in great dispute. These compromises may be far more acceptable to those involved in the negotiations—the political and military elites and international mediators—than they are to most victims. They often contradict or undermine precepts of international law that call for investigation and punishment of acts that constitute war crimes, genocide, torture, and crimes against humanity. Recent events, including the reaction to the publication of South Africa's Truth and Reconciliation Commission report and the arrest of General Augusto Pinochet in London, have illustrated the complexities of these trade-offs.

In El Salvador, the UN Truth Commission's report was hastily followed by a sweeping amnesty law, which has been understood to foreclose not only criminal prosecutions but also judicial investigations to determine the fate of victims. Despite the FMLN's emphasis on ending military impunity and its insistence on the formation of the Ad Hoc and Truth Commissions, the parties had understood that the peace process would eventually include a broad amnesty. Concerned with creating the conditions for consolidating democracy for the future and fearful that its own members could be prosecuted, the FMLN was willing to sacrifice its calls for accountability. No reparations have been provided to victims of human rights violations or their family members. These compromises leave survivors and society without any recourse against those responsible for heinous crimes. They may also complicate efforts to build the rule of law.

Since the 1970s, international bodies have decried the weakness of the Salvadoran judicial system in failing to confront rampant human rights abuses. Yet not until the Truth Commission issued its March 1993 report blaming the judiciary for complicity in the massive human rights violations that occurred during the war, were the failings of the legal system widely understood as a crucial institutional problem that needed to be overcome if more democratic structures were to take root in El Salvador. According to the Truth Commission:

None of the three branches of Government—judicial, legislative or executive—was capable of restraining the military's overwhelming control of society. The judiciary was weakened as it fell victim to intimidation and the foundations were laid for its corruption; since it had never enjoyed genuine institutional independence from the legislative and executive branches, its ineffectiveness steadily increased until it became, through its inaction or its appalling submissiveness, a factor which contributed to the tragedy suffered by the country.[10]

The Commission found that the judiciary bore "tremendous responsibility" for "the impunity with which serious acts of violence such as those described in this report occurred."[11]

Although the pressures of wartime and the heightened military control over supposedly civilian institutions exacerbated and focused attention on the subservient status of the judicial system, the lack of justice in El Salvador is often cited as one of the root causes of the war. A justice system seen as capable of protecting rights and redressing wrongs *regardless of the power of those responsible*—a system that had never existed in El Salvador—is a necessary component of a democracy. While no justice system is above criticism in this regard, there is a vast difference between a system that enjoys general credibility but fails in some cases, and one that forgoes serious investigation if it would affect powerful interests.

Although certain kinds of abuses are likely to become less prevalent (or disappear) because the war ended, failure to transform the judiciary leaves the citizenry without an essential protection against arbitrary treatment and might limit the success of other basic reforms, such as the new civilian police. The escalation in common crime that appears to accompany postwar or post-authoritarian periods accentuates the need for an effective justice system.

This book focuses on the judicial system, a critical weakness in the Salvadoran institutional structure, and the related decision by Salvadoran political actors to forgo any domestic effort to establish accountability for the thousands of human rights abuses committed during the war. Although not a traditional focus of study in the literature on democratic transitions, an

10. *From Madness to Hope, the 12-Year War in El Salvador,* Report of the Truth Commission for El Salvador (San Salvador and New York: United Nations, 1992–1993), appendix to UN Doc. S/25500, April 1, 1993, 172. This report was released in New York on March 15, 1993.
11. Ibid., 177.

effective and independent justice system is increasingly recognized as crucial to the consolidation of democracy.[12] The international community and many Salvadorans now recognize the importance of an independent judiciary, yet transforming this branch of government in El Salvador has been particularly difficult.

Ironically, in El Salvador the judiciary has proven more resistant to reform than the military. There are a number of explanations for this phenomenon, including the institutional nature and history of the judiciary and the complex relation between other aspects of a society and its legal system. A justice system is usually less susceptible to outside pressure than is the military, which is likely to be more reliant on outside support. Moreover, judicial reform involves more players in different branches of government. International pressure is most effective on the executive branch. International actors tend to be more knowledgeable about the military, which they may have trained and supplied, and with whom they are likely to have maintained a collegial relationship through military attachés, training, or even joint maneuvers.

In the Salvadoran case, other complicating factors include the limited attention given to this topic in the negotiations; the resistance of the head of the Salvadoran judiciary to reforms and outside pressure; and the apparent sensitivity of judicial reform, especially when international actors are seen to be promoting it. In contrast to the judiciary's nonparticipation in the negotiations, representatives of the armed forces were at the negotiating table and played a crucial role in ensuring a successful outcome. On a formal level, the armed forces are part of the executive branch and subordinate to the president; the Supreme Court is not. Although eight years have passed since the signing of the Salvadoran peace agreements, the transition process remains incomplete: justice reform is a work in progress, and El Salvador has yet to decide how to pay its "debt to the past."

Reflecting the importance the international community now gives to improving the administration of justice as a prerequisite for sustainable development, the United Nations Development Program (UNDP), the World Bank, and the Inter-American Development Bank (IDB) have recently incorporated within their mandates projects to improve the administration

12. See Irwin P. Stotzky, ed., *Transition to Democracy in Latin America: The Role of the Judiciary* (Boulder: Westview Press, 1993); Alejandro M. Garro, "Nine Years of Transition to Democracy in Argentina: Partial Failure or Qualified Success?" *Columbia Journal of Transnational Law* 31 (1993): 1, 5.

of justice.[13] International donors are becoming increasingly aware of the complexity of assuring the independence, fairness, and reliability of the judiciary in countries in which the judiciary has never played a significant role in controlling abuses by the executive branch.[14] Yet, as one U.S. AID official put it, nobody doubts the importance of judicial reform, but nobody really knows how to make it work.

The Salvadoran case raises key questions about the role of the international community in ensuring accountability and promoting judicial reform. Practical questions of strategies and determining how change can be effected must be accompanied by discussion of which activities or roles are appropriate for international actors and which should be reserved for domestic players. How can international involvement help build domestic capacity and institutions so that peace and development will be sustainable?

This book first describes the context for recent reform efforts spurred by the United States and the peace negotiations by looking at the state of the judicial system before reforms were undertaken. The second chapter addresses U.S. and, to a lesser degree, Salvadoran efforts initiated during the war years. Chapter 3 examines how justice and accountability issues were addressed in the peace process. Chapter 4 looks at how different parts of the peace accords relating to these issues have been implemented: the temporary bodies established by the accords, the new permanent institutions designed to safeguard human rights, and reforms to the justice system. The final chapter attempts to draw some lessons about the complexities of international involvement and the role of civil society.

13. See Edmundo Jarquín and Fernando Carrillo, eds., *Justice Delayed: Judicial Reform in Latin America* (Washington, D.C.: Inter-American Development Bank, 1998) (hereafter *Justice Delayed*); *Justice and Development in Latin America and the Caribbean* (1994), proceedings from a 1993 seminar sponsored by the Inter-American Development Bank in San José, Costa Rica (hereafter *Justice and Development*); Jorge Obando, "Reform of the Justice Sector," in *Governance and Democratic Development in Latin America and the Caribbean* (New York: UN Development Program, 1997).
14. See Stotzky, *Transition to Democracy*; Garro, "Nine Years of Transition," 72.

1

THE CONTEXT FOR EARLY REFORM EFFORTS

The Salvadoran Legal System in Historical Perspective

The lack of justice in El Salvador became internationally known in the 1980s because of the war. There is no indication, however, that the legal system was ever independent, efficient, reliable, or accessible to the vast majority of Salvadorans. Instead, abuse of power by state actors and their powerful allies and a lack of legal recourse against such abuses are frequently cited among the causes of the war.

The Salvadoran legal system, like others in Latin America, was based on European models at the time of independence from Spain (1821). In the past two hundred years, European nations have undergone profound changes, which have been reflected in their legal systems. The French Revolution introduced continental European legal systems to the Anglo-Saxon model of a public, accusatory, adversarial process ending in a jury trial. More recently, in the wake of the horrors of World War II and the end of long periods of fascist rule in Spain and Portugal, European countries have introduced reforms designed to make their legal systems better able to protect democratic institutions and individual rights against potential abuses by the executive branch.

In the 1980s criminal justice procedures in most Latin American countries remained essentially as they were before the French Revolution. Beset with internal conflicts, political instability, and the repeated intervention of the armed forces in the political sphere, most Latin American countries continued to rely on authoritarian models of criminal justice.[1] Judges continued to manage investigations, act as prosecutors, and conduct trials based on written documents. Abuses by police remained common, and government accountability, elusive. The absence of structural reforms in Latin America ensured that justice would be slow, inefficient, and imperfect.[2]

Despite the claims of their constitutions, few Latin American countries evolved into functioning democracies or accepted the notion that government — or those with economic power — should be subject to the rule of law. Most remained authoritarian, with power concentrated in the executive. Land ownership remained highly concentrated, creating extreme disparities of wealth. The legal systems in Latin America were part of these societies, upholding the claims of the privileged and using their power against the downtrodden. The vast majority of the population had no access to justice. Compliant courts showed little concern about state corruption and the suppression of individual rights.

Early Salvadoran statutes and regulations reflected the role of law in a distinctly undemocratic society. Salvadoran police regulations in 1843 reveal governmental control over the indigenous class and pressure to force them to work on haciendas. Mayors and police were to take special care to see that day laborers in their jurisdiction went to work each Monday on the haciendas. Vagrancy laws provided punishment for those who failed to work. Mayors and municipalities were obliged to provide plantations with laborers upon request. Likewise, women vagrants (without employment) were to be apprehended by mayors, police chiefs, criminal judges, and commissioners and sent to serve or grind corn in houses that needed them.[3] Police rules of August 6, 1824, provided that day laborers who without just

1. For a more thorough discussion of the historical background, see Keith S. Rosenn, "The Protection of Judicial Independence in Latin America," *Inter-American Law Review* 19 (1987): 1; Luis Salas and José María Rico, *Administration of Justice in Latin America: A Primer on the Criminal Justice System* (Miami: Florida International University, Center for the Administration of Justice, 1993), 11–15 (hereafter *Primer on Criminal Justice*). Jaime Williams, Marco Augusto Sarmiento, and Leopoldo Schiffrin, "Análisis de Identificación de Areas de Reforma Legal y Constitucional," San Salvador: Checchi and Company Consulting, Inc., presented to USAID El Salvador, June 1991, 7–9; Alberto M. Binder, *Justicia Penal y Estado de Derecho* (Buenos Aires: Ad-Hoc, SRL, 1993).

2. Harry Blair and Gary Hansen, *Weighing In on the Scales of Justice: Strategic Approaches for Donor Supported Rule of Law Programs* (Washington, D.C.: USAID, 1994), 29.

3. Isidro Menéndez, Presbítero, Doctor y Licenciado, *Recopilación de Leyes de El Salvador* (Guatemala: Imprenta de L. Luna, plazuela del Sagrario), Libro 4, 206–7.

cause failed to go to work would be punished, the first time with fifteen canings, the second time with twenty, and thirty for repeat offenses. They were also required to pay the costs of their capture and would be turned over to the person for whom they were to work. Likewise, domestics who deserted were to be pursued by the local authorities and forced to continue in service if their masters so desired or be jailed for eight to fifteen days.[4] Of course, slavery remained legal in the United States during the same period.

In El Salvador in the late nineteenth century, the oligarchy relied on the courts to force peasants off land that was to be concentrated in private hands to increase coffee production and to force the landless peasants to serve as cheap seasonal labor.[5] An 1881 decree created the rural justices of the peace who had the authority to order peasants to work on coffee plantations as they were needed.[6] The landed oligarchy controlled the government and suppressed a series of uprisings.

The unequal distribution of wealth in El Salvador was such that in 1931 the U.S. attaché for Central American military affairs wrote, "I imagine the situation in El Salvador today is very much like France was before its revolution, Russia before its revolution and Mexico before its revolution. A socialist or even communistic revolution in El Salvador may be delayed for several years, ten or even twenty, but when it comes it will be a bloody one."[7] In a 1932 Indian peasant uprising, brutally crushed by General Maximiliano Hernández Martínez, as many as 30,000 peasants are thought to have died. For the next forty-seven years, the military governed directly to protect the interests of the oligarchy. El Salvador maintained its reputation as one of the least democratic countries in the Americas. In the late 1970s, El Salvador had the most unequal distribution of incomes in Latin America. The wealthiest 5 percent of the country's families received 38 percent of national income, while 40 percent enjoyed only 7.5 percent of the country's income.[8]

4. Ibid., 210–15.
5. For a thorough account of how legal decrees were used to concentrate traditional communal lands in the hands of the oligarchy while the majority of the population was reduced to the status of landless peasants forced to work on the coffee plantations, see David Browning, *El Salvador, Landscape and Society* (London: Clarendon/Oxford University Press, 1971), 203–26.
6. Tommie Sue Montgomery, *Revolution in El Salvador: Origins and Evolution* (Boulder: Westview Press, 1982), 42. The 1883 constitution, article 26, provided that work was obligatory, except on Sunday and national holidays. The 1886 constitution, article 19, prohibited the use of caning as punishment.
7. Major R. A. Harris, cited in Raymond Bonner, *Weakness and Deceit: U.S. Policy and El Salvador* (New York: Times Books, 1984), 16.
8. Ibid., 16–17. For background on the socioeconomic conditions, see also Richard A.

The trappings of democracy provided in the different Salvadoran constitutions—such as the division of powers—did not alter the authoritarian nature of government.[9] Likewise, the modifications to the inquisitorial criminal process did not substantially change it. Before looking at reform efforts initiated during the 1980s, it may be useful to understand certain aspects of the formal legal structure and how they functioned in practice.

In the late 1970s, in an effort to better its human rights image, El Salvador ratified a number of international human rights instruments: the International Covenant on Civil and Political Rights, the International Covenant on Social and Economic Rights,[10] the American Convention on Human Rights,[11] and the Protocols Additional to the Geneva Conventions of 1949.[12] The 1983 constitution provided that international treaties would take precedence over domestic law and theoretically guaranteed many fundamental rights, but it also left many loopholes.[13] This constitution—and its predecessors—established three theoretically independent branches of government; however, that independence was to a large degree illusory. The armed forces were the de facto power in El Salvador. Permission to travel or hold events

Haggerty, ed., *El Salvador: A Country Study* (Washington, D.C.: Federal Research Division, Library of Congress, 1990); Tommie Sue Montgomery, *Revolution in El Salvador: Origins and Evolution*, 2d ed. (Boulder: Westview Press, 1995); Robert Armstrong and Janet Shenk, *The Face of Revolution* (Boston: South End Press, 1982); Rafael Guidos Véjar, *El Ascenso del Militarismo en El Salvador*, 4th ed. (San Salvador: UCA Editores, 1980).

9. Since independence, El Salvador has had fourteen constitutions. See Keith S. Rosenn, "The Success of Constitutionalism in the United States and Its Failure in Latin America: An Explanation," *Inter-American Law Review* 22 (1990), app. A. Between 1930 and 1990 the government of El Salvador was changed by extraconstitutional means seven times (ibid., app. B).

10. Both covenants were ratified on November 23, 1979, by the civilian/military junta that took power after the October 1979 coup. See discussion *infra* at 43ff.

11. Ratified on June 23, 1978, with the reservation that El Salvador would recognize the jurisdiction of the Inter-American Court on Human Rights only on a case-by-case basis.

12. Ratified on July 4, 1978. El Salvador ratified the four Geneva Conventions of 1949 on December 10, 1952.

13. The 1983 constitution was drafted by a constituent assembly elected in 1982 when the civilian/military junta installed after the October 1979 military coup called for elections. It was modeled on the 1962 constitution, although it included some innovations. See "Exposición de Motivos," *1983–1993 Diez Años de la Constitución de la República de El Salvador 1983* (San Salvador: Unidad Técnica Ejecutora, 1993), Tomo III, Anexo III. Deficiencies in the protection of individual rights included, among others, a provision protecting freedom of expression "unless it subverts the public order" (article 6); a provision allowing the detention for reeducation or readaptation of persons who, through antisocial, immoral, or harmful activity, show themselves to be in a "dangerous state" and pose an imminent risk to society or individuals (article 13); and a provision giving military courts jurisdiction over civilians accused of political crimes when constitutional guarantees were suspended (article 30). Only the last of these was eliminated through the peace process.

throughout the country had to be obtained from military, not civilian, authorities. Judges outside the capital routinely checked with local military commanders before proceeding with required investigative steps. When representatives of the United Nations High Commissioner for Refugees sought the release of imprisoned repatriates in 1987, they went to the Ministry of Defense rather than to the courts.

Breaking this tradition of military rule, whether overt or covert, was a top priority of the FMLN during the peace negotiations. Rather than a transition from authoritarian military dictatorship to democracy, El Salvador sought to change from a formal democracy to a functional democracy, with various guarantees to ensure civilian control over the military and a democratic system that would not exclude any political parties from participation.

Actors in the Criminal Justice System

This chapter describes the different actors in the Salvadoran criminal justice system: the courts, the Public Ministry (which includes the attorney general's or public prosecutor's office), and the police, focusing on the historic lack of judicial independence and its implications for human rights protection.

The Judicial Branch

The judicial branch, headed by the president of the Supreme Court, is one of three "independent" branches of government in El Salvador. The numerical composition, tenure, and procedures for electing the court have varied in the country's numerous constitutions.[14] As in many Latin American countries, Salvadoran constitutions have long entrusted the legislative branch with the appointment of Supreme Court justices.[15] In many of these countries,

---

14. In 1824 the National Constituent Assembly of the State of El Salvador elected the first Salvadoran Supreme Court. The first Salvadoran constitution (June 12, 1824) called for popular election of Supreme Court magistrates, who did not need to be lawyers. The 1841 constitution required that members of the Supreme Court be lawyers named by the legislature and that their appointments would be permanent (as long as they maintained "good behavior").

15. See Salas and Rico, *Primer on Criminal Justice*, Table 5, p. 34. Despite the executive's domination of political power in most of Latin America, the executive has unfettered discretion to name all judges only in Peru. Other countries provide for presidential selection with congressional approval.

including El Salvador, the legislature was subservient to the executive. In reality, the degree of judicial independence is often associated with a country's political and social development.[16]

The judicial branch consisted of the Supreme Court, second instance appellate courts for each region of the country, first instance courts in population centers, and justices of the peace in all municipalities. Justices of the peace were called on to perform initial investigations, to examine the dead or injured, and to resolve minor cases and local land disputes. Traditionally, most were political appointments with little or no legal training. First instance judges could also investigate cases from the outset and were required to do so in important cases. Those with criminal jurisdiction were responsible for all stages of the criminal process: investigation, the plenary, presiding over jury trials, and sentencing.

Lack of Independence of the Judiciary

In recent years a number of international principles to ensure judicial independence have been developed. For example, the second principle of the United Nations Basic Principles on the Independence of the Judiciary provides that

> the judiciary shall resolve matters before it impartially, on the basis of facts and in accordance with the law, without any restrictions, improper influences, inducements, pressures, threats or interference, direct or indirect, from any quarter or for any reason.

As this principle suggests, different actors may subvert judicial independence. Owen Fiss has set forth three principles of judicial independence: (1) "party detachment"—a judge should not be vulnerable to influence or control by the parties in litigation (e.g., through corruption); (2) individual autonomy—one judge should not be subject to another's influence; and (3) political insularity—judges should be free from pressures from other branches of government.[17] Others have described the forms of judicial independence using different categories: "internal independence" to exercise authority based on the law and a judge's personal values without undue

---

16. Ibrahim Shihata, "The World Bank," in *Justice Delayed,* ed. Edmundo Jarquín and Fernando Carrillo (Washington, D.C.: Inter-American Development Bank, 1998), 120.

17. Owen Fiss, "The Limits of Judicial Independence," *University of Miami Inter-American Law Review* 25 (1993): 55–58.

influence from any quarter (the parties to the litigation, other branches of government, other judges, associations of any kind, the media, political parties, etc.); independence of the judicial branch in terms of planning and implementation; and bureaucratic independence so that judges can devote their time to judging rather than judicial administration.[18] The Salvadoran judiciary met none of the criteria for judicial independence.

External Independence or Political Insularity

El Salvador's Supreme Court never enjoyed true independence. Traditionally, the legislature appointed justices for short terms.[19] Executive domination meant that the president would designate Supreme Court justices by providing a list of names to the Assembly. The 1983 constitution provided that all fourteen Supreme Court justices were to be appointed for renewable five-year terms that coincided almost exactly with presidential terms.

Lack of job tenure often compromises the judiciary's independence from the political branches of government. Aware of this problem, lawyers involved in drafting the 1983 constitution recommended giving Supreme Court justices life tenure up to the age of 70 as long as they observed conduct befitting their duties. While lifetime tenure might be desirable to shield justices from concerns about reappointment, its success depends on an appointment process designed to ensure the selection of qualified candidates. The traditional Salvadoran appointment process allowed the majority party in the legislature to select the entire Supreme Court.

The Supreme Court president from 1989 to 1994, Mauricio Gutiérrez Castro, was a leader of the governing ARENA party who had served as one of three vice presidents of the country from 1982 to 1984. His predecessor, Francisco José Guerrero (1984–89), was awarded the presidency of the Supreme Court after a failed bid for the presidency in 1984 as the candidate of the *Partido de Conciliación Nacional* (PCN), traditionally allied with the military.

18. Jorge Obando, "Reform of the Justice Sector," in *Governance and Democratic Development in Latin America and the Caribbean* (New York: United Nations Development Program, 1997), 124.

19. Article 47, no. 8, and article 91 of the 1962 constitution provided that Supreme Court justices as well as first and second instance judges were to be appointed by the legislature for three-year terms. After three successive appointments, the incumbents could only be removed for legal cause. This stability in office proved illusory. See "Exposición de Motivos," Constitución de El Salvador (1983).

The 1983 constitution established that the Supreme Court would have a Constitutional Chamber, responsible for ruling on the constitutionality of laws.[20] While prior constitutions had empowered the court to propose any kind of law, the 1983 constitution limited this authority to laws related to the judicial branch. Under the 1962 constitution, all proposed legislation designed to interpret, reform, or derogate any provision in Salvadoran law was to be reviewed by the Supreme Court before it could be enacted. The 1983 drafting commission explained that the reform removing this responsibility from the court was designed to strengthen the court's independence, because the prior arrangement had led to agreements and negotiations between the Supreme Court and the executive branch. The commission emphasized that the spirit of the new constitution called for separating the Supreme Court from all politically partisan actions. Under the earlier scheme, petitions arguing the unconstitutionality of laws were futile since the court had preapproved all laws.

Still, the terms of the 1983 constitution and the military's domination of the country limited the judiciary's role. It entrusted the armed forces with responsibility for "maintaining peace, tranquility and public security and compliance with the constitution and other laws in force....It will especially ensure that the republican form of Government and the representative democratic regime is maintained, that the rule requiring that the President of the Republic not be the same person twice in succession, and that freedom to vote and respect for human rights are guaranteed."[21] When members of the military were responsible for human rights violations, the judiciary knew better than to investigate. Moreover, the "auxiliary bodies for the administration of justice" — fundamentally the three military security forces — were hardly reliable independent investigators.[22] The judicial branch lacked any investigative capacity under its own control.

20. The Court's other chambers were Criminal, Civil, and Administrative Review.

21. Article 211. This article was replaced by the constitutional reforms negotiated in 1991. Reformed article 212 defines the armed forces' mission as the defense of national sovereignty and territorial integrity. The government could call on the armed forces to carry out measures it had adopted in fulfilling constitutional duties, and the executive could also have it collaborate in public works. The armed forces is still to aid the population in cases of national disaster (article 212). Responsibility for security functions was transferred to a civilian police force, no longer part of the Defense Ministry, and the army was no longer to have a role in enforcing the constitution or other laws. Articles 211 and 212 were substituted by Legislative Decree 152, D.O. 19, Tomo 314, January 30, 1992.

22. Article 11 of the Código Procesal Penal (1973) listed the órganos auxiliares de la administración de justicia (auxiliary bodies of the administration of justice) for criminal investigations: the National Guard, the National Police and Scientific Police Institute, the Treasury

The judiciary also suffered from an extremely limited budget. As a result, judicial salaries were low, forcing judges to engage in other employment and encouraging corrupt practices.

Internal Independence or Individual Autonomy

Traditionally in Latin America, either the Ministry of Justice (within the executive branch) or the highest court is responsible for judicial governance. In El Salvador this responsibility has been firmly vested in the Supreme Court. The Ministry of Justice, part of the executive branch, played no role in the courts. Its authority included responsibility for the country's prison system and preparation of draft legislation to be submitted to the legislature.

Lower court judges were dependent on the Supreme Court for their appointments, continued tenure, discipline, and sanctions as well as for review of their decisions. Judges were chosen based more on political criteria and family ties than on professional qualifications. The Supreme Court exerted a powerful influence over the entire judicial branch.[23] Lower court judges were often advised by the Supreme Court how to handle cases, or they sought advice to avoid future problems. The judiciary's highly vertical structure discouraged any independent action. This lack of internal independence may be even more prejudicial than a lack of independence from other branches of government. As Professor Zaffaroni has noted, the executive and politicians in general tend to be interested only in certain conflicts, whereas the judicial bodies that impose internal dictatorships tend to use their power on an ongoing basis.[24]

Combining the Supreme Court's responsibility for constitutional and appellate control with responsibility for judicial administration and government impinges on the internal independence of judges and seriously

---

Police, Customs Police, and tax administrators. The peace accords called for the dissolution of the National Guard and Treasury Police, and the replacement of the National Police by the new Civilian National Police.

23. See, e.g., Report on the Situation of Human Rights in El Salvador, prepared by the Independent Expert of the Commission on Human Rights in accordance with paragraph 12 of Commission resolution 1992/62 of 3 March 1992 and Economic and Social Council decision 1992/237 of 20 July 1992, UN Doc. A/47/596, November 13, 1992, par. 155 (hereafter Independent Expert's November 1992 Report on Human Rights in El Salvador); Marcelo A. Sancinetti, Jorge A. Bacqué, and Marco A. Castro Alvarado, *Programa para una estrategia de reforma judicial de US AID* (San Salvador: Checchi and Company Consulting, Inc., March 10, 1991), 35–38.

24. Eugenio Raúl Zaffaroni, "Dimensión política de un poder judicial democrático," Comisión Andina de Juristas, Boletín no. 37 (June 1993):17.

prejudices the most important functions of higher court judges, such as the control of constitutionality. In these combined structures, the more time-consuming administrative duties inevitably take precedence over judicial functions.[25]

To enhance internal and external judicial independence, reformers have proposed transferring responsibility for government of the judiciary to a body other than the executive and the highest court. The UN's former Independent Expert on El Salvador, Pedro Nikken, echoed these concerns, emphasizing: "[the] unsoundness of a vertical structure in the judicial system which makes the judge administratively subordinate to the very instance which will review his judgements in appeal proceedings. If the judge is aware that his appointment and, especially, his dismissal, depend on the Supreme Court, he will inevitably be subject to the Court's influence, whether that influence is direct or implicit."[26]

The 1983 constitution took only a minuscule step to modify this situation by establishing an auxiliary body, the National Judiciary Council, designed to provide the Supreme Court with lists of candidates for first and second instance judgeships. Yet the constitutional drafting commission gave great importance to the role of the judicial branch, particularly the control of constitutionality and the legality of governmental acts, and put considerable effort into reforms. It considered the judicial branch "the axis around which the democratic order turns. It is the courts which give citizens the guarantee that law will be enforced, not only against private citizens, but also against anyone who holds power and violates the law."[27] However, the judiciary's actions during the subsequent years did little to reflect these concerns.

Party Interference: Corruption

Some prominent Salvadoran jurists insist that the judiciary was one of the least corrupt institutions until the 1970s. Nonetheless, stories of the ease with which juries and judges could be bought abound. Low salaries made offers from parties to litigation attractive. Likewise, threats and intimidation by powerful litigants were frequently used to ensure particular results. Without structures to ensure independence and accountability, corruption could easily flourish.

25. Ibid., 35.
26. Independent Expert's November 1992 Report on Human Rights in El Salvador, par. 155.
27. "Exposición de Motivos," Informe Unico, Capítulo III, El Organo Judicial, Constitución de la República de El Salvador (1983), Anexo III (author's translation).

Judicial Tolerance of Executive Abuses

Throughout the 1980s, including the period when repression was most intense, few members of the Salvadoran Supreme Court appeared to waver in the belief that the threat of terrorism justified the suspension of rights guaranteed by the constitution and international law. The judiciary rarely questioned the use of torture and routinely failed to investigate, even when suspects were brought before judges with obvious physical injuries inflicted by their captors.

Comparative analysis indicates that the judiciary has rarely distinguished itself for standing up during periods of widespread and serious human rights violations. As one study of Latin American criminal justice put it, "During the military period, the independence of Latin American courts was tested, and judiciaries failed the test as persons seeking their protection were ignored and military crimes went unpunished."[28] In some cases, the judiciary made no effort to stand up to military rulers; in others, its efforts produced no results.

The executive's predominance and the lack of independence of the judiciary from the political branches of government are some of the principal explanations offered for the judiciary's acquiescence. Under authoritarian regimes, judges can either be marginalized or be subordinated to the dominant party. The legal culture, training, and constitutional philosophy also contribute to the general weakness of judicial review in Latin America.[29] The hierarchical structure of the judiciary makes it difficult for lower court judges to act when the highest court is complicit with an authoritarian regime. Still, in other Latin American countries courageous members of the judiciary did occasionally seek to investigate human rights cases, despite opposition from the military and Supreme Court.[30] No such examples can

28. Salas and Rico, *Primer on Criminal Justice*, 53.

29. Alejandro M. Garro, "Nine Years of Transition to Democracy in Argentina: Partial Failure or Qualified Success?" *Columbia Journal of Transnational Law* 31 (1993): 56–58.

30. In Chile, Appellate Judge Carlos Cerda pursued an investigation of the 1976 disappearance of ten members of the Communist Party. In 1986 the Supreme Court agreed with the defendants that the 1978 amnesty barred prosecution and ordered Cerda to close the case. Cerda refused and was suspended for two months. In 1990, after General Pinochet's defeat in a plebiscite and the election of Patricio Aylwin as president, Cerda resumed his investigation. The Supreme Court reaffirmed its prior order. Cerda stopped the proceedings but refused to dismiss the case. The Supreme Court's attempt to require the president to remove Cerda was met with such a strong public outcry that the Supreme Court was ultimately forced to back down, although Cerda had to apologize to the court. See Owen Fiss, "The Right Degree of Independence," in *Transition to Democracy in Latin America,* ed. Irwin P. Stotzky (Boulder: Westview Press, 1993), 70, n. 40.

be cited in El Salvador. International observers have sometimes credited individual Salvadoran judges with valor for going forward against the triggermen in high-profile cases, but their actions, however risky, were mandated by high-level political decisions taken in response to unrelenting international pressure.[31] Without strong political backing, judges occasionally initiated investigations but were quickly intimidated by threats or stonewalling. The fear of violence was very real: some judges responsible for sensitive cases were attacked and killed.

The Chilean Supreme Court was known for its autonomy and enjoyed life tenure, yet it failed to take a stand against the grave human rights violations committed under General Pinochet's rule after the 1973 coup in Chile and quashed lower court efforts to take action. The "corporate autonomy" enjoyed by the Chilean judiciary must be distinguished from the independence of the judiciary that implies the ability of each individual judge to make a decision free of outside influences and control.[32] A strong "corporatist spirit" can lead to isolation of the judiciary from political sectors and social demands. Excessive corporate autonomy can result in a lack of transparency and make it difficult for judges to adapt to changes or to understand social demands for change.[33] Despite the notorious human rights situation then existing in Chile, in 1975 the president of the Supreme Court attributed Chile's international reputation for abusing human rights to "bad Chileans or foreigners with political interests."[34] Thousands of habeas corpus petitions remained unresolved.[35]

31. Judge Bernardo Rauda, who presided over the May 1984 trial of five National Guardsmen convicted and sentenced to thirty years in prison for the December 1980 murder of four U.S. churchwomen, is often cited as an example of this kind of courage. The case was investigated and shepherded through the judicial process by U.S. officials. After the verdict, Judge Rauda was transferred to a court in Chalatenango, which required a considerably longer commute to a conflictive part of the country. Interviewed in 1985, Judge Rauda noted that despite the difficulties inherent in the new location, the dearth of lawyers in Chalatenango meant that he could earn substantial sums as a notary. In 1995 the Supreme Court decided that Judge Rauda was unfit to remain on the bench. There was no indication that this removal had anything to do with his role in the churchwomen's case.

32. Comisión Andina de Juristas, *Chile: Sistema Judicial y Derechos Humanos* (May 1995), 21. See also Jorge Correa Sutil, "The Judiciary and the Political System in Chile: The Dilemmas of Judicial Independence During the Transition to Democracy," in *Transition to Democracy*, ed. Irwin P. Stotzky (Boulder: Westview Press, 1993), 90; W. D. Zabel, D. Orentlicher, and D. E. Nachman, "Human Rights and the Administration of Justice in Chile," *Recordings of the Association of the Bar of the City of New York* 42 (1987): 431, 436.

33. Jorge Correa Sutil, "Modernization, Democratization, and Judicial Systems," in *Justice Delayed*, ed. Jarquín and Carrillo (Washington, D.C.: Inter-American Development Bank, 1998), 106.

34. Comisión Nacional de Verdad y Reconciliación (1991), 96.

35. Between September 1973 and January 1990, 8,900 habeas corpus petitions were

In Honduras, the Commissioner for Human Rights found that during the 1980s judges failed to conduct investigations or process habeas corpus petitions in cases of forced disappearances. They ignored information that clearly indicated who might have been responsible.[36] In the wake of the 1976 military coup in Argentina, the new military authorities changed the composition of the Supreme Court, the Attorney General (*Procurador General de la Nación*), and the higher provincial courts. To be named or confirmed, each judge was required to first swear fidelity to the goals and decrees (*actas*) of the military government.[37] The Argentine truth commission concluded that during the period when the military carried out massive disappearances "the judicial route became an almost non-operational recourse."[38] The Supreme Court of Argentina became totally frustrated by the refusal of military authorities to provide information to the judiciary about disappeared persons and actually stated that the country was experiencing an "absence of justice" because "judges are being deprived of those necessary conditions to enable them to exercise their jurisdictional powers."[39] The Colombian Supreme Court distinguished itself by ruling that the trial of civilians in military courts was unconstitutional.[40]

In Guatemala, a few members of the judiciary attempted to uphold the rule of law and prosecute human rights violators. Many of those who took courageous and principled stands were themselves threatened and killed. For example, after President Jorge Serrano attempted to dissolve the congress and the courts in May 1993, Guatemala's Constitutional Court continued to meet and, under the leadership of Epaminondas González Dubón, declared Serrano's action unconstitutional, a ruling seen as key to precluding the success of Serrano's move. On April 1, 1994, González Dubón was killed in an attack on a highway. The investigation of his killing was riddled with

---

presented in Santiago alone on behalf of persons arrested or kidnapped. Less than ten of these were taken up by the judicial authorities (Comisión Andina de Juristas, *Chile: Sistema Judicial y Derechos Humanos*, 10).

36. Leo Valladares, *The Facts Speak for Themselves: Preliminary Report of the Commissioner for Human Rights in Honduras* (trans.) (Washington, D.C.: Center for Justice and International Law and Human Rights Watch/Americas, 1994).

37. Argentine National Commission on the Disappeared, *Nunca Más, The Report of the Argentine Commission on the Disappeared* (New York: Farrar, Straus and Giroux, 1986), 391.

38. Ibid., 392.

39. Pérez de Smith y otros, 300 Fallos 1283 (1978) (Argentina). See Alejandro Garro, "The Role of the Argentine Judiciary in Controlling Governmental Action Under a State of Siege," *Human Rights Law Journal* 4 (1983): 332–37.

40. Decisión de 5 de marzo 1984, Sala Plena in 16 Jurisprudencia y Doctrina 492, cited in Keith S. Rosenn, "Protection of Judicial Independence in Latin America," *Inter-American Law Review* 19 (1987): 1, 24.

inconsistencies.[41] Guatemalan judges also risked disciplinary proceedings or transfers to less desirable positions in response to their attempts to protect human rights.

Military Jurisdiction

Unlike many Latin American countries, El Salvador has not recently used military jurisdiction to shield members of the armed forces from prosecution. Military jurisdiction may have been unnecessary in El Salvador since civilian courts showed no inclination to prosecute cases where members of the armed forces were suspects. Under the 1983 Salvadoran constitution, when a state of emergency was declared, civilians suspected of political offenses could be placed under military jurisdiction. These military proceedings lacked rudimentary due process protections and denied civilians accused of political crimes access to an impartial tribunal. Military judges of instruction were active-duty or retired military officers, often without legal training. They resolved most of the cases referred to them by negotiating a "fine" with family members, so that the suspected "subversive" could be released. Military judges of first instance were lawyers or regular judges with jurisdiction over military cases and civilians accused of political crimes under a state of emergency. Their courts were in San Salvador, but they had national jurisdiction. These judges enjoyed no special protection: one was killed in 1985, presumably by an urban guerrilla commando; another was murdered in 1988, either by persons connected to a kidnapping ring comprised of military and far-right civilians or by an FMLN commando. No one was ever prosecuted in either case.

The Public Ministry

The 1939 constitution established the Public Ministry and placed it under the Ministry of Justice in the executive branch. The head of the office was the Chief State Counsel (*Procurador General de la República*), who had the apparently contradictory responsibilities of representing and defending the state and society's interests while defending minors, indigents, and the disabled and promoting judicial actions where appropriate. The 1962

41. For this and other cases in which judges were killed, threatened, or suffered reprisals, see, e.g., *Informe Anual 1994*, Oficina de Derechos Humanos, Arzobispado de Guatemala, 28–29, 47–57.

constitution separated these functions, establishing two divisions within the Public Ministry: the Attorney General (*Fiscal General de la República*) and the Chief State Counsel for the Poor (*Procurador General de Pobres*). Both were named by the executive.

The 1983 constitution removed the Public Ministry from the executive branch, entrusting the legislature with responsibility for electing both officials. The drafter's report noted that the decision to have the attorney general elected by the legislature was intended to give the office greater independence since it was supposed to oversee the legality of executive actions. According to the framers of the 1983 constitution, the attorney general was to be vigilant of citizens' rights and was to denounce or prosecute officials who violated the law. The attorney general was also responsible for oversight and intervention in criminal investigations from the initial police involvement, as well as for the organization and direction of specialized organisms for criminal investigation.

The transfer of appointment power to the legislature did nothing to shield these posts from partisan politics. ARENA founder Roberto D'Aubuisson, known for his role in organizing death squads, headed the Constituent Assembly when the new constitution went into effect. His close ally José Francisco Guerrero, who was named attorney general, plainly had no interest in solving cases where death squads or the military were involved. A subsequent Christian Democratic attorney general was unceremoniously removed from office by the legislature after an unsuccessful attempt to reopen the investigation of the murder of Archbishop Romero. In 1989 an ARENA-controlled Assembly appointed Mauricio Eduardo Colorado as attorney general after his predecessor was killed by an FMLN commando. Colorado's extreme right-wing views colored his actions: after six Jesuit priests, their cook, and their cook's daughter were murdered by the armed forces in November 1989, Colorado wrote a letter to the pope urging that he withdraw San Salvador's bishops from the country. Colorado argued that the archdiocese's support for liberation theology placed the bishops in danger, and he urged that they be removed for their own protection.

Aside from the extreme politicization of the post, the attorney general continued to play a very limited role. Despite his constitutional mandate, the attorney general made no effort to prosecute officials who violated the law. Prosecutors did not oversee or intervene in police investigations, nor did they carry out their own investigations. Poorly paid and trained, with no conception of what a more active role might entail, prosecutors played a largely passive role, deferring to police and to the courts.

Militarized Police

Militarized police forces were responsible for carrying out criminal investigations. A centralized law enforcement with a militarized police inclined toward national security rather than public safety was common throughout the continent. The Salvadoran police were part of the armed forces, and the judiciary exercised no control over them. Article 11 of the Criminal Procedure Code provided that the three militarized security forces—the National Police, National Guard, and Treasury Police—would be "auxiliary organs of the administration of justice" for criminal investigation. In reality, however, the police conducted their investigations autonomously, rarely providing information to the courts. As part of the state security apparatus dedicated to the struggle against subversion, the security forces routinely tortured suspects. Their intelligence sections (S-2), charged with carrying out investigations, were heavily involved in death-squad activities and operated outside legal constraints.[42]

Because of their military ties, the security forces were particularly unsuited to investigating crimes committed by the military. The Commission to Investigate Criminal Acts, established in 1985 as the most important piece of the U.S.-funded judicial reform effort, was meant to overcome some of these problems. Yet the commission was structured to keep investigations under military control. It devoted more of its time to investigating common crimes than human rights cases. It failed to conduct any investigation of many crimes thought to have been committed by the military and conducted patently inadequate investigations of others.[43]

In the only two human rights cases in which officers were ordered to stand trial during the war for actions committed as part of military operations, it was not the Commission to Investigate Criminal Acts that identified those who would be prosecuted. Instead, when outside pressure made it impossible to deny military responsibility, special ad hoc military "honor commissions" composed of officers of different ranks were charged with investigating. Thus the military determined who should be prosecuted for

42. See *From Madness to Hope: The 12-Year War in El Salvador*, Report of the Truth Commission for El Salvador (San Salvador and New York: United Nations, 1992–1993), appendix to UN Doc. S/25500, April 1, 1993, 131–38.

43. See Martha Doggett, *Underwriting Injustice: AID and El Salvador's Judicial Reform Program* (New York: Lawyers Committee for Human Rights, 1989), 51; Margaret Popkin, *El Salvador's Negotiated Revolution: Prospects for Legal Reform* (New York: Lawyers Committee for Human Rights, 1993), 25–28.

these offenses and limited the scope of the investigation to those individuals. Ranking officers who may have given the orders or participated in the cover-up were protected from inquiry.[44]

In general, police failed to carry out basic investigative steps, often failing even to initiate a formal inquiry. Their main sources of incriminating evidence were confessions, often coerced, and uncorroborated witness statements.

Salvadoran Criminal Procedures: The Quasi-Inquisitorial Model

Salvadoran criminal procedures blatantly failed to protect human rights and often contributed to serious rights abuses. All have been subject to debate in recent years and most have undergone some change.

The Extrajudicial Confession

Confessions made to police, known as "extrajudicial confessions," have been widely accepted in Latin America. In an Inter-American Institute of Human Rights study published in 1986, Professor Zaffaroni found that although confessions were routinely coerced, they were accepted as evidence in almost all Latin American countries. He recommended legal reforms prohibiting the use of confessions taken by the police and establishing that only confessions rendered before a judge and in the presence of a lawyer would have evidentiary value.[45]

44. In September 1988, soldiers from the Jiboa Battalion of the army's Fifth Infantry Brigade executed ten peasants whom they had detained as guerrilla collaborators. The army's initial position was that the deaths had resulted from combat. Its revised position was that the guerrillas had ambushed the army and its captives, resulting in the death of the ten peasants. The brigade commander, who almost certainly gave the order to eliminate the peasants, was not prosecuted. Although defendants were identified in this case in early 1989, no one was ever tried. The trial judge and the appellate court freed all the defendants except the major alleged to have given the orders to the others. The court never set a trial date for Major Beltrán, who hinted that he would implicate higher-ups. Since the major was not dismissed from the army until November 1992, he was not held in a Salvadoran prison but at an army base. In April 1993 he was granted amnesty. The other case involved the November 1989 murder of six Jesuit priests and two women. See discussion at 52–56.

45. Eugenio R. Zaffaroni, *Sistemas penales y derechos humanos en América Latina*, Final Document of the research program conducted by the Inter-American Institute for Human Rights, 1982–86 (San José, Costa Rica: Inter-American Institute for Human Rights, 1986), 157. These recommendations have been followed in several countries. The 1986 Guatemalan

The Salvadoran criminal justice system has relied heavily on confessions. Nonetheless, article 12 of the Salvadoran constitution provided that "statements obtained against a person's will have no value; whoever obtains statements in this form and uses them will incur criminal responsibility." No one disputed that the acceptance of extrajudicial confessions as evidence promoted the use of coercive police methods, including torture. Still, efforts to completely invalidate extrajudicial confessions as evidence met with great resistance.

The 1973 Criminal Procedure Code permitted extrajudicial confessions as "sufficient evidence" in common crimes if they were witnessed by two people "worthy of belief" who stated that the suspect was not subject to physical force or intimidation, if the confession was consistent with other evidentiary elements that might exist in the case, and if it was taken within seventy-two hours of detention.[46] When constitutional guarantees were suspended, the period for taking an extrajudicial confession was extended from seventy-two hours to fifteen days. In proceedings for common crimes, the extrajudicial confession could be sufficient evidence to decree provisional detention and to submit the case to an adversary hearing or to the jury.[47] In other words, the extrajudicial confession could be sufficient evidence for a conviction, as shown by the Criminal Procedure Code's provision that a conviction based solely on an extrajudicial confession could not be the basis for application of the death penalty.[48]

A 1957 reform suppressed the use of extrajudicial confessions rendered before the police.[49] This reform was short-lived, however, because the security forces adopted the position that it was not worth making arrests only to have suspects freed by a judge after the 72-hour period of administrative

---

constitution, article 9, invalidated the extrajudicial confession, as does Guatemala's new Criminal Procedure Code, which entered into effect in 1994. Other Latin American countries that have rejected the extrajudicial confession include Argentina, Bolivia, Nicaragua, Paraguay, and Uruguay. See Ministerio de Justicia, Dirección General de Asistencia Técnico Jurídica, *La Confesión Extra-judicial* (San Salvador: Ministerio de Justicia, 1993), 15.

46. Although the Código Procesal Penal (1973), article 496, did not allow extrajudicial confessions in political cases, the special procedural laws in effect when constitutional guarantees were suspended permitted their use as a basis for continued detention. See, e.g., Decree 50, article 28.

47. Código Procesal Penal, article 496.

48. Article 27 of the 1983 constitution abolished the death penalty for all but certain military crimes committed in the context of an international war.

49. Legislative Decree No. 2510 of November 1, 1957, article 415 of the Código de Instrucción Criminal.

detention. After only three months the extrajudicial confession was reinstated.[50] This history suggests that in the 1950s the extrajudicial confession
to the police must have been almost the exclusive method of proof. The
original Criminal Procedure Code of 1973 required that the witnesses who
had to testify to the spontaneity and freedom of the extrajudicial confession
could not belong to any branch of the "security forces that instruct the
process." A 1977 reform of article 496 removed this restriction.[51] After that
time, police agents regularly appeared as witnesses of suspects' confessions,
routinely assuring the court that they had been voluntarily rendered. This
reform was enacted the same year as the Law for the Defense and Guarantee
of Public Order, which was designed to crack down on "terrorism."

The failed effort to prohibit extrajudicial confessions in police custody
served to confirm an entrenched belief in El Salvador that because the police
lack scientific methods, they must be allowed to rely on extrajudicial confessions or criminals will go free.

The Right to Defense

Historically, the right to defense has been severely limited in El Salvador.
Following the Latin American model, Salvadoran law only required the
appointment of counsel for defendants when the case entered the contradictory or plenary phase—after all the evidence had been gathered.[52] The 1983
constitution, however, included a provision guaranteeing the assistance of
defense counsel from the time a person was detained by "auxiliary bodies"
(the police).[53] A 1990 reform called for defendants to name their lawyer
when the judge decreed provisional detention if they had not done so before.
If the defendant failed to name counsel, the judge was to appoint a lawyer at
the next hearing.[54] Nonetheless, defense counsel almost never had access
to detainees until they were brought to court. In practice, during the crucial
period of administrative detention when extrajudicial confessions were taken
or elaborated, the suspect remained incommunicado. Lawyers representing
suspects arrested for "subversive" activities were routinely threatened by
security force personnel if they sought to communicate with their clients.

Those accused of political crimes could seek legal representation from

50. Williams et al., "Análisis," 47.
51. Legislative Decree 381, D.O. 158, Tomo 257, October 24, 1977.
52. Código Procesal Penal, article 62.
53. Constitution of El Salvador (1983), article 12.
54. Decree 524, D.O. No. 163, Tomo no. 309, July 5, 1990.

the handful of private lawyers willing to take on political cases or from law students and a few lawyers employed by human rights organizations. Often lawyers were not present when suspects were brought to court to give statements, since they had no way of knowing when their clients would arrive. In many cases, indigent family members were unable to secure an attorney to represent the suspect in the early and critical stages of the proceedings. Throughout the war years, there was no meaningful public defense.[55]

Abuse of Preventive Detention

The vast majority of prisoners were awaiting trial. Release pending trial was sometimes available to those accused of crimes for which the punishment did not exceed three years in prison.[56] However, for certain crimes, including virtually all political crimes, pretrial release was not allowed.[57] Judicial failure to comply with prescribed procedural time periods meant that pretrial detainees might be imprisoned for as long or longer than the maximum sentence they might receive. Defendants routinely remained incarcerated from the time of arrest until the resolution of their case, regardless of the nature of their crime, the likelihood that they would flee, or any other considerations.

These practices failed to respect the principle of the presumption of innocence guaranteed by the Salvadoran constitution and human rights treaties ratified by El Salvador. Delays in criminal cases violate the rights of those arrested to a speedy trial or release and to be tried without delay. Instead of being the exception, pretrial detention was the norm.[58] The AID consultants who reviewed the criminal justice system in 1991 found that it was "absolutely necessary to harmonize legislation regarding provisional liberty with constitutional norms and treaties in effect which are gravely violated by the current system."[59] Many earlier constitutions had guaranteed defendants the right to conditional liberty during criminal proceedings.[60]

55. A public defenders program funded by AID declined to represent defendants accused of political offenses and other selected crimes.

56. Código Procesal Penal, article 250.

57. Código Procesal Penal, article 251, 60.

58. International Covenant on Civil and Political Rights, articles 9(3) and 14(3)(c); American Convention on Human Rights articles 7(5) and 8(1); see also the Principles for the Protection of All Persons Under Any Form of Detention or Imprisonment adopted by the UN General Assembly in its resolution 43/173 of December 9, 1988, which further establishes the exceptional nature of pretrial detention. See principles 36(2), 37, 38, and 39.

59. Williams et al., "Análisis," 43.

60. The Federal Constitution of 1824, article 166; Reformed Federal Constitution of 1835,

An Inter-American Human Rights Institute study on penal systems and human rights in Latin America called for prohibiting pretrial detention of more than two years unless the delays were attributable to arbitrary actions of the accused or the defense. The study further suggested that regional constitutions include a provision limiting normal pretrial detention to four months.[61]

Combination of Investigative and Sentencing Functions

Salvadoran law and practice traditionally combined the investigatory, accusatory, and sentencing functions in the same judge. Thus the judge would decree the defendant's provisional detention, gather the evidence, issue the order finding sufficient evidence to take the case to the plenary or trial stage (*auto de elevación a plenario* or *llamamiento a juicio*), and then agree with his or her previous orders in the sentence.

The failure to separate investigative or preliminary steps from sentencing has been found to violate article 8, section 1, of the American Convention on Human Rights and article 14, section 1, of the International Covenant on Civil and Political Rights. The European Court of Human Rights has ruled that this kind of situation is incompatible with the European Convention on Human Rights because it violates the right to an impartial and "objective" sentencing judge.[62]

In recent years a number of Latin American countries, including Argentina, Costa Rica, Ecuador, Peru, the Dominican Republic, and Guatemala, have created separate sentencing and instruction courts.

The Adversarial Stages of Salvadoran Criminal Proceedings

In Latin American criminal proceedings, the addition of an adversarial "plenary" stage and even a jury trial had little effect when, in reality, only the evidence produced in the investigatory (instruction) stage mattered. The evidence period of the plenary phase lacked importance, and the plenary was

---

article 161; Salvadoran Constitution of 1841, article 86; Salvadoran Constitution of 1864, article 91; Salvadoran Constitution of 1871, article 117; Salvadoran Constitution of 1872, article 35; and Salvadoran Constitution of 1880, article 31. Later constitutions no longer included this guarantee.

61. Zaffaroni, *Sistemas penales y derechos humanos*, 149ff.

62. DeCubber case, October 26, 1984; see also Tribunal Constitucional del Reino de España, sentence No. 88, April 28, 1988.

at best a discussion of evidence produced in the instruction, with mandatory participation of the parties. In El Salvador, the judge had up to 120 days to complete the instruction phase of the criminal process. Ninety days was supposed to be the norm. However, these time limits were routinely ignored. The plenary stage was far shorter, with an evidence period of fifteen days (shortened to eight days in 1990). In the traditional Salvadoran process, it was only in this stage that a defendant would be provided court-appointed counsel and that participation of the parties became mandatory. Although the parties could propose evidentiary steps (witnesses, confrontations of witnesses, etc.), the judge determined which to carry out and whether the results would be included in the summary of the case to be presented to the jury.

Despite the strong inquisitorial mode of Salvadoran criminal justice, an 1872 constitutional provision established jury trials for "common crimes determined by law."[63] Trial by jury was not actually introduced until 1906. No provision was made to require the concentrated and direct presentation of evidence before the jury. Trials continued to be based on written evidence collected in the earlier *sumario* phase of the proceedings and selected by the judge. Even when defendants, witnesses, experts, and victims were present in court, they were not likely to testify. Only the jury could decide to question them. The reading of the file was the norm; questioning witnesses was conceived of as simply a means of clarification. The jurors were not provided with jury instructions and were given virtually no guidance about how to reach their verdict. Rather than urge them to focus on the facts and the law, they were invited to ignore the facts and the law and decide the case based on their "intimate conviction."[64]

63. Constitution of 1872, article 114. This provision was maintained in the constitutions of 1880, 1883, 1886, 1939, 1945, 1950, 1962, and 1983 (article 189). While the use of juries is not common in Latin America—criminal jury trials were introduced in Brazil, Colombia, Mexico, Nicaragua, and Panama—the jury system has not distinguished itself in any of these countries. In Brazil, where jury trials are restricted to felonies against life, human rights groups have criticized Brazilian juries' repeated refusals to convict men who kill their adulterous wives caught in the act of adultery; judges have tended to defer to the jury's "sovereignty." See Americas Watch, *Criminal Injustice: Violence Against Women in Brazil* (New York: Human Rights Watch, 1991), 24–29. Despite a Mexican constitutional provision authorizing juries for certain crimes, jury trials rarely occur in Mexico. The use of juries was abolished in Nicaragua in 1988 and in Colombia in 1989. See Garro, "Nine Years of Transition," 45–46, n. 143.

64. Código Procesal Penal, article 363: "The Law does not ask jurors to explain how they arrived at their opinion; the law does not prescribe for them the rules they should apply to deduce whether evidence is sufficient; it tells them to question themselves silently and with calm reflection, and search in the sincerity of their conscience their impression of the evidence produced against and in defense of the defendant. The Law does not say to them: Do you find

The introduction of the jury system in El Salvador produced no real change, since it was simply tacked on to a written proceeding in which the evidence was taken by the court in the instruction phase. As before, only the case file mattered. Compounding this situation, the instruction itself was normally limited to confirming the police investigation. Intended as a protection against judicial arbitrariness, the jury system instituted in El Salvador instead introduced another element of chance. This denaturalized jury trial gave priority to the written investigative phase and took no interest in the direct search for the truth through the public trial of a case.[65] The irrational union of a jury trial with a highly inquisitorial system effectively produced the appearance of a democratic safeguard—allowing fellow citizens to determine the truth—and the reality of widespread abuse.

Because jurors were called from outdated lists, the court often found itself unable to seat the requisite five jurors, especially during the war years when many people abandoned their homes. The parties were not given an opportunity to look for possible juror bias. Only a majority vote—three of five—was necessary for conviction or acquittal. Criminal lawyers frequently recounted stories of juries that were influenced through money or intimidation. Other problems with jury trials stemmed from the country's high rate of illiteracy. The requirement that jurors be able to read and write precluded large sectors of the population from serving and skewed the jury pool toward the more educated sectors of the population.

Habeas Corpus

Salvadoran constitutions have long included the guarantee of habeas corpus. In practice—as in many other Latin American countries—it has been an ineffective remedy for arbitrary detentions and disappearances.[66] The formalistic procedure provided was completely inappropriate for achieving the intended goal of habeas corpus: immediately ending the violation. Over time it was perverted into a recourse that served more as an alternate appeal

this to be the truth? It puts only one question to define the extent of their duties: Do you have an intimate conviction?" (author's translation). This provision was sharply criticized by observers who attended the Jesuit trial. See *infra*, 54, note 17.

    65. Williams et al., "Análisis," 13.

    66. Francisco Bertrand Galindo, José Albino Tinetti, Silvia Lizette Kuri de Mendoza, and María Elena Orellana, *Manual de Derecho Constitucional*, Tomo I (San Salvador: Centro de Investigación y Capacitación, Proyecto de Reforma Judicial, 1992), 333, noting that the remedy has been "in large measure only historic and formal." The term *habeas corpus* first appeared in El Salvador's second constitution of 1841, article 83.

procedure for defendants challenging judicial resolutions than as an immediate remedy for unlawful detentions.[67] The problems with habeas corpus
procedures derived from the law itself, as well as practice.

Article 11 of the 1983 constitution provides that "everybody has the
right to habeas corpus when any authority or individual illegally restricts
his or her liberty." Article 247 of the constitution established that habeas
corpus petitions could be brought before the Constitutional Chamber of the
Supreme Court or appellate courts (Second Instance Chambers) outside the
capital. In practice, virtually all petitions were filed with the Supreme Court.
Under existing law, the Constitutional Chamber (or appellate court)
appointed an unpaid *juez ejecutor* to locate the beneficiary and determine
whether his or her freedom had been illegally restricted. In practice, the *juez
ejecutor* was normally a private individual, often a law student. The writ of
habeas corpus called for exhibiting the beneficiary to the *juez ejecutor* and
required that the entity responsible for restricting the beneficiary's freedom
explain the basis for the detention.[68] While time limits were set for the different stages of the proceedings, these time limits—too long to begin with—
were routinely ignored, thereby defeating the intent of habeas corpus to
serve as a quick and timely mechanism to protect individual freedom and
personal integrity.[69]

Salvadoran law rendered habeas corpus ineffective during the critical
days of administrative detention, which could be extended to fifteen days
when a state of emergency was in effect.[70] The Constitutional Procedures
Law prohibited the *juez ejecutor* from seeing the person on whose behalf the

---

67. A June 1993 study by the Human Rights Division of the UN Observer Mission in El
Salvador (ONUSAL) documented this phenomenon. It found that none of 138 habeas corpus
resolutions issued by the Supreme Court's Constitutional Chamber during a six-month period in 1992 referred to police, municipal, or administrative (prison) authorities. ONUSAL's
Human Rights Division had found that arbitrary detentions for police misdemeanors constitute the major violation of personal liberty, yet habeas corpus was so ineffective as a remedy
that it was not even used in these cases. See ONUSAL, "El Habeas Corpus en El Salvador:
Aproximación a la Actual Ineficacia," unpublished report on file with the author, 9.

68. Ley de Procedimientos Constitucionales, article 44.

69. The law gave the *juez ejecutor* twenty-four hours in which to present the detaining
authority with the writ (article 45). Within fifteen days of notification of the writ of habeas
corpus, the *juez ejecutor* was to return the case to the court with a certification of his or her
resolution and a report on the actions carried out (articles 66, 69, 70). The Supreme Court's
Constitutional Chamber or Appeals Court then had to resolve the writ within five days, unless
the court decided to request the case file, in which case the five-day period ran from receipt
of the case record (article 71). See, e.g., ONUSAL, "El Habeas Corpus en El Salvador," 6.

70. Constitution of El Salvador (1983), article 29, paragraph 2.

writ was issued during the legally authorized inquiry period.[71] In the past, during this period of incommunicado detention, the judge executor could only seek confirmation of the specific authority detaining the person named in the petition. In practice, the problem was still greater. The security forces and military installations rarely allowed *jueces ejecutores* to see detainees. Instead, they were shown ledgers with the names of people detained and the date of detention.[72] Salvadoran law and practice were incompatible with the decision of the Inter-American Court on Human Rights, which held that habeas corpus guarantees cannot be suspended even under a state of emergency.[73]

States of Emergency and Political Detentions

Throughout Latin America in the 1970s and 1980s, de facto governments declared long-term "states of emergency" during which many procedural guarantees were suspended. Although these suspensions often undermined constitutionally guaranteed rights, they were rarely questioned by the judiciary. When guarantees were suspended, civilians could be subject to military court jurisdiction, prolonged incommunicado detention, relaxed evidentiary standards, and presumptions of guilt. This chapter reviews how such decrees were implemented in El Salvador and the implications for those detained on political charges.

States of Emergency

In 1977 El Salvador enacted the "Law for the Defense and Guarantee of Public Order" as a legal tool to control growing political and labor unrest. The law's preamble described it as a response to "the serious situation created by terrorist acts and events instigated by international subversion."[74]

71. Ley de Procedimientos Constitucionales, article 46.

72. See Hillary Richard, "Right Without a Remedy: Habeas Corpus During the State of Siege in El Salvador, July 1984–August 1987" (May 1988), unpublished manuscript on file with the author, 8.

73. Inter-American Court of Human Rights, Habeas Corpus in Emergency Situations, articles 27(2), 25(1), and 7(6), American Convention on Human Rights, Advisory Opinion OC-8/87 of January 30, 1987.

74. The law was based on "article 158, paragraph 2, of the Constitution [which] prohibits propaganda advocating anarchistic or antidemocratic doctrines ... the Government of the

This law established a series of political offenses conceived so broadly that they could be applied to all kinds of government opposition. The crimes listed included spreading or disseminating abroad news or information considered biased or false and intended "to disturb the constitutional or legal order, the tranquility or security of the country, the economic and monetary system, or the stability of public values or effects."[75] Courts were authorized to order provisional arrest based on "any presumption or indication of the participation of the person or persons charged" with this offense.[76] Those charged under this law could not be released on bond while proceedings were pending.[77] Nor was the arrest order subject to appeal. Admissible evidence under this law included "the evident or notorious acts that may be in the public domain because massive information has been given about them."[78] Thus unsubstantiated news accounts could serve as evidence. As Amnesty International noted, the law seemed to have been designed to restrict the actions of labor unions, the political opposition, and human rights monitors, including those in the Catholic Church who reported human rights violations or advised members of peasant organizations.[79]

The Supreme Court, consulted by the legislature before enactment of the law, expressly approved its contents, thus putting the imprimatur of legality on a decree that gravely limited freedom of expression as well as due process rights.[80] A constitutional challenge to the law brought by an opposition political party sat for many months in the Supreme Court and was never resolved.[81]

Given the Supreme Court's prior approval of the law, it is hardly surprising that the Salvadoran judiciary failed to protect the rights of those in

---

Republic must have the legal instruments that will ensure the exercise of individual rights and the freedom of the members of the community, thereby satisfying the just demands of morality, public order, and the general welfare of society, fully respecting the Universal Declaration of Human Rights, approved and proclaimed by the United Nations General Assembly on December 10, 1948" (Preamble to Decree No. 407, November 25, 1977).

75. Decree 407, article 1, no. 15.
76. Decree 407, article 15.
77. Decree 407, article 6, final paragraph.
78. Decree 407, article 21.
79. *Amnesty International Report 1978,* 121.
80. Inter-American Commission on Human Rights (IACHR), *Report on the Situation of Human Rights in El Salvador,* OEA/Ser.L/V/II.46, doc. 23 rev. 1 (November 17, 1978), 18. Article 61 of the 1962 constitution required such consultation.
81. "La Derogatoria de la Ley de Defensa y Garantia del Orden Público," March 30, 1979, reprinted in Universidad Centroamericana José Simeón Cañas Instituto de Derechos Humanos, *Recopilación de Trabajos Publicados en la Revista Estudios Centroamericanos (ECA), Volumen II: Comentarios y Documentos,* 12.

clandestine detention. When the Inter-American Commission on Human Rights (IACHR) of the Organization of American States visited El Salvador in 1978, the Supreme Court justices explained that this draconian law was necessary because of "the campaign that had been launched abroad in connection with alleged violations of human rights in El Salvador."[82]

At the executive's initiative, the law was derogated on February 27, 1979, after the IACHR had visited El Salvador. However, the law's repeal did not signal a greater respect for the human rights of political suspects, many of whom were never seen again following their detention.

On December 3, 1980, the governing junta issued Decree Law 507,[83] which allowed political suspects to be held incommunicado during an "investigation" period of 195 days[84] and wholly denied their right to a defense. Decree 507 permitted a military judge of instruction to order that a person be held in corrective detention for 120 days, even if no grounds were found for the detention during the inquiry period.[85] Sufficient evidence of membership in a subversive association could come from "any communication media, national or foreign." Ironically, Salvadoran authorities pointed to this law as an advance. Before the enactment of Decree 507, suspected subversives were routinely tortured and executed, often after spending prolonged periods in abysmal conditions of clandestine detention.[86] Thus the decision to have political prisoners, even if they were denied all due process protections, could be pointed to as an improvement.[87]

Largely because of the provision for 195 days of incommunicado detention and the serious abuses that occurred during that period, Decree 507 was sharply criticized by domestic and international human rights

82. IACHR, Report on Human Rights in El Salvador (1978), 18.

83. *Diario Oficial,* Tomo 269, December 3, 1980.

84. Suspects could first be held for a 15-day administrative detention period, followed by a 180-day investigation period.

85. Decree 507, article 6. Two of the signatories to this law were Christian Democratic party leaders José Antonio Morales Erlich and José Napoleón Duarte.

86. In this regard, see IACHR, Report on Human Rights in El Salvador (1978); Ana Guadalupe Martínez, *Las Cárceles Clandestinas de El Salvador* (San Salvador: UCA Editores, 1992). Martínez, a commander of the People's Revolutionary Army (ERP), and a fellow ERP leader were released from clandestine detention in 1977 only after the ERP kidnapped industrialist Roberto Poma and arranged a prisoner exchange. (Poma died as a result of wounds inflicted at the time of his capture.) Other prisoners held with Martínez were never released and were presumably executed.

87. See A. W. DeWind and S. L. Kass, "Justice in El Salvador: Report of a Mission of Inquiry of the Association of the Bar of the City of New York," *Recordings of the Association of the Bar of the City of New York* 38 (1983): 112.

observers.[88] When a new constitution was enacted in 1983, it called for the replacement of Decree 507.[89] Its successor, Decree 50, again established special military tribunals for suspected political offenders, extended the period of incommunicado police detention from seventy-two hours to fifteen days, and limited the right to a defense.[90]

During the 1980s, the declaration of a state of emergency and suspension of certain constitutional guarantees became the norm. When the land reform program went into effect in March 1980, the governing junta declared a state of siege as an emergency measure "to avoid abuses and alterations of the public order."[91] Both the 1962 and the 1983 constitutions provided that "in case of war, territorial invasion, rebellion, sedition, catastrophe, epidemic or other general calamity, or grave disturbances of public order," certain constitutional guarantees could be suspended.[92] The 1983 constitution further permitted the suspension of certain procedural guarantees for criminal suspects with the agreement of three fourths of the deputies in the Legislative Assembly. The 72-hour limit on administrative detention could be lengthened to a maximum of fifteen days. Both constitutions provided that once constitutional guarantees were suspended, special military tribunals would be granted jurisdiction over crimes against the existence or

88. See, e.g., U.S. Department of State, Country Reports on Human Rights (1983), 496; Report of the Human Rights Committee to the UN General Assembly, 1984, UN Doc. A/39/40, par. 78; DeWind and Kass, "Justice in El Salvador"; "El Decreto 507, una Monstruosidad Jurídica," Estudios Centroamericanos (January–February 1981); "La Nueva Corte Suprema de Justicia y los Reos Políticos," Estudios Centroamericanos (August 1982).

89. Constitution of El Salvador (1983), article 251.

90. Decree 50, February 24, 1984, D.O. 41, Tomo 282, February 27, 1984; Decree 339, D.O. 44, Tomo 286, March 1, 1985; Decree 293, D.O. 33, Tomo 290, February 19, 1986. For an analysis of Decree 50 and its application, see Margaret Popkin, Waiting for Justice: Treatment of Political Prisoners Under El Salvador's Decree 50 (Washington, D.C.: International Human Rights Law Group, 1987). Military judges of instruction were military officers (active or retired) appointed for one-year terms by the Minister of Defense (Decree 50, article 9). No prior legal training or experience was required, although a Defense Ministry lawyer was assigned to work with these officers. Prisoners not released by the military judges of instruction during the 60-day investigation phase were turned over to a military judge of first instance (Decree 50, article 19). These judges were lawyers nominated by the Defense Ministry and appointed by the Supreme Court for three-year terms.

91. Decree 155, March 7, 1980. Thirty-day suspensions remained in effect with only brief interruptions until February 1987.

92. Constitution of El Salvador (1962), article 175. Although the constitutional order was interrupted by the October 1979 coup, Decree No. 114 of February 11, 1980, confirmed the validity of the 1962 constitution (Constitution of El Salvador [1983], article 29). Both allowed for suspension of the guarantees of freedom of movement into and within the country, not to be obliged to change residence without a judicial order, freedom of expression, freedom of association, and the inviolability of correspondence.

organization of the state and public peace.[93] This provision was used to give military courts jurisdiction over civilians accused of political crimes or membership in subversive organizations.

The Salvadoran suspensions of constitutionally guaranteed rights exceeded those allowed by the International Covenant on Civil and Political Rights and the American Convention on Human Rights, both of which include specific provisions authorizing the suspension of the exercise of certain rights in emergency situations.[94] Moreover, El Salvador failed to follow the procedures mandated for declaring a state of emergency.[95] The Inter-American Commission on Human Rights found that the "right of justice" has "been deeply affected by the state of emergency that governs in El Salvador." The Commission noted that "the American Convention does not authorize the suspension of judicial guarantees necessary to protect fundamental rights, even less so when that suspension is in force for unduly long periods, as has happened in El Salvador."[96]

Political Prisoners

When suspects were detained as alleged subversives or terrorists, the legal provisions seemed irrelevant. Until 1980, the popular movement often responded to detention of its leaders, whether or not acknowledged, by occupying San Salvador's cathedral or foreign embassies. In certain situations the FMLN—or before 1980, the different political/military organizations that later came together to form the FMLN—abducted important figures, often connected to the government or military, in order to negotiate a prisoner exchange. Thus in September 1985 a guerrilla group kidnapped Inés Duarte, daughter of President José Napoleón Duarte. She was freed six weeks later in exchange for the release of twenty-one FMLN leaders then in government custody and safe-conduct for ninety-six wounded FMLN combatants to

93. 1962 constitution, article 177; 1983 constitution, article 30.

94. International Covenant on Civil and Political Rights, article 4; American Convention on Human Rights, article 27.

95. *Annual Report of the Inter-American Commission on Human Rights 1984–85*, 143. Report of the Human Rights Committee to the UN General Assembly, 1984, UN Doc. A/39/40, par. 75 ("With reference to article 4 of the Covenant, it was noted from the report that the state of emergency in El Salvador had been extended several times but that its proclamation and extension had never been notified to the other States parties to the Covenant in conformity with article 4 of the Covenant").

96. *Inter-American Commission on Human Rights Annual Report 1983–84*, OEA/Ser.L/ V/II.63, doc. 10 (September 24, 1984), 98.

leave the country. As part of this exchange, the FMLN also released twenty-one municipal officials in its custody. Shortly thereafter, the FMLN kidnapped Colonel Omar Napoleón Avalos, who was held until February 2, 1987, when he was released in exchange for the release of fifty-seven prisoners, including members of humanitarian organizations, trade unionists, and *campesino* leaders. As a result of those negotiations, forty-two wounded FMLN combatants were granted safe passage out of the country. International pressure was often brought to bear and was sometimes effective in winning the release of detainees not yet consigned to prison. Perhaps the majority of those imprisoned on political charges won their release through bribes.

This situation reinforced the notion that there was no rule of law. People could be arbitrarily arrested and held indefinitely without trial, only to be released under ad hoc prisoner exchange agreements, while less problematic cases of arbitrary detentions were resolved by payment of a "fine" to a military judge or his secretary. Hundreds more won their freedom as the result of broad amnesty laws passed in 1983, 1987, and 1992.[97] Supposedly meant to reincorporate political prisoners and FMLN members into civilian life, these laws became better known for their application to state-sponsored crimes.

The 1987 "Amnesty Law to Achieve National Reconciliation," passed in response to the Esquipulas II Central American peace agreement, went far beyond freeing political opponents. It provided the basis for freeing the few military men convicted or accused of killing civilians. The investigation of other cases was dropped in response to the amnesty law. At the insistence of the Catholic Church, the only case specifically exempted from the terms

97. Decree 210 of the Constituent Assembly of May 4, 1983, the "Amnesty and Citizen Rehabilitation Act presented by the President of the Republic," granted amnesty to any rebel who abandoned the armed struggle before July 4, 1983. Amnesty was also granted to persons charged with an offense or offenses against the state for which the maximum penalty did not exceed four years, and who had completed six months in custody. According to the head of the Amnesty Board, 1,137 persons benefited from the amnesty; of these 554 were political offenders, and 583 were armed insurgents. See "Final Report on the Situation of Human Rights in El Salvador," submitted to the UN Commission on Human Rights by Professor José Antonio Pastor Ridruejo in fulfillment of the mandate conferred under Commission Resolution 1983/29, E/CN.4/1984/25, Jan. 19, 1984, par. 159.

Legislative Decree 805 was passed on October 27, 1987, purportedly to comply with the Central American ("Esquipulas") Peace Plan of August 1987 (*Diario Oficial* 199, Tomo 297, October 28, 1987). In the wake of the peace accords, the "National Reconciliation Law" was quickly passed by the legislature on January 23, 1992 (Legislative Decree 147, *Diario Oficial* 14, Tomo 314). Forty-two of sixty recognized political prisoners were released pursuant to this amnesty (Popkin, *Prospects for Legal Reform*, 82).

of this broad law was the murder of Archbishop Romero.[98] Based on the amnesty, 462 prisoners accused of FMLN ties were released; however, the law contained no provisions for reincorporation of those amnestied into civil society and no measures to achieve reconciliation. After freeing the vast majority of political prisoners, the Ministry of Justice ended the policy of maintaining a separate sector of San Salvador's "La Esperanza" (Mariona) prison for political prisoners, instead dispersing those arrested on political charges among the general prison population throughout the country. The Minister of Justice insisted that all those arrested were common criminals.

The numbers of persons arrested and held on political charges varied during the decade. In January 1984 there were roughly five hundred prisoners held in the political sections of Mariona and Ilopango prisons; by the end of 1986 there were 1,174. Many more people were arrested for suspected involvement in subversive activities and released within days: arrests averaged 340 per month in 1986.[99]

Convictions were rare. Cases generally bogged down in the instruction phase, and prisoners awaited extrajudicial resolutions. Political arrests in El Salvador did not lead to long prison sentences. Instead, special procedural laws enacted to combat subversion permitted arbitrary mass arrests that served the function of intimidating individuals and groups, destabilizing organizations, and securing information through interrogations and torture. These state of emergency laws permitted the Salvadoran military to carry out a counterinsurgency effort that had little to do with trial and punishment. Wittingly or unwittingly, the judiciary collaborated in this effort.

Entrenched Impunity

Looking back after the war, the Truth Commission found that "[w]ith the passage of time, the military establishment and, more specifically, some elements within the armed forces ... ended up totally controlling the civilian

---

98. U.S. pressure succeeded in avoiding the application of the amnesty to the five National Guardsmen convicted of killing four U.S. churchwomen in 1980 as well as FMLN members charged with killing four U.S. Marines and nine other people in the "Zona Rosa" case.

99. See Americas Watch, El Salvador's Decade of Terror (New Haven: Yale University Press, 1991), 76.

authorities, frequently in collusion with some influential civilians."[100] The vicious circle of violence led to a "situation in which certain elements of society found themselves immune from any governmental or political restraints and thus forged for themselves the most abject impunity."[101]

Many on the left claim to have resorted to violent methods because no legal recourse for abuse of power existed. The military took direct control of the government in 1931 and killed thousands to crush a communist-led peasant uprising the following year.[102] The armed forces, in alliance with civilian economic elites, governed the country directly until 1979. Blatantly fraudulent elections in 1972 and 1977 led opposition parties to withdraw from participation in the political process as many of their leaders were forced into exile.[103]

The National Guard operated in the countryside, assisted by the paramilitary organization ORDEN.[104] The formation of rural death squads grew out of the National Guard, which was itself created in 1910. The Guard always cooperated closely with large landowners, engaging in periodic crackdowns against peasant organizations.

Local National Guard commanders "offered their services" or hired out guardsmen to protect landowners' material interests. The practice of using the services of "paramilitary personnel" chosen and armed by the army or the large landowners began soon afterward. They became a kind of "intelligence network" against "subversives" or a "local instrument of terror."[105]

In its 1978 report, the Inter-American Commission on Human Rights called for the dissolution of ORDEN.[106] In its response to the IACHR, the Salvadoran government defended ORDEN for its role in fighting terrorism.[107]

100. *From Madness to Hope*, 172.
101. Ibid., 173.
102. See Thomas P. Anderson, *Matanza: El Salvador's Communist Revolt of 1932*, (Lincoln: University of Nebraska Press, 1971).
103. See, e.g., Michael McClintock, *The American Connection*, Vol. 1: *State Terror and Popular Resistance in El Salvador* (London: Zed, 1985), 165–87. Among those exiled was Christian Democratic leader José Napoleón Duarte, who apparently would have won the presidency for the UNO coalition in 1972 had the military not intervened to stop the vote count.
104. ORDEN, the Democratic Nationalist Organization, was formed between 1967 and 1969 by Gen. José Alberto Medrano, head of the National Guard. A principal function of the organization was to identify and eliminate purported communists among the rural population. General Medrano also organized the national intelligence agency ANSESAL.
105. *From Madness to Hope*, 133.
106. Inter-American Commission on Human Rights, *Report on the Situation of Human Rights in El Salvador* (1978), 167.
107. Ibid., 173.

Death squads operated freely in the years before the war, targeting peasants who organized to better their living conditions, priests and religious workers who worked with peasants and the urban poor, the Jesuit order and the Jesuit-run Central American University—vilified for its role in supporting an early attempt at land reform—labor and student leaders. In San Salvador, shadowy death squads actually composed of members of intelligence services issued communiqués and sentenced labor, religious, and political leaders to death.[108]

The 1979 Coup and El Salvador's First Truth Commission

Responding to massive human rights abuses and civil unrest, a group of young officers carried out a coup against President Humberto Romero on October 15, 1979. The coup came just four days before the IACHR was to discuss its devastating report on human rights in El Salvador at the OAS General Assembly in La Paz, Bolivia. Ending forty-eight years of direct military rule, the coup leaders replaced Romero with a civilian/military junta. In an initial proclamation, the armed forces explained that it had overthrown a government that had violated human rights, promoted and tolerated corruption in public administration and the justice system, created a real economic and social disaster, and profoundly damaged the prestige of the country and the armed forces. Its emergency program called for human rights guarantees and an end to violence and corruption.[109]

At least two of the initial acts of the new government responded directly to recommendations of the IACHR. The governing junta established after the October 1979 coup quickly disbanded ORDEN,[110] although the paramilitary organization was dissolved only on paper. No steps were taken to dismantle ORDEN's network or to disarm its members. Instead, the intelligence network and paramilitary control of the countryside continued, often under the guise of civil defense.

Shortly after taking power, in response to intense social pressure and the

108. For a history of death squad organizations in El Salvador, see, e.g., McClintock, *State Terror and Popular Resistance.*

109. Proclama de la Fuerza Armada de El Salvador, October 15, 1979.

110. Decree no. 12 of November 6, 1979. At a news conference the following day, junta member Guillermo Ungo explained that ORDEN had been a part of the "repressive machinery" and that a staff of forty people had directed its operations from the Presidential Palace, although the organization had no statutes or legal status. *Amnesty International Report 1980,* 136. Ungo resigned from the junta on January 3, 1980, and became a leader of the Democratic Revolutionary Front (FDR), which formed an alliance with the FMLN.

IACHR's recommendation, the revolutionary junta created a special commission to investigate the whereabouts of persons disappeared for political reasons, clandestine prisons, clandestine sites used for the practice of torture, and clandestine cemeteries.[111] Along with the public demand, members of the new government felt strongly about this issue. Some of the disappeared were well known to them because they had studied together at the university.[112]

A little-known precursor to more recent "truth" commissions, the special commission was composed of the newly appointed attorney general, Roberto Suárez Suay; Luis Alonso Posada, a designate of the newly appointed Supreme Court; and Roberto Lara Velado, president of the nongovernmental Human Rights Commission, an honorable citizen named by the governing revolutionary junta. When the commission opened its doors, it was overwhelmed with cases. Based on information it received about clandestine burial sites, the commission undertook a series of exhumations and efforts to identify cadavers.[113] The commission met with a total lack of cooperation from the security forces. While it could not determine individual responsibility for specific acts, it found evidence indicating the responsibility of prior governments. Its preliminary report, issued less than three weeks after it began work, recommended the prosecution of former presidents Armando Arturo Molina and Carlos Humberto Romero for their responsibility as commanders-in-chief of the armed forces and the prosecution of the directors of the National Guard, Treasury Police, and National Police during the Molina and Romero regimes. It further recommended that detention facilities inside security force and military garrisons be prohibited because they were likely to be used for illegal detentions and torture; that a Military Honor Committee be formed to collaborate with the special commission in investigating the whereabouts of persons possibly detained in security force jails and those disappeared for political reasons; and that measures be taken to compensate the families of missing political prisoners whose deaths could be confirmed or presumed.

Much as the Truth Commission would do thirteen years—and tens of thousands of deaths—later, the commission ended its preliminary report expressing its harsh condemnation ("*acre censura*") of the members of the

111. Decree no. 9, October 26, 1979.
112. Author's interview with Rubén Zamora, who was appointed minister of the presidency during the first civilian/military junta, July 4, 1994, San Salvador.
113. Informe de la Comisión Especial Investigadora de Reos y Desaparecidos Políticos, November 23, 1979, reprinted in *Estudios Centroamericanos* (January–February 1980).

Supreme Courts of Justice in office during the preceding regimes for their "culpable negligence." By failing to fulfill their duties to assure compliance with the constitution and laws, they had failed to protect the fundamental rights of the population of the republic.

In response to issuance of the report, Minister of the Presidency Rubén Zamora announced that the Attorney General's office had been instructed to investigate and obtain sufficient evidence to bring the heads of the security forces of the two prior administrations to justice and to investigate the responsibility of the two former presidents. He further announced that the families of missing persons and police killed in confrontations with the guerrillas would be compensated. As the Inter-American Commission on Human Rights noted, however, no proceedings were undertaken to determine the responsibility of former presidents Romero and Molina and the heads of their security forces. According to Zamora, the military's response to the special commission's recommendations was decisive: it was the military's declaration of war against the progressive forces represented in the junta. Another former government minister described the 1979 commission as "somewhat suicidal," given that it was carrying out its work while the death squads were in full action and the army still believed that it could and should crush all opposition.[114]

The special commission succeeded in locating sixty-seven bodies, twenty-five of whom were identified as disappeared prisoners. No living political prisoners were found. In its final report, issued on January 3, 1980, the commission called for modifications to the headquarters of the three security forces so that existing cells could no longer be used as clandestine detention sites. Because recent events (including the failure to heed the commission's earlier recommendations) rendered further efforts useless, the commission dissolved itself.

The special commission had acted with great valor, urging that responsibility be determined at the highest levels. But the military was far from willing to submit to examination of its actions and still believed it was entitled to use any means available to destroy the opposition. In this context, there was simply no possibility that the recommendations of the commission would be heeded. Overwhelmed though it was by the political moment, the commission remains the only Salvadoran institutional effort to examine the fate of the disappeared and determine responsibilities. By the time another

114. Author's interview with Ernesto Arbizú Mata, appointed treasury minister by the first governing revolutionary junta, San Salvador, July 13, 1994.

truth commission was finally formed as a result of the peace negotiations, expectations were far lower, and foreigners were called on to undertake the task.

State Violence During the War

Despite the reformist coup, killings and disappearances actually increased after October 1979.[115] Hard-line military officers assumed control over the governing junta as they rejected the efforts and findings of the special commission. Faced with this situation, recently appointed Supreme Court justices joined cabinet ministers and other government officials in resigning on January 3, 1980. Civilian leaders who did not resign, like the U.S. policymakers who supported them, sacrificed human rights concerns to the effort to defeat the growing insurgency and restore order. The lack of military support for the special commission was a critical element in undercutting the legitimacy of the junta. As the country moved inexorably toward civil war, unrestrained death-squad violence contributed to the determination of large sectors of the opposition that the only path remaining was armed struggle.[116]

The death squads' most famous victim was San Salvador's Archbishop, Monsignor Oscar Arnulfo Romero, shot and killed on March 24, 1980, as he said a memorial mass in a hospital chapel.[117] No one was ever tried for the murder of the Archbishop. The first judge assigned to investigate the case fled the country after an attempt on his life. The Supreme Court thwarted an effort to reopen the case seven years later by rejecting new testimony and throwing out an extradition petition on technical grounds. The Truth Commission confirmed that ARENA party founder Roberto D'Aubuisson, who died of cancer in February 1992, masterminded the killing. The ARENA party vehemently disputed that finding.

The Truth Commission found that the death squads "gained such control that they ceased to be an isolated or marginal phenomenon and became an instrument of terror used systematically for the physical elimination of

115. For a comprehensive analysis of the relationship between political developments in this period and the use of repression, see William Stanley, *The Protection Racket State: Elite Politics, Military Extortion, and Civil War in El Salvador* (Philadelphia: Temple University Press, 1996).

116. See, e.g., Enrique Baloyra, *El Salvador in Transition* (Chapel Hill: University of North Carolina Press, 1982), 91ff.

117. See *From Madness to Hope*, 127–31; Robert Weiner, *A Decade of Failed Promises: The Investigation of Archbishop Romero's Murder* (New York: Lawyers Committee for Human Rights, 1990).

political opponents. Many of the civilian and military authorities in power during the 1980s participated, encouraged and tolerated the activities of these groups."[118]

In the countryside during the early years of the war, the Salvadoran armed forces massacred thousands of *campesinos* in guerrilla zones in a deliberate strategy to terrorize the peasant population and eliminate sources of supply and information for the guerrillas. Salvadoran and U.S. authorities dismissed reports of massacres as guerrilla propaganda. No official investigations were undertaken. Deaths went unrecorded as survivors fled the area and, often, the country. When apprised of mass killings in the countryside, local justices of the peace were easily discouraged from fulfilling their duties. Even in urban areas, judicial investigations of deaths resulting from political violence rarely proceeded beyond identification of the victim and a cursory determination of the cause of death. Judicial authorities did not carry out autopsies and basic investigative steps.

The only politically motivated killings investigated and prosecuted during the 1980s were those in which U.S. citizens were victims. The U.S. government's role in downplaying human rights abuses committed by the Salvadoran military while insisting on prosecutions when U.S. citizens were killed also contributed to cynicism about the role of the judicial system. Perhaps the best-documented example of U.S. cover-up of Salvadoran abuses came in the wake of the December 1981 "El Mozote" massacre. During a massive military operation, the U.S.-trained Atlacatl Battalion engaged in wholesale, systematic slaughter of civilians in a remote area of northeastern El Salvador.[119] No official investigation of the killings at El Mozote was undertaken despite persistent reports of a massacre and accounts provided by U.S. journalists who visited the site weeks later.[120] U.S. government officials vigorously disputed the reports of a massacre. Embassy officials had failed to reach the site of the killings, yet nonetheless believed that something serious had happened at El Mozote.[121] Danner's account shows how the failure of U.S. embassy officials to confirm the deeds became the basis for the Reagan administration's attacks against the journalists and proof that no massacre

118. *From Madness to Hope*, 132.
119. Ibid., 114–21; Mark Danner, *The Massacre at El Mozote* (New York: Vantage Books, 1994).
120. Accounts of the massacre by Ray Bonner of the *New York Times* and Alma Guillermoprieto of the *Washington Post*, both of whom traveled to the area of the massacre, saw evidence of mass killings, and interviewed survivors, were published on the front pages of their respective newspapers on January 27, 1982.
121. Danner, *The Massacre at El Mozote*, 126ff.

had occurred. The handling of this case graphically illustrates the willingness of the Reagan administration to minimize or discount atrocities committed by the Salvadoran armed forces because of its overriding commitment to support the effort to defeat the leftist insurgency.

At times the Salvadoran military's wanton disregard for human rights became a political problem in Washington, as the Reagan administration sought increased aid for its Salvadoran allies.[122] This massive increase in aid came in the wake of the January 1984 "Report of the National Bipartisan Commission on Central America," known as the "Kissinger Commission" report, which urged a huge increase in military and economic assistance to El Salvador. From a total of $64.2 million in fiscal year 1980, only $6 million of which was military aid, U.S. assistance climbed to $412.5 million in 1984, almost half of which ($196.6 million) was military aid. In 1985 the total aid package was $570.2 million. In large part because of massive U.S. aid to the Salvadoran army, U.S.-based human rights groups focused on abuses in El Salvador. Two of the largest U.S.-based human rights organizations, Human Rights Watch and the Lawyers Committee for Human Rights, cut their teeth on the Salvadoran conflict.[123]

---

122. See Americas Watch, *El Salvador's Decade of Terror*, 141, app. A.

123. See, e.g., Americas Watch and American Civil Liberties Union, *Report on Human Rights in El Salvador, January 26, 1982*; Americas Watch, *The Continuing Terror: Seventh Supplement to the Report on Human Rights in El Salvador*, September 1985; *Draining the Sea: Sixth Supplement to the Report on Human Rights in El Salvador*, March 1985; *Nightmare Revisited, 1987-88: Tenth Supplement to the Report on Human Rights in El Salvador*, September 1988; *Settling into Routine: Human Rights Abuses in Duarte's Second Year: Eighth Supplement to the Report on Human Rights in El Salvador*, May 1986; *A Year of Reckoning: El Salvador a Decade After the Assassination of Archbishop Romero*, March 1990; Americas Watch and American Civil Liberties Union, *As Bad as Ever: A Report on Human Rights in El Salvador, Fourth Supplement*, January 31, 1984; *Supplement to the Report on Human Rights in El Salvador*, July 20, 1982; *Third Supplement to the Report on Human Rights in El Salvador*, July 19, 1983; Americas Watch and Lawyers Committee for Human Rights, *Free Fire: A Report on Human Rights in El Salvador, Fifth Supplement*, August 1984; Americas Watch, *El Salvador's Decade of Terror*; Lawyers Committee for International Human Rights, *Update: The Case of Four U.S. Churchwomen Murdered in El Salvador in December 1980* (1984); Lawyers Committee for Human Rights, *El Salvador Certification: Summary of the Cases of Ten U.S. Citizens Killed Since 1980* (1984); Lawyers Committee for Human Rights, *Justice Denied: A Report on Twelve Unresolved Human Rights Cases in El Salvador* (1985); Lawyers Committee for Human Rights, *El Salvador: Human Rights Dismissed: A Report on Sixteen Unresolved Cases* (1986); Doggett, *Underwriting Injustice*; DeWind and Kass, "Justice in El Salvador."

2

CRIMINAL JUSTICE AND REFORM EFFORTS DURING THE WAR YEARS

Press reports of atrocities in El Salvador and the unstinting efforts of human rights advocates raised concerns in the U.S. Congress. From late 1981 to late 1983, Congress conditioned U.S. military aid to El Salvador on a semiannual administration report that the Salvadoran government was "making a concerted and significant effort to comply with internationally recognized human rights" and "achieving substantial control over all elements of its own armed forces so as to bring to an end the indiscriminate torture and murder of Salvadoran citizens by these forces."[1] The Reagan administration made four such certifications despite overwhelming evidence of continuing serious violations and a total failure to investigate past violations.[2]

1. International Security and Development Cooperation Act of 1981, Pub. L. No. 97–113, Section 728, 95 Stat. 1519, 1555 (1981). See, generally, Kenneth H. Anderson, "Action Specific Human Rights Legislation for El Salvador," *Harvard Journal of Legislation* 22 (1985): 255–68.

2. The certification requirement ended when President Reagan pocket vetoed legislation containing it in late 1983, although the Reagan administration provided "voluntary" certifications in January and July 1984. The certification process has been termed a "clumsy tool for reducing human rights violations" because the statute itself was vague, no mechanism was established for congressional review of the executive's certification, and the only alternative to authorization of full military aid was a complete cutoff of that aid at a time when U.S. policy mandated support of the Salvadoran government (Anderson, "Action Specific Human Rights Legislation," 261).

This chapter looks at how the U.S. involvement in the war in El Salvador led to pressure to achieve justice in selected cases and an ambitious, large-scale but fundamentally flawed judicial reform effort. Salvadoran officials also proposed justice reforms during the 1980s, but none designed to address the serious failings of the criminal justice system.

U.S. Efforts to Curb Human Rights Abuses: The Big Case Focus

The families of four U.S. churchwomen killed in 1980, along with church and human rights groups, demanded that those responsible be brought to justice.[3] Members of the National Guard abducted Ita Ford, Maura Clarke, Dorothy Kazel, and Jean Donovan as they left El Salvador's airport on December 3, 1980. They raped and murdered the four women, who were subsequently found buried in a shallow grave. Ultimately, Congress conditioned 30 percent of 1984 military aid appropriations on a trial and verdict in the churchwomen's case.[4] Six months later, in May 1984, five low-level National Guardsmen were convicted. U.S. experts were instrumental in the investigation and prosecution of the case. Still, those who gave the order to kill the four women and the officers who covered up the crime were never identified or prosecuted.

During the 1980s the only other case of political murder that led to a trial and convictions of the triggermen was the murder of the head of the Salvadoran agrarian reform agency (ISTA) along with two land reform advisors from the American Institute for Free Labor Development (AIFLD). The three were gunned down in the coffee shop of the Sheraton Hotel in January 1981. Only because AIFLD assigned a full-time investigator to the case

3. The tortuous progress of this investigation is recorded in a series of reports by the Lawyers Committee for International Human Rights, which represented the families of the murdered women. See Lawyers Committee for International Human Rights, *Update: The Case of Four U.S. Churchwomen Murdered in El Salvador in December 1980* (New York, 1984); Michael Posner and Scott Greathead, "Justice in El Salvador: A Report of the Lawyers Committee for International Human Rights on the Investigation into the Killing of Four U.S. Churchwomen," *Columbia Human Rights Law Review* 14 (1983): 191.

4. Act of November 14, 1983, Pub. L., No. 98–151, 97 Stat. 970 (1983). The amendment was introduced by Sen. Arlen Specter - R. Pa., and Rep. Clarence D. Long - D. Md. See Cynthia Arnson, *Crossroads: Congress, the President, and Central America 1976–1993*, 2d ed. (University Park: Pennsylvania State University Press, 1993), 140.

was sufficient evidence developed to convict the triggermen, two former National Guardsmen. Those who planned the killings, gave the orders, and covered up the crime, including several officers known to be involved in death-squad activities, were never tried.[5] A judge permitted one of the officers involved to change his appearance so that he would not be identified by witnesses in a lineup.[6] Another officer, who confessed his involvement in the killings to various people, including investigators from the United States, relied on his uncle, a powerful member of the Supreme Court, to avoid prosecution.[7]

The human rights groups that pushed for justice in these cases hoped that successful, albeit limited prosecutions would lead to investigations and prosecutions in other cases. Yet Salvadoran institutions demonstrated no inclination to fulfill their responsibilities when U.S. pressure was not brought to bear or when it was relaxed. Various elements contributed to the lack of prosecutions. One was a general and well-founded conviction that those responsible for death-squad activities were beyond the reach of law. Witnesses and judges received warnings not to risk their lives foolishly. Without the kind of intense U.S. involvement seen in these two cases, there was not even a minimal aura of protection for witnesses who might give information. Security forces did not investigate crimes committed by other security force or military personnel. They failed to carry out basic investigative steps, such as securing forensic evidence and conducting timely and thorough witness interviews.

While many aspects of Salvadoran criminal procedure can and have been questioned, the fundamental weakness was that cases were simply not investigated in any serious way. This pattern did not change despite prodding by the United States that led to the 1984 formation of a commission under the executive charged with investigating five cases.[8] In 1985 its responsibilities

5. See *From Madness to Hope,* Report of the Truth Commission for El Salvador (San Salvador and New York: United Nations, 1992–1993), 144–47.

6. Ibid., 146; Lawyers Committee for Human Rights, *Justice Denied: A Report on Twelve Unresolved Human Rights Cases in El Salvador* (New York, 1985), 31.

7. Lawyers Committee, *Justice Denied,* 35–36.

8. The "Cestoni" Commission, headed by Government Human Rights Commission president Benjamín Cestoni, was charged with investigating: (1) the murder of Archbishop Romero; (2) the January 1981 murder of two U.S. agrarian reform advisors and the head of the Salvadoran agrarian reform institute in the Sheraton Hotel; (3) the disappearance and murder of U.S. journalist John Sullivan in December 1980; (4) the killing of various people by Civil Defense men in the Armenia area in 1981, known as the Armenia "well" case; and (5) the Las Hojas massacre in which at least sixteen peasants were killed in a combined Civil Defense and army operation. Only in the "Sheraton" case was anyone convicted, and after years of U.S. pressure

were transferred to the newly formed Commission to Investigate Criminal Acts, the linchpin of a $9.2 million U.S.-funded judicial reform project.[9]

The Jesuit Case

The need for a "show" trial for domestic and international consumption was most clear after uniformed soldiers entered the campus of the Central American University in the predawn hours of November 16, 1989, and murdered six Jesuit priests—including the University rector, vice rector, and director of the Human Rights Institute—their cook, and her daughter.[10] The murders occurred five days into the largest FMLN offensive of the war. The armed forces, unprepared for the magnitude of the guerrilla attacks, vented their wrath against those they perceived as civilian supporters of the guerrillas. Military leaders attempted to blame the crime on the FMLN.

Undeterred by overwhelming evidence of military responsibility, U.S. authorities—despite their stated desire to get to the bottom of the case—repeatedly engaged in actions that impeded the investigation and failed to provide Salvadoran authorities with all the information available to them.[11] The U.S. Embassy's legal officer worked closely with the U.S.-funded Commission to Investigate Criminal Acts that investigated the murders and staunchly defended the officer in charge of that unit, even when his participation in a cover-up became apparent.

---

and assistance, it was only the triggermen who faced trial. Efforts to prosecute officers involved in the case and civilians reportedly involved in the planning were thwarted at every turn. In late 1991, thirteen Civil Defensemen were finally tried and acquitted in the Armenia "well" case. Prosecutors cited the jurors' proximity to the defendants and military presence outside the courtroom as intimidating factors. In late 1987 the Supreme Court quashed efforts to proceed against at least one of the former officers reportedly involved in the Romero killing when it voided an extradition request and rejected new testimony on the case. Efforts by the Attorney General's office to proceed in the Las Hojas case in 1987 were abruptly halted by the application of a broad amnesty law, and no progress was ever made in the Sullivan case.

    9. See discussion *infra* at 63–64.

    10. For an authoritative account of the background to the murders, the subsequent investigation, and the U.S. role, see Martha Doggett, *Death Foretold: The Jesuit Murders in El Salvador* (Washington, D.C.: Georgetown University Press, 1993). For another comprehensive account of the Jesuit murders, the role of the Jesuits in El Salvador, and the investigation and trial, see Teresa Whitfield, *Paying the Price* (Philadelphia: Temple University Press, 1994).

    11. For an account of the ambivalent U.S. role, see Doggett, *Death Foretold*, 209–36; see also Martha Doggett, "The Assassination of the Jesuits: What the United States Knew," paper presented at Latin American Studies Association meetings, Atlanta, Georgia, March 10, 1994, based on information contained in classified documents released by the U.S. government in late 1993—after publication of the Truth Commission report.

In the Jesuit murder investigation, forensic personnel carried out ballistics tests on rifles provided by the troops involved in the killing yet were unable to match any of the weapons to the suspects who confessed to being the triggermen. The Truth Commission subsequently revealed that the chief investigator, Col. Manuel Antonio Rivas Mejía, had advised other officers how to ensure that the ballistics tests would be meaningless.[12]

The Jesuit murders tested the Salvadoran judicial system. Investigations were undertaken, but strictly within the limits set by the military. An armed forces Honor Commission identified the nine defendants who were to stand trial, while it simultaneously limited those responsible to the nine soldiers and officers selected. Under strong international pressure to carry out a credible prosecution, the judge assigned to the case proceeded against the nine defendants identified by the military Honor Commission, but failed to develop significant additional evidence in the face of military lies and stone-walling. The chief investigator's role in the cover-up ensured that relevant documentary evidence was destroyed and that high-ranking military officers remained outside the purview of the investigation. When the judge ordered the arrest of a lieutenant colonel who, according to testimony, had ordered the destruction of key records, the military was slow to turn him over to the court, and coup rumors abounded. The Truth Commission subsequently determined that this officer had actually organized the entire operation.[13]

In August 1990 Congressman Joseph Moakley, who headed a congressional task force formed to monitor the murder investigation, released a statement accusing the High Command of engaging "in a conspiracy to obstruct justice."[14] Salvadoran military officers had "withheld evidence, destroyed evidence, falsified evidence and repeatedly perjured themselves in testimony before the judge." According to Moakley, "The High Command's goal, from the beginning, had been to control the investigation and to limit the number and rank of officers who will be held responsible for the crimes."[15]

12. *From Madness to Hope*, 51.

13. Ibid., 53.

14. Shortly after the murders, House Speaker Thomas Foley formed a democratic congressional task force to monitor the Jesuit murder investigation in El Salvador. This was the first time a congressional group was charged with monitoring a human rights case in another country. The Moakley task force played a vital role by following developments closely and by releasing a series of timely and strongly worded reports and statements that forced Salvadoran authorities to take further actions. Nonetheless, the Moakley task force was unsuccessful in persuading the Salvadoran government to investigate the role of ranking officers involved in ordering the murders and the subsequent cover-up.

15. Congressman Joe Moakley, Statement on the Jesuits' Case and the Salvadoran Negotiations, Aug. 15, 1990, 1.

In reaction to Moakley's statement, the United States urged the Salvadoran military to show that it was serious about investigating the case. The 1993 release of previously classified U.S. documents showed that the U.S. Embassy and Congressman Moakley had already received information indicating that then army chief of staff Col. Rene Emilio Ponce had played a key role in the decision to kill the Jesuits. The army High Command held a publicized meeting with the Supreme Court president and (investigating and trial) Judge Ricardo Zamora to discuss ways to facilitate the investigation. Given that several of those at the meeting should have been defendants in the case, the results were predictably meaningless.

Efforts to question the official limits established for the case met with strong resistance. Two young prosecutors who sought to question military officers and focused on the inexplicable weaknesses in the police investigation found their role in the case rapidly reduced. When they resigned from their jobs and subsequently were contracted by the Jesuits to serve as private prosecutors on behalf of the victims' families, their motives were widely impugned.[16]

Since the highest levels of the Salvadoran armed forces were behind the decision to kill the Jesuits, it is not surprising that the judicial system was ill equipped to hold them accountable. Nonetheless, the unprecedented show trial offered up by Salvadoran authorities revealed myriad weaknesses in the legal system, which were noted by international observers.[17]

The outcome of the trial itself suggested a political bargain rather than a judicial resolution based on the facts and law. The president of the Supreme Court orchestrated the proceedings throughout the case. The jury trial of the nine defendants selected by the military was held just outside the Supreme Court president's chambers. The trial was broadcast on national television, allowing the nation to see eight uniformed defendants and hear readings of

16. Doggett, *Death Foretold*, 177–80.

17. See, e.g., International Commission of Jurists, *A Breach of Impunity, the Trial for the Murder of Jesuits in El Salvador, Report of the Observer for Latin America of the International Commission of Jurists* (Geneva, 1992); François Crepeau, "Rapport d'un observateur international dans l'affaire du meurtre des Jesuites a la Universidad Centroamericana de San Salvador," *McGill Law Journal* 37 (1992): 835; Amnesty International, "El Salvador Army Officers Sentenced to 30 Years for Killing Jesuit Priests," AMR 37/WU 01/92a5 (February 7, 1992); José María Tamarit, "Informe sobre el proceso judicial por los asesinatos de Seis Jesuitas y dos Colaboradoras en El Salvador," prepared for Ministry of Foreign Affairs of Spain (1991), unpublished manuscript on file with the author; Robert Kogod Goldman, "Report to the Lawyers Committee for Human Rights on the Jesuit Murder Trial," in Doggett, *Death Foretold*, app. C; *El Proceso por el Asesinato de los Sacerdotes Jesuitas en El Salvador, Informe del Observador Eduardo Luis Duhalde,* Asociación Americana de Juristas, Buenos Aires, November 15, 1991.

the triggermen's confessions, which detailed how the crime was committed. The jury's verdict was inexplicable, given the evidence presented. Colonel Benavides, who allegedly gave the order and was in charge of the troops involved on the night in question, was convicted for all eight counts of murder. A lieutenant who served with him was convicted for the murder of the teenage girl, although no evidence linked him directly to any of the killings. All the other defendants, most of whom had confessed, were acquitted on all charges.

A cynical reading of this verdict suggests an understanding that the colonel had to be convicted to satisfy U.S. demands. The conviction of Lt. Mendoza only for the murder of the girl—for which he was no more responsible than for any of the other deaths—suggested to some a belief that the Jesuits had earned their fate, and that the girl's mother had made a conscious choice to work with them, while her fifteen-year-old daughter was an innocent victim of circumstances. The defense devoted much of its energy to attacking the Jesuits and defending the armed forces. The jurors heard no evidence directly. In accordance with Salvadoran practice, the judge had selected certain parts of the record to be read to them. The jurors declined to exercise their option to ask that witnesses be called for clarification.

International observers who attended the trial could find no logical basis for the verdict. Some speculated that the jury might have been fixed. One of the jurors, all of whom remained anonymous and invisible, was reportedly an employee of the Supreme Court. While many observers lauded the conviction of two officers as a break in the tradition of military impunity, the failure to identify and prosecute those who gave the orders and to convict the confessed triggermen suggested that impunity had not been overcome.

A year and a half after the jury verdict, the Truth Commission confirmed that members of the High Command and other ranking officers planned and ordered the murders and orchestrated the cover-up.[18]

The justice system charged with responsibility for investigating the case had actually served primarily as a vehicle for a political decision. Because of the insistence of the Jesuits, particularly Father José María Tojeira, provincial of the Central American province, and the courage of the young former prosecutors who took on the private prosecution, the legal case provided an opportunity to challenge publicly the official version of the killings as an isolated act not ordered by higher-ups. Despite the failure to prosecute higher-ups, the private prosecution broke new ground in El Salvador by focusing on this issue. Relying on Salvadoran law as well as on international

18. *From Madness to Hope*, 45–54.

definitions of command responsibility and legal arguments used in the trials of the Argentine military commanders, the private prosecutors called for the investigation of ranking officers.[19] In a highly unusual move requested by the private prosecution, retired Argentine colonel José Luis García, who had served as a witness in the trials of the Argentine military commanders, testified during the plenary evidence period as an expert on the structure and function of a Latin American military. His testimony reinforced the notion that this kind of military operation could not have been carried out without the approval of the highest levels of command. Yet his testimony was not officially presented to the jury because the judge did not include it in the material to be read.

Rather than establishing a new standard for Salvadoran justice, the Jesuit case highlighted key problems in the judicial system. First and foremost, it once again revealed the military domination of civil society. The armed forces could murder the Jesuits, determine who would be tried, where they would be detained and under what conditions, who would testify and what they would say, and—conceivably—the outcome. The jury trial itself focused largely on defending the armed forces as an institution, and a noisy pro-army demonstration outside the courthouse was fully audible to the jury as defense counsel presented their arguments. The police investigation graphically illustrated the lack of an independent (non-military) criminal investigative body. Following Salvadoran custom, the primary evidence against the defendants consisted of extrajudicial confessions given while in police custody with no defense attorney present. Defense attorneys represented multiple defendants, whose interests were not always identical. In keeping with Salvadoran procedure, the judge in charge of the investigation also presided over the trial and sentenced the defendants. The judge alone determined what evidence would be read to the jury. The jury system revealed a series of deficiencies related to jury selection, lack of judicial direction, lack of opportunity to hear witnesses testify, and the possibility of arbitrary verdicts and jury tampering.

The Big Case Strategy in Retrospect

Even these exemplary cases graphically illustrated the extent of military impunity and the weakness of the justice system. While publicity about the

---

19. See pleadings presented to the 4th Criminal Court, San Salvador, by Alvaro Henry Campos Solorzano and Edward Sidney Blanco Reyes, May 22, 1991.

cases provided important information for domestic and international observers, the attempts to force prosecutions yielded minimal results. The focus on high-profile cases never produced results that created confidence in the judicial system. Instead, a consistent pattern emerged. In the rare cases that were investigated, foreign—usually U.S.—pressure was instrumental. Those who ordered the killings, the "intellectual authors," were never prosecuted. In most cases, even the triggermen escaped conviction. Salvadoran authorities became adept at waiting out U.S. interest in particular cases, and when absolutely unavoidable—as in the cases cited above—they offered up half or quarter loaves, or more often, crumbs.

This pattern may actually have increased cynicism about the possibility of achieving justice. Even in cases that had been the object of strong international pressure, justice was not achieved. And in cases not subject to international pressure, no one expected justice. The trials and verdicts in the high-profile cases did not have a national impact comparable to the trials of the Argentine generals or the Chilean prosecution of the officers responsible for the murder of former Foreign Minister Orlando Letelier and his assistant Ronni Moffitt (killed by a car bomb in Washington, D.C.). Once democracy was restored in the Southern Cone, at least a few of the intellectual authors of heinous crimes were put on trial. Moreover, the justice system was seen as capable of being an independent player, not merely a vehicle to carry out a political decision.

The Administration of Justice (AOJ) Project in El Salvador

Background

U.S. efforts to promote judicial reform developed in response to U.S. frustration with the Salvadoran justice system's difficulties in bringing those responsible for high-profile murders to justice.[20] Based on U.S. concerns,

20. U.S. GAO, *Foreign Aid: Efforts to Improve the Judicial System in El Salvador*, Report to the Chairman, Subcommittee on Western Hemisphere Affairs, Committee on Foreign Affairs, House of Representatives, GAO/NSIAD–90–81, May 1990. For a thorough critique of the U.S. AOJ program in El Salvador, see Doggett, *Underwriting Injustice*; see also Thomas Carothers, *In the Name of Democracy* (Berkeley and Los Angeles: University of California Press, 1991); and *Elusive Justice: The U.S. Administration of Justice Program in Latin America*, report on a workshop sponsored by the American University School of International Service and the Washington Office on Latin America (May 1990); Marcelo Sancinetti, Jorge A. Bacque,

millions of dollars were allocated for justice reform. From fiscal year 1984 through fiscal year 1989, a total of $13.7 million was authorized for the Administration of Justice program in El Salvador, although only $5 million was actually spent. A State Department lawyer involved in these programs notes that the original congressional earmark of $9.23 million was a completely disproportionate amount to provide for something the Salvadorans were not prepared to do. The El Salvador Project originally had four components: a Commission to Investigate Criminal Acts, a commission to reform Salvadoran legislation (CORELESAL), a judicial protection unit, and judicial administration and training.

With the El Salvador project, AID launched a new Administration of Justice (AOJ) program that, in theory, should have benefited from the critiques of an earlier law and development strategy in Latin America.[21] AID's new strategy was intended to avoid the pitfalls of the law and development programs of the 1960s and '70s, which had been based on the idea of transforming Latin American legal education through U.S. models, and exchanges of law professors and lawyers between the United States and Latin America. Those involved in this effort discovered that Latin American legal education had not been transformed, nor had their efforts seriously contributed to economic revitalization. Instead, these efforts came to be seen as ethnocentric, lacking in understanding, and interventionist. U.S. lawyers found themselves serving U.S. foreign policy goals to facilitate "stable and predictable commercial transactions within an implicit liberal capitalist economy."[22]

Among the lessons AID purportedly drew from its earlier experience were: the AOJ Program would be "strictly for democratic governments" with elected officials truly committed to the improvement of the administration of justice;[23] AID would "support local initiatives, not create demand for assistance where none exists";[24] efforts would involve Latin Americans themselves rather than imposing U.S. models; the AOJ program would give

and Marco A. Castro Alvarado, *Programa para una estrategia de reforma judicial de US AID* (San Salvador: Checchi and Company Consulting, Inc., 1991); Arthur Mudge et al., *Evaluation of the Judicial Reform Project, No. 519-0296, USAID/El Salvador* (1987).

21. See José E. Alvarez, "Promoting the 'Rule of Law' in Latin America: Problems and Prospects," *George Washington Journal of International Law and Economics* 25 (1991): 281.

22. James A. Gardner, *Legal Imperialism: American Lawyers and Foreign Aid in Latin America* (Madison: University of Wisconsin, 1980), 6, 9.

23. Bureau of Latin America and the Caribbean, "Agency for International Development Action Plan for Administration of Justice and Democratic Development" (1986), 15.

24. Ibid., 16.

priority to improvement of criminal proceedings because of the human rights consequences of deficiencies in this area; and the complexity of AOJ reform efforts called for a "contextual approach" that would assure that judicial reforms related to "the society generally."[25]

The lessons learned from the earlier law and development efforts were not applied in El Salvador. Alvarez notes that the "hurried design" of the Salvador AOJ project, which responded to congressional calls for a "quick fix," appeared to violate "virtually every tenet of AID's AOJ strategy."[26] In 1995 a State Department lawyer involved in these programs from the outset similarly noted that "we were violating our policy from the outset; perhaps we were all being used."

U.S. policymakers seemed to believe that justice reform could remedy problems of political violence rooted in ingrained economic and social structures, and political and cultural traditions.[27] They failed to take into account that those charged with implementing the reforms had far stronger interests in preserving the status quo. In Washington, the decision to initiate a judicial reform effort in El Salvador was based on the thinking of policymakers such as the authors of the 1984 Report of the National Bipartisan Commission on Central America (the "Kissinger Commission"), who recommended that the United States help to strengthen Central American judicial systems as part of the overall effort to defeat communism and maintain order by "shaping existing governments into more democratic forms."[28] This decision was not based on a realistic assessment of the needs of the Salvadoran justice system or the feasibility of introducing reforms in the existing context.

Thus, rather than set a new standard for administration of justice programs as the vanguard of a new generation of justice reform projects, the Salvador project responded almost exclusively to political concerns in Washington. As some State Department officials have since observed, it was not an AOJ project. In objective terms, the proposal for judicial reform in El Salvador was seen as something necessary in order to obtain far more important military and economic aid.

Nonetheless, the new generation of AOJ projects begun in El Salvador emerged as the largest set of democracy assistance projects in Latin America during the 1980s and involved AID, the State Department, the United States Information Agency (USIA), and the Justice Department.

25. Ibid., 17.
26. Alvarez, "Promoting the Rule of Law," 306, n. 186.
27. Carothers, *In the Name of Democracy*, 218.
28. Ibid., 223.

The Proposed Project

In its original El Salvador Project Paper, U.S. AID described the breakdown of the Salvadoran criminal justice system as a recent phenomenon. It noted that fewer than 20 percent of all cases brought before a jury result in convictions and that the "dysfunction" of the system has led to increasing reliance on extrajudicial (violent) means to resolve disputes or redress grievances.[29] The underlying premise of the paper was that the justice system was not investigating those responsible for death-squad actions because of its limited technical capacity. The proposed project focused on establishing order and promoting trust in the system through the resolution of exemplary cases.

As Thomas Carothers, a former State Department lawyer who worked on the program, has written:

> Creating a judicial assistance program to get at the problem of right-wing political violence was a way of addressing the problem without confronting the fundamental issue of the configuration of power in El Salvador.... The Salvadoran justice system did not break down as a result of the civil war and thereby cause the torrent of political violence of the late 1970s and early 1980s. The justice system has never exercised independent authority over the dominant sector of Salvadoran society. The massive political violence that occurred in the civil war merely highlighted the justice system's long-standing inadequacy; it did not result from it.[30]

The U.S. analysis assumed that those in power in El Salvador wanted to stop death-squad actions and that the reason these actions were going unpunished was because of a weak judiciary. Yet death squads were formed to serve as paid protectors of powerful interests unwilling to accept change; they had close links to the armed forces and powerful civilians. The judiciary alone had little possibility of being effective in preventing the actions of paramilitary death squads. These groups relied on the collaboration or toleration of the police and armed forces and would not hesitate to threaten or attack judges who had the temerity to investigate their deeds. In this context, the withdrawal of official approval for such groups was plainly the key prerequisite to their suppression.

29. U.S. AID, *El Salvador Project Paper—Judicial Reform*, AID/LAC/P-175, Project no. 519–0296, p. 4.
30. Carothers, *In the Name of Democracy*, 224.

Despite the Salvadoran government's unwillingness or inability to tackle the underlying issues, those involved in the AOJ project proposal claimed to have found the requisite political will on the part of the government. In substantial part, AID rested its hopes on the enactment of Decree 50, a less draconian procedure for processing those suspected of political crimes than its predecessor Decree 507, but far from meeting international human rights standards.[31] AID nonetheless maintained: "It is the general opinion of legal experts, both Salvadoran and others, that the passage of Decree 50 shows a willingness on the part of the Salvadoran government to make the necessary reforms and revisions of the law in order to ensure a fair and workable criminal justice system."[32]

Other Salvadoran initiatives cited as evidence of the government's commitment to judicial reform were the successful 1984 prosecution of five members of the Salvadoran National Guard accused of murdering four American churchwomen in 1980; passage of a new constitution in December 1983 that assured a more independent judiciary by mandating that future judges be chosen from a list compiled by an independent commission rather than by the legislature; and the creation of two separate commissions in 1983, one by the Supreme Court and the other by interim President Alvaro Magaña, to review Salvadoran criminal codes and make recommendations for changes that would improve the administration of justice.[33]

It is hard to understand how any of these developments could have been interpreted as showing a commitment to judicial reform. The limited prosecution of the churchwomen's killers owed much more to U.S. persistence and conditioning of aid than to the Salvadoran judicial system. The "independent commission" mandated by the 1983 constitution was not established until 1989 and was hardly independent since it was controlled by the Supreme Court, which was responsible for naming lower court judges.[34] The various commissions set up to review Salvadoran criminal codes and improve the administration of justice did virtually nothing. AID's finding of sufficient commitment to carry out judicial reform in 1984 seems to have been, at best, based on wishful thinking and unfulfilled commitments.

31. See discussion and cites *supra,* 38, note 90.
32. U.S. AID, *El Salvador Project Paper,* 5.
33. Ibid., 12.
34. By 1984 it seemed likely that this commission—the National Council on the Judiciary—would serve as no more than an advisor to the Supreme Court. By that time Supreme Court justices had shown themselves unable to agree about whether the Council's recommendations would be binding on the court. See CORELESAL, *Consejo Nacional de la Judicatura* (June 1988), 270–87.

Acknowledging to some degree that political will remained an issue, AID wrote:

> While the unwillingness of any society to correct the defects in its social institutions cannot be compensated for, the inability to correct problems due to lack of resources and training can be dealt with. This project proposes to assist El Salvador to strengthen its judiciary and related institutions through the provision of necessary resources—financial and technical assistance, equipment, and training—so that it can make its system of criminal justice work for the general welfare and security of its citizens.[35]

Yet judicial reform was not on the Salvadoran national agenda at the time, and as a result, there were virtually no Salvadoran initiatives under way. In this context, the U.S. proposal focused on technical capacity. The United States proposed to form a crack police unit that would be incorruptible. According to the U.S. analysis, police needed improved scientific methods, the judiciary needed protection and training, and the laws needed to be improved. A 1993 General Accounting Office (GAO) report noted: "AID projects focused on easier-to-manage technical assistance, such as judicial training seminars and computerized caseload management, rather than working on the institutional, political and attitudinal changes necessary for fundamental, sustainable reform."[36]

Responding to the criticism that it had undertaken judicial reform in El Salvador without any Salvadoran political commitment to undertake substantive reforms, AID explained that "the program's strategy was to foster commitment, not to wait until it was present."[37] Rather than honestly evaluate the willingness of different actors in El Salvador to promote judicial reform, the AID project assumed such willingness on the part of the Christian Democratic Party (PDC). The PDC's hold on power was always tenuous, with frequent rumors of military coups. Throughout the Duarte administration, forces further to the right controlled the Supreme Court. For a three-year period (1985–88), the PDC enjoyed a majority in the Legislative Assembly, but it did not take this opportunity to push through reforms. Weakened by internal divisions, corruption, serious economic problems, a debilitating war, and an overweening military, the PDC accomplished little.

35. U.S. AID, *El Salvador Project Paper*, 5.
36. U.S. General Accounting Office, *Foreign Assistance: Promoting Judicial Reform to Strengthen Democracies*, GAO/NSIAD–93–149 (September 1993), 17.
37. Ibid., 34–35.

Having made its partnership with the Christian Democrats, who controlled only the executive branch, U.S. judicial reform assistance was channeled through the executive. The new police unit designed to tackle sensitive cases (in which military involvement was suspected) was thus placed under a Commission to Investigate Criminal Acts headed by the minister of justice. The attorney general, who under the constitution was responsible for overseeing criminal investigation, was an associate of ARENA leader Roberto D'Aubuisson, known for his involvement in death squads. The judiciary, which was responsible for prosecutions, was headed by Francisco José Guerrero, a leader of the National Conciliation Party (PCN), which had long been the ally of the armed forces. The decision to channel funding based on Salvadoran political lines, to favor the "centrist" Christian Democrats regardless of the institutional logic involved, thus created a heavily politicized Special Investigative Unit in the executive branch that was not trusted by the courts and did not work with the Attorney General's office. Understandably, the United States had little desire to channel funding to an attorney general closely identified with ARENA founder Roberto D'Aubuisson or to a Supreme Court dominated by the right.

This situation again reflected the hopelessness of the massive judicial reform effort that the United States proposed in 1984. Little or no effort was made to identify individuals and groups who might have been interested in judicial reform or develop potential interest within nongovernmental organizations, including lawyers' groups and law schools.

The Special Investigative Unit

Intended to tackle sensitive human rights cases, the Special Investigative Unit of the Commission to Investigate Criminal Acts (known in English as the "SIU") was made up of members of the security forces under the direction of an army officer. U.S. and Salvadoran authorities justified this arrangement as necessary for effective investigation of the military. In practice, military officers controlled all investigations and shielded their colleagues from inquiry.[38] Any political will that the civilian members of the commission might have had to investigate military crimes was undermined by the recalcitrance of the armed forces, which retained control over the new investigative unit.

38. See Doggett, *Underwriting Injustice* (New York: Lawyers Committee for Human Rights, 1989), 43–55, for a thorough critique of the Commission to Investigate Criminal Acts. See also Popkin, *Prospects for Legal Reform*, 23–35, and discussion *infra* at 181–86.

As a result, the SIU devoted most of its efforts to cases of common crime. U.S. officials, heavily invested in terming it successful, refused to acknowledge that the SIU was not an effective investigative body when members of the military were suspects.

In several cases in which the SIU, with substantial U.S. assistance, actually undertook investigations of members of the military or powerful individuals, the courts found ways to ensure impunity. Thus the Supreme Court effectively quashed a 1987 effort to reopen the investigation of the murder of Archbishop Romero, including the extradition of a former officer purported to have been involved in the plot. This effort had been spearheaded by a Christian Democratic attorney general and based on investigations by the SIU. The Truth Commission found that the Supreme Court "ensured ... impunity for those who planned the assassination."

In 1990 U.S. officials expressed outrage when two major cases fell apart in the courts and suspended all programs with the Supreme Court, choosing to work instead with the Public Ministry. In a notorious kidnapping-for-profit case, a first instance judge dismissed charges and freed the defendants. The defendants were military officers and well-connected members of the ARENA party linked to death-squad activities who were charged with kidnapping wealthy businessmen for ransom and attributing their actions to the FMLN. Because the judge's actions in this case did not concord with procedural requirements, he was replaced by another judge, who reinstated the charges, but not before one of the principal defendants succeeded in fleeing. Rumors in El Salvador suggested that the judge involved had been bribed— or threatened and bribed. A military judge and three suspects in the kidnapping case had previously met violent deaths; two of the suspects killed were in police custody at the time.[39] The other case involved the September 1988 army killing of ten peasants outside the town of San Sebastian. Because of intense U.S. pressure—including a visit by Vice President Dan Quayle, who called for punishment of those responsible—the army was eventually forced to identify some of those involved. Based on the army's belated investigation, the judge ordered the detention of nine soldiers and officers. The same judge subsequently released all but two of them. An appellate court confirmed this decision and ruled that only the major accused of ordering the killings should stand trial.[40]

Military interference and a complicit judiciary thus assured that those with power and influence would continue to be protected.

39. Americas Watch, *El Salvador's Decade of Terror*, 98–100.
40. *From Madness to Hope*, 80–86.

The Judicial Protection Unit

The judicial protection unit, composed of poorly trained prison guards and never really operational, was ill conceived from the outset and incapable of addressing the very real security concerns of Salvadoran judges, prosecutors, and witnesses.[41]

Judicial Administration and Training

The effort to improve judicial administration and training also suffered from conceptual problems. AID commissioned a major assessment of the Salvadoran court system carried out by the United Nations Latin American Institute for the Prevention of Crime and the Treatment of Offenders (ILANUD) and the Center for Administration of Justice at Florida International University.[42] The study, while thorough and replete with statistics, failed to address or even mention many key problems affecting the independence of the judiciary and due process. It devoted a relatively small percentage of its attention to problems affecting the criminal justice system, despite their centrality to the issues purportedly of concern to the United States.[43] Major concerns included the case-flow problems and the failure to comply with legal time periods.

In its section on criminal justice, the report recommended such reforms as reducing the fifteen-day plenary period to speed up the process, naming alternate judges to take the place of absent first instance judges, obliging law students to serve as defense counsel, and improving jury lists. A reform reducing the plenary evidence period to eight days and revising the jury selection system was subsequently proposed by the law reform unit (CORELESAL) and enacted by the legislature.[44] In the Jesuit case—a rare example of a case in which the private prosecution sought to introduce additional evidence during the plenary evidence period—lawyers for the Jesuits found themselves severely limited by this reform that further compounded the tendency to regard the instruction period as the only time when evidence could be received. Most delays actually occurred during the far lengthier period of

41. Doggett, *Underwriting Injustice*, 67–71.
42. Their 170-page report, "Diagnóstico sobre el órgano judicial en El Salvador," was presented in September 1987.
43. The study looks at all the country's courts and addresses the issues of case-flow, budget, human resources, administration, and material resources.
44. Código Procesal Penal, article 300, Decree 524, D.O. 163, Tomo 309, July 5, 1990.

instruction. No proposals were made to ensure that time periods for the instruction were observed.

The study did not rely on international standards, explain how these recommendations would contribute to respect for human rights, or enhance the independence of the judiciary. It did not address such urgent matters as the need to institute mechanisms for pretrial release, to separate investigative and sentencing judges, or to end arbitrary sentencing practices for misdemeanors. The report called for prohibiting judges from serving as notaries and increasing their salaries to compensate for loss of notarial income,[45] extending court hours, monitoring by the Supreme Court to make sure courts were actually open during business hours, and requiring justices of the peace to live in the jurisdictions of their courts.[46] No mention was made of the need to increase the external and internal independence of the judiciary, establish objective criteria for the selection and evaluation of judges, or protect them from arbitrary actions of the Supreme Court. The study mentioned without comment that civilians accused of political crimes could be subject to proceedings in military courts when constitutional guarantees were suspended.

The focus on administration and case management ignored fundamental sources of injustice and did little to ensure that administrative reforms would contribute to protection of individual rights. While some of these issues may have been outside the intended scope of this report, the failure to address them meant that the reforms proposed could, at best, have only a very limited impact on the overall deficiencies of the judiciary.

The Revisory Commission on Salvadoran Legislation (CORELESAL)

Established under the executive, CORELESAL came under the domination of the Supreme Court, which opposed many reforms. Although common in Latin America, the involvement of Supreme Court justices in the preparation of legislation also undermined the constitutional separation of powers. The

---

45. This reform was included in the constitutional reforms negotiated in April 1991.

46. This recommendation ignored the reality of the wartime situation in which many justices of the peace from conflict zones, where the insurgents often exercised political and military control, were unable to live in their communities because the FMLN did not recognize their authority and viewed them as part of the (enemy) state apparatus. Twenty-four justices of the peace were reported to have been murdered during the 1980s. See *From Madness to Hope*, 170.

1983 constitution had sought to remove the Supreme Court from this sphere precisely so that it would be able to serve as an outside and presumably impartial arbiter of the constitutionality of laws.

After five years of work, CORELESAL could point to few tangible results.[47] It failed to tackle the most pressing problems in Salvadoran criminal justice and had a poor track record in winning legislative approval for its proposals. Some of its draft bills were ultimately approved in a form so distinct from that proposed by CORELESAL that their intent was completely undermined. Along these lines, CORELESAL's attempt to mitigate the criminal procedure law for states of exception by increasing protections for suspects was rejected when the legislature approved a new law at the height of the 1989 FMLN offensive.[48]

The law reform unit was to give priority to criminal justice reform, yet despite extensive analyses of existing problems, it declined to confront fundamental problems in criminal proceedings. For example, no effort was made to suppress the extrajudicial confession or establish mechanisms for pretrial release of detainees. CORELESAL adopted the view that extrajudicial confessions were a necessary evil, despite having recognized in 1987 that "it is also a well known fact in this country, that in the majority of cases, [the extrajudicial confession] is obtained by the auxiliary organs through violence or intimidation."[49] In 1990 CORELESAL concluded that the extrajudicial confession should not be modified:

> [I]t is evident that in our country the problem of the extra-judicial confession is primarily cultural; we would propose taking away all value from that rendered in the auxiliary organs were it not for the lack of a true scientific police which applies the most modern techniques to investigate crime. For that reason we believe that it should be maintained as an institution.[50]

47. In September 1990, AID listed nine laws drafted by CORELESAL that had won legislative approval: the definition of a small farmer; a state of exception criminal procedure law; use of surname law; national council for the judiciary; reforms to the jury system and plenary phase of the criminal procedure; procedural law for the imposition of arrests and administrative fines; amendments to criminal, criminal procedure, and minors codes in relation to protection of the family and minors; amendments to criminal procedure code in relation to reversals and absolute nullity declarations; and the judicial career law.

48. Decree 376, November 16, 1989, D.O. 216, Tomo No. 305.

49. CORELESAL, *Reformas Inmediatas al Código Procesal Penal*, July 1987, primera parte, Tomo II, 389, cited in Williams et al., "Análisis," 46.

50. Ibid., 402, 421, and 424.

In evaluating legal reforms, it is relatively straightforward to compare proposed changes to internationally accepted standards as well as to assess their feasibility and likely effectiveness in light of institutional constraints. Because the U.S. effort did not rely on a human rights perspective, it did not necessarily give priority to reforms designed to improve human rights performance. For example, despite the well-known ineffectiveness of habeas corpus as a protection against arbitrary detention, disappearances, and abuses of detainees, CORELESAL prepared a proposal for habeas corpus reform that failed to address key deficiencies. Its proposed legislation would not have required a public hearing, nor would it have made the remedy more accessible.

The few criminal procedure reforms enacted were superficial. In some cases, they actually exacerbated existing problems.[51] When CORELESAL proposals were overruled in favor of maintaining the status quo, the law reform unit was largely silent, and AID officials still included the changed laws as project accomplishments in its list of proposed legislation enacted into law.

In the area of judicial governance, CORELESAL again identified key problems but failed to act on them. A CORELESAL treatise warned of the need for the Supreme Court to entrust many of its administrative duties to another body with sufficient specialized personnel, the most appropriate being the National Council on the Judiciary. Ending this concentration of functions would permit the Supreme Court to dedicate more time to its own jurisdictional duties.[52]

Despite CORELESAL's identification of the Supreme Court's excessive powers as a fundamental problem, the AOJ project had never focused on addressing this situation. In 1989—six years after the 1983 constitution called for establishment of a National Judiciary Council—the legislature passed an altered version of a CORELESAL proposal of enabling legislation that gave effective control of the council to the Supreme Court. This legislation did nothing to limit the court's control over the rest of the judiciary.[53] Even the draft bill prepared by CORELESAL gave the council less authority and fewer responsibilities than an earlier proposal drafted by the previous Supreme Court over the objection of some of its members.[54]

---

51. The reduction in the length of the plenary evidence period further contributed to making evidence obtained during the instruction phase dispositive.

52. CORELESAL, *Problemática de la Administración de la Justicia en El Salvador* (San Salvador, 1990), 107, 108.

53. Decree 348, October 5, 1989, D.O. 194, Tomo 305.

54. See CORELESAL, *Consejo Nacional de la Judicatura* (San Salvador, 1988), 105ff., 271ff.

A 1991 evaluation commissioned by AID observed:

> In order that the Supreme Court—over a period of time that should be accompanied by a real change in the structures of power aimed at the democratization of the country—can become increasingly independent and the judges at all levels can become independent of it, all disciplinary and contracting authority over members of the judicial branch should be in the hands of a body other than the Court itself; for example, the National Council on the Judiciary.[55]

This report found that under the existing system the implementation of any reform effort would be obstructed, because "virtually all Salvadoran lawyers are immersed in the context of a structure of authoritarian power, from which it is difficult for them to separate themselves, and in which a good part of their possibilities for employment depend on submission to these structures."[56]

CORELESAL's limited achievements were not due primarily to technical deficiencies, but rather to a lack of political will. CORELESAL carried out valuable studies and included a number of staff members committed to improving guarantees in Salvadoran justice. Two laws passed subsequent to its demise—a new Family Code and a law requiring defense counsel for suspects from the time of arrest—included substantial advances in the protection of citizens' rights. Those working on the technical issues in El Salvador were competent and understood the need for reform. Those with political responsibility did not share the same concerns; however, they were willing to accept the U.S. dollars and have well-paid lawyers work on studies and proposed reforms, even though they had no intention of implementing them. In this context, a group of professionals was funded by AID to carry out thorough studies and draft proposed legislation—legislation that was unlikely to be enacted into law if it meant any significant alteration of power relations in the country or limitation of arbitrary state action.[57]

After a negative 1990 evaluation by Argentine Professor Marcelo Sancinetti, AID apparently took many of its evaluator's criticisms seriously. It ceased funding CORELESAL on June 1, 1991, more than a year before the

---

55. Sancinetti, Bacqué, and Alvarado, *Programa para una estrategia*, 61.
56. Ibid., 10.
57. The first significant reform proposed by CORELESAL that was enacted into law was the public defense law. It unexpectedly won legislative approval in May 1992, after the peace accords were in effect and CORELESAL had been replaced by the ATJ. See discussion *infra* at 227–31.

project's scheduled termination date. The Supreme Court made an unsuccessful attempt to absorb the unit.[58] AID instead provided funding to the
Ministry of Justice for a smaller law reform unit, known as the ATJ (technical legal assistance).

Identification with U.S. Political/Military Goals

During the war years, U.S. sponsorship of judicial reform inevitably tainted
the effort. The United States was a key player in the war, planning and assisting with the counterinsurgency effort. In the 1991 study commissioned by
AID, the evaluators concluded that the top U.S. priority should be pressure
to assure the success of the peace process and the inclusion in the agreements
of "fundamental institutions necessary for the rule of law." The report noted
that U.S. financial support for an army that failed to comply with the principles of the rule of law meant that AID-sponsored efforts were necessarily
perceived by Salvadorans (on all sides) as an instrument of counterinsurgency. As a result, any discrete institutional modifications AID might be able
to achieve would encounter great resistance and the risk of their possible
neutralization through strategies designed to undermine the real application
of the new norms. The report noted: "It is ... military aid, rather than any
deficiencies in AID's AOJ program that ensures the futility of any program
to democratize the judicial system."[59]

In this situation, the United States was neither willing nor able to draw in
nongovernmental sectors that might have supported and lent vitality to a
more serious judicial reform effort. The degree of isolation is illustrated by
Sancinetti's experience in early 1991, when he led the three-member delegation conducting a review of the AID project. AID officials made no effort to
arrange for him to meet with representatives of nongovernmental human
rights organizations or to provide him with materials critical of the AID-
sponsored program prepared by NGOs. It was only through the initiative of
a U.S. Embassy legal officer that two members of the delegation had a minimal opportunity to discuss their mission with one nongovernmental human
rights organization.

During the war years, the "bunker mentality" of U.S. officials in El Salvador made it hard for them to view criticism of their project as anything

58. See CORELESAL, *Terminación de Labores e Información del Trabajo Realizado por
la Comisión Revisora de la Legislación Salvadoreña*, Memoria, San Salvador, October 31,
1991, 1–5.
59. Sancinetti, Bacqué, and Alvarado, *Programa para una estrategia*, 74–76.

other than politically motivated. Even after the September 1991 Jesuit murder trial, an AID official dismissed international observers' criticisms of the conduct of the investigation and trial as politically motivated. By that time, however, foreign consultants working with AID were incorporating many of the same human rights standards relied on by the observers into proposals for reform.

Under these circumstances, it is hardly surprising that the Salvadoran AOJ project failed to achieve its lofty goals. The project's goal of achieving an independent, responsible, and reliable justice system remained elusive. The expenditure of millions of dollars between 1985 and 1991 did little to lessen the risks of arbitrary repression or to overcome the historic impunity enjoyed by state actors and influential perpetrators of serious crimes. Much of the project's resources were diverted into less controversial areas, but even in these progress was minimal.

The problems in implementation of the project and the lack of oversight raise issues that go beyond the unique situation in El Salvador during the Reagan administration. Despite its obvious lack of success, there was very little controversy about the Salvadoran AOJ project during its early years. The program was seen as harmless (in contrast to military aid). And a bipartisan consensus reflected in the Kissinger Commission report saw an AOJ project as an integral part of U.S. assistance to Central American countries struggling against communist insurgencies. In part, AID's slowness to recognize its project's defects is explicable because of the war and the U.S. role in supporting the Salvadoran government, which made it politically impossible for the United States to be objective about its erstwhile ally. For the amount of money appropriated, very little oversight was provided. Those involved in the project in Washington say that reporting of progress on the project was always inadequate. During his tenure, Ambassador Edwin Corr reportedly declined to grant country clearance to the State Department and AID personnel charged with overseeing the program so that they could visit El Salvador.[60]

Ignorant of the workings of the legal system and stubborn in the refusal to admit that their chosen counterparts might have greater reason to maintain the status quo than to change it, U.S. officials repeatedly allied themselves with sectors indifferent or opposed to reform. As former Ambassador Walker put it, "Too often USG players allow themselves to be fooled, manipulated into working with the wrong crowd. This propensity for self-deception and

60. Author's interview with State Department official, March 1995.

gullibility—especially among neophytes to the game—can be a significant factor for things not working out as originally proposed."[61]

Those on the ground in El Salvador tended to lose any critical perspective. U.S. authorities were reluctant to admit the failings observed by others in the institutions they had created. The closeness of U.S. officials to their Salvadoran counterparts may have led to a loss of objectivity. U.S. officials often focused narrowly on technical skills without looking at the big picture: what a unit was actually doing, to whom it was really responsible, and whether oversight mechanisms were in place and functional. Mistakes that should have been examined were instead excused. Such behavior was particularly evident in the Jesuit murder investigation, during which the embassy legal officer, under Ambassador Walker, worked closely with the SIU chief in charge of the investigation and was unwilling to admit that the investigation was fundamentally flawed.[62] Although a focus on technical skills may be a rational response to the impossibility of creating political will, it leads to a focus on the success of transmission of those skills, rather than on how or whether the skills are ultimately put to use to achieve meaningful results. Improved technical skills may become a smoke screen to hide the lack of more fundamental changes. Thus time and again FBI experts lauded the technical capacity of the SIU in fingerprinting and ballistics work yet ignored the implications of its inability to make progress on sensitive human rights cases.

In El Salvador the United States appears to have promoted judicial reform without measurable guidelines for achievement.[63] International treaties in effect in El Salvador establish minimum due process requirements. These internationally recognized guidelines provide a basis for measuring whether reforms are contributing to respect for human rights. Without such guidelines, any reform can be classed as an achievement, efficiency itself can become the goal or the number of judges who have attended training sessions

61. See William Graham Walker, *Justice and Development: A Study* (January 1995), 13.

62. See discussion *supra* at 52–53. In its 1992 Project Paper for Judicial Reform II, Project No. 519–0376, September 1992, AID still claimed that the SIU was recognized in Central America and by the U.S. Justice Department as a "highly competent criminal investigative agency." More objective observers found serious fault with the unit's structure and performance.

63. Alvarez notes that AID reported on the number of training hours and material or books provided, but "there is little to suggest that either bilateral or regional AOJ projects are having a demonstrable impact on the overall competence or efficiency of the judiciary. Part of the problem lies in finding 'coherent, measurable' and undebatable indicators of success. Expedited case-processing or increased material support for the judiciary are not necessarily indicators of an 'improved' or more independent judiciary" ("Promoting the 'Rule of Law,'" 310).

the yardstick, without any demonstrable improvement of the quality of justice imparted.[64]

In 1990 assistance to the Supreme Court was temporarily suspended to express U.S. displeasure with developments on certain key cases, and the U.S. Congress eventually suspended funding to the SIU, pending approval of a plan to civilianize the institution. These suspensions did not, however, constitute an overall assessment of U.S. AOJ efforts in El Salvador to determine whether project goals were being furthered and whether the Salvadoran authorities had demonstrated the political will to implement reforms that would enhance judicial independence, procedural safeguards, and effective investigation and prosecution of those responsible for human rights violations.

The AOJ program in El Salvador during the war years graphically illustrated the risks inherent in making decisions about an AOJ project, not on its potential contribution to the rule of law, but on the basis of U.S. political needs and as part of a broader counterinsurgency effort.

Salvadoran Efforts to Promote Judicial Reform During the War Years

During the 1980s there was no indigenous effort to promote comprehensive reform of the justice system in El Salvador, yet certain issues were repeatedly raised and some reforms introduced. Lawyers who worked on drafting the 1983 constitution were particularly concerned about increasing the independence of the judiciary to overcome its traditional submissiveness to the executive branch. The 1983 constitution removed the Public Ministry, which includes the Attorney General's office, from the executive branch. A Constitutional Chamber was established within the Supreme Court, and the court's role in proposing or reviewing law reforms was limited to matters related to the judicial branch. For the first time, the constitution included a National Judiciary Council that was to assist in the selection of lower court

---

64. In his critique of earlier law and development efforts, Gardner noted the failure of the Chile Law Program to "develop notions of 'higher' international and human rights law that would be applicable to a given nation state.... Indeed, the failure to develop any cogent standard of legal thought and social justice by which arbitrary or repressive exercise of power—whether by social and economic groups or by the state—might be understood and challenged was a fundamental failure of American legal assistance in Chile, and a reflection of the vulnerability of the legal engineer and instrumental models carried abroad" (*Legal Imperialism*, 190).

judges. The comments of the drafters included in the *Informe Unico* testify to their concern about these issues. Not all of their recommendations— which included lifetime tenure for Supreme Court magistrates—were accepted; those that were did not achieve the desired results. These were certainly not matters that had been widely discussed at the time, and public consciousness about them was minimal.

Although few reforms to the criminal justice system advanced during the 1980s, the business sector in El Salvador pushed through reforms in areas important to them. At the private sector's urging and in the wake of publicity about a string of kidnappings committed by individuals tied to the military and to the ARENA party, the legislature enacted legal reforms in 1987. To enhance the likelihood of conviction in kidnapping, extortion, and certain drug-related crimes, reforms made codefendant testimony admissible and removed these cases from juries.[65] Salvadoran criminal procedure traditionally barred codefendant testimony as inherently unreliable.[66] The bar against codefendant testimony had been raised repeatedly to explain the failure to pursue those responsible for ordering and planning political killings. In response, U.S. officials and U.S.-based human rights groups had urged repeal of this restriction. At the time, San Salvador Archbishop Arturo Rivera y Damas expressed concern about the lack of interest in guaranteeing equally effective prosecutions in cases of political murder.

The 1987 reforms also limited the special privileges normally enjoyed by military defendants. While members of the armed forces ordinarily remained in detention in their garrison (or under the control of the armed forces) throughout criminal proceedings, the 1987 reforms required that those accused of kidnapping, extortion, and drug-related crimes be sent to prison.[67] Military men accused of political murder, such as the soldiers and officers prosecuted in the Jesuit case, were not discharged from the armed forces or sent to regular prisons. Instead, they remained in security force headquarters, under direct military control, with substantially greater privileges than other prisoners. Only after two officers were convicted in the Jesuit case were they transferred to prison. Had the same defendants been charged with kidnapping members of the economic elite, they would have been dismissed from the army and transferred to prison at the outset. The 1987 reforms reflected the concerns of the country's economic elite, calling for needed reforms only in those crimes of particular concern to them.

65. Código Procesal Penal, article 499–A.
66. Código Procesal Penal, article 499.
67. Código Procesal Penal, article 246.

In 1989 the new ARENA government initiated efforts to strengthen antiterrorist legislation, in some cases harking back to provisions of earlier discredited laws.[68] Proposed reforms would have extended the definition of terrorist acts to cover nonviolent protests, criminalized international human rights reporting, and created presumptions of involvement in "terrorist" activities. Domestic and international human rights groups attacked these proposals as inconsistent with international human rights norms. Most were never enacted into law.

During this same period, the Salvadoran Supreme Court undertook a series of reforms. Under the leadership of Supreme Court President Mauricio Gutiérrez Castro, the court initiated a section to maintain and provide information about persons detained throughout the country. It also assigned judicial officers to the principal prisons (*jueces de vigilancia penitenciaria*) to review the situation of prisoners and facilitate communication between them and the courts, itinerant judges to assist backed up courts, and judicial auditors to review court statistics. The Supreme Court did amass substantial statistical information, but these efforts appeared to have little impact on substantive problems. The percentage of prisoners awaiting sentence did not decrease significantly during this period, nor was the widespread problem of backlogs meaningfully addressed. During Gutiérrez Castro's tenure dozens of new court facilities were constructed and inaugurated, greatly improving the judiciary's physical facilities. Vehicles were provided to some judges. Computer systems were introduced in the Supreme Court, although trial courts continued to labor with antiquated manual typewriters. Aside from the improved physical facilities, there was no noticeable improvement in justice at the local level: justices of the peace remained notorious for their failure to fulfill their obligations.

Many of the Supreme Court's initiatives reflected genuine needs of the justice system, but they were so poorly implemented that they achieved few substantive results. For example, the court established a medical forensic institute that became known for its lack of professionalism. The institute failed to carry out court-ordered autopsies in a timely manner and gave out unsolicited and erroneous information on sensitive cases. While forensic anthropologists were unearthing small children's remains at the site of the El Mozote massacre, the institute's director, Dr. Juan Mateu Llort, assured the news media that the dead had been guerrilla combatants or civilians caught in cross fire.

68. Proposed reform of Penal Code article 373, in article 9 of "Proyecto de Reformas al Código Penal," undated document on file with the author since 1989.

Any positive aspects of the reforms introduced by Gutiérrez Castro were overshadowed by mounting criticism of corruption, interference in lower court cases for political or personal reasons, and a general manipulation of the judiciary.

Judicial Reform Moves onto the Salvadoran Political Agenda

AID's original judicial reform project failed to recognize the importance of building social consciousness of the need for reform and underestimated the resistance to change. At the time the AOJ project was initiated, few Salvadorans in government or outside it were committed to working for judicial reform. It simply was not on the national agenda.

Furthermore, AID's judicial reform effort was not well known in El Salvador. The scope of the project was little known outside the government circles involved in it. The project did not disseminate its early products, such as CORELESAL's useful studies and those prepared by the Dirección General de Asistencia Técnico Jurídica (ATJ), the Justice Ministry's law reform unit. Salvadorans outside of government interested in promoting the rule of law were generally unfamiliar with the project's overall scope, the difficulties encountered, and its advances. Reflecting this lack of transparency, many of the documents obtained for this study came from unofficial sources and were not readily available in El Salvador at the time.[69]

ARENA's 1989 electoral victory opened the possibility of meaningful peace negotiations with the FMLN. While serious movement toward reaching a peace agreement did not occur until after the FMLN's November 1989 offensive, President-elect Cristiani met with UN envoy Alvaro de Soto on the eve of his June 1989 inauguration. The early months of the Cristiani administration saw no initiatives to undertake fundamental judicial reform; instead, legislators discussed draconian antiterrorist legislation, declared a new state of emergency once the FMLN offensive was under way, and enacted new legislation for processing those suspected of political offenses, which again violated due process rights. After the offensive, when both sides recognized the need to engage in serious negotiations and the UN was asked to mediate, the climate for judicial reform began to improve markedly.

69. In 1997 the Friedrich Ebert Foundation published the first Salvadoran evaluation of USAID's judicial reform efforts. Francisco Eliseo Ortiz Ruiz, *Diez Años de Reforma Judicial en El Salvador (1985–1995): Aproximación a un Diagnóstico* (San Salvador, 1997).

A combination of factors contributed to a heightened Salvadoran consciousness of the need for profound judicial reform. The negotiations process itself spurred efforts to diagnose some of the major ills in the justice system. Representatives of the different political parties worked together in the *Inter-partidaria*, an ad hoc group made up of representatives of the different political parties, created to contribute to the negotiations process, identify major problems in the justice system, and make recommendations for reforms. In July 1990 five nongovernmental groups concerned with human rights and the justice system came together to publish a "First Working Document about Human Rights and the Administration of Justice in El Salvador."[70]

Around the same time that the peace process began to take shape, significant changes were also taking place in the U.S.-funded judicial reform effort. Starting in 1990, El Salvador began to benefit from interchange with proponents of profound judicial reform from Ibero-America. In recent years, as many Latin American countries have been undergoing transitions to democracy, attention has focused on the need for profound reform of the administration of justice for the consolidation of democracy. The kind of reform contemplated was radically different from that proposed by AID in 1984. Along with the restoration of democracy in Argentina, attention focused on the need for a major reform of the criminal justice system. Although the Argentine reformers initially met with limited success in enacting their proposals, their efforts were subsequently enlisted to revive AID's judicial reform projects in Central America. This unprecedented confluence of divergent judicial reform efforts gave new impetus to a stagnant program in El Salvador that had achieved virtually none of its objectives despite the outlay of millions of dollars. Yet given the roots of AID's interest in judicial reform, there was an inevitable tension in this alliance. U.S. promotion of democracy had traditionally been tied to a deeper interest in maintaining order and promoting economic development in a market economy rather than to consistent advocacy of international human rights standards.

Since the reform effort had been so totally identified with U.S. policy and objectives, it was not until the peace process was well under way that AID made an effort to reach out to nongovernmental sectors. Likewise, the NGO community did not begin to explore the possibility that the reform effort might contribute to democratic consolidation until peace was on the horizon.

The 1990 evaluation of AID's project carried out by Sancinetti, Bacqué,

70. "Primer Documento de Trabajo sobre los Derechos Humanos y la Administración de Justicia en El Salvador," *El Mundo*, July 3, 1990.

and Castro Alvarado constituted a turning point in AID's efforts. Sancinetti's team was the first of many knowledgeable Ibero-Americans, committed to fundamental judicial reform and the protection of human rights, to
visit El Salvador in this period. AID's decision to bring in experts with this
kind of perspective raises fascinating questions, given that U.S. policy had
not yet fundamentally changed and that the war was still ongoing. New
leadership in AID's office of democratic initiatives in El Salvador and the
involvement of Costa Rican lawyer Jorge Obando seem to have been key
factors. Obando came to El Salvador in 1990 to head the office of AID's
contractor for judicial reform, which later established a training center in
San Salvador. He conditioned his involvement in El Salvador on authorization to bring in Ibero-American experts interested in the relationship
between the rule of law and the consolidation of democracy. Precisely
because it is difficult for those within a system to recognize the need for fundamental change, the interchange with Ibero-American jurists facing similar
problems with the legal systems in their own countries opened up new hori-
zons in a country with extremely limited exposure to modern currents of
legal thought. In turn, the Ibero-American jurists, though not always sufficiently versed in Salvadoran reality, better understood the weaknesses of the
Salvadoran system than did U.S. reformers, whose understanding of the Salvadoran criminal justice system was, at best, limited.

Benefiting from the advice of the Ibero-Americans, AID and the Salvadoran Ministry of Justice began a serious effort to reform the criminal justice
system.[71] Heeding several of Professor Sancinetti's recommendations, the
ministry's law reform unit, the ATJ, gave priority to criminal justice reform,
incorporated foreign consultants, and sought—albeit with minimal success—
to improve mechanisms for winning legislative approval of proposals.

Ideally a justice reform effort should not be exclusively "government
property." Particularly in a country as polarized as El Salvador, there is a real
danger that the reform effort will be seen as belonging to the right wing—
in this case the ARENA party. (Although the project was initiated under
Christian Democratic leadership, the serious effort to propose fundamental
criminal justice reforms began under the ARENA government.) This result is
ironic because many of the reforms proposed (and the foreign consultants
proposing them) sought to establish human rights safeguards not normally

71. See U.S. AID Project Paper, "Judicial Reform II." Under the 1991/1992 agreement for
U.S. Economic Support Funds, U.S. economic assistance was conditioned on progress in three
specific areas: development and adoption of a comprehensive legal reform agenda, increased
independence of the judiciary, and heightened public awareness of the need for legal reform.

associated with a political party whose roots were distinctly undemocratic. ARENA "ownership" of the justice reform effort—although some in ARENA have been staunchly opposed—tended to raise automatic doubts or at least preclude wholehearted support from opposition sectors that would normally have been expected to support such reforms.

As the following chapters discuss, the U.S. role and the (real and perceived) partisan nature of justice reform efforts in El Salvador during the 1980s limited the extent to which they would be incorporated into the peace process.

3

ADDRESSING JUSTICE ISSUES
IN THE PEACE NEGOTIATIONS

The deficiencies of Salvadoran criminal justice and the extent of impunity, particularly for crimes involving the military, were well documented by the time the peace negotiators tackled these issues. Its independence compromised and subject to political and military manipulation, the criminal justice system needed a major overhaul. At the same time, the negotiators faced the daunting task of ending impunity while building confidence in the possibility of peace.

Leading international human rights experts became deeply involved in the Salvadoran peace process. Venezuelan jurist Pedro Nikken was the UN's advisor on human rights during the peace negotiations and subsequently the UN's Independent Expert on the Situation of Human Rights in El Salvador. He was a member of the Inter-American Court on Human Rights when the *Velásquez Rodríguez* case was heard and decided. In this landmark decision finding state responsibility for forced disappearances in Honduras, the Inter-American Court found that, under the American Convention on Human Rights, a state has a "legal duty ... to use the means at its disposal to carry out a serious investigation of violations committed within its jurisdiction, to identify those responsible, to impose the appropriate punishment and to ensure the victim adequate compensation." The court held that "if the State apparatus acts in such a way that the violation goes unpunished ... the State has failed to comply with its duties to ensure the free and full exercise of those rights to the persons within its jurisdiction."[1]

French Judge Philippe Texier, who had been the UN Independent Expert on Haiti, served as the first director of the Human Rights Division of the UN Observer Mission in El Salvador (ONUSAL). Peruvian jurist Diego García-Sayán, the executive director of the Andean Commission of Jurists, was the second director of ONUSAL's Human Rights Division. Truth Commission member Thomas Buergenthal, a U.S. professor of law, had been president of the Inter-American Court on Human Rights when *Velásquez Rodríguez* was decided and is a leading scholar in the human rights field. On an ad hoc basis during the negotiations process, the UN also drew on the expertise of leading figures in a variety of international NGOs.

During this period the AID project focused on law reform, particularly the reform of the criminal justice system. While this effort was ongoing during the negotiations process, it operated essentially on a parallel track, with few opportunities for intersection. The Ministry of Justice provided the negotiators with its reform agenda and proposed interim reforms, which included such items as the suppression of the extrajudicial confession, reduction of the period of administrative detention, and separation of instruction and sentencing courts. The negotiators sought to tackle fundamental human rights issues, establish a UN verification mechanism, and enhance the independence of the judiciary. Some important constitutional reforms were approved, but many other areas—including the entire realm of criminal justice—were simply not addressed by the negotiators.

The Human Rights Accord

The peace negotiations that led to the signing of a final peace agreement on January 16, 1992, in Mexico's Chapúltepec Palace formally began on April 4, 1990, when the Salvadoran government and the FMLN signed an agreement in Geneva to enter into UN-mediated peace talks.[2] When the

1. *Velásquez Rodríguez* case, Judgment of July 29, 1988, Ser. C. No. 4 (1988), reprinted in 28 I.L.M. 291 (1989), *Human Rights Law Journal* 9 (1988): 212.
2. See Geneva Agreement. For background on the negotiations process, see George Vickers, "The Political Reality After Eleven Years of War," in *Is There a Transition to Democracy in El Salvador?* ed. Joseph S. Tulchin and Gary Bland (Boulder: Lynne Rienner Publishers, 1992);

negotiations agenda was set in May 1990, the FMLN included the judicial system and human rights among the topics to be addressed.[3]

The first substantive agreement between the FMLN and the Salvadoran government was the San José Human Rights Accord signed on July 26, 1990. The accord was intended as a confidence-building measure that would immediately improve the human rights situation in the country as well as aid in the negotiations process, because discussions about reform of the armed forces were at an impasse, and negotiators thought it essential to reach a substantive agreement.

The San José agreement recognized El Salvador's human rights commitments under domestic and international law, thus explicitly incorporating into the peace accords the parties' agreement to be bound by internationally recognized human rights standards.[4] The parties committed themselves to taking "all necessary steps and measures" "to avoid any act or practice which constitutes an attempt upon the life, integrity, security or freedom of the individual," including the elimination of any practices that involved forced disappearances or abductions.[5] Priority was to be given to the investigation of such cases and to the identification and punishment of those responsible. The agreement also specified various measures to protect against arbitrary detentions and mistreatment or torture of detainees.[6] No one was to be arrested for the lawful exercise of political rights. Arrests

---

Vickers, "El Salvador: A Negotiated Revolution," *NACLA Report on the Americas* 25, no. 5 (May 1992); Terry Lynn Karl, "El Salvador's Negotiated Revolution," *Foreign Affairs* 71 (1992): 147.

3. The negotiating agenda established in the Caracas Agreement of May 21, 1990, foresaw a two-stage process of political agreements followed by a cease-fire. The agenda items for the first stage were armed forces, human rights, judicial system, electoral system, constitutional reform, socioeconomic problems, and United Nations verification. The purpose of the process was "to end the armed conflict by political means as speedily as possible, promote the democratization of the country, guarantee unrestricted respect for human rights and reunify Salvadoran society." Report of the Secretary-General on the Situation in Central America, UN Doc. A/45/706-S/21931, November 8, 1990, Annex II; *The UN and El Salvador 1990–1995*, Document 11, p. 117.

4. "For the purposes of the present political agreement, 'human rights' shall mean those rights recognized by the Salvadoran legal system, including treaties to which El Salvador is a party, and by the declarations and principles on human rights and humanitarian law adopted by the United Nations and the Organization of American States" (San José Agreement on Human Rights, 1. Respect for and Guarantee of Human Rights, UN Doc. A/44/971-S/21541, August 16, 1990, *The UN and El Salvador 1990–1995*, Doc. 9, p. 108). See Enrique Ballasteros Bernales and Roberto Garreton, *Aplicación de las Normas Internacionales de Derechos Humanos* (San Salvador: ONUSAL-PDDH, 1994), 66–67.

5. San José Agreement on Human Rights I.1.

6. Ibid. I.2(a–f).

could only be carried out by properly identified officers, based on written orders of the competent authority and in accordance with law. Those arrested were to be immediately informed of the reasons for their detention and of the charges they faced. Arrests were no longer to be used as a form of intimidation, and nighttime arrests were specifically prohibited except in cases of those caught in flagrante delicto. Suspects could not be held incommunicado and must have the right to prompt assistance of counsel and to communicate freely and privately with counsel. No one could be subject to torture or other cruel, inhuman, or degrading treatment or punishment. In general terms, the agreement called for giving the "fullest possible support" to ensure "the effectiveness of the remedies of amparo and habeas corpus."[7]

Since the frame of reference for the San José agreement was the Salvadoran constitution and international human rights treaties, its terms both specified and amplified provisions of the constitution. In the San José agreement, the parties pledged to carry out the agreement's terms and provided in detail for a UN verification mission that would serve as an enforcement mechanism.

The agreement granted the UN verification mission broad powers to collect information and make recommendations to the parties as part of its oversight of the accord's implementation. Its specific functions included helping to "improve the judicial procedures for the protection of human rights and increase respect for the rules of due process of law."[8] Originally slated to begin after a cease-fire, the UN mission, known as ONUSAL, was actually established in July 1991, almost five months before the cease-fire agreement was signed.[9] The San José Accord did not resolve the more

7. Ibid., I.4. Habeas corpus addresses violations of the right to liberty (i.e., illegal detentions), while amparo provides a remedy for violations of other constitutional rights. The San José agreement also specifically protected the right of free association, trade union freedom, and freedom of expression and the press; it provided that displaced persons and returned refugees would be provided with legal identity documents and guaranteed freedom of movement as well as freedom to carry on their economic activities and to exercise their political and social rights within the country's legal framework. All persons were to be guaranteed freedom of movement in the areas involved in conflict, and inhabitants of these areas were to be provided with legal identity documents. Finally, the parties recognized the need to guarantee the effective enjoyment of labor rights and stated that this subject would be considered under the agenda item on economic and social problems (articles I.5–9).

8. San José Agreement, article 14(h).

9. For a comprehensive critique of ONUSAL, see Lawyers Committee for Human Rights, *Improvising History: A Critical Evaluation of the United Nations Observer Mission in El Salvador* (New York: Lawyers Committee for Human Rights, 1995); for an analysis of the UN's role, see Ian Johnstone, *Rights and Reconciliation: United Nations Strategies in El Salvador* (Boulder and London: Lynne Rienner Publishers, 1995); for an account by a director of ONUSAL's

sensitive and equally pressing issue of how past human rights violations would be dealt with, leaving this matter to a subsequent agreement.

Confronting Past Impunity in the Peace Negotiations

Background

By the mid-1990s peace processes were expected to include mechanisms for addressing past human rights and humanitarian law violations. In recent years much has been written about the need for, and challenge of, attaining truth and justice as different countries have made the transition from authoritarian to democratic rule or from internal conflicts to postconflict situations.[10] Yet it is worth remembering how little of this material was available to the Salvadoran negotiators in 1990. Moreover, the international community had not been involved in any such efforts since the end of World War II.

The proposition that successor regimes have a duty under international law to prosecute those responsible for serious human rights violations in the

Human Rights Division, see Diego García-Sayán, "The Experience of ONUSAL in El Salvador," in *Honoring Human Rights and Keeping the Peace: Lessons from El Salvador, Cambodia and Haiti,* ed. Alice H. Henkin (Washington, D.C.: Aspen Institute, 1995); Reed Brody [the final director of ONUSAL's Human Rights Division], "The United Nations and Human Rights in El Salvador's 'Negotiated Revolution,'" *Harvard Human Rights Journal* 8 (Spring 1995): 153; regarding ONUSAL's first year, see Americas Watch, *El Salvador — Peace and Human Rights: Successes and Shortcomings of the United Nations Observer Mission in El Salvador (ONUSAL)* (Washington, D.C.: Human Rights Watch, 1992).

10. See, e.g., Lawrence Weschler, *A Miracle, A Universe: Settling Accounts with Torturers* (New York: Pantheon Books, 1990); Jaime Malamud-Goti, "Punishment and a Rights-Based Democracy," *Criminal Justice Ethics,* (Summer–Fall 1991); Alice H. Henkin, ed., *State Crimes: Punishment or Pardon* (Washington, D.C.: Aspen Institute, 1989); David Pion-Berlin, "To Prosecute or to Pardon? Human Rights Decisions in the Latin American Southern Cone," *Human Rights Quarterly* 16 (1994): 105; Jon M. Van Dyke and Gerald W. Berkeley, "Redressing Human Rights Abuses," *Denver Journal of International Law and Policy* 2 (1992); José Zalaquett, "Balancing Ethical Imperatives and Political Constraints: The Dilemma of New Democracies Confronting Past Human Rights Violations," *Hastings Law Journal* 43 (1992): 425; Diane F. Orentlicher, "Addressing Gross Human Rights Abuses: Punishment and Victim Compensation," in *Human Rights: An Agenda for the Next Century, Studies in Transnational Legal Studies,* No. 26, ed. Louis Henkin and John Lawrence Hargrove (Washington, D.C.: The American Society of International Law, 1994) 425–75; Naomi Roht-Arriaza, *Impunity and Human Rights in International Law* (New York: Oxford University Press, 1995); Neil J. Kritz, ed., *Transitional Justice: How Emerging Democracies Reckon with Former Regimes* (Washington, D.C.: United States Institute of Peace, 1995); James A. McAdams, ed., *Transitional Justice and the Rule of Law in New Democracies* (University of Notre Dame Press, 1997).

prior regime is now widely accepted.[11] The right to know the truth about what happened to the victims of human rights abuses has also been increasingly recognized under international law and in some national courts.[12] In practice, however, newly elected governments have encountered difficulties in holding accountable those responsible for past human rights violations. Outgoing regimes have relied on broad amnesty laws, which have rarely been annulled. Moreover, military threats of destabilization have proved powerful inducements to end prosecution efforts.

The Salvadoran negotiators had the benefit of the experience of a few other countries, notably Argentina and Chile. In both of those countries, newly elected presidents who replaced military dictators created independent commissions of national notables from diverse political perspectives. In each case, the commission members worked together to examine and reach common conclusions about the most serious human rights abuses committed during preceding periods of military rule. In Argentina the National Commission for Disappeared Persons (CONADEP), also known as the "Sábato" Commission, was charged with investigating the fate of those who were forcibly disappeared during the period of military dictatorships. The Chilean National Commission for Truth and Reconciliation or "Rettig" Commission was assigned the task of investigating cases of disappearances, executions, and torture that resulted in death. Both commissions were able

11. See the Inter-American Court's decision in *Velásquez Rodríguez* case; Robert K. Goldman, "International Law and Amnesty Laws," *Human Rights Internet Reporter* 12 (1988): 9; Diane F. Orentlicher, "Settling Accounts: The Duty to Prosecute Human Rights Violations of a Prior Regime," *Yale Law Review* 100 (1991): 2537; Naomi Roht-Arriaza, "State Responsibility to Investigate and Prosecute Grave Human Rights Violations in International Law," *California Law Review* 78 (1990): 451; Douglass Cassel, "Lessons from the Americas: Guidelines for International Response to Amnesties for Atrocities," *Law and Contemporary Problems* 59 (1996): 191.

12. See, e.g., Inter-American Commission on Human Rights, Annual Report 1985–1986, chapter 5, "Areas in which steps need to be taken towards full observance of the human rights set forth in the American Declaration of the Rights and Duties of Man and the American Convention on Human Rights"; Jo M. Pasqualucci, "The Whole Truth and Nothing but the Truth: Truth Commissions, Impunity, and the Inter-American Human Rights System," *Boston University International Law Journal* 12 (1994): 321; Carlos Chipoco, "El Derecho a la Verdad, un Análisis Comparativo," paper presented at the 18th LASA International Congress, Atlanta, March 1994; Memorial en Derecho Amicus Curiae Presentado en la Camara Federal en lo Criminal y Correccional de la Capital Federal por Human Rights Watch/Americas y el Centro por la Justicia y el Derecho Internacional, en los Autos; Mignone, Emilio F., S/Presentación en Causa No. 761, "Hechos Denunciados Como Ocurridos en el Ambito de la Escuela Superior de la Mecánica de la Armada (ESMA), *El Derecho* (Buenos Aires), September 14, 1995; Martín Abregú, "La tutela judicial del derecho a la verdad en la Argentina," *Revista IIDH* 24 (1996): 12–47.

to write an authoritative version of the events that took place under military rule.

The Salvadoran context called for a somewhat different approach. In Argentina, after military rulers were discredited by the armed forces' poor performance in the Malvinas (or Falklands) war, Raúl Alfonsín campaigned for the presidency on a human rights platform, vowing to hold accountable those responsible for violating human rights during the dictatorship. He formed a national commission to investigate the fate of the people who were detained and "disappeared" during the military dictatorship. The CONADEP report did not include the names of those found responsible, but the list of names was leaked to the press and published. Alfonsín also called for the prosecution of those responsible for human rights violations during the dictatorship. The information collected by CONADEP was provided to the courts. Much has been written about the deficiencies of the Argentine prosecution of the generals—the slow start as the original responsibility for prosecution was entrusted to military courts, the due obedience and *punto final* laws that limited and ended the prosecutions, and the pardons granted by Alfonsín's successor, Carlos Menem. While Alfonsín's supporters argue that he did as much as was possible given the real danger of a military uprising, the human rights community faulted Alfonsín's government for not using the weight of its initial mandate to go farther in upholding the rule of law.[13]

13. See, e.g., Carlos H. Acuña and Catalina Smulovitz, "Guarding the Guardians in Argentina: Some Lessons About the Risks and Benefits of Empowering the Courts," in *Transitional Justice*, ed. McAdams, 93; Garro, "Nine Years of Transition to Democracy in Argentina," *Columbia Journal of Transnational Law* 31 (1993): 56–58; Carlos Santiago Nino, "Human Rights in Context: The Case of Argentina," *Yale Law Journal* 100 (1991): 2619, and Diane F. Orentlicher, "A Reply to Professor Nino," *Yale Law Journal* 100 (1991): 2641; Jaime Malamud-Goti, "Trying Violators of Human Rights: The Dilemma of Transitional Democratic Governments," in *State Crimes: Punishment or Pardon* (Washington, D.C.: Aspen Institute, 1989), 82; Jaime Malamud-Goti, "Transitional Governments in the Breach: Why Punish State Criminals?" *Human Rights Quarterly* 12 (1990): 1; Carlos Santiago Nino, "The Human Rights Policy of the Argentine Constitutional Government: A Reply," *Yale Journal of International Law* 11 (1985): 217; Alejandro M. Garro and Henry Dahl, "Legal Accountability for Human Rights Violations in Argentina: One Step Forward and Two Steps Backward," *Human Rights Law Journal* 8 (1987): 283; Emilio F. Mignone et al., "Dictatorship on Trial: Prosecution of Human Rights Violations in Argentina," *Yale Journal of International Law* 10 (1984): 118; George C. Rogers, "Argentina's Obligation to Prosecute Military Officials for Torture," *Columbia Human Rights Law Review* 20 (1989): 259; Kathryn Lee Crawford, "Due Obedience and the Rights of Victims: Argentina's Transition to Democracy," *Human Rights Quarterly* 12 (1990): 17; Americas Watch, *Truth and Partial Justice in Argentina* (New York: Human Rights Watch, 1991). For a legal analysis of the Argentine court proceedings and judgment, see Marcelo A. Sancinetti, *Derechos Humanos en la Argentina Post Dictatorial* (Buenos Aires: Lerner Editores Asociados, 1988).

The Argentine example of prosecutions seemed inapplicable to El Salvador, which had neither a defeated nor wholly discredited military, a new government committed to the redress of human rights violations, nor a judicial system capable of imparting justice.

The Chilean model, in which the military retained significant power during the transition and a truth commission largely substituted for justice, seemed closer to the Salvadoran situation.[14] Yet there were significant differences. In Chile, General Augusto Pinochet agreed in 1988, under mounting pressure, to hold a plebiscite, which he lost. A broad center-left coalition backed the winning Christian Democratic candidate, Patricio Aylwin, who took office in 1990. While in power, Pinochet rewrote the constitution to ensure that those loyal to him continued to exercise significant power in the legislature and the Supreme Court. Under the transition agreement, he remained as head of the army until March 1998, when he became a senator-for-life. Unlike its Chilean counterpart, the Salvadoran armed forces would have to undergo a major transformation and submit to a purge of the officer corps. Yet the governing party in El Salvador did not change with the war's end.

The nature of the conflict in El Salvador—a twelve-year civil war with many combat-related casualties—distinguished it from the situation in both Argentina and Chile. In contrast to the situation in the Southern Cone, the Salvadoran government had not changed and was not committed to seeking truth or justice about past violations. The Cristiani government, itself implicated in many violations, made no move to form a national commission. Instead, the sensitive topic of how to address past abuses was left to the negotiating table.

Another factor that complicated the task in El Salvador was that the number of victims far exceeded those in either Argentina or Chile. Although exact figures for the numbers of victims of political violence in El Salvador do not exist, an estimated 75,000 people died as a result of political violence

14. Jorge Correa Sutil, " 'No Victorious Army Has Ever Been Prosecuted . . .': The Unsettled Story of Transitional Justice in Chile," in *Transitional Justice,* ed. McAdams; Jorge Correa Sutil, "Dealing with Past Human Rights Violations: The Chilean Case After Dictatorship," *Notre Dame Law Review* 67 (1992): 1455; Americas Watch, *Chile: The Struggle for Truth and Justice for Past Human Rights Violations* (New York and Washington, D.C.: Human Rights Watch, July 1992); Americas Watch, *Human Rights and the "Politics of Agreements": Chile During President Aylwin's First Year* (New York: Human Rights Watch, 1991); David Weissbrodt and Paul Fraser, "The Report of the Chilean National Commission on Truth and Reconciliation," *Human Rights Quarterly* 14 (1992): 601; Robert Quinn, "Will the Rule of Law End? Challenging Grants of Amnesty for the Human Rights Violations of a Prior Regime: Chile's New Model," *Fordham Law Review* 62 (1994): 905.

during the twelve-year civil war. The Truth Commission obtained some documentation or received testimony about 22,000 victims. In Chile, the Rettig Commission and its successor, the National Corporation of Reparation and Reconciliation, documented 3,129 cases that resulted in death under the military regime.[15] While human rights groups' estimates of the total number of victims were considerably higher, they did not approach the numbers cited in El Salvador, despite a larger total population. In Argentina, the CONADEP was able to document almost 9,000 cases of disappearances, again considerably less than the 15,000 to 30,000 estimated by human rights groups.

The Argentine and Chilean militaries justified their excesses as necessary in the war against subversion. Yet the Salvadoran armed forces fought the FMLN on the battlefield as well as through the "dirty war" tactics of their South American colleagues. Tens of thousands died in combat. A country emerging from civil war inevitably views the issue of human rights violations that occurred in the context of that war somewhat differently than does a country emerging from a period of authoritarian rule. In addition to the risk that military men who found themselves under scrutiny for past acts might destabilize a transition process, El Salvador had to assure the FMLN's participation in the political process. In Argentina and Chile there were not two warring factions that had to agree to a cease-fire and devise a way to live together in the future.

Negotiating History

The FMLN apparently decided early on that justice would be symbolic, at best, and placed greater emphasis on forward-looking measures. Nonetheless, an April 1990 FMLN document made ending the impunity of military leaders a prerequisite to a cease-fire. Specifically, it called for prosecutions and exemplary punishments in four of the most notorious crimes committed by government forces or death squads: the November 1989 murder of the Jesuits, the January 1990 murder of Democratic Convergence Leader Héctor Oquelí,[16] the October 1989 bombing of the labor federation FENASTRAS

---

15. See Human Rights Watch/Americas, *Chile: Unsettled Business, Human Rights in Chile at the Start of the Frei Presidency* (New York: Human Rights Watch, 1994), 2.

16. Héctor Oquelí was a leader of the National Revolutionary Movement (MNR), a social democratic party that helped found the Democratic Convergence in 1987 when leaders who had been in exile decided to return to El Salvador to participate in the political process. In Guatemala in January 1990, in the wake of the FMLN offensive, Oquelí and Gilda Flores, a Guatemalan Social Democrat, were abducted and murdered.

in which nine unionists died and dozens more were wounded,[17] and the March 1980 assassination of Archbishop Romero. It called, as well, for the investigation of massacres and other notorious human rights violations committed by the armed forces to determine those responsible, although not all needed to be prosecuted. The FMLN document noted that after the exemplary resolution of the four cited cases, a broad amnesty would be appropriate. When the FMLN's proposal became known, *campesino* and human rights activists objected to its elitist focus. The FMLN then added to the list two of the most notorious army massacres of *campesinos*: the "El Mozote" massacre of December 1981 and the 1980 "Sumpul" massacre.[18]

The negotiations never addressed the need to reach a common understanding of what had happened to people during the war; determine the fate and, in many cases, the whereabouts of victims; provide reparations; and restore the good name of victims. Neither side seemed particularly concerned about protecting the rights of victims or creating an ongoing process. This is in sharp contrast to the Chilean commission, which sought to determine the fate of the disappeared and proposed a series of measures to compensate those affected.

The Salvadoran government argued that impunity was not exclusive to the armed forces and should instead be addressed as part of the negotiations on reforming the justice system. The government countered the FMLN's list with its own list that included the four cases originally raised by the FMLN as well as four others attributed to the FMLN: mayors assassinated by the FMLN;[19] Dr. José Antonio Rodríguez Porth, age 74, murdered in June 1989, days after President Cristiani named him Minister of the Presidency;[20] the killing of 73-year-old Dr. Francisco Peccorini,[21] and the June 1985 murder

17. On October 31, 1989, a mid-day blast destroyed the San Salvador offices of the union federation FENASTRAS. As a result of this attack, the FMLN broke off peace talks with the Salvadoran government. Days later, it launched its biggest offensive of the war on November 11, 1989. Despite the magnitude of the crime, no serious investigation of the FENASTRAS bombing was undertaken; those responsible have never been identified.

18. On May 14, 1980, Salvadoran soldiers, National Guardsmen, and members of ORDEN deliberately killed at least three hundred noncombatants as they tried to flee to Honduras across the Sumpul River in Chalatenango (see *From Madness to Hope*, 121).

19. From 1985 to 1988 the FMLN carried out a policy of killing mayors whom it considered to be active in counterinsurgency efforts (ibid., 148); Americas Watch, *Nightmare Revisited* (New York: September 1988), 41ff.

20. Dr. Rodríguez Porth was assassinated in San Salvador on June 9, 1989. At the time, the FMLN denied responsibility for the killing. The crime was never properly investigated, and those responsible have not been identified.

21. Francisco Peccorini was a 73-year-old philosophy professor, known for his outspoken attacks against the FMLN. The FMLN later acknowledged responsibility for his March 1989 murder.

of four U.S. marines and nine civilians in San Salvador's "Zona Rosa."[22] The government proposal called for supporting existing judicial proceedings in order to have exemplary trials in these cases, but it insisted that the 1987 amnesty barred prosecution of other cases.[23]

Early on, the UN proposed a special commission to be appointed by the secretary-general, which would itself determine the cases to be examined.[24] Although the working paper was part of the same document as the proposal that served as a basis for the July 1990 San José Agreement on Human Rights, an agreement to form a UN Truth Commission was not signed until April 1991, when the agreement on constitutional reform—only the second substantive agreement—gave new impetus to the negotiation process.

Weeks after the San José agreement was signed, the FMLN set forth its toughest position on the issue of impunity. The FMLN had been criticized for signing the San José Accord because it did not provide for immediate UN verification and therefore seemed to many to do nothing but repeat El Salvador's obligations to respect human rights. At the request of both the FMLN and the government, the UN subsequently agreed to initiate its verification mission before a cease-fire was in place.

In an August 1990 communiqué, the FMLN called for the trial and punishment, in an exemplary manner and prior to agreement on a cease-fire, of the intellectual and material authors in the six cases they had previously listed as well as any murder, massacres, or bombings of civilians that might take place during the negotiations process. The FMLN document further called for opening a process of investigation and bringing to trial the intellectual and material authors of all crimes, massacres, and forced disappearances committed since 1979 and including acts committed by prominent members of the private sector and paramilitary groups linked to them. It then listed a number of cases, including some that occurred prior to 1979.[25]

22. The victims were gunned down at an outdoor cafe in a wealthy San Salvador neighborhood in a June 1985 FMLN attack. Three young men were arrested and convicted for their alleged participation in the crime, but those who planned and ordered the killings were never brought to justice.

23. Ley de Amnistía para el Logro de la Reconciliación Nacional, Decree 805. The 1987 amnesty, passed to comply with the regional Esquipulas peace accords, granted amnesty to persons accused of having participated in political crimes, common crimes connected to political crimes, or common crimes in which at least twenty individuals participated. Only the murder of Archbishop Romero was specifically excluded from its terms. See Hillary Richard, "The Salvadoran Amnesty Bill," *Human Rights Internet Reporter* 12 (Winter 1988): 71.

24. See "Documento de Trabajo, Tema: Derechos Humanos," prepared for the July 1990 negotiating session in San José, Costa Rica (on file with the author); author's interview with Pedro Nikken, March 31, 1994, New York.

25. See FMLN, "Posición del FMLN para Desmontar el Militarismo, Alcanzar el Cese de

In this document the FMLN called for the formation of a special tribunal to
try and punish all cases

> which have gone unpunished and war crimes committed by the
> Armed Forces and paramilitary groups.... [The] tribunal, in order to
> overcome the inability and the absence of moral standing of the cur-
> rent judicial system and legal order, must have exceptional powers
> to establish proceedings and penalties. Its composition would be
> decided upon by consensus among the political forces, the Govern-
> ment and the FMLN.

At the time, the FMLN affirmed that without investigation and trial of those
responsible for all these cases, "the negotiations for a definitive end of the
conflict will not be considered concluded."[26]

In a letter to the Salvadoran political parties, the FMLN explained its
negotiating position and called for the total demilitarization of the country.
According to the FMLN's analysis,

> [I]mpunity is a systematic policy and resource of the Armed Forces as
> an institution. The officers who give orders or carry out crimes cover
> up for each other and foreclose, through intimidation and terror, any
> possibility that these acts will be investigated. This is the root of all
> the deformations and ineffectiveness of the judicial system against
> military power. The guarantees that these crimes will not be investi-
> gated or judged functions in the entire Armed Forces, from the high-
> est level to the lowest ranks; and this guarantee provides the basis for
> all the repression, the framework of the death squads and the main-
> tenance of structurally unjust and antidemocratic regimes.[27]

The FMLN further insisted that the punishment of these crimes and massacres was not a legal matter, but fundamentally political:

> In the current situation, the judicial or police emphasis to cover up or
> prove responsibilities is a form of evading justice and maintaining

---

Fuego y Avanzar a la Democracia sin Armas," dated August 17, 1990 (on file with the author),
25–27, 32.

26. Ibid.

27. Letter of August 14, 1990, to members of political parties of El Salvador from the
FMLN, signed by Schafik Jorge Handal, 2 (on file with the author).

impunity. The responsibility for these crimes is political and the Armed Forces itself should come forward with those who gave and executed the orders that resulted in the commission of these crimes. The army needs to be profoundly cleansed of those who have committed abuses of power, who have created obstacles to justice and have corrupted and enriched themselves from the war.

The FMLN explained that the agreements about the armed forces—especially relating to impunity and purging as key elements to initiate a total demilitarization—constituted the fundamental pillar of the negotiations for peace founded on democracy and justice.

The FMLN maintained that the special commission should examine serious acts of violence committed by members of the armed forces or paramilitary groups but did not initially accept that cases for which it was responsible also be examined. In its view, impunity—protection from prosecution and punishment—differed qualitatively from the simple failure to punish. Impunity normally implies that state agents or those protected by them (e.g., death squads) are not punished for their acts. Police know that they are not to investigate, judges find technical reasons to release suspects or dismiss cases, and so on.

Another FMLN concern was the risk of creating a false symmetry when the vast majority of violations were committed by government forces or those allied with them. Governments tend to excuse past violations of state agents by arguing that the armed opposition committed equally vile acts, espousing what was known in Argentina as the theory of "the two devils." If both sides are held to be equally culpable, then blanket forgiveness for all becomes the logical response. Yet this argument ignores both the qualitative and quantitative differences between state-sponsored violations and those of other actors. It also ignores international law requirements that certain violations must be prosecuted and punished.

The government's response to the FMLN's initial proposal pointed toward a "two devils" position by proposing that the Truth Commission examine four cases attributable to each side. Even if the commission was not expressly limited to examining government violations, the FMLN proposed that it be provided with the list of six cases as the focus for its work. Not knowing who would be on the special commission or how the commission would decide to function, the FMLN was anxious to ensure that serious cases of military and paramilitary impunity would be the commission's focus.

From a more self-interested point of view, the FMLN may well have wished to avoid scrutiny of its violations of international humanitarian law and principles. Unlike the African National Congress in South Africa, the FMLN never initiated a public process to investigate reports of abuses committed by its members. Internal investigations were carried out during the war and punishments imposed. Human rights groups criticized these proceedings for their lack of due process protections and failure to abide by the standards of international humanitarian law.[28] But the FMLN found itself unable to control the potential consequences of identifying those within its ranks who had committed violations. This dilemma was illustrated in the 1991 case of two FMLN combatants identified by the FMLN as having been responsible for the execution of two wounded U.S. military advisors whose helicopter the FMLN had shot down. The FMLN unsuccessfully sought an alternative forum to try the two accused in accordance with international humanitarian standards, but ultimately it turned them over to Salvadoran authorities. The unreliability of the justice system and the likelihood that FMLN members would face prosecution, while those in the armed forces responsible for serious human rights violations would go free, contributed to the FMLN's reluctance to identify wrongdoers within its ranks. As a practical matter, there was no way that the government would agree to have its violations scrutinized if the FMLN were not to be subject to the same process.

In April 1991, during the Mexico negotiations, both parties accepted a UN proposal to form a "truth commission," conditional on the other party's unconditional acceptance. It seems likely that neither side expected the other to accept this formulation without modification. This agreement was, in the words of an FMLN negotiator, a "blank check" for the UN. It left the commission to be named by the UN Secretary-General free to determine how to examine the most serious acts of violence that had occurred since 1980. The commission was assigned the task of "investigating serious acts of violence that have occurred since 1980 and whose impact on society urgently demands that the public should know the truth." Its mandate included "recommending the legal, political or administrative measures which can be inferred from the results of its investigation. Such recommendations may include measures to prevent the repetition of such acts, and initiatives to promote national reconciliation." The commission was free to select and investigate cases, determine the nature of its report, and recommend prosecutions or other measures. The terms of the agreement neither required the commission to name the individuals responsible nor barred them from doing

---

28. See Americas Watch, *Violation of Fair Trial Guarantees by the FMLN's Ad Hoc Courts* (New York: Human Rights Watch, 1990).

so. The parties pledged to carry out its recommendations. The commission was not to function as a judicial body, but it was also not to preclude judicial actions. Its creation was

> without prejudice to the obligations incumbent on the Salvadoran courts to solve such cases and impose the appropriate penalties on the culprits.... The provisions of this agreement shall not prevent the normal investigation of any situation or case, whether or not the Commission has investigated it, nor the application of the relevant legal provisions to any act that is contrary to law.

The decision to establish a truth commission reflected an understanding by the parties that the judicial system had failed to confront the "serious acts of violence" that had occurred during the war—and remained inadequate to the task.

Although not specifically stated in the accord, the parties agreed that, because of the extreme polarization of Salvadoran society, the commission would be international in composition. After consultation with the parties, the UN Secretary-General named former Colombian President Belisario Betancur, former Venezuelan Foreign Minister Reinaldo Figueredo, and U.S. law professor and former Inter-American Court President Thomas Buergenthal to the commission.

The Ad Hoc Commission

For the FMLN one of the pillars of the negotiations was the need to purge the armed forces of those responsible for massive human rights violations. This issue was on the negotiating table from the outset, but it proved so controversial and complicated that it was not resolved until the very end of the negotiations.[29] In this case, unlike the Truth Commission, the negotiators could not look to other Latin American countries for models. Overall, reforming the armed forces was the topic that occupied most of the negotiators' time. The FMLN presented many proposals and was able to win important concessions from the government. Among these was the agreement to form a civilian commission to review the human rights record of

---

29. A UN official involved in the negotiations process estimated that 30 percent of the negotiators' time was devoted to the need to develop a mechanism to clean out the armed forces. The agreement on the Ad Hoc Commission was reached on December 31, 1991, just before the final peace agreement was announced.

military officers and make binding recommendations for the dismissal or transfer of those found to have violated human rights.

As they had in their proposals for addressing past human rights abuses, the FMLN argued for the presentation of a list of officers who should be purged. This was the concept U.S. authorities had used when then Vice President Bush was sent to El Salvador in December 1983 with a list of officers to be transferred out of command positions because of involvement in death-squad activities. The FMLN focused primarily on the *tandona*, the officers from the large 1966 military academy graduating class who then dominated the armed forces.[30] Following the same logic it had applied to the establishment of the Truth Commission, the UN suggested that a mechanism be designed to carry out an evaluation and purge. The armed forces were reluctant to accept civilian control of this process. Much of the debate centered on the composition of such a commission. The government initially proposed an internal military review. Government negotiators argued that civilians would not be capable of carrying out this kind of evaluation (judging professional qualifications) and that the army would never accept it.

For the commission to succeed, its members had to be accepted by both sides. In contrast to the Truth Commission, this was to be a task carried out by Salvadorans who were to use "objective criteria" to evaluate officers. Although Salvadorans would not have the same capacity as foreign dignitaries to exert pressure, their judgments were expected to be better accepted by the armed forces, which would not have tolerated foreigners carrying out this task. After lengthy negotiations, the criteria agreed to for the evaluations were: (1) the officer's professional history; (2) any violation of human rights either directly committed, ordered to be committed by subordinates, or committed by troops under command and condoned; and (3) the officer's capacity to exercise his functions in the new reality of peace.[31]

30. The *tandona* was the focus of a 1990 staff report to the Arms Control and Foreign Policy Caucus of the U.S. Congress. *Barriers to Reform: A Profile of El Salvador's Military Leaders* (May 21, 1990) found that twelve of the fifteen primary commanders were members of the *tandona*: "This unprecedented concentration of power permits the *tandona* to protect its members from removal for corruption, abuses or incompetence. The *tandona* at times shows more loyalty to its members than to the rule of law or even to the President."

31. The final Chapúltepec peace agreement provided: "The evaluation shall take into account the past performance of each officer, including in particular: (1) his record of observance of the legal order, with particular emphasis on respect for human rights, both in his personal conduct and in the rigor with which he has ordered the redress and punishment of unlawful acts, excesses or human rights violations committed under his command, especially if there have been serious or systematic omissions in the latter respect; (2) his professional competence; and (3) his capacity to function in the new situation of peace, within the context of a

Eventually, discussions led to a decision to form a mixed group with three civilians and two military officers who would have a limited role. The military officers would be excluded from the processes of obtaining information, investigation, and decision making but could have access to the information collected and provide explanations.

The government was concerned that due process be respected. The agreement provided that officers reviewed be interviewed, but it did not establish an appeal process for those named or require that the commission justify its conclusions. This was in no sense meant to be a judicial process. The government's negotiating position was to term this process simply an "evaluation"; only at the very end did it accept the notion that the evaluation would lead to a purge.

Negotiating Judicial Reform

Throughout the war years and before, international bodies had decried the weaknesses of the Salvadoran judicial system—particularly its inability to confront grave human rights violations. Despite its inclusion of this topic in the negotiating agenda, the FMLN had devoted scant attention to the justice system and had virtually no expertise in this area. A guerrilla insurgency with minimal experience in the legal system is not the ideal protagonist for profound judicial reform. Yet the peace negotiations represented a unique opportunity to introduce far-reaching reforms in Salvadoran institutions and constitution or, in the words of some of those involved in the negotiations, to "jump-start" the judicial system. The idea of a jump start implies that there is something ready to begin functioning properly once it receives a salutary shock to the system. In reality, however, the Salvadoran justice system was in need of more than getting back on track: it had not simply been stalled or derailed by the exigencies of war. An independent, efficient, accessible, and impartial justice system had never existed in El Salvador. A profound transformation was called for, not simply the correction of certain aspects of the system.

---

democratic society, and to promote democratization of the country, guarantee unrestricted respect for human rights and reunify Salvadoran society, which is the common purpose agreed upon by the Parties in the Geneva Agreement." Chapúltepec Agreement, Chapter 1 Armed Forces, 3(A).

The Negotiations Process

In October 1989—before the FMLN's November 1989 offensive and the subsequent initiation of more serious negotiations under UN auspices—the FMLN had formulated only one demand to initiate a process of judicial reform: the election of a new Supreme Court and a new attorney general based on consensus between the government and opposition parties.[32] In April 1989, following the FMLN's assassination of Attorney General Roberto García Alvarado, the Assembly named Mauricio Eduardo Colorado to the post. He was to distinguish himself after the murder of the Jesuits by a public letter urging the pope to withdraw Archbishop Rivera and Bishop Rosa Chávez from El Salvador for their own protection. ARENA leader Mauricio Gutiérrez Castro, who has been linked to individuals active in death squads, was named president of the Supreme Court in June 1989.[33]

By March 1991 the FMLN had incorporated additional elements for judicial reform in its proposal for constitutional reforms: requiring a two-thirds majority legislative vote for election of Supreme Court justices and the attorney general; establishing instruments and institutional mechanisms under the direct authority of the Supreme Court to assure prompt and full justice, including a technical body for investigations; creating a human rights ombudsman; and increasing the flexibility of the procedure for constitutional reform, notably establishing a procedure for a plebiscite.[34]

Because of political realities in El Salvador and AID's identification with the counterinsurgency effort, the negotiators failed to take advantage of the excellent analyses prepared by foreign consultants working with the AID judicial reform project during this period.[35] At the time negotiations were conducted on the issue of judicial reform, there was still virtually no contact between the AID project and nongovernmental sectors.

After the negotiations process began in earnest, input was provided by

32. FMLN, "Puntos Fundamentales de la Propuesta de Reforma Constitucional del FMLN," October 16, 1989 (on file with the author).
33. See, e.g., *Los Escuadrones de la Muerte en El Salvador* (San Salvador: Editorial Jaragua) 1994.
34. FMLN, "Principales Reformas a la Constitución que el FMLN Considera Necesarias," March 16, 1991 (on file with the author).
35. These included the evaluations carried out by Marcelo Sancinetti, Jorge A. Bacqué (who had been an Argentine Supreme Court magistrate at the time of the trials of the Argentine military), and Costa Rican magistrate Marco A. Castro Alvarado, as well as the analysis of the criminal justice system and urgent needs for reform prepared by Argentine judge Leopoldo Schiffrin et al.

representatives of the different political parties, who met in a subcommission of an interparty body established to address issues raised in the peace negotiations.[36] The UN also organized a brainstorming session in Geneva attended by members of the international human rights community and a few Salvadoran lawyers. Based on these analyses, the UN prepared a working document on judicial reform.

The UN working document suggested a wide range of measures, noting that the "Salvadoran judicial situation is particularly critical, but it is not unheard of in Latin America, as there are similar cases." The UN proposal noted that El Salvador could serve as a "test-case."[37] This document emphasized the need for new human resources in the judiciary, chosen by nonpartisan methods and with a new judicial spirit, to help create in a short period of time a renewed and independent atmosphere in the judicial branch. It called for replacement of the Supreme Court by a less politicized court that could enjoy consensus and collective trust. It further called for the evaluation of judges and replacement of those most notorious for not fulfilling their duties. The UN document urged the creation of separate investigatory (instruction) courts as well as a human rights ombudsman. The document also called for a lifetime exclusion from any police duties of those who could be identified as responsible for human rights violations. Proposed procedural reforms would have given victims a greater role in criminal proceedings, stripped all value from the extrajudicial confession, provided mandatory defense, rewarded those who cooperated in clarifying a crime, eliminated the disqualification of codefendant testimony, and simplified the procedures for amparo and habeas corpus. The UN document noted that the UN itself could play an important role during the transition period by, for example, designating advisors to support reform and train judges.

Agreements on judicial reform were almost entirely limited to those included in the constitutional reforms negotiated in April 1991 in Mexico. The Salvadoran constitution of 1983 established rigid requirements for constitutional change: any reforms had to be approved in two successive

36. The April 1990 Geneva Agreement called for the parties to the negotiations to maintain mechanisms for exchanging information and consulting with the political parties in El Salvador. In response, the political parties formed the "Inter-partidaria" to join in looking for solutions to the national crisis. This interparty commission then formed three subcommissions: electoral, democratic liberties, and administration of justice. The administration of justice subcommission began meeting in May 1990 and prepared a series of reports that were provided to the negotiators.

37. Temas para Acuerdos Políticos sobre el Sistema Judicial de El Salvador, undated document from the negotiations (on file with the author).

legislatures—in the first by majority vote, and in its successor by a two-thirds majority of all deputies.[38] The negotiators, who had neglected the issue of constitutional reform as they focused on issues related to the armed forces, realized that they were facing an important deadline. Because of constitutional article 248 and the imminent end of the Assembly's term on April 30, 1991, any constitutional reforms intended to take effect before 1994 would have to be approved prior to expiration of the current Assembly's term. During the April 1991 Mexico negotiations, the parties hotly debated a proposal to modify the procedure for constitutional reform. Groups dedicated to legal reform in El Salvador, notably the Center for the Study of Applied Law (CESPAD), pushed hard for a constitutional reform that would have permitted further reforms without the cumbersome process of approval by two successive assemblies. Such a reform would have obviated the need for agreement on a range of specific reforms during the month of April 1991, thus permitting a broader and lengthier debate and reflection about the constitutional reforms actually needed.

The government nonetheless took an unbending position that article 248 was not subject to reform.[39] A paid ad in the Salvadoran newspapers left space for the names of the legislators who would be charged with treason if they introduced such a reform. Ultimately, the procedure for constitutional reform was left untouched, while a series of discrete constitutional reforms were hurriedly agreed to. It was at this point that the government rejected UN proposals that would have ended the concentration of functions in the Supreme Court by transferring the court's administrative responsibilities to the Judiciary Council. Government negotiators claim credit for proposing constitutional reforms such as earmarking 6 percent of the country's budget for the judiciary and calling for a qualified legislative majority to elect Supreme Court justices.[40] The government refused to negotiate an agreement to provide for replacement of the existing Supreme Court, although it

38. Salvadoran Constitution of 1983, article 248.
39. See letter from President Alfredo Cristiani to UN Secretary-General Javier Pérez de Cuéllar, April 19, 1991. Among other things, this letter points out that "in view of the legal debate on the constitutionality of the reform, there is a risk that a declaration on its unconstitutionality would totally preclude the possibility of constitutional reform until after the 1994 elections" (*The UN and El Salvador 1990–1995* [New York: UN Blue Book Series, 1995], Doc. 17, p. 139).
40. Author's interviews with David Escobar Galindo, October 25, 1993, and then Foreign Minister Oscar Santamaría, July 20, 1994, San Salvador. No one interviewed provided any document containing proposals prepared by the government. Throughout the negotiations, the government negotiating team presented very few written proposals.

did agree to a new formula for selecting Supreme Court justices to avoid one-party control.

Unprepared in this terrain, and far more determined to win concessions related to the armed forces, the FMLN agreed to forgo many of the proposed reforms. Given the unalterable opposition of Supreme Court President Gutiérrez Castro, the parties may have opted to avoid confrontation with him.[41]

The judicial reforms included in the constitutional reform package negotiated in April 1991 changed the formula for electing judges at all levels; increased the independence of the National Judiciary Council and gave it additional responsibilities for the nomination of judges and magistrates as well as the Judicial Training School; increased the budget of the judiciary; prohibited judges from serving as notaries; required a two-thirds legislative majority for the election of Supreme Court justices, the attorney general, and the state counsel; established a new human rights ombudsman; gave the attorney general greater responsibility for directing criminal investigations; and ended military court jurisdiction over civilians accused of subversive activities when constitutional guarantees are suspended.[42] Additional political agreements set forth guidelines designed to restructure the National Judiciary Council "to guarantee its independence from the organs of State and from political parties" and to include in the council persons not directly related to the administration of justice. These agreements also called for transforming the Judicial Training School and reforming the career judicial service law.[43]

Although the Mexico Accords noted that "the set of political agreements on the judicial system envisaged by the Parties in the Caracas Agenda has still to be negotiated,"[44] further agreements were never negotiated. The final Chapúltepec agreement included a one-page chapter on the judicial system that reiterated the prior agreement on the National Judiciary Council and the Judicial Training School, emphasizing the need to ensure its academic

41. This view was expressed by UN mediator Alvaro de Soto during a presentation sponsored by the Council on Foreign Relations, Washington, D.C., April 28, 1995.

42. For details on the provisions included in the peace accords, see Popkin, *El Salvador's Negotiated Revolution: Prospects for Legal Reform* (New York: Lawyers Committee for Human Rights, 1993).

43. Letter dated October 8, 1991, from El Salvador transmitting the text of the Mexico Agreement and annexes signed on 27 April 1991, by the Government of El Salvador and the FMLN, A/46/553–S/23130, October 9, 1991, reprinted in *The UN and El Salvador 1990–1995*, Doc. 29, p. 167.

44. Ibid., 168.

independence and openness to various schools of legal thought.[45] This section also set a time period for election of the new National Counsel for the Defense of Human Rights, entrusted the National Commission for the Consolidation of Peace (COPAZ)[46] with preparing draft enabling legislation for the new entity, and called for incorporation into that legislation of the parties' pledge (in the San José Human Rights Accord) to identify and eradicate groups that engage in the systematic practice of human rights violations.

Far more was done to modify and limit the role of the armed forces. Among other measures, responsibility for public order was assigned to a new civilian police, no longer under the authority of the Defense Ministry.[47] The Peace Accords called for disbanding the National Guard and Treasury Police, while the National Police was to be phased out as the civilian police was gradually deployed throughout the country.

Proposals not accepted included the immediate replacement of the Supreme Court and the attorney general; a process for evaluating all judges and cleaning out the judiciary; limiting the functions of the Supreme Court so that it would no longer be responsible for naming judges and court personnel, and supervising the legal profession; eliminating the extrajudicial confession; separating investigative and sentencing functions; making procedures for habeas corpus and amparo more accessible and efficient; guaranteeing the right to defense; permitting codefendant testimony; and allowing some form of reduced sentence or reward for cooperation with a judicial investigation. According to UN expert Pedro Nikken,

> In the negotiations, the United Nations working document dealing
> with the judiciary was subject to the greatest change of all. To obtain

45. Peace Agreement between the Government of El Salvador and the FMLN, letter dated January 27, 1992, from El Salvador, transmitting the entire text of the Peace Agreement between the Government of El Salvador and the FMLN, signed at Chapúltepec Castle in Mexico City on January 16, 1992, A/46/864–S/23501, January 30, 1992, reprinted in *The UN and El Salvador 1990–1995*, Doc. 36, p. 205.

46. COPAZ was created in the September 25, 1991, New York agreement as a mechanism to oversee implementation of the peace agreements. It was composed of two representatives of the government (one of whom was to come from the armed forces), two representatives of the FMLN, and one representative of each party or coalition in the Legislative Assembly. See UN Doc. A/46/502–S/23082, September 26, 1991, reprinted in *The United Nations and El Salvador 1990–1995*, Doc. 25, p. 159.

47. The attributes of the National Civilian Police were set out in the final Chapúltepec Agreement of January 16, 1992, which established that it was to be "a new force with a new organization, new officers, new education and training mechanisms, and a new doctrine." Among other innovations, the PNC was to be made up of limited numbers of former National Police and FMLN combatants, and a majority of recruits who had not taken part in hostilities.

more provisions and stronger language in the constitutional reform related to the military, the FMLN made greater concessions with respect to the judiciary. Therefore, judicial reform was left relatively weak; even if all the reforms had been implemented, they would not have been sufficient. It would have made more sense if the judicial reforms were part of a separate agreement, as in the case of human rights.[48]

UN mediator Alvaro de Soto has attributed the parties' failure to make greater progress on judicial reform to their mutual fear of Supreme Court President Gutiérrez Castro, who rejected the possibility of further reforms and maintained that the negotiators were trampling on the constitution.

The Supreme Court: An Obstacle to Negotiated Reforms

One of the most controversial issues raised was the need to make an immediate change in the Supreme Court.

The FMLN had agreed to negotiations within the framework of the 1983 constitution, a major concession from an insurgency that had always challenged the legitimacy of a constitution promulgated at the height of the war by a constituent assembly that included no representation from left parties. Under the 1983 constitution, the existing Supreme Court had been selected by a simple majority of the ARENA-dominated Legislative Assembly in 1989. The Supreme Court played no role in the negotiations, and Supreme Court President Mauricio Gutiérrez Castro repeatedly dismissed the peace agreements as mere political accords between the executive and the FMLN, which could have no binding effect on the judicial branch. At several points, sectors affected by the peace process threatened legal challenges in the Supreme Court, a threat the executive and others seemed to take seriously. For example, officers included in the Ad Hoc Commission's purge list threatened constitutional challenges. It is likely, however, that this threat was exaggerated and manipulated to allow the government to take tougher stands. In practice, it functioned much like periodic threats of military uprisings or coups—unlikely to be carried out, given national and international realities, but sufficiently credible to limit the parameters for debate on certain key issues.

48. Gary Bland, Conference Report: *El Salvador: Sustaining Peace, Nourishing Democracy* (Washington, D.C.: Woodrow Wilson Center Latin American Program, Washington Office on Latin America, 1993), 33.

The proposal to replace the Supreme Court had strong support: with the exception of ARENA, all parties represented in the interparty subcommission on the administration of justice coincided in calling for replacement of the incumbents.[49] The subcommission specified that the lawyers chosen should have no links with decision-making bodies of political parties and, preferably, not belong to any political party.

The new constitutional formula approved in April 1991 and ratified in October of that year called for the appointment of Supreme Court justices for staggered nine-year terms by a two-thirds majority vote of the legislature, limited to candidates proposed by the National Judiciary Council (half of whom were to come from the bar associations).[50] While the negotiators failed to agree on when this change would be implemented, the legislature introduced a transitional provision that called for the election of the new Supreme Court within ninety days of the expiration of the sitting Court's term.[51] Aside from indicating that the incumbent court would be allowed to finish its term, this provision also made it possible for the Assembly elected in 1991 (before the Peace Accords were signed) to choose the new court. (It was, however, its successor Assembly that finally carried out this task.) In this transitional provision, the legislature also assigned itself authority to determine which justices would serve for three, six, and nine years, rather than leaving this to lot, as had been proposed.

Despite the legislature's addition of this transitional provision, the issue of replacing the Supreme Court before the end of its term appeared in negotiating documents until the peace talks were nearly complete. Ultimately, it proved impossible to replace sitting justices before the end of their term. ARENA's refusal to accede reflected the Supreme Court's adamant insistence that its constitutional mandate could not be altered by political agreements. Given that the Assembly was also dominated by ARENA, including many hard-liners allied with Supreme Court President Gutiérrez Castro, any attempt to impeach sitting justices would have failed. Within the constitutional framework, the court could not be forced to resign.

---

49. Comisión Interpartidaria, Subcomisión de la administración de justicia, Primer informe de la subcomisión de la administración de justicia, San Salvador, June 6, 1990, 4.

50. Reformed article 186, substituted by D.L. No. 64, October 31, 1991, D.O. 217, Tomo 313, November 20, 1991.

51. Decreto No. 64, article 39.

4

THE CHALLENGE OF IMPLEMENTING THE AGREEMENTS TO END IMPUNITY

The negotiations were hastily completed in December 1991 to meet a some-what artificial December 31 deadline. The San José Human Rights Accord was already in effect, and the UN Observer Mission, ONUSAL, was on the ground and functioning. The large UN presence played a critical role in keeping the implementation process on track. Beyond its responsibilities in the human rights area, ONUSAL also verified all other aspects of the accords, including the demobilization of the FMLN, military reductions and elimination of different military and security forces, land transfers, and the conduct of elections.

As outlined above, the peace accords prescribed a combination of temporary ad hoc bodies as well as constitutional and institutional reforms. The Ad Hoc Commission to purge the military of human rights violators and the broader Truth Commission were to initiate their work in the months following the signing of the peace accords. The new permanent institutions designed to play key roles in ensuring protection of human rights, the National Civilian Police and the National Counsel for the Defense of Human Rights, were to be built from scratch, starting in the weeks following the signing of the accords. The few judicial reforms agreed to were implemented over a longer period of time.

Purging the Military

Implementing the agreement to purge the military of human rights violators was a daunting task. The secretary-general named the Ad Hoc Commission's three civilian members: renowned corporate lawyer and founder of the Christian Democratic Party Abraham Rodríguez; Eduardo Molina Olivares, an educator formerly associated with the Christian Democrats; and Reynaldo Galindo Pohl, a respected international lawyer who served as the UN's Special Rapporteur on Iran. President Cristiani chose two former defense ministers as the military representatives.

With three months to complete their work, the three commissioners were faced with the challenge of evaluating the records of 2,293 army officers. The agreement gave the commission the authority to recommend the discharge or transfer of officers reviewed and called for the Salvadoran government to put these recommendations into effect. The commission could use any information from any source it considered reliable; no criteria were set forth for the standard of evidence to be used. The commission chose to focus on the army's upper echelons and those individuals about whom it had obtained information, approximately 10 percent of the total. The Ad Hoc Commission's confidential report was submitted to President Cristiani and UN Secretary-General Boutros-Ghali on September 23, 1992. The commission went farther than either of the parties had anticipated. Achieving compliance with its recommendations proved to be one of the greatest challenges to the peace process. The Ad Hoc Commission called for the discharge or transfer of 103 officers, including virtually the entire High Command of the Salvadoran Armed Forces.[1] Army officers decried the commission's recommendations as an attack on the institution. President Cristiani failed to carry out the recommended actions in the time frame established in the peace accords, nor did he honor a subsequent commitment to the UN Secretary-General. The president said that the commission had violated officers' legal rights and had failed to justify its recommendations for dismissals or transfers. As a consequence, he claimed that officers would have been able to mount legal challenges to their discharges. He also suggested that officers who felt they had been unfairly "purged" might react violently.[2]

1. One officer was no longer a member of the armed forces. See Letter dated January 7, 1993, from the Secretary-General Addressed to the President of the Security Council, UN Doc. S/25078, January 9, 1993. Of the 102 remaining, 26 officers were recommended for transfer and 76 for discharge.

2. Shirley Christian, "Salvador Says It Needs More Time to Purge Army," *New York*

In a public letter to the UN Security Council, Secretary-General Boutros-Ghali rejected the measures taken regarding fifteen of the named officers as not in compliance with the Ad Hoc Commission's recommendations. Seven of these had been assigned as military attachés in Salvadoran embassies, and eight were to remain in their posts during the "transition period," understood as the remainder of President Cristiani's term in office.[3] Among those in dispute was the defense minister, General René Emilio Ponce, credited with playing a crucial role in the armed forces' acceptance of the peace process, but who would subsequently be named by the Truth Commission (in March 1993) as having ordered the killing of the Jesuit priests. Some FMLN leaders, notably from the People's Revolutionary Army (ERP), voiced their willingness to allow certain officers to stay on longer than agreed in the peace accords in the interests of stability and to obtain additional benefits for midlevel FMLN commanders. The UN, various governments involved in the peace process, the Jesuit-run Central American University, and human rights groups all urged full compliance with the recommendations, which, they maintained, were not subject to negotiation.[4] Despite UN pressure, it was not until April 1, 1993—after the Truth Commission issued its report—that the government advised the UN of its plan to implement the outstanding Ad Hoc Commission recommendations by June 30, 1993.

The Ad Hoc Commission's recommendations constituted an unprecedented civilian review of military officers. The commission's role must be understood in conjunction with that of the Truth Commission. The Ad Hoc Commission's "report" was a confidential list of officers to be discharged and transferred. Thus it was in no sense a truth-telling process. Yet it was designed to introduce a measure of accountability and to send a message to the armed forces. Since the process could not possibly constitute a thorough or systematic review of the entire officer corps, it was instead a symbolic cleansing. Other officers long cited for their involvement in death-squad activity continued to serve in official posts as, for example, military attachés. Still, as Truth Commission member Thomas Buergenthal notes, because of the Ad Hoc Commission's recommendations, "some individuals implicated

---

Times, January 6, 1993, A3; Shirley Christian, "El Salvador's Leader Says Purge of Army Skipped Defense Chief" (Alfredo Cristiani to retain General René Emilio Ponce), *New York Times*, January 7, 1993, A7, 11.

3. UN Doc. S/25078, January 9, 1993.

4. In some aspects of implementation of the peace accords, the UN brokered revised calendars and revised plans (particularly in the land transfer program and some aspects of the Public Security Academy) to overcome deliberate or circumstantial delays and technical difficulties.

in serious acts of violence no longer felt sure that they would be protected" and subsequently opted to provide information to the Truth Commission.[5] The commission's unanticipated decision to focus on the highest ranking officers increased the symbolic impact at the same time that it heightened resistance to implementation of its recommendations.

The need for a purging process reflected the failure of Salvadoran institutions to hold military officers accountable for human rights violations. Neither the armed forces nor civilian authorities had made any serious effort to punish officers implicated in human rights abuses. Most of the officers in leadership positions in the armed forces at the time of the peace agreement had been implicated in serious human rights violations. Because no existing institution was capable of addressing this situation, a special commission was necessary. Reforms generated by the peace process were supposed to ensure that the criminal justice system would be equipped to identify and sanction future wrongdoers within the military.

Although the three Salvadorans appointed to the Ad Hoc Commission showed great courage in their decision to review the highest echelons of the armed forces, without international pressure their recommendations would not have been fully implemented. In addition to the UN's public pressure and other diplomatic efforts, the Clinton administration froze $11 million in U.S. military aid in February 1993 until the Ad Hoc Commission's recommendations were carried out. When General Ponce offered his resignation on March 12, he angrily cited "foreign pressures."[6] An important lesson is that without a change of government, this kind of effort is likely to be successful only when sufficient outside pressure can be brought to bear to force compliance with the recommendations. Without the added pressure of the public Truth Commission report and the U.S. action, it is not at all clear how the government would have dealt with the officers in dispute.

Even after publication of the Truth Commission report, the Ad Hoc Commission's recommendations were implemented in such a way that neither the government nor any officers admitted wrongdoing. Instead, officers were allowed to take their normal retirement and honorable discharges. Furthermore, the outgoing High Command had much to say about who would succeed it. Two years after publication of the Truth Commission report, Defense Minister General Humberto Corado still maintained that the "armed forces have nothing to apologize for, since their conduct was consistent with

5. Thomas Buergenthal, "The United Nations Truth Commission for El Salvador," *Vanderbilt Journal of Transnational Law* 27 (1994): 517.

6. *El Diario de Hoy*, March 15, 1993.

the principles of a war in which a clandestine enemy attacks regular military patrols."[7]

The Truth Commission's Work

The Salvadoran Truth Commission had an enormous impact in the international arena and is often touted as a model of what the international community can accomplish. Its groundbreaking and controversial decision to name those found responsible for abuses and its far-reaching recommendations have generated both admiration and criticism.[8] A truth commission negotiated as part of a pacted transition is now commonly seen as a solution for the sensitive problem of dealing with past human rights violations quickly and relatively comprehensively without confronting the evidentiary, legal, institutional, and political problems posed by prosecutions. In the Salvadoran case, what the commission recommended and what actually happened as a result have not always been distinguished. Likewise, insufficient attention has been given to consequences of using a temporary, entirely international commission as a substitute for any societal effort to address the past.

Goals

The lofty goals of the Truth Commission were established in the April 1991 agreement drafted by the UN and signed by the parties:

> *Reaffirming* [the parties'] intention to contribute to the reconciliation of Salvadoran society;

7. Quoted in (El Salvador) *Proceso*, May 10, 1995.
8. For descriptions and analysis of the Salvadoran Truth Commission, see, e.g., Mike Kaye, "The Role of Truth Commissions in the Search for Justice, Reconciliation, and Democratisation: The Salvadorean and Honduran Cases," *Journal of Latin American Studies* 29 (1997): 693–716; Buergenthal, "The UN Truth Commission"; Margaret Popkin and Naomi Roht-Arriaza, "Truth as Justice: Investigatory Commissions in Latin America," *Journal of Law and Social Inquiry* 20 (1995): 79; Priscilla B. Hayner, "Fifteen Truth Commissions—1974 to 1994: A Comparative Study," *Human Rights Quarterly* 16 (November 1994): 597; Americas Watch, *El Salvador: Accountability and Human Rights: The Report of the United Nations Commission on the Truth for El Salvador* (Americas Watch—News from the Americas, August 10, 1993); Douglass Cassel, "International Truth Commissions and Justice," *Aspen Institute Quarterly* 5 (1993): 69.

Recognizing the need to clear up without delay those exceptionally important acts of violence whose characteristics and impact, and the social unrest to which they gave rise, urgently require that the complete truth be made known and that the resolve and means to establish the truth be strengthened;

... *Agreeing* on the advisability of fulfilling that task through a procedure which is both reliable and expeditious and may yield results in the short term, without prejudice to the obligations incumbent on the Salvadoran courts to solve such cases and impose the appropriate penalties on the culprits.[9]

In the final January 1992 peace agreements, the parties included another reference to the Truth Commission's mandate:

The Parties recognize the need to clarify and put an end to any indication of impunity on the part of officers of the armed forces, particularly where respect for human rights is jeopardized. To that end, the parties refer this issue to the Commission on the Truth for consideration and resolution. All of this shall be without prejudice to the principle, which the Parties also recognize, that acts of this nature, regardless of the sector to which their perpetrators belong, must be the object of exemplary action by the law courts so that the punishment prescribed by law is meted out to those found responsible.[10]

Thus the Truth Commission was called on: (1) to make the complete truth known and strengthen the means and resolve to establish the truth; (2) to overcome impunity on the part of officers of the armed forces; (3) to achieve quick results without preempting the role of the courts; and (4) to promote reconciliation (not necessarily in that order).

On their face, these goals seem to go far beyond the reach of any ad hoc

---

9. Preamble to Truth Commission agreement, Mexico Accords, 173.

10. Chapúltepec Agreement, Chapter 1, Armed Forces, Section 5, End to Impunity, Doc. 36, p. 196. The explicit reference to overcoming impunity on the part of the armed forces gave a very different role to the Salvadoran Truth Commission than that assigned to the Chilean commission. While the preamble bears some resemblance to the preamble to the Chilean decree establishing the Commission on Truth and Reconciliation, there are important differences. For example, the Salvadoran preamble is far less explicit than the Chilean version in differentiating between the roles of the commission and the courts, it does not and could not focus on the importance of building a collective version of the truth, and it does not mention the need to vindicate victims and provide compensation for the harm caused.

commission with a six-month mandate. Derived from the logic of the negotiations process, they focused on the need for reconciliation (so that the warring parties could live together in the future), the need to establish an official "truth" in certain key cases, the need to end military impunity, and the need to strengthen Salvadoran judicial institutions. As the only mechanism designed to address El Salvador's tragic history of human rights violations, the Truth Commission's stated goals, even had they been feasible, appear inadequate to address the magnitude of that history. Neither the UN nor the parties to the conflict made any systematic effort to consult with Salvadoran civil society, victims and their relatives, or even Salvadoran human rights groups. Nor did the parties appear to recognize that the right to truth and justice could not be foreclosed by their negotiations.

As the following discussion suggests, the Truth Commission's success in accomplishing its stated goals was limited. In large part, the Truth Commission could not have fulfilled these goals. Beyond the goals set for the Truth Commission, the adequacy of its mandate to address the massive human rights violations that had taken place in El Salvador during the armed conflict must be examined.

Making the Complete Truth Known and Strengthening the Resolve and Means to Establish the Truth

"Up to a certain point, the Truth Commission told the truth ... it assigned some blame to everybody."[11]

Undoubtedly the Truth Commission established some measure of truth. Unfortunately, in El Salvador too little attention has been given to the commission's fact-finding and conclusions. While not a judicial authority, the commission nonetheless established some important precedents in holding commanders responsible for the actions of their troops and in focusing on who gave the orders and who covered up for violations. It placed particular emphasis on the complicity and failures of state institutions charged with investigating and prosecuting those responsible for violations.

The limited investigations previously undertaken in a few cases had confined themselves to identifying the material authors of certain crimes. In selected cases, the Truth Commission worked hard to get beyond the triggermen, at times successfully. Truth Commission member Thomas Buergenthal notes that the commission's power to make recommendations concerning

11. Author's interview with Rubén Zamora, July 4, 1994, San Salvador.

prosecutions and amnesties and to help individuals obtain asylum abroad led a few current or former members of the military to begin to provide important information to the commission.[12] Establishing who gave the orders when these did not follow an official chain of command can be very difficult for a court of law, especially when witnesses are unwilling to testify publicly for fear of reprisals. Thus the commission was able to do something that would have been virtually impossible for a Salvadoran court to accomplish.[13]

The Truth Commission's Methodology: Naming Perpetrators

The Salvadoran Truth Commission focused on investigating particularly notorious and representative cases. Although the commission invited and received testimonies from anyone who wished to present them, it did little more than catalog most of these statements.[14] The commission did use these testimonies to establish patterns and help establish the facts in the individual cases it chose to examine. In most cases, however, no independent verification was undertaken. The commission attempted to resolve a smaller universe of cases, selecting them either for their impact and importance or as examples of patterns. Thirty-two cases were written up in some detail by the Truth Commission. One of the three commissioners, Professor Thomas Buergenthal, has explained that they were following the wishes of the negotiating parties, who wanted "an investigation that focused on some of the most egregious acts and a set of recommendations to help ensure that the past would not repeat itself."[15]

How this was understood by the negotiating parties nonetheless seems to have differed considerably. The FMLN conceived of a limited number of cases—perhaps eight—to be thoroughly investigated. Most of these cases would involve army or death-squad actions. The government, on the other

12. Buergenthal, "The UN Truth Commission," 517.
13. Aside from the issue of a witness's willingness to testify in court, Salvadoran law and practice did little to encourage such testimony. A broadly interpreted exclusion of codefendant testimony hampered efforts to proceed against higher-ups, while there was no legal basis for granting lenient treatment or foreign asylum to those who cooperated in an investigation.
14. "The Commission . . . registered more than 22,000 complaints of serious acts of violence that occurred in El Salvador between January 1980 and July 1991. Over 7,000 were received directly at the Commission's offices in various locations. The remainder were received through governmental and non-governmental institutions. . . . Those giving testimony attributed almost 85 percent of cases to agents of the State, paramilitary groups allied to them, and the death squads. . . . The complaints registered accused FMLN in approximately 5 percent of cases (*From Madness to Hope*, 43).
15. Buergenthal, "The UN Truth Commission," 501.

hand, saw a symmetrical treatment of a limited number of cases that would lead to the proposition that terrible things happen on all sides during wars and the best way to deal with them is through a comprehensive amnesty. After issuance of the Truth Commission report, President Cristiani insisted that it had been designed as a mechanism to discover "the historical truth in the armed conflict." The chief government negotiator claims that he did not expect names to be named.[16]

Nonetheless, the language of the accord did not bar naming names, and the provision regarding the "need to clarify and put an end to any indication of impunity on the part of officers of the armed forces, particularly in cases where respect for human rights is jeopardized" seemed to call for establishing individual responsibility.

The Salvadoran Truth Commission considered determining individual responsibility a crucial part of its mandate. The agreement itself called for the commission to make known the "complete truth." Professor Buergenthal writes:

> [O]ur initial contacts with the Parties indicated that they assumed we would identify individuals responsible for serious acts of violence. The government representatives, including President Alfredo Cristiani and members of the Military High Command, told us repeatedly during our initial visits to El Salvador that our task was to identify the "rotten apples" within the institution. The Institution itself had to be protected. The government representatives told us: "Individuals and not the 'Institution' were responsible for the violations that the government side committed." The FMLN also repeatedly made it clear that the guilty had to be identified. Of course, neither side expected our investigation to be very thorough or to contain much evidence implicating the "big fish."[17]

Once it became aware of some of the names likely to be included in the commission's report, the Salvadoran government launched a diplomatic offensive to try to convince the commission not to name individuals.[18] Supporting

16. Author's interview with Foreign Minister Oscar Santamaría, San Salvador, July 20, 1994.

17. Buergenthal, "The UN Truth Commission," 520.

18. For a description of this campaign and the arguments it raised, such as the danger to the peace process and national reconciliation, the possibility of a military coup, and the government's claimed inability to protect from retaliation those who provided information to the commission, see ibid., 521.

the Salvadoran government's argument, Guatemalan government officials argued that the El Salvador Truth Commission's inclusion of names of military officers would hamper Guatemalan efforts to achieve a negotiated peace settlement. The Salvadoran government was most concerned about protecting then Defense Minister, General René Emilio Ponce, and other members of the High Command found by the Truth Commission to have participated in the 1989 conspiracy to kill the Jesuits. As leader of the armed forces and of the powerful 1966 military academy graduating class known as the *tandona*, General Ponce had played an essential role in ensuring the military's acceptance of the peace agreements.

Well aware of the Salvadoran precedent, negotiators in neighboring Guatemala agreed to what seemed to be a more limited truth commission, the "commission to clarify past human rights violations and acts of violence that have caused the Guatemalan population to suffer."[19] In the preamble to the Guatemalan Historical Clarification Commission accord, the parties referred to "the right of the Guatemalan people to know the full truth about these events whose clarification will contribute to preventing the repetition of these sad and painful pages and to fortifying the process of democratization in the country." The Guatemalan accord provided that individuals responsible for violations would not be identified and limited the commission's mandate to violent acts related to the armed conflict. The Guatemalan commissioners were left with the task of interpreting these limitations. Without naming names, for example, the Guatemalan commission was still able to assign institutional responsibility.

What it means to reveal the complete truth remains a disputed issue, closely connected to the question of how a truth commission's work relates to the judicial system. In theory, there is a certain appeal to the argument that a truth commission should quietly pass the information it has collected on individual responsibilities to the courts charged with conducting judicial investigations according to law. But the danger is that the judiciary may not fulfill its obligations. The political branches of government may preclude prosecutions through an amnesty law. Even without amnesty, lack of faith in the justice system, limited resources, witnesses' fears of testifying, and military obstruction may make successful prosecutions almost impossible. Experience shows that successful prosecutions are indeed rare: a truth commission may provide the only opportunity to establish the "official" truth.

19. Agreement on the establishment of the commission to clarify past human rights violations and acts of violence that have caused the Guatemalan population to suffer, June 23, 1994, UN Doc. A/48/954, S/1994/751, July 1, 1994, Annex II.

The Chilean Rettig Commission rejected the possibility of naming those responsible for crimes as an impermissible intrusion on the jurisdiction of courts.[20] José Zalaquett, a member of the Rettig Commission, maintains that the "global truth" about what happened under the dictatorship can come from a truth commission report, while the truth about each individual case should emerge from a judicial process.

Investigatory commissions established after the Salvadoran Truth Commission have grappled with this problem. In Honduras, the Commissioner for Human Rights named those he could identify and urged state institutions to carry out investigations and prosecutions in accordance with law. The Human Rights Prosecutor in Honduras initiated a test prosecution based on the commissioner's findings, but other Honduran institutions did little to implement his recommendations. The Guatemalan accord barred the identification of individuals responsible but (arguably) left open the possibility that information could be provided to the courts. The Colombian "Trujillo" commission was specifically authorized to weigh the inculpatory and exculpatory evidence against those presumed responsible, their accomplices, and other identified participants, as well as the extent of state responsibility in these acts.[21]

20. The preamble to the decree establishing the Rettig Commission explains the government's intentions in forming such a body. Among the reasons given for forming the commission were that basic demands for justice and the creation of the indispensable conditions for true national reconciliation could only be satisfied over the foundation of the truth; that only knowledge of the truth will rehabilitate the public perception of the victims' dignity, give their relatives the possibility of honoring them appropriately, and permit some measure of reparation of the harm caused; that apart from judicial actions (necessary to establish the crimes that may have been committed, identify those responsible, and apply the appropriate sanctions), in a relatively short period the country needs to obtain an overall appreciation of what occurred during the years of military rule; that the prompt formation of a serious collective concept of what occurred is necessary for the reunification of Chilean society; and that without prejudice to the role of the courts, it is the president's duty to do everything in his power to contribute to the most rapid and complete clarification of the truth. See Executive Decree 355, April 25, 1990, creating the Commission of Truth and Reconciliation, *Diario Oficial de la República de Chile*, May 9, 1990.

21. The "Trujillo" commission was set up to examine a series of violent incidents that occurred in the municipality of Trujillo between 1988 and 1991 as part of a friendly settlement of case no. 11.007, pending before the Inter-American Commission on Human Rights. An agreement to form the commission was signed in September 1994, and it was established in December 1994. It worked for less than three months before delivering its report to the IACHR. The commission was comprised of nineteen members, including representatives of state entities and the government as well as nongovernmental organizations. It found the state responsible for the actions and omissions of public servants as well as for judicial and disciplinary failures to collect pertinent evidence, rulings contrary to the evidence in the case, and other serious irregularities that impeded the identification and sanctions of those responsible for serious violations of human rights in Trujillo.

The Haitian truth commission's mandate charged it with responsibility for identifying the material authors of serious human rights violations and crimes against humanity as well as their accomplices and those who instigated these crimes. Unlike prior commissions, the Haitian commission was authorized to seek assistance from judicial or police authorities against those who refused to cooperate with its efforts. Information about suspected perpetrators was not included in the public version of the Haitian commission's report. Instead it was turned over to Haitian authorities so that they could proceed with investigations and prosecutions. Its report, published in 1996, was not widely circulated, and two years after its publication, efforts to implement its recommendations had encountered many obstacles. While some prosecutions have taken place in Haiti, they have been fraught with myriad difficulties.

The South African Truth and Reconciliation Commission (TRC), established in 1995, has gone further than any other in its quest to establish the complete truth. Well funded and initially authorized to operate for two years, the TRC held public hearings throughout the country. The provision for amnesty, which required full disclosure by those requesting its protection, encouraged many of those involved in violent acts to come forward. If the TRC determined that an application met the requirements for amnesty, no prosecution could follow. In South Africa, in contrast to most of Latin America, the carrot of amnesty was accompanied by the stick of a real possibility of prosecution. Those who did not seek amnesty during the relevant period, as well as those who were denied amnesty by the TRC, could, at least in theory, face prosecution.

Given the difficulty of attaining justice in many transitional situations, it seems appropriate for truth commissions to go as far as they can to discover the complete truth, including the identity of those responsible for serious violations. But reliance on confidential sources and failure to provide due process guarantees may deprive their findings of necessary fairness, transparency, and even credibility. Under these circumstances, their findings are more akin to the decision of a prosecutor or a grand jury to indict than to an ultimate finding of guilt after a public trial with due process guarantees. The credibility of the commission's findings will rest on that of its members and the manner in which it is perceived to have carried out its task.

Understood in this context, the identification of perpetrators should ideally serve as a spur to the justice system. Using the information provided by the truth commission as background, the appropriate institutions should undertake official investigations to determine responsibilities according to law.

In El Salvador, the commissioners unanimously agreed that "unless both Parties decided to amend our mandate, we were legally and morally obligated to identify those we found to be guilty of the serious abuses we had been investigating."[22] Not to have done so in cases where reliable testimony existed, and especially when the persons identified continued to occupy important positions and perform official functions, would "reinforce the very impunity to which the Parties instructed the Commission to put an end."[23]

Choice of Cases

Perhaps inevitably, the Truth Commission's choice of cases satisfied few in El Salvador. The Lawyers Committee for Human Rights found that the report "reveals arbitrary case selection criteria and uneven, inconsistent methodology."[24] For the government and its allies, too few FMLN cases were examined, and those that were examined generally received a more cursory treatment than those involving government agents. In large part, the numerical discrepancy stemmed from the commission's finding, which it apparently did not anticipate, that the vast majority of violations were attributable to the Salvadoran armed forces or paramilitary groups allied with them.[25] The commission also encountered a dearth of information about FMLN violations and was surprised to discover that neither Salvadoran nor U.S. authorities had significant evidence about responsibilities in these cases.[26] In certain cases, the FMLN took responsibility for its actions without naming the specific perpetrators. In several cases, the Truth Commission simply accepted these admissions without further investigation. Nor did it assign command responsibility in these cases even when the FMLN organization responsible had been identified.[27]

In cases where FMLN responsibility was suspected but not admitted, the commission failed to make significant progress.[28] Some cases important to

22. Buergenthal, "The UN Truth Commission," 522.
23. *From Madness to Hope*, 25.
24. Lawyers Committee for Human Rights, *Improvising History: A Critical Evaluation of the United Nations Observer Mission in El Salvador* (New York: Lawyers Committee for Human Rights, 1995), 129.
25. Buergenthal, "The UN Truth Commission," 528–29.
26. Ibid., 514.
27. Professor Buergenthal notes that the guerrillas' clandestine chain of command was more difficult to penetrate than the military's and the use of pseudonyms further compounded the problem (ibid., 507, 531).
28. See *From Madness to Hope*, "Violence against opponents by the Frente Farabundo Martí para la Liberación Nacional," 148–71.

the government, notably the 1989 murder of Minister of the Presidency José Antonio Rodríguez Porth, were simply not addressed.[29] This was one of the four cases listed in the government's proposals. The Truth Commission's mandate did not require it to examine the cases proposed by the parties. Nonetheless, the six cases listed by the FMLN were included, although the Truth Commission was unable to identify specifically those responsible for killing Hector Oquelí or to determine responsibility for the bombing of the FENASTRAS labor federation office.

The Truth Commission failed to shed significant light on what may well have been the FMLN's most widespread violations—those committed against its own ranks. These practices, which included summary executions without due process protections, were hardly examined by the Truth Commission. The commission included the well-known but atypical case of the murder of "Miguel Castellanos," a guerrilla commander who switched sides after his 1985 arrest. Far more common were cases of combatants or civilian collaborators in rural areas who, rightly or wrongly, were accused of being informants, often after having been arrested by the military. The victims were usually *campesinos*, whose disappearances or deaths were often not documented by human rights groups. Despite persistent reports suggesting that the FMLN executed a large number of combatants and civilian collaborators as supposed informants in San Vicente department in 1987, the commission did not address these allegations.

The commission did break new ground when it found that international human rights norms could be applied to the insurgents under certain conditions:

> It is true that, in traditional theory, international human rights law is applicable only to governments, while in some armed conflicts international humanitarian law is binding on both sides: in other words, binding on both insurgents and Government forces. However, it must be recognized that when insurgents assume government powers in territories under their control, they too can be required to observe certain human rights obligations that are binding on the State under international law.[30]

29. *From Madness to Hope*, 92–100. The other three cases listed by the government were included in the commission's report, although the case of Dr. Peccorini was treated in a summary fashion, merely stating that FMLN representatives had acknowledged responsibility for his killing (ibid., 163).
30. Ibid., 20.

The Truth Commission's limitations in addressing FMLN violations reflect the difficulties of handling violations by an insurgent force in this context. Given that the commission's mandate specifically included overcoming impunity on the part of members of the armed forces and that it was to address the most notorious cases, its work was necessarily weighted toward official abuses. As the commission itself pointed out, its chief recommendation to the FMLN—that it demobilize its forces and reintegrate into civil society—was already a key component of the peace process. Yet the government's notion that the FMLN should have been found equally culpable and its violations handled in identical fashion left the Truth Commission open to criticism on this score. Because with a few notable exceptions little had been done to investigate cases in which FMLN responsibility was presumed, less evidence was readily available to the commission. The Truth Commission might have blunted some criticism had it clarified these issues in its report. It also might have recommended that the FMLN establish a mechanism to help families find out what had happened to their relatives.

All these factors suggest that violations by an insurgent force might better be addressed, at least initially, separately from government violations: perhaps something closer to the ANC's decision in South Africa to undertake an examination of violations committed in its camps outside the country. The Motsuenyane Commission held public hearings that were widely reported in the press. The ANC expressed its profound sense of regret, collective moral responsibility, and apology to all those who suffered as a consequence of the violations established by the commission.[31]

The ANC rejected the idea of pursuing "partial" prosecutions and sanctions or providing reparations when abuses of the apartheid regime had yet to be examined, and it called for the establishment of a global truth commission. The Motsuenyane Commission and its predecessor, the Skweyiya Commission, did much to establish the truth about violations that occurred in the ANC camps but were unable to initiate efforts to achieve justice outside the context of a global truth commission. Still, the ANC's effort went far beyond what any other contemporary insurgency has done in this regard. This promising beginning has since been undermined by the ANC's unfortunate October 1998 attempt to block publication of the TRC report because some of its leaders were found responsible for serious human rights violations.

The Salvadoran Truth Commission's failure to name most of the civilians

---

31. African National Congress, National Executive Committee's Response to the Motsuenyane Commission's Report, August 28, 1993.

who financed and planned death-squad activities drew criticism from the left but also from members of the military who claimed it was unfair to place the blame only on the military. A Supreme Court justice asserted that it was unfair to attack the judiciary so harshly when those behind the death squads remained unscathed.[32] There was widespread speculation in El Salvador that the commission, for political reasons, had deliberately suppressed information about civilians linked to death-squad activities since some of those expected to be named were members of the ARENA government or close allies. The commission maintained that it simply lacked sufficient corroborating evidence to publish most of the names provided to it.

The Truth Commission could not have satisfied everybody. The commission's work was limited by time and resource constraints as well as by unfamiliarity with the terrain. These problems were exacerbated by a well-intentioned but questionable decision to avoid too much contact with Salvadoran human rights groups or others knowledgeable about the events to be examined. Internal administrative problems also complicated the commission's task. Some of the cases chosen were inevitable: for example, Archbishop Romero, the Jesuits, the El Mozote and Sumpul massacres. Yet the cases selected seemed to reflect an excessive number involving foreign victims, perhaps because of pressure from their governments and the availability of information.[33] Indisputably, some of these cases, precisely because they had been investigated, yielded important information about death-squad or military practices.[34] Still, more of the commission's time could have been dedicated to unmasking those behind the death squads and establishing the truth in some of the cases where responsibility remained in dispute. Perhaps this would have called for criminal investigative capabilities beyond those of the commission. Yet the commission, with its unprecedented access to information and witnesses, constituted a unique opportunity to establish the truth. To the disappointment of many observers, the commissioners determined that their mandate did not include addressing U.S. responsibility for training and supporting the abusive Salvadoran military.

32. Author's interview with Atilio Ramírez Amaya, Magistrate of the Criminal Chamber, April 1993, San Salvador.

33. In 9 of the 32 cases selected at least some of the victims were foreigners.

34. For example, the deaths of José Rodolfo Viera, Michael Hammer, and Mark Pearlman were only investigated because the two U.S. victims were working for AIFLD, although the principal target of the assassins was Viera, then head of the Agrarian Transformation Institute (ISTA). The investigation revealed a great deal of information about the manner in which death-squad operations were conducted by a parallel structure within the National Guard. See *From Madness to Hope*, 136–38.

The Commission's International Composition and the State's Failure to Embrace Its Findings

Official acknowledgment of the truth is considered a crucial element in addressing past human rights violations.[35] But to what extent can an authoritative international body fulfill this role when the government fails to adopt its findings? In Chile, President Aylwin presented the Rettig Commission report on national television, apologizing in the name of the government for the actions of state agents. In Colombia in 1995, President Ernesto Samper recognized the state's responsibility for the serious human rights violations documented in the Trujillo report.

In contrast, in El Salvador, President Cristiani voiced his dissatisfaction with the Truth Commission's report and urged an immediate and total amnesty. His military commanders took to the airwaves to denounce the commission's report, as did the entire Supreme Court. Minister of the Presidency Oscar Santamaría, who headed the government's negotiating team, termed the report "an insult to Salvadoran society ... and very explosive." General Mauricio Vargas, who represented the military on the negotiating team, called the report "biased, incomplete, unfair, totally unacceptable." Nelson García, then president of the Salvadoran Lawyers Federation, found that the commission's report did "not even meet the requirements of the Inquisition." President Cristiani deplored the commission for "exceeding its mandate." The entire leadership of the armed forces appeared on national television to blast the report as "unfair, incomplete, illegal, unethical, partisan and insolent."[36]

The FMLN's reaction to the report was complicated because all the current FMLN leaders named belonged to a single organization, the People's Revolutionary Army (ERP). Six ERP leaders were found responsible for an FMLN policy of killing mayors who were considered political opponents.[37]

35. See José Zalaquett, "Confronting Human Rights Violations Committed by Former Governments: Principles Applicable and Political Constraints," in *State Crimes: Punishment or Pardon* (Washington, D.C.: Aspen Institute, 1989); Aryeh Neier, "What Should Be Done About the Guilty?" *New York Review of Books* 32 (February 1, 1990).

36. Popkin, *Prospects for Legal Reform*, 69–71.

37. *From Madness to Hope*, 148. The only FMLN commander named in the commission's report who was not an ERP member was Pedro Antonio Andrade, who had been a commander of the Central American Workers Revolutionary Party (PRTC) until he was detained by security forces and decided to cooperate with them and with U.S. intelligence. The Truth Commission found that Andrade had participated in planning the Zona Rosa killings of four U.S. marines (nine civilians and one of the attackers were also killed). He was deported from the United States in 1997, after families of the murdered marines and Senator Richard C. Shelby,

The ERP maintained that its leadership had been unfairly singled out precisely because they had been more cooperative in providing information to the Truth Commission than the other FMLN organizations. Professor Buergenthal dismissed this claim as "simply not true" and noted that they had been identified largely because they were "more careless than the others in covering their tracks." The ERP leadership was apparently named because the killing of mayors had been an official and public policy. Still, it is not clear why political killings that the Truth Commission attributed to members of other FMLN organizations were not analyzed in the same fashion. In many cases, a lack of readily available documentation and no known official policy were undoubtedly contributing factors. Regardless of the commission's reasons for naming the ERP leaders,[38] the effect was to create a serious problem within the FMLN. Existing tensions among the different factions were exacerbated as ERP leaders felt themselves unfairly singled out and said so. Still, the FMLN's public statements generally supported the report's conclusions and accepted its findings.

Given the reaction to the report, it is reasonable to ask why El Salvador resorted to an international commission for such a sensitive task. The continuing polarization of Salvadoran society made it difficult to conceive of three Salvadorans who would have been acceptable to both sides. Many witnesses might not have come forward. Yet relying on internationals meant that respected Salvadorans of divergent opinions did not come together to write a common history of the abuses that occurred during the period under examination, as was done in Chile and Argentina. Nor was there official Salvadoran "ownership" of the report's findings. The Salvadoran government made no effort to distribute or disseminate the report. Nongovernmental organizations made some efforts to distribute the report itself, as well as popular, comic book versions. Seven years later, the report was not widely available or read.

The international nature of the Truth Commission facilitated international support for the undertaking and also allowed international pressure to be brought to bear to achieve compliance with the report's recommendations. But international pressure could not force official acceptance of the commission's findings, however authoritative they might be. Indeed, with the attribution of responsibility for notorious human rights violations to

---

chairman of the Senate Intelligence Committee, had raised an outcry about the U.S. government's decision to grant him safe haven in the United States.

38. Buergenthal, "The UN Truth Commission," 532, n. 73.

ARENA founder Roberto D'Aubuisson and others associated with the party, to virtually the entire military High Command, and to the Supreme Court for its complicity, it would have been extremely difficult for President Cristiani's government to have accepted the report's conclusions.

International efforts to attain truth and justice have become commonplace since the Salvadoran Truth Commission issued its report. Yet no other country has chosen to rely on an entirely international commission to undertake this task. The UN itself has undertaken efforts in the former Yugoslavia and in Rwanda to investigate and prosecute in international tribunals those responsible for grave breaches of international humanitarian law and crimes against humanity. These efforts did not come from a concerted agreement of the parties involved but were instead initiatives of the international community in response to horrifying and well-publicized levels of bloodshed. In Honduras, the commissioner for human rights, himself a member of the Inter-American Commission on Human Rights, relied on international technical assistance to undertake a preliminary investigation of the disappearances that occurred in Honduras during the early 1980s. His office continued its investigation after publication of a preliminary report, and the Human Rights Prosecutor's Office sought to prosecute military officers implicated in human rights violations.

In 1997 the UN-sponsored Historical Clarification Commission (HCC) in Guatemala was established with a mixed composition. The peace accords provided that one member would be from the UN, while the other two were to be Guatemalans.[39] The HCC's investigative staff was also mixed, with an international delegate heading each regional office. Beyond its Guatemalan staff, the HCC sought to work closely with Guatemalans. Ideas for potential HCC recommendations were discussed and debated at a May 1998 forum in which more than four hundred people representing approximately one hundred and fifty organizations participated. Moreover, the HCC enjoyed the benefit of several civil society initiatives to address the past. Concerned about the limitations in the HCC's negotiated mandate, and eager to contribute to the peace and reconciliation process, the Guatemalan Catholic Church launched its Recovery of Historical Memory (REMHI)

---

39. The UN subsequently named Christian Tomuschat, a German expert on international human rights who had previously served as the UN Independent Expert on Guatemala, to head the commission. The two Guatemalan members, Edgar Alfredo Balsells Tojo and Otilia Lux de Cotí, were named by the UN with the agreement of the negotiating parties. The commission was installed on August 1, 1997, and its initial six- to twelve-month mandate was eventually extended until January 31, 1999.

project in 1995. This interdiocesan project trained layworkers to take testimonies, mostly in indigenous languages, that captured people's experience and understanding of the years of violence. The 1400-page REMHI report, *Guatemala: Nunca Más*, was publicly released on April 24, 1998. Two days later, Bishop Juan Gerardi, who had overall responsibility for the effort, was brutally murdered. To the surprise of most observers, the official HCC report proved to be an unexpectedly powerful indictment of the Guatemalan military's violent actions against the civilian population during thirty-six years of armed conflict. Among the commission's findings was that the Guatemalan army carried out acts of genocide against particular Mayan communities in specific geographic areas between 1981 and 1983. The commission's far-reaching recommendations included the establishment of a presidential commission to review the actions of individual military officers during the armed conflict and the investigation of the fate of the disappeared, the implementation of an active policy of exhumations, and the identification and location of children forcibly separated from their families during the conflict. The Guatemalan government's initial response to the report was quite defensive and rejected any recommendations that were not already included in the 1996 peace accords. Unlike the Salvadoran negotiators, the parties to the Guatemalan peace accords did not explicitly commit to carrying out the recommendations of the Historical Clarification Commission.

Haiti's seven-member truth commission included three members chosen in close consultation with the UN and the OAS and had a mixed staff as well. In contrast, the seventeen commissioners on the South African Truth and Reconciliation Commission (TRC) were South African. Extensive consultation with international experts preceded the commission's creation and continued throughout its mandate. Unfortunately, ANC officials have not wholeheartedly endorsed the TRC report because of their belief that the TRC failed to adequately distinguish violations committed in the struggle against apartheid from those committed to maintain the apartheid state.

Undoubtedly, El Salvador's international commission (under UN auspices) helped to encourage key witnesses to provide information they would have been unlikely to give to Salvadorans. It also raised the profile of the commission, which encouraged international funding and calls from the international community for compliance with its recommendations.

Nonetheless, the reality that no other country has chosen to rely on a wholly international commission in the wake of the Salvadoran Truth Commission undoubtedly reflects some of the complexities of that experience.

The Truth Commission's "Binding" Recommendations

Unable to force the Salvadoran government to accept the Truth Commission's conclusions, the UN focused instead on the report's "binding" recommendations. These recommendations were binding in the sense that both parties had agreed that they would carry them out. As part of the peace accords, implementation of the recommendations was subject to UN verification. As a consequence, there was substantial international pressure on both parties to comply with the terms of the accords they themselves had signed. Indubitably, the involvement of the UN, the four friends of the UN Secretary-General, and the United States made noncompliance more difficult. Mexico, Spain, Colombia, and Venezuela were the "friends" of the Salvadoran peace process. They played an active role throughout various stages of the process and provided significant support to the Truth Commission. Both the Salvadoran government and the FMLN cared deeply about their international image: neither wanted to be seen as flouting the peace accords. Thus, the practical solution was to focus more on the recommendations (i.e., creating conditions that would make recurrences impossible) than on the still controversial and divisive past.[40] Even so, many of the Truth Commission's recommendations met with great resistance.

The UN largely treated the Truth Commission recommendations as an integral part of implementation of the peace accords and included implementation of certain key recommendations in periodic rescheduling of commitments. This follow-up involved a selection process based on the importance and feasibility assigned to different recommendations. Some were allowed to fall by the wayside, while others have been the subject of intense UN pressure. Because the Truth Commission recommendations were not the product of direct negotiations between the parties, government representatives maintained that they did not constitute an absolute obligation. In a May 1993 note to the Inter-American Commission on Human Rights, the Salvadoran government explained that President Cristiani would "comply with the recommendations of the Truth Commission insofar as they are consistent with the constitution and laws of El Salvador and serve the interests of national reconciliation and contribute to what the majority of the Salvadoran people

---

40. Even before the publication of the report, the Democratic Convergence, a center-left coalition, circulated a letter urging all political parties in the Assembly to focus on the report's recommendations and try to reach consensus on those that could be implemented.

want, which is to promote national reconciliation by forgiving and forgetting a painful past that has caused so much damage."[41]

The Truth Commission's varied recommendations were divided into four categories: (1) those stemming from the results of the investigation, (2) those aimed at eradication of structural causes linked directly to the acts examined, (3) institutional reforms to prevent the repetition of such acts, and (4) steps toward national reconciliation. Perhaps not surprisingly, given the reaction to the report's findings, among the most controversial were several recommendations resulting from the investigation.

Recommendations Stemming from the Results of the Investigation

In its findings, the Truth Commission named members of the military, government officials, FMLN leaders and combatants, civilians, and judges for their participation in, responsibility for, or complicity in, the acts of violence examined. The commission called for dismissing those named who remained in the armed forces, the civil service, or the judiciary. It further called for disqualifying all those named from holding any public office or post for at least ten years and permanently from any activity related to public security or national defense.[42] Noting that it lacked the power to apply such a provision directly, the commission recommended to COPAZ that it prepare a draft bill along these lines for presentation to the Legislative Assembly. Based on its finding that the judiciary bore "tremendous responsibility" for the impunity with which serious acts of violence were committed, the commission urged the justices of the Supreme Court to resign from their posts so that a new court could be selected in accordance with the constitutional reforms.[43]

The government simply rejected these recommendations. Military officers named by the Truth Commission included some who had been singled out by the Ad Hoc Commission, notably Defense Minister Ponce and others in the High Command found to have participated in the conspiracy to kill the Jesuits. The Truth Commission report and international pressure provided the necessary impetus so that those named by the Ad Hoc Commission who remained in the armed forces were given retirement dates. Many of the others named were no longer in active service. According to an October

41. Inter-American Commission on Human Rights, *Report on the Situation of Human Rights in El Salvador*, OEA/Ser.L/V/II.85, doc. 23 rev. (February 11, 1994), 74.
42. *From Madness to Hope*, 176.
43. Ibid., 177.

1993 UN report, only eight officers named by the Truth Commission remained in the armed forces after full implementation of the Ad Hoc Commission recommendations.[44] Some of these, including former SIU chief Col. Manuel Antonio Rivas, continued to occupy command positions. Still fewer civilians named were employed by the government. The Supreme Court explicitly rejected the commission's findings regarding members of the judiciary.[45] Rodolfo Parker, the civilian lawyer for the armed forces found to have altered confessions in the Jesuit case, was subsequently assigned to represent the government in COPAZ and, along with General Ponce, in its successor, FUNDAPAZ.

Aside from the factual disagreements, the government and others disputed these recommendations as a matter of principle. For some, the commission had exceeded its mandate and violated constitutional guarantees by seeking to impose administrative sanctions without due process of law. Government representatives argued that the Ad Hoc Commission had the exclusive responsibility to determine which members of the armed forces were to be dismissed. According to this view, the Truth Commission had no authority to revisit this point.[46] Moreover, the government and others noted that it was unfair that some individuals had been named, while others who were equally culpable escaped mention.[47] President Cristiani maintained that the commission had usurped exclusive functions of the courts by judging, imposing sanctions, classifying criminal acts, evaluating evidence, and establishing degrees of participation. By so doing, the commission, according to the president, infringed on the institutional order.[48]

44. Annex to Further Report of the Secretary-General on the UN Observer Mission in El Salvador, UN Doc. S/26581, Oct. 14, 1993. This document reviews implementation of the Truth Commission's recommendations.

45. Resolution of the Supreme Court of Justice (El Salvador), March 22, 1993, signed by all fourteen members of the Supreme Court.

46. Among the Truth Commission's specific tasks was the following: "The Parties recognize the need to clarify and put an end to any indication of impunity *on the part of officers of the armed forces, particularly in cases where respect for human rights is jeopardized.* To that end, the Parties refer this issue to the Commission on the Truth for consideration and resolution" (Article 5 of the Chapúltepec Agreement). The Ad Hoc Commission's work was to be without prejudice to the Truth Commission's undertaking.

47. Truth Commission staff member Carlos Chipoco countered that the commission only named those individuals about whom it had sufficient confirmation of their participation; failing to name them because not everyone could be named would have thwarted the accord's intention. See Gary Bland, *El Salvador: Sustaining Peace, Nourishing Democracy* (Washington, D.C.: Woodrow Wilson Center Latin American Program, 1993), 44–45.

48. Letter from President Cristiani to UN Secretary-General, March 30, 1993, *The United Nations and El Salvador 1990–1995*, Doc. 68, p. 415.

The decree establishing the Haitian truth commission specifically authorized it to recommend that those identified as responsible for serious violations be removed from public service and/or that they be barred from future public service, "all in conformity with law and the principles of justice and without prejudice to the obligations and attributes of Haitian courts in these matters."

In El Salvador the proposal that those named be banned from public office for ten years met with a particularly cool reception, as it arguably violated the Salvadoran constitution. A UN analysis found that this recommendation could not be implemented because it conflicted with the provisions of the constitution and international human rights instruments that do not allow citizens to be deprived of their political rights in the manner recommended.[49] One proposed solution was that all those named simply refrain from seeking office or holding public posts for the ten-year period. The FMLN as well as the government had difficulty with this recommendation, since its implementation would have disqualified six top ERP leaders from holding political posts for ten years. Aside from the legal arguments against this provision, many voiced concern that it would run counter to the peace accords' effort to allow all parties to the conflict full participation in the country's political life. Ana Guadalupe Martínez, a former ERP commander named by the Truth Commission as one of those responsible for an ERP policy of killing mayors, was elected to the Legislative Assembly in March 1994, where she was selected as a vice president.[50]

In international fora, commentators often state that all those named in the Salvadoran Truth Commission report have been excluded from public office. This is simply not the case. In 1997 several of those named were elected to the Legislative Assembly either as deputies or alternates, including Colonel José Antonio Almendariz Rivas and Dr. Mauricio Gutiérrez Castro. For the 1999 presidential elections, the Christian Democratic Party nominated attorney Rodolfo Parker, who had been named by the commission for his purported role in altering suspects' statements in the Jesuit murder investigation.

49. Further Report of the Secretary-General, par. 5.

50. The Truth Commission's inclusion of Martínez in this context came as a surprise, because she had been out of the country and serving as a diplomatic representative during the period in question. The other five ERP leaders named did not run for public office in 1994. Three of the five top FMLN commanders (the leaders of the five component organizations) did not run for office in 1994; the other two were elected to the Legislative Assembly. All continued to play active roles in the country's political life.

The judiciary, apparently orchestrated by Supreme Court president Gutiérrez Castro, resoundingly rejected the suggestion that the Supreme Court step down to permit the election of its replacement under the new constitutional formula. Viewing himself as unfairly attacked, Supreme Court President Gutiérrez Castro vociferously rejected the commission's report and said in no uncertain terms that he would not step down before the end of his term.[51] The report had singled out Gutiérrez Castro for unprofessional conduct and for his "inappropriate and negative" interference in the investigation of the 1981 El Mozote massacre. The president, as he repeatedly pointed out, had no power to remove the Supreme Court. Nor was the ARENA-dominated legislature likely to undertake impeachment proceedings. The commission's suggestion must be viewed more as a moral condemnation of the conduct of the Supreme Court than as a recommendation likely to be followed.

Replacing the Supreme Court had been an issue of contention during the negotiations. Government negotiators saw it as a proposal that had been rejected at the negotiating table and therefore inappropriate for a Truth Commission recommendation. Yet the peace accords placed no restrictions on the recommendations the Truth Commission could make. Cristiani insisted, however, that the constitutional reforms negotiated in April 1991 constituted "the basic agreement of the peace negotiations" and established that all political agreements subsequently adopted would be in harmony with the constitutional reforms.[52] The recommendation to replace the Supreme Court was based on the Truth Commission's findings of improper conduct and the utter failure of the judiciary—headed by the president of the Supreme Court—to confront the problem of impunity. Although the commission's investigation provided an objective basis for the recommendation, this unenforceable recommendation became a kind of lightning rod for those who argued that the commission had violated national sovereignty and exceeded its mandate.

Despite the vehement rejection of the Truth Commission's recommendation regarding the Supreme Court, this recommendation was perceived as having had a powerful effect. The commission's findings validated widespread criticism of the Supreme Court and especially of its president, amidst charges of corruption, favoritism, and failure to protect human rights. The effects of the commission's recommendation became evident a little more

---

51. *From Madness to Hope*, 125.
52. Letter from President Cristiani to UN Secretary-General, March 30, 1993.

than a year later, when the Supreme Court's term ended. Despite having orchestrated a substantial campaign on his own behalf, Supreme Court president Gutiérrez Castro failed to marshal much support; neither he nor any members of his court were seriously proposed for reelection by the legislature. Throughout the difficult process of selecting a new Supreme Court by consensus, discussion centered on the need to clean out and transform the judiciary so that it could play a leading role in overcoming, rather than maintaining, impunity.[53]

Among the recommendations arising from the results of its investigation, the Truth Commission also included the need to reform the Career Judicial Service Act to incorporate a provision for a rigorous evaluation of judges by the National Judiciary Council so that those who lacked the requisite aptitude, efficiency, and concern for human rights and failed to demonstrate necessary independence, judicial discretion, honesty, and impartiality would be removed from the judiciary.[54] The commission's decision to devote more than half of this section to issues related to the judiciary reflected the gravity of the problem.

Recommendations Aimed at Eradication of Structural Causes Linked Directly to the Acts Examined

Truth Commission recommendations designed to eradicate the structural causes of the acts it had examined were clearly meant to complement other peace accord commitments. The commission included some recommendations related to reforms in the armed forces to ensure its subordination to civilian authority, "democratic control over promotions to senior ranks and positions of command, rigorous budgetary management, greater decentralization of the military structure, application of the new doctrine and new educational system of the armed forces, and steady professionalization of officers." The report called for reforms in military legislation, including a specific limitation of the concept of "due obedience" to make clear that it does not exonerate a person who carries out an order that is clearly illegal. Other recommendations addressed military training and the need to eradicate any vestigial relationship between members or retired members of the

53. For a discussion of the politics of electing the new Supreme Court, see Margaret Popkin et al., *Justice Delayed: The Slow Pace of Judicial Reform in El Salvador* (Washington, D.C., and Cambridge, Mass.: Washington Office on Latin America and Hemisphere Initiatives, 1994), 3–5.

54. *From Madness to Hope,* 177.

armed forces and paramilitary organizations. The commission urged that the guidelines for the new civilian police be scrupulously followed and that, as a measure to prevent the resurgence of death squads, a further investigation be undertaken of "illegal armed groups" with the assistance of foreign police. It proposed a domestic commission to follow up on the question of death squads, a recommendation that was belatedly implemented but was limited to the period after the peace accords (a period outside the scope of the Truth Commission's mandate).[55]

Recommended Institutional Reforms to Prevent the Repetition of Such Acts

The Truth Commission proposed additional reforms in the administration of justice to prevent the repetition of the kinds of violent acts it had examined. It recommended various measures to reinforce the right to due process, including the invalidation of the extrajudicial confession, and to enforce maximum time limits for administrative and preventive detention. Other recommendations again reinforced or complemented peace accords commitments. The commission called for giving the "utmost priority" to the "proper functioning of the Judicial Training School" and noted that this is an area "susceptible to constructive, tangible international cooperation."[56] It also called for strengthening the new office of the National Counsel for the Defense of Human Rights and making the remedies of habeas corpus and amparo accessible to the population.

The commission recommended changes to the system of administrative detention to clarify which officials are authorized to carry out detentions and for what causes, to limit the duration of administrative detention, and to end the practice of police imposing penalties involving deprivation of liberty for "police misdemeanors." The commission's focus on police misdemeanors clearly came from ONUSAL's findings rather than from its own investigations. ONUSAL had found rampant abuses under the existing system and had termed the constant arbitrary detentions for police misdemeanors the "central problem involving violations of the right to liberty."[57]

55. This recommendation and its eventual implementation are discussed in the section on criminal investigation, *infra* at 186–89.

56. *From Madness to Hope*, 182.

57. Report of the Director of the Human Rights Division of ONUSAL up to January 31, 1993, UN Doc. A/47/912, S/25521, April 5, 1993 (ONUSAL, Sixth Human Rights Report) at par. 124. Those detained were generally poor and were held for such crimes as vagrancy, public

Recommendations called for legislative reforms to enhance human rights protections, as well as the ratification of a number of international instruments and recognition of the compulsory jurisdiction of the Inter-American Court on Human Rights.[58] El Salvador was the only Central American nation not to have accepted the Court's compulsory jurisdiction.

Some recommendations called for constitutional reforms rejected by the government during the peace negotiations. These included constitutional reforms designed to transfer responsibility for judicial administration to the Judiciary Council and end the Supreme Court's control over the legal profession, to make habeas corpus and amparo more accessible to the population, and to strengthen the independence of the Judiciary Council. The government considered these proposals foreclosed by the April 1991 agreement on constitutional reforms.

Beyond reiterating the importance of establishing the National Civilian Police in accordance with the peace agreements, the commission called for making every effort to ensure prompt implementation of the new criminal investigation mechanism involving the combined action of the Attorney General's office and the civilian police. It also recommended the dissolution of the Commission for the Investigation of Criminal Acts (the SIU), based on the Truth Commission's finding that this entity had helped to cover up serious human rights violations through its omissions.[59]

---

drunkenness, "known thief," and prostitution. ONUSAL found these detentions arbitrary because they violated the principle of legality as persons continue to be detained for conduct not specified in the law, minimal procedural safeguards are not observed (there are no legal proceedings prior to imposition of punishment), and those carrying out detentions have no legal authority to do so. See Report of the Director of the Human Rights Division of ONUSAL covering the period from 1 November 1993 to 28 February 1994, UN Doc. A/49/116, S/1994/385, April 5, 1994 (ONUSAL Tenth Human Rights Report) at pars. 59–71. Under existing practice, police automatically imposed sanctions without presentation of any evidence, a hearing, any right to present a defense, or a formal record of the decision. No appeal was allowed, and habeas corpus procedures were ineffective. An ONUSAL effort to work with police failed to change existing practices significantly, and an 1886 Police Law used to justify these practices had yet to be repealed, despite ONUSAL's repeated recommendations to this effect. ONUSAL insisted that misdemeanors should be handled through the judicial system rather than by the police.

58. The commission listed the Optional Protocol to the International Covenant on Civil and Political Rights; Optional Protocol to the American Convention on Human Rights; Conventions nos. 87 and 98 of the International Labor Organization; Convention on the Non-Applicability of Statutory Limitations to War Crimes and Crimes Against Humanity; United Nations Convention Against Torture and Other Cruel, Inhuman, or Degrading Treatment or Punishment; and the Inter-American Convention to Prevent and Punish Torture.

59. For further discussion of the Commission to Investigate Criminal Acts, see *infra* 180–86.

Recommended Steps Toward National Reconciliation

National reconciliation is a complex undertaking and a long-term process. Eight years after the war's end, there are more signs of societal than of individual reconciliation in El Salvador. Former battlefield enemies now deal with each other as political adversaries and work together in the new civilian police. After the March 1997 municipal and legislative elections, the majority of the population found itself living in municipalities governed by FMLN coalitions. Yet at the level of individuals, few perpetrators of heinous crimes have asked for pardon, and few survivors have had the opportunity to decide whether they are able to forgive those responsible for the fate of their loved ones, since the perpetrators have not been identified. Unlike Argentine army chief General Martín Balza, who in April 1995 offered a public apology to the country for the crimes committed by the army during the dirty war, the Salvadoran High Command has never recognized institutional responsibility for harm done during the war, nor have civilian leaders recognized state responsibility.

In neighboring Guatemala, President Alvaro Arzú issued an appeal for forgiveness two months before the truth commission issued its report. The Historical Clarification Commission report called on the president "to recognise, before the whole of Guatemalan society, before the victims, their relatives and their communities, those acts described in the report, ask pardon for them and assume responsibility for the human rights violations connected with the internal armed confrontation, particularly those committed by the Army and state security forces."[60]

The Guatemalan commission's recommendations likewise called on the former guerrillas to ask forgiveness for acts of violence their forces had committed that caused the Guatemalan population to suffer. Shortly after the HCC's report was released, the former guerrillas responded to that recommendation: "With great pain and humility, we ask pardon in the memory of the victims, their relatives and their communities that suffered irreparable damage, injustices or offenses because of any kind of excess, mistakes or irresponsible acts committed in the course of the armed conflict by any of our members."[61]

60. *Guatemala: Memory of Silence, Report of the Commission for Historical Clarification, Conclusions and Recommendations* (Guatemala City 1999), 49.

61. URNG, "De la Verdad Histórica a la Reconciliación," communiqué of March 12, 1999 (on file with the author).

The South African experience has demonstrated the extent to which victims have differing needs. Some victims want to know what happened to their relatives and who was responsible so that they can forgive them. Others, upon learning the facts and who was involved in torturing or murdering their loved ones, become far more determined to seek justice. Many of those who testified to the TRC said that doing so had reopened old wounds, leaving them in a worse psychological state than before.

The Salvadoran Truth Commission expressed its hope that knowledge of the truth and the immediate implementation of those recommendations directly related to its investigation would be an adequate starting point for national reconciliation and the reunification of Salvadoran society. The commission's words seemed to suggest that its findings and recommendations regarding those identified as responsible could in some sense satisfy demands for truth and justice. Yet these were among the recommendations most strongly rejected by the government.

The timing of the Truth Commission's work, though essential for the peace process, was premature for reconciliation for many in El Salvador, especially those who had suffered the brunt of wartime abuses. The Truth Commission began its work less than six months after the war's end. Many people were still going through the difficult transition from war to peace, not yet believing that peace would endure and struggling to find a new way of life or return to one they had left behind years ago. Many FMLN combatants remained in demobilization camps. Still suffering from the effects of years of war and trauma, and accustomed to suppressing grief, many relatives of victims did not choose to go to the Truth Commission. In some areas of the country, human rights activists engaged in preparatory work, encouraging victims to take their cases to the Truth Commission. In many areas, wartime leaders did not urge people to go to the commission. In any case, with a six-month mandate and limited human resources, the commission was able to determine the "truth" in only a fraction of the cases presented to it; it was hardly in a position to investigate a larger universe of cases. The commission did not propose any mechanism for addressing the thousands of cases it had not been able to take on.

The Truth Commission's hoped-for immediate implementation of the recommendations directly related to its investigation was not to be. The Salvadoran government not only rejected these recommendations but also appeared largely to reject the commission's findings. Nor were most victims given a basis for reconciliation: most of their cases were not resolved, their dignity was not restored, and the government failed to acknowledge state responsibility or provide any form of moral or material reparations.

The Truth Commission recommended that reparations be provided by the establishment of a special fund and that at least one percent of all international assistance sent to El Salvador be earmarked for this purpose. The commission further called for moral compensation through the construction of a national monument bearing the names of all the victims of the conflict, the recognition of the good name of the victims and of the serious crimes committed against them, and the institution of a national holiday in memory of the victims of the conflict that would also serve as a symbol of national reconciliation.

Rather than act on these recommendations, the government pushed through the amnesty law in the name of national reconciliation. Its scope and timing showed that it was intended to cover up the truth and preclude any kind of justice, including civil liability. More than six years after issuance of the report, no steps had been undertaken to provide either material or moral compensation to victims or their families.

The Salvadoran Truth Commission's recommendation that one percent of foreign assistance be set aside to compensate the relatives of victims has not been implemented. A draft bill prepared by the nongovernmental Human Rights Commission has languished in the Assembly since 1993.

Aside from the apparent reluctance of many international donors to earmark assistance for such a fund, no mechanism was established to determine who would be eligible or what kind of compensation would be appropriate. Given the number of victims and the lack of any mechanism to verify their claims, it would be difficult to establish a fair distribution system. An April 1995 work program to complete implementation of the peace accords included no agreement in this area.[62] The FMLN simply stated its belief that the victims of human rights violations should be compensated in accordance with the Truth Commission's recommendation and that a reasonable formula for doing so should be determined.[63]

In 1995 a fund was established to provide payments to the war-wounded and to certain relatives of fallen combatants. The land transfer program included in the peace accords could arguably be seen as a kind of compensation for those in areas most affected by the war. This program was targeted at those who participated in the war or those who had occupied land in guerrilla-controlled areas. Nonetheless, Norma de Dowe, who headed El Salvador's reconstruction effort, claimed that victims of the war are already

---

62. Programa de Trabajo para Finalizar la Ejecución de los Acuerdos de Paz, April 27, 1995.

63. Ibid., 10.

covered in the reinsertion program for excombatants.[64] These programs were intended to promote national reconciliation but were not specifically designed to compensate survivors of human rights violations. Most families of victims were not among the beneficiaries of these programs. No such programs were established in urban areas, also greatly affected by repression. Nor has any special official effort been made to dedicate resources to the communities that bore the brunt of army massacres or other particularly heinous crimes. A special focus on some of these communities might have helped to create and preserve a national memory of the victims and the horrible events that occurred at the same time that it would have served to revitalize these areas and to reintegrate individuals displaced during the war.

The failure to make any attempt in this direction reflects the state's failure to acknowledge what actually happened during the war and take responsibility for state-sponsored abuses. Again, the government seemed more willing to address issues related to the war per se (for example, the need to reintegrate former combatants) than to take any responsibility for the suffering of thousands of campesino families. An amnesty in the name of national reconciliation did nothing to alleviate the suffering of these families on a moral, emotional, or material basis.

In his five-year assessment of the Salvadoran peace process, the UN Secretary-General noted that the Truth Commission's recommendations aimed at national reconciliation "were largely ignored" and termed this a "disappointing failure to respond to the unique opportunity" to further "a climate of national reconciliation."[65] But the international community had not placed great emphasis on these recommendations. While many of the forward-looking reforms proposed for the justice system and other Salvadoran institutions either reinforced or complemented aspects of the peace accords and had some constituency, the reforms regarding national reconciliation seemed to have little political support. The government was decidedly uninterested, regarding the passage of a broad amnesty law as the embodiment of reconciliation and an end to discussion of the past. Opposition political parties, including the FMLN, seemed more interested in the recommendations for legal and institutional reform. As Teresa Whitfield has observed, the UN mission took its lead from Salvadoran society: "As none was forthcoming, little progress was made in building on the work of the Truth Commission."[66]

64. *La Voz*, monthly magazine of the El Salvador Human Rights Commission, 3, no. 19 (1995): 6.
65. July 1997 Secretary-General report, par. 26.
66. Teresa Whitfield, "Staying the Course in El Salvador," in *Honoring Human Rights:*

Even a commission set up to focus largely on accountability, as was the Salvadoran Truth Commission, could propose alternatives to allow family members a mechanism to discover the fate of their relatives. Some in El Salvador have objected that such a mechanism would have created unrealistic expectations and toyed further with the emotions of relatives. An ongoing effort to determine the fate of victims is something that has been undertaken after many wars, including World War II with its millions of civilian victims. The African National Congress established a "Missing Persons Committee" in 1991 to investigate and report to families as well as to provide counseling and assistance. The impossibility of determining the fate of a certain percentage of victims should not preclude the undertaking.

The efforts of Chile's Rettig Commission in this regard are instructive. A follow-up foundation was established to determine the fate of individual victims and the circumstances of their families and to award compensation to relatives. The Chilean commission reviewed the situation of each family, the impact of their relative's death or disappearance, and their current circumstances. The Rettig Commission's recommendations on reparation led to the passage of the 1992 Reparation Law, under which 4,000 relatives of victims identified in the report receive monthly benefits from the government, 821 receive education grants, and 63 were provided with homes.[67]

Responding to rulings by the Inter-American Court and the Inter-American Commission on Human Rights finding state responsibility for disappearances in the 1980s and calling for the payment of compensation, the Honduran government eventually agreed to make payments to relatives of the disappeared. In addition to the government's greater willingness to heed the findings and recommendations of the Inter-American human rights bodies, the smaller number of victims in Honduras made compensation payments more feasible.[68]

In Colombia, the "Trujillo" commission was charged with recommending the terms and means through which compensation and restitution should be provided to victims. The commission called for providing reparations to

---

From Peace to Justice—Recommendations to the International Community, ed. Alice H. Henkin (Washington, D.C.: Aspen Institute, 1998), 182.

67. Human Rights Watch/Americas, *Chile: Unsettled Business, Human Rights in Chile at the Start of the Frei Presidency* (New York: Human Rights Watch, 1994), 1.

68. Mike Kaye, "The Role of Truth Commissions in the Search for Justice, Reconciliation, and Democratisation: The Salvadorean and Honduran Cases," *Journal of Latin American Studies* 29 (1997), 707; Freddy Cuevas, "Honduras to Pay Kin of Kidnapped," Associated Press, February 23, 2000.

individuals injured as well as to relatives of those disappeared and murdered. The commission took the view that everybody in Trujillo and Colombia had been harmed by the killings there. To compensate the community of
Trujillo and Colombian society, the commission recommended that the
government design and develop a broad program of social investment in the
zone, make a public apology on behalf of the state, and publish the commission's report as well as a summary in the mass media. It also called on the
government to design and carry out a program of return or relocation of
those displaced, assure their integration with specific programs of work,
provide free educational opportunities for children of victims in state estab-
lishments, and provide necessary services to persons or families forcibly displaced. Unfortunately, four years later, the government had shown little
political will to implement the recommendations.

South Africa's Truth and Reconciliation Commission proposed various
forms of monetary and moral reparation. Victims in dire need were to be
provided with "urgent interim reparation" to provide them with access to
services and facilities. The TRC recommended that each victim of a gross
human rights violation receive a financial grant to be paid over a six-year
period. It also called for symbolic reparation measures to facilitate the communal process of remembering and commemorating the pain and victories
of the past, including a national day of remembrance, the construction of
memorials and monuments, and the development of museums. In addition,
the TRC called for legal and administrative measures to assist individuals in
obtaining death certificates and expunging criminal records. Other recommendations included community rehabilitation programs to promote heal-
ing and recovery of individuals and communities that have been affected by
human rights violations. In theory, the South African situation seems more
favorable for these measures, given that the ANC, which formerly represented
the majority of the victims, is the ruling party. Nonetheless, many of the decisions confronting the TRC, including its reparations policy, were the object
of bitter debate in South Africa. Within the human rights community, some
groups advocated a more individualized reparations policy that would assess
actual need, while others insisted that all victims should be treated equally.

Guatemala faces similar issues as it seeks ways to compensate victims of
state-sponsored repression. Unlike the Salvadoran government, the Guatemalan government committed itself to providing some form of reparations
to victims.[69] How much the government would actually provide and in what

69. National Reconciliation Law, article 9.

form remained to be determined. The commission recommended the establishment of a national reparations program that would include both individual and collective forms of reparation, economic compensation for the most serious injuries or losses, measures for psychosocial rehabilitation and reparations, and steps to restore individual dignity. The commission proposed that the program have a board of directors with representatives of the executive and legislative branches, the National Counsel for Human Rights, and nongovernmental organizations.[70] The commission further recommended that the government initiate an active policy of exhumations and undertake investigations into the fate of the disappeared and missing children, including those who were illegally adopted, or separated from their families.

Implementing a reparations policy was somewhat less challenging in the Southern Cone. The Chilean effort involved far fewer victims and a country with a far stronger economy. Although the lack of criminal convictions in Argentina precluded civil judgments, the Menem government began providing substantial reparations, first to seventy former detainees in response to a case before the Inter-American Commission on Human Rights, and then, following an act of congress, to eight thousand former detainees held during the dictatorship. These reparations were later extended to families of the disappeared, who were not required to rely on the presumption of death after seven years of absence. These numbers, while larger than Chile's, still do not compare with the potential beneficiary population in El Salvador.

As UN Secretary-General Kofi Annan observed in his five-year assessment of the peace process: "Reconciliation will rest on shaky foundations if the specific needs of the population that suffered the impact of the war most directly are not addressed. The measures contemplated for material and moral compensation for victims of violations of human rights . . . are an area of the pending accords that casts a particularly long shadow over the recognized successes of the process as a whole."[71]

The measures proposed and undertaken in other countries provide a range of potential models that could be adapted to the specific Salvadoran situation with its large number of victims and serious economic constraints. If El Salvador were to give priority to such an effort, surely some forms of reparations, both material and moral, could be devised. In early 1998 the first stone of a memorial to the civilian victims of human rights violations during the war was dedicated in a San Salvador park. This was the fruit of a

70. *Guatemala: Memory of Silence*, 50.
71. Report of the Secretary-General, July 1, 1997 at par. 63.

nongovernmental coalition's efforts and the agreement of San Salvador's mayor to allow its construction in a city park. At that time, the NGOs behind the effort had no funds with which to erect the memorial. On December 10, 1998, "Human Rights Day," San Salvador Mayor Héctor Silva joined with the NGOs united in the effort to preserve historic memory and announced that construction of the monument would soon begin. (Silva was elected mayor in 1997 as the candidate of a coalition between the FMLN and several smaller parties.) As it stands, honoring the memory of the victims remains a strictly nongovernmental or local effort—a reminder of the continuing polarization of Salvadoran society, rather than its reconciliation.

The Commission's Report, the Role of the Courts, and the Amnesty Law

The peace agreements, in more than one place, insisted that the Truth Commission's work in uncovering the truth was to be "without prejudice to the obligations incumbent on the Salvadoran courts to solve such cases and impose the appropriate penalties on the culprits." Yet instead of encouraging prosecutions, the Salvadoran legislature followed President Cristiani's lead and enacted a sweeping amnesty law days after publication of the Truth Commission report.

The Truth Commission itself did not recommend prosecution of those identified in its report, nor did it turn over information to the judiciary or the attorney general. The commission noted that

> El Salvador has no system for the administration of justice which meets the minimum requirements of objectivity and impartiality so that justice can be rendered reliably. This is a part of the country's current reality and overcoming it urgently should be a primary objective for Salvadorian society.
>
> The Commission does not believe that a reliable solution can be found to the problems it has examined by tackling them in the context which is primarily responsible for them.[72]

72. *From Madness to Hope*, 178.

For the commission, attempts at prosecution "in the current context, far from satisfying a legitimate desire for justice, could revive old frustrations, thereby impeding the achievement of that cardinal objective, reconciliation."[73] The Salvadoran Truth Commission in effect saw itself as a one-shot deal, with no hope of prosecutions. From this perspective, it did little to encourage existing Salvadoran institutions to undertake investigations of those named.

Even with the best of intentions, it would have been impossible to punish more than a sampling of those responsible for past human rights violations. The sheer numbers involved, the lack of documentation and witnesses willing to come forward, and the sorry state of the judiciary all ensured that few prosecutions would have been possible.

Had political will existed, the Salvadoran justice system would still have been hard-pressed to duplicate the Truth Commission's work. Because of its reliance on confidential sources and its real and supposed access to classified documents,[74] the commission's relative success depended on attributes not enjoyed by Salvadoran institutions. The commission itself was acutely aware that many of the witnesses who provided information to it would not have trusted Salvadoran authorities or risked testifying in public. In large part, this distrust reflected the reality that the structures of power had not been altered by the peace accords. As Professor Buergenthal put it:

> It is important to recall that the very governmental institutions and the individuals responsible for many of the most egregious acts of violence in El Salvador remained in place and in power, which explains the fear of the vast majority of individuals who appeared before the Commission. The situation would have been quite different had a transition government assumed power after the signing of the peace accords, or if a change had occurred in the leadership of the military and security forces as well as in the judiciary. But none of

73. Ibid., 178–79.
74. According to Professor Buergenthal, all parties assumed that the commission was privy to a great deal more information than it actually had received. This belief led many to come forward (Buergenthal, "The UN Truth Commission," 518, n. 285. The United States reinforced the notion that classified information is rarely accessible by granting a security clearance only to Professor Buergenthal. In the Jesuit murder case, the U.S. government was slow to provide relevant documents, which only came to light because of the work of the congressional "Moakley" task force. See Martha Doggett, *Death Foretold: The Jesuit Murders in El Salvador* (Washington, D.C.: Georgetown University Press, 1993), 226–32.

that happened in El Salvador while the Commission was exercising its functions. That explains, of course, why the Commission was appointed in the first place, and why it had to proceed as it did in order to discharge its responsibilities.[75]

Under these circumstances, the military witnesses who provided information that allowed the commission to establish that the upper echelons of the Salvadoran armed forces planned, ordered, and covered up the Jesuit murders were not willing to testify in court.

In general, the Truth Commission was unable to establish a usable model to demonstrate that through adequate investigation it is possible to determine responsibility for human rights violations. Still, in the commission's investigation of the El Mozote massacre, the use of forensic evidence combined with witness testimonies established authoritatively that the armed forces had been responsible for the murder of hundreds of civilians.[76] These findings and others included in the commission's report constitute a major advance in establishing the truth about who was responsible for particularly egregious crimes and practices. This effort contributed to promoting the use of forensic science in El Salvador, despite the attempts at interference by officials such as former Supreme Court president Gutiérrez Castro and forensics institute director Juan Mateu Llort.[77] Unfortunately, Salvadoran NGOs were unable to take advantage of the presence of the Argentine Forensic Anthropology Team to develop a Salvadoran NGO team. This contrasts with the experience in neighboring Guatemala, where several Guatemalan forensic teams, initially trained by the Argentine team, now operate.

Throughout the war years in El Salvador, few human rights cases were pursued by the courts. In many cases the dead were not even examined, and the cause of death was never officially determined. This is strikingly different from Argentina and Chile, where complaints were routinely filed even under military rule, and cases clogged the courts once democracy was restored.[78]

75. Buergenthal, "The UN Truth Commission," 512.

76. In an unprecedented effort in El Salvador, the renowned Argentine team of forensic anthropologists worked with Salvadorans to unearth skeletal remains buried in a burned convent. The remains of at least 143 people were found, most of them minors. U.S. forensic experts participated in examining the remains, determining the cause of death, and analyzing ballistic evidence. See *From Madness to Hope*, "El Mozote: Reports of the Forensic Investigation," Annex, Volume 1, 117–20.

77. Ibid., 120.

78. The Rettig Commission transmitted new evidence to the courts in about 220 cases. Before the Rettig Commission's report was released, President Aylwin wrote to the Supreme

In South Africa, the reality that a large percentage of amnesty applicants were imprisoned or facing prosecution reflected a far more functional justice system, although not one that could be relied on to provide justice to all.

Political considerations aside, any call for prosecutions in El Salvador would have encountered the reality that the judiciary was wholly unequipped to handle human rights investigations and trials. In this aspect, countries such as El Salvador, Guatemala, and Haiti must be distinguished from countries with stronger legal systems, such as Chile and Argentina. In a country that lacks a sufficiently independent and credible judiciary, either a way must be found to bolster the court system so that it can carry out at least some credible and exemplary prosecutions, or some alternative method of transitional justice must be developed.[79]

In Chile, a broad 1978 "self-amnesty" law complicated attempts at prosecution. With no definitive interpretation of the 1978 amnesty law, Chilean courts have taken inconsistent positions on their ability to pursue prosecutions or simply investigate the fate of the disappeared. In some cases, judges ended investigations after establishing that a crime was committed and that the perpetrators were members of the military acting on higher orders. In others, they continued the investigation until the perpetrators were individually identified. The Chilean situation was further complicated by continuing military court jurisdiction over crimes committed by members of the

---

Court president urging that he instruct the courts to reopen the investigations. When he presented the report on television, Aylwin said, "I hope they [the courts] duly exercise their function and carry out an exhaustive investigation, to which in my view, the amnesty law in force is no obstacle" (Americas Watch, *Unsettled Business*, 8 n. 17).

In Argentina the 1986 *punto final* law was designed to limit prosecutions through extraordinary procedural standards. Human rights groups and the courts worked overtime to carry out the required steps so that—to the Government's surprise—hundreds of officers still faced charges after the time period established in the law. The Due Obedience law, enacted on June 5, 1987, ended most of these prosecutions by instructing courts that "due obedience" should be treated as a presumption of innocence in that defendants were acting in error about the legitimacy of orders they had received (Americas Watch, *Truth and Partial Justice*, 47–52).

79. For a discussion of developments and trends in this area, see Diane F. Orentlicher, "Addressing Gross Human Rights Abuses," in *Human Rights: An Agenda for the Next Century*, ed. Henkin and Hargove (Washington, D.C.: American Society of International Law, 1994). Under Orentlicher's analysis, international law prohibits wholesale impunity for atrocious crimes committed on a massive scale but leaves prosecutors a broad realm of discretion in determining the scope of action to be undertaken (p. 440). Even a limited program of exemplary punishment should be able to serve the desired deterrent function. See Diane F. Orentlicher, "The Role of the Prosecutor in the Transition to Democracy in Latin America," in *Transition to Democracy in Latin America*, ed. Stotzky (Boulder: Westview Press, 1993), 249–68.

armed forces. Until 1998, the Supreme Court consistently maintained that the 1978 amnesty barred further investigation once military involvement was established. The Supreme Court had overturned a 1994 appeals court ruling that held that international law, in particular the Geneva Conventions, has primacy over domestic law and bars the application of amnesty to crimes considered grave breaches of those conventions.[80] In September 1998, however, a Supreme Court ruling ordered the reopening of a disappearance case based on a Geneva Conventions argument.[81] (The composition of the court had changed between the two holdings.) Since the October 1998 arrest of General Pinochet in London, Chilean courts have undertaken efforts to prosecute other military officers responsible for human rights crimes committed during the dictatorship. By September 1999, twenty-five officers had been arrested on charges of murder, torture, and kidnapping.[82]

Given the ambiguous state of the law, the resistance of the military, and the passivity of the judiciary, little progress had been made in establishing responsibility for individual cases. President Aylwin and the Rettig Commission gave priority to the establishment of the truth and other forms of justice, such as reestablishing the victims' good name and various forms of compensation to the relatives of victims. Criminal responsibility was to be determined "to the extent possible" (*en la medida de lo posible*).[83] In a few exceptional cases, Chilean courts did carry out investigations and convict perpetrators. The former head of military intelligence is serving a prison term for his role in the 1976 Washington, D.C., murder of former foreign minister Orlando Letelier and his assistant, Ronni Moffitt.[84] The parameters for criminal investigation had not been further limited by a post-1978 amnesty, but they had also not been expanded by a frontal attack on or a limitation of the earlier amnesty law. Thus, the vast majority of human rights violations committed under the military dictatorship had neither been adequately punished nor expressly pardoned.

Despite the various initiatives undertaken by the successor democratic government in Chile, the Inter-American Commission on Human Rights

80. Uribe Tambley, Corte Suprema de Chile (October 26, 1995).

81. The case involved the July 1974 detention and disappearance of Pedro Poblete, member of the Frente Obrero Revolucionario.

82. Clifford Krauss, "Chilean Military Faces Reckoning for Its Dark Past," *New York Times*, October 2, 1999; Francesc Relea, "La detención del ex dictador ha provocado cambios en la política y la justicia Chilena," *El País*, September 27, 1999.

83. See Comisión Andina, *Chile: Sistema Judicial y Derechos Humanos* (May 1995), 33.

84. See Jorge Correa Sutil, "Justice in Chile," in *Transitional Justice and the Rule of Law*, ed. James McAdams (Notre Dame: University of Notre Dame Press, 1997), 143–44.

found that Chile has not lived up to its obligations under the American Convention on Human Rights. The commission found that "the Government's recognition of responsibility, its partial investigation of the facts, and its subsequent payment of compensation" were insufficient, unless the right to justice was also satisfied, to meet the state's obligations under the convention.[85]

If trials are not feasible immediately after a democratic transition or the end of an armed conflict, potential alternatives include waiting until the justice system is sufficiently strengthened to take on such a challenge and the political will exists to do so. Postponing the possibility of trials undermines the notion that identifying and punishing at least some of those responsible for the worst crimes is a necessary step in the process of societal reconciliation.[86] While trials of Nazi war criminals continue to this day, the delay in bringing perpetrators to justice makes it unlikely that such trials will serve to help consolidate democracy, heal victims so that they can contribute to this effort, and establish the rule of law during the transition from an authoritarian regime. Still, recent events in Chile and Argentina suggest that demands for justice do not dissipate in a matter of years, and they may actually intensify. In response to the British Law Lords' initial November 1998 ruling that General Pinochet did not enjoy immunity from charges that he was responsible for serious crimes, including torture, Chilean government officials argued that their country was now serious about putting the general on trial if only he were allowed to return to Chile. At the time, the record of the Chilean courts and the legal obstacles facing any attempt to try Pinochet in Chile undermined these arguments.[87] Nonetheless, Pinochet's arrest spurred Chilean courts to pursue cases against military officers, including the general himself. And for the first time, moderate military officers

85. Inter-American Commission on Human Rights, Annual Report 1996, Report No. 36/96 (Chile), case 10843.

86. Jaime Malamud-Goti has suggested that punishment of past rights violators, rather than serving as a deterrent to potential wrongdoers or as simple retribution, is essential to make former victims capable of assuming their rights and responsibilities in a democracy. Under this "victim-centered theory of punishment," punishment of state criminals is necessary to overcome the victim's loss of purpose and sense of worth. Unless the victims regain these attributes, they are unlikely to be able to contribute to consolidating democratic values ("Human Rights Abuses in Fledgling Democracies: The Role of Discretion," in *Transition to Democracy in Latin America*, ed. Stotzky [Boulder: Westview Press, 1993], 225–48). In a subsequent book, Malamud-Goti concludes that the Argentine trials did not actually contribute to the consolidation of democracy in part because they focused responsibility for repression too narrowly (*Game Without End: State Terror and the Politics of Justice* [Norman: University of Oklahoma Press, 1996]).

87. See Human Rights Watch, "Pinochet in Chile: Guaranteed Impunity."

have been willing to acknowledge that human rights abuses did occur. Army commander General Ricardo Izurieta and other military leaders have entered into negotiations with human rights lawyers designed to lead to establishing what happened to the disappeared and who was responsible. The military hoped to obtain a new amnesty agreement in exchange for providing this information.[88]

If early passage of an amnesty decree can be avoided, a prudential waiting period has some advantages. In El Salvador, as the Truth Commission found, witnesses remained highly fearful of offering their testimony, thus posing a major obstacle to prosecutions. With sufficiently changed conditions in the country, including a credible judiciary, prosecutions might become feasible at some future time. To do so would require applying the Salvadoran constitution and international law to set aside, or limit the scope of, the amnesty law and overcoming a ten-year statute of limitations for homicides. Advances in the interpretation of international law, reflected in rulings from the International Criminal Tribunals for the former Yugoslavia and Rwanda, the International Criminal Court treaty signed in 1998, and developments following the 1998 arrest of General Pinochet, make this an increasingly real possibility.

Recent decisions and interpretations of international law have placed increasing emphasis on the obligation of governments, including successor regimes, to prosecute those responsible for genocide, torture, war crimes, and crimes against humanity. As a result of the arrest of Pinochet in London and the Law Lords' decision that he is not immune from prosecution, courts in other countries are more likely to exercise universal jurisdiction to hold accountable perpetrators who have been protected from prosecution in their own countries. Even before the Pinochet decision, a French court had found that the Salvadoran amnesty did not bar it from issuing arrest orders in a case examined by the Truth Commission that involved the murder of a French nurse by Salvadoran air force troops.[89] The fallout in Chile from Pinochet's arrest in London suggests that national courts may be more inclined to undertake prosecutions of military officers suspected of human rights violations if they understand that they may otherwise be prosecuted outside the country.

88. Krauss, "Chilean Military Faces Reckoning."
89. The French court's action was reported in the Salvadoran weekly *Primera Plana*, May 5, 1995, p. 7. In the wake of the Spanish effort to extradite General Pinochet from Great Britain, the French court sent letters rogatory to El Salvador, asking for the Salvadoran government's assistance in obtaining evidence to determine responsibilities in the case ("Juez francés quiere investigar asesinato ocurrido en El Salvador en 1989," *Co-Latino*, March 26, 1999).

An emerging international law precept recognizes that survivors and society as a whole have the right to know the truth. Even if sanctions remain barred, an amnesty law can be understood to permit investigations with the goal of determining the facts and identifying those responsible, but with the understanding that punishment cannot be imposed. This argument was accepted by the Federal Chamber in Buenos Aires in response to renewed efforts to establish the fate of the disappeared in 1995. In 1998 former junta leader General Jorge Rafael Videla was placed under house arrest in Buenos Aires during a judicial investigation of his and other commanding officers' roles in creating new identities for babies born to women held in clandestine detention centers. The Argentine court found that this crime was not included in the exculpatory laws enacted to end the military prosecutions. In March 1998, the legislature took the symbolic step of derogating but not annuling the exculpatory laws.

In 1999, for the first time, the Argentine Supreme Court confirmed a court ruling awarding a substantial sum to Daniel Tarnopolsky, whose family had been kidnapped and disappeared in 1976. The court rejected the state's argument that the statute of limitations barred the action, noting that forced disappearance is a continuing crime until the fate or whereabouts of the disappeared is established.[90] A recent Supreme Court decision in Chile has recognized that forced disappearance is a continuing crime until the victim's fate or whereabouts is known and therefore may not be subject to a statute of limitations or an amnesty decree that covers crimes that occurred before a cutoff date.

Demands for justice may be greatest at the moment of transition, but they clearly have a far better possibility of concretion if there is a change of regime. Often these coincide. In the case of a negotiated settlement to an armed conflict, however, a situation such as that found in El Salvador can occur.

Even when a new democratically elected government takes over, real and self-imposed constraints are likely to limit the possibility of prosecutions.[91] This dilemma confronted the Aristide and Preval governments in Haiti. In exile, President Aristide had made achieving justice for past human rights abuses a key goal. Aristide explained that bringing human rights violators to justice under a fair system would further the democratic process by demonstrating that a democratically elected government could redress past wrongs.

90. Francesc Relea, "Massera tendrá que indemnizar a las víctimas de la dictadura Argentina," *El País,* September 3, 1999.
91. See, e.g., David Pion-Berlin, "To Prosecute or to Pardon? Human Rights Decisions in the Latin American Southern Cone," *Human Rights Quarterly* 16 (1994).

Although an amnesty law was decreed as part of the transition agreement, it has not been applied to human rights violations. Nonetheless, initial attempts to prosecute human rights violators met with a variety of setbacks, including a lack of U.S. government cooperation.[92]

El Salvador combined the disadvantages of a peace process that did not involve a change in government with a compromised judiciary. The conclusion of a civil conflict in which neither side emerged victorious appears to have further decreased the likelihood of prosecutions. Neither the political will nor the institutional framework was adequate to the task.

The explicit references in the Salvadoran peace accords to maintaining the role of the courts and the need for "exemplary prosecutions" were simply ignored: no role was assigned to the courts. The government's rapid passage of an unusually broad amnesty decree sought to completely preempt judicial action.

While declining to recommend prosecutions in the existing context, the Truth Commission did not recommend amnesty either. In its recommendations regarding national reconciliation, however, the commission noted:

> [S]ince it is not possible to guarantee a proper trial for all those responsible for the crimes described here, it is unfair to keep some of them in prison while others who planned the crimes or also took part in them remain at liberty. It is not within the Commission's power to address this situation, which can only be resolved through a pardon *after justice has been served.*[93] (Emphasis added)

Salvadoran legislators, lawyers, and judges had expected the Truth Commission to take a position on cases that should be prosecuted or amnestied, as suggested by the wording of the 1992 amnesty law, which specifically

---

92. Likening the situation of the Haitian people to that of Holocaust survivors, Aristide wrote in 1993: "The need for a judicial system that will bring [those responsible for massive human rights violations] to justice is the major concern, the major desire, and the major issue for most Haitians" ("The Role of the Judiciary in the Transition to Democracy," in *Transition to Democracy*, ed. Stotzky, 36). See Reed Brody, "International Aspects of Current Efforts at Judicial Reform: Undermining Justice in Haiti," in Méndez et al., eds., *The (Un)Rule of Law and the Underprivileged in Latin America* (Notre Dame: University of Notre Dame Press, 1999).

93. *From Madness to Hope*, 185. Because convictions were so rare, the only cases examined by the Truth Commission in which defendants had been sentenced and remained in prison were the Jesuit murders, the killing of four U.S. churchwomen, the killing of human rights activist Herbert Anaya, and the "Zona Rosa" killings of four U.S. marines and nine others.

excepted cases to be included in the Truth Commission's report from its terms. By discarding the possibility of prosecutions, and with the rejection of its recommendations about the individuals it had named, the commission's recommendations left few alternatives for establishing accountability. Had it chosen to do so, the commission might have pointed out that certain crimes are not subject to amnesty under international law. It might have distinguished civil responsibility from criminal responsibility or judicial investigations designed to determine the facts of a case from the imposition of punishment. Or it might have suggested the formula proposed in South Africa, which would permit granting amnesty only to those whose offenses were related and proportional to political objectives and who fully admitted their responsibility and told what they knew. Or, as the Guatemalan commission later did, it might have called for prosecutions of those crimes not eligible for amnesty under international law.

The Truth Commission indicated that whether to grant amnesty was a decision for the Salvadoran people. This is an arguable point, particularly in light of recent developments in international law. While the decision to grant an amnesty may be a political one, the scope of an amnesty is subject to legal restriction. Aryeh Neier, former executive director of Human Rights Watch, has insisted that this should in no sense be a political decision.[94] The majority may opt for an amnesty when a minority group has been the focus of repression. This was not the case in El Salvador, where human rights violations were so widespread that few people were not connected to a victim. There is a sense in El Salvador, however, that politicians have largely abandoned the victims. Those most ready to "put the past behind us" tend to be those most desirous of participating in the political process—or those who might be objects of prosecution. In this respect, the FMLN—a political entity eager to take part in the country's political process and with its own concerns about potential prosecutions—is not an adequate representative of the victims and their relatives. Representatives of civil society, including Salvadoran human rights groups, lacked sufficient clout to keep these issues on the political agenda.

94. At the Aspen Institute's 1988 conference on State Crimes and Punishment, Neier maintained that "punishment is the absolute duty of society to honor and redeem the suffering of the individual victim. . . . As a matter of law we simply have to say we are not going to grant clemency to the most grotesque criminals" (Lawrence Weschler, *A Miracle, A Universe: Settling Accounts with Torturers* [New York: Pantheon, 1990], 244–45). Neier also disagreed with the notion that a principal reason for seeking justice should be related to ensuring the future stability of a reconstituted democracy.

The Amnesty

Rather than implement the Truth Commission's recommendations regarding the individuals named, President Cristiani said that the report failed to meet the expectations of the Salvadoran people with respect to national reconciliation, "to forgive and forget this painful past," and called for a "general and absolute" amnesty. In a March 18, 1993, address to the nation, President Cristiani justified the call for a sweeping amnesty in the following terms:

> [O]ne also has to consider that the Report of the Truth Commission examines only a part of everything that happened in all those years of violence. And because the Report speaks of only certain cases and mentions only certain people, we have to think much more carefully about what course of action we should take. *What is most important now is to see what has to be done to erase, eliminate and forget everything in the past.* Our position is that it would be unjust to take legal or administrative measures against some but not others, simply because the latter did not figure in the cases examined in the Truth Commission's Report. In this sense, our position is not to blame specific individuals, but to consider all the facts and not act on only part of the problem; it is preferable to look for an overall solution that will embrace everyone.... Therefore, we are again calling upon all sectors in the country to support a general and absolute amnesty, so that we can turn that painful page in our history and seek a better future for our country.[95] (Emphasis added)

Applying this reasoning and over the objections of opposition forces, the governing ARENA party pushed through a sweeping amnesty law days after the Truth Commission report was released.[96] When the peace accords were signed in January 1992, all Salvadoran political parties had agreed that a

95. Quoted in IACHR El Salvador Report (1994), 69–70 (emphasis added).
96. Legislative Decree 486, March 20, 1993, published in D.O. 56, Tomo 318, March 22, 1993. The Salvadoran constitution, article 131, 260, authorizes the legislature to "grant amnesty for political crimes or common crimes related to them, or for common crimes committed by 20 people or more." Salvadoran law defines political crimes as "punishable acts against the international or internal personality of the State"; common crimes related to political crimes are "those that have a direct or immediate relation with the political crime or are a natural and common means of preparing, carrying out, or promoting it" (Salvadoran Penal Code [1973], article 151). Examples of common crimes connected to political crimes include the acquisition of weapons and munitions, the possession or transportation of weapons of war for the crime of rebellion.

general amnesty would be approved in the future. The 1993 amnesty followed an earlier law passed in the wake of the peace accords. Because of the immediate need to legalize the situation of FMLN leaders who were returning to the country and would be involved in implementing the peace accords, on January 23, 1992, the political parties rushed through a partial amnesty, the "National Reconciliation Law."[97] That law amounted to a delayed general amnesty. It excluded from its benefits: (1) persons convicted by juries (to prevent the release of the two officers convicted four months earlier for the killing of six Jesuit priests, their cook, and her daughter); and (2) those named in the Truth Commission report as being responsible for serious human rights violations, to allow the Truth Commission to carry out its work before the application of amnesty in all cases. (The National Reconciliation Law was passed on January 23, 1992; the Truth Commission report was not made public until March 15, 1993.)

According to the National Reconciliation Law, these exceptions could be overruled by the Legislative Assembly six months after the Truth Commission issued its report. Human rights groups expressed reservations about the law, which permitted amnesty for crimes that cannot be amnestied under international and Salvadoran law. Nonetheless, the exceptions to the 1992 law were explicitly overruled by the 1993 amnesty, and the six-month waiting period for legislative action was eliminated. Instead of calling for a national debate on the issue, the ARENA party used the Truth Commission report to insist on an immediate amnesty with a very broad scope.

Although the Truth Commission provided some measure of truth, the government—despite its oft-stated concern for the sanctity of the judicial process—barred any form of justice, based either on the Truth Commission report or court proceedings. In effect, the judiciary was given no opportunity to act on cases investigated by the Truth Commission or the thousands of others not addressed. The judiciary was thus excluded from the process of determining the truth and seeking justice.

The government's argument that the Truth Commission had invaded the jurisdiction of the judicial branch would have been more compelling had it not advocated an immediate blanket amnesty but instead encouraged the courts to proceed in meting out justice.

The General Amnesty Law for the Consolidation of Peace expressly provided for the extinction of civil as well as criminal responsibility.[98] For the

97. Legislative Decree 147, January 23, D.O. 14, Tomo 314, No. 14, January 23, 1992.
98. Legislative Decree 486, article 4. Amnesty laws do not usually sweep this broadly. In Argentina, for example, neither an amnesty law nor a pardon precludes the continuation or

purposes of this law, the definition of political crimes was broadened to cover "crimes against the public peace," "crimes against the activities of the courts," and "crimes committed on the occasion of or as a consequence of the armed conflict, without regard to political condition, militancy, affiliation or ideology."[99] Among the crimes classed as "political" and potentially covered are a series of "crimes against the activities of the courts,"[100] including perjury, false expert opinions and reports, false evidence, procedural fraud, bribery, cover-ups, punishable omissions, prevarication, and delays of justice.

The UN Secretary-General expressed concern and noted that it would have been preferable to have achieved a broad degree of national consensus before approving an amnesty law.[101] While maintaining that the amnesty did not violate any of the Truth Commission's recommendations, Professor Buergenthal found the haste with which it was rushed through the Salvadoran legislature, "with no time or opportunity for a full national debate on the subject ... unseemly at the very least, indicative of a lack of respect for democratic processes, and thus incompatible with the spirit of the peace accords."[102] According to Professor Buergenthal, the amnesty neither affected the commission's recommendations nor overrode those that called for the dismissal of individuals named in the report.

As the government pointed out, Salvadoran political parties had signed an agreement in early 1992 providing that a general amnesty would be enacted after publication of the Truth Commission report. Opposition political parties nonetheless disputed the timing, the scope, and the relationship of the amnesty to the Truth Commission's recommendations.

Salvadoran human rights groups unsuccessfully petitioned the Supreme Court to declare the amnesty unconstitutional.[103] Among the provisions

---

initiation of civil actions seeking monetary compensation from public officials for crimes committed in connection with their office (Salvadoran Criminal Code [1973], articles 61, 68). The claims of former political prisoners were initially dismissed as barred by the statute of limitations, but the claims were accepted after a petition filed with the Inter-American Commission on Human Rights resulted in a friendly settlement process (Alejandro M. Garro, "Nine Years of Transition to Democracy in Argentina," *Columbia Journal of Transnational Law* 31 [1993], 22–23, n. 63).

99. Legislative Decree 486, article 2.

100. Salvadoran Penal Code, articles 460–479.

101. United Nations, Report of the Secretary-General on the United Nations Observer Mission in El Salvador, UN Doc. S/25812/Add.1, May 24, 1993.

102. Buergenthal, "The UN Truth Commission," 538.

103. The nongovernmental Human Rights Commission of El Salvador filed a petition with the Supreme Court on April 21, 1993, while Socorro Jurídico Cristiano "Archbishop Oscar A. Romero" and the Human Rights Institute of the Central American University filed another

challenged was the enlargement of the concept of political crime beyond the categories specified in the constitution to include crimes against the activity of the courts and "those committed because or as a result of the armed conflict, without taking into consideration the condition, membership status, affiliation or political ideology" of those responsible. The Salvadoran human rights groups argued that the amnesty violated the Salvadoran constitution's guarantees of judicial protection, due process, and the right to seek compensation. Furthermore, it ignored the constitutional responsibilities of public officials, both civilian and military, to report "official crimes" committed by their subordinates or face sanctions for cover-up.[104] The Salvadoran constitution specifically prohibits the granting of amnesty to civilian or military officials who commit constitutional crimes during the incumbent president's term.[105] The human rights groups also maintained that the amnesty violated El Salvador's obligations under international conventions to which it is a party, which take precedence over Salvadoran laws.[106]

In holding that the amnesty law was a political matter not subject to judicial review, the Salvadoran Supreme Court's Constitutional Chamber nonetheless cited article 6(5) of Protocol II Additional to the Geneva Conventions as a basis for granting the broadest possible amnesty to persons who took part in the armed conflict or are deprived of liberty, interned, or detained for reasons related to the conflict. After the Salvadoran Supreme Court's ruling, the Chilean and South African Supreme Courts also interpreted this article in the same manner.[107] In August 1995, the Criminal Chamber of the new (1994–97) Supreme Court applied similar reasoning to uphold the granting of amnesty to three former FMLN combatants charged with having killed two wounded U.S. military advisors after shooting down their helicopter in January 1991. The court's decision relied heavily on its interpretation of article 6(5) of Protocol II Additional to the Geneva Conventions.[108]

---

petition on May 11, 1993. Both petitions were denied, and the court ruled that the constitutionality of the amnesty presented a nonjusticiable political question. See Resolution of the Petition for Unconstitutionality ("Demanda de Inconstitucionalidad") presented by Joaquín Antonio Caceres Hernández, Sala de lo Constitucional de la Corte Suprema de Justicia, Inconstitucionalidad No. 10-93, May 20, 1993.

104. Salvadoran Constitution (1983), article 241.

105. Ibid., article 244.

106. Ibid., article 144.

107. See Naomi Roht-Arriaza and Lauren Gibson, "The Developing Jurisprudence on Amnesty," *Human Rights Quarterly* 20 (1998): 847.

108. Criminal Chamber of the Supreme Court of El Salvador, appeal in proceedings for the aggravated homicide of David Henry Pickett and Ernest Gene Dawson Jr., August 16, 1995.

The International Committee of the Red Cross (ICRC) has since provided its own interpretation of this article, which differs from the reasoning of the Salvadoran Supreme Court. In 1995, at the request of Justice Richard Goldstone, then chief prosecutor for the international criminal tribunals for the former Yugoslavia and Rwanda, the ICRC stated that article 6(5)'s call for broad postwar amnesties does not extend to violations of international humanitarian law.[109]

In 1992 the Inter-American Commission on Human Rights (IACHR) ruled that amnesties granted in Argentina and Uruguay violated provisions of the American Convention on Human Rights, which establishes the state's duty to investigate, prosecute, and sanction violations of human rights.[110] The IACHR also ruled that the 1987 Salvadoran amnesty did not free El Salvador of the obligation to prosecute and sanction those responsible for the Las Hojas massacre.[111]

Following the same line of reasoning, in a 1994 report, the IACHR found the amnesty incompatible with El Salvador's obligations under the American Convention on Human Rights because it extinguishes criminal and civil liability and disregards the legitimate rights of the victims' relatives to reparation. It found that the amnesty would do nothing to further reconciliation and that it was inconsistent with the provisions of articles 1, 2, 8, and 25 of the American Convention on Human Rights. The IACHR pointed out that under article 27 of the Vienna Convention on the Law of Treaties, a state cannot unilaterally invoke provisions of its domestic law to justify its failure to carry out the legal obligations imposed by an international treaty.[112]

The IACHR found no justification for the inclusion of crimes against

---

109. Letter from Dr. Toni Pfanner, Chief, ICRC Legal Division, to the author, April 15, 1997.

110. Inter-American Commission on Human Rights Annual Report 1992–93, Reports 28/92 and 29/92. At the request of the governments of Argentina and Uruguay, the Inter-American Court subsequently confirmed that the Inter-American Commission on Human Rights was competent to address the issue of whether domestic laws are compatible with the American Convention on Human Rights. Inter-American Court of Human Rights, Advisory Opinion OC-13/93, July 16, 1993. "Certain attributes of the Inter-American Commission on Human Rights (articles 41, 42, 46, 47, 50, and 51 of the American Convention on Human Rights)"; requested by the Governments of Argentina and Uruguay. The court noted that "the authority of the Commission is in no way constrained by the manner in which the Convention is violated" (ibid., par. 27).

111. Inter-American Commission on Human Rights, Report No. 26/92, Case No. 10.287 El Salvador, OAS/Ser.L/V/II.82, Doc. 22, September 24, 1992, citing the decision of the Inter-American Court for Human Rights in the Velásquez Rodríguez case.

112. IACHR, El Salvador Report (1994), 73. Article 144, paragraph 2 of the Salvadoran constitution provides that "the law shall not modify or derogate that agreed upon in a treaty in effect in El Salvador. In the event of a conflict between the treaty and the law, the treaty will prevail."

"the activity of the courts" within the amnesty's scope. On the issue of civil liability, the IACHR noted the generally recognized principle that the rights of victims should be safeguarded in amnesty laws. It reiterated its earlier conclusion that "[e]very society has the inalienable right to know the truth about past events, as well as the motives and circumstances in which aberrant crimes came to be committed, in order to prevent repetition of such acts in the future. Moreover, the family members of the victims are entitled to information as to what happened to their relatives."[113] The IACHR also concluded that

> regardless of any necessity that the peace negotiations might pose and irrespective of purely political considerations, the very sweeping General Amnesty Law passed by El Salvador's Legislative Assembly constitutes a violation of the international obligations it undertook when it ratified the American Convention on Human Rights, because it makes possible a "reciprocal amnesty" without first acknowledging responsibility (despite the recommendations of the Truth Commission); because it applies to crimes against humanity, and because it eliminates any possibility of obtaining adequate pecuniary compensation, primarily for victims.[114]

In 1996 the IACHR went still further, finding not only that the amnesty decreed by Chile's de facto military government violated the American Convention, but that the successor democratic regime's legislature was in violation of its obligations to bring the law into line with the convention's precepts.[115] In 1999 the IACHR held that the Salvadoran Truth Commission's work could not be considered an adequate substitute for judicial proceedings. Because the commission did not act as a judicial body in its investigations and actions, its work could not relieve the state of its obligation to investigate to ensure that the truth would be made known and to prosecute and punish perpetrators.[116]

113. IACHR, El Salvador Report (1994), 75, citing Inter-American Commission on Human Rights, Annual Report 1985–1986, Chapter 5: "Areas in which steps need to be taken towards full observance of the human rights set forth in the American Declaration of the Rights and Duties of Man and the American Convention on Human Rights."

114. Ibid., 77.

115. Inter-American Commission on Human Rights Annual Report 1996, Report No. 36/97, Case 10.843.

116. Inter-American Commission on Human Rights, Report No. 1/99 (El Salvador) (Case No. 10.480, January 27, 1999), pars. 145, 155; Report No. 136/99 (El Salvador) (Case No. 10.488, December 22, 1999) (Jesuit case).

Despite the IACHR's strong stance against blanket amnesties for past human rights violations,[117] very little has been done to enforce the obligation to undertake criminal prosecutions. The IACHR has no enforcement powers of its own and relies on moral suasion. In 1995, relying largely on the jurisprudence of the Inter-American system and the Argentine constitution, the Federal Chamber in Buenos Aires recognized the right of family members and society to know the truth, and the right of relatives to mourn their dead. Preceding the new court cases, a former navy captain's account of his participation in "death flights" during which disappeared persons were drugged and dropped from airplanes into the sea had given impetus to a new effort to force an official investigation about the fate of the disappeared despite the exculpatory laws passed in 1986.[118]

For fifteen years El Salvador distinguished itself by its disregard for the findings and recommendations of the IACHR. As the IACHR's 1994 report on El Salvador noted, in none of the many individual cases that the IACHR approved and subsequently published during the period of armed conflict "did the [Salvadoran] authorities respond to the Commission's recommendations, follow up on its requests or recognize the compulsory jurisdiction of the Inter-American Court of Human Rights, despite the Commission's recommendations to that effect."[119] The Salvadoran government also thwarted planned IACHR visits by such ploys as informing the commission shortly before a scheduled visit that none of the officials with whom it planned to meet would be available. The passage of a broad amnesty law that failed to distinguish crimes that can be amnestied from those not subject to amnesty ignored El Salvador's obligations under international law and continued its long-standing practice of disregarding the IACHR.

In El Salvador there was a widespread perception that the hastily passed and overly broad amnesty law undermined the Truth Commission's recommendations. A public opinion poll carried out by the Jesuit-run Central

---

117. See Inter-American Commission on Human Rights, Report No. 29/92 (Uruguay), 82nd Sess., OEA/Ser.L/V/II.82, doc. 25 (October 2, 1992); Report No. 24/92 (Argentina), 82nd Sess., OEA/Ser.L/V/II.82, doc. 24 (October 2, 1992); Report No. 36/96 (Chile), 95th Sess., OEA/Ser.L/V/II.95 (October 15, 1996); Douglass Cassel, "Lessons from the Americas: Guidelines for International Response to Amnesties for Atrocities," *Law and Contemporary Problems* 59 (1996): 4.

118. Captain Scilingo's account was published in Horacio Verbitsky, *El Vuelo* (Buenos Aires: Planeta, 1995); in English, *The Flight: Confessions of an Argentine Dirty Warrior* (New York: New Press, 1996); Martín Abregú (1996), "La tutela judicial del derecho a la verdad en la Argentina," *Revista IIDH* 24 (1996): 11.

119. IACHR, El Salvador Report (1994), 21.

American University in June 1993 found public sentiment against the amnesty law (55.5 percent), with 77 percent of those polled favoring punishment of those who violated rights.[120] With no acknowledgment of wrongdoing by the individuals named or by the government on behalf of the state agents identified, the amnesty sought to impose a veil of forgetting and forgiving. Chief government negotiator Oscar Santamaría termed the amnesty law "the achievement of the peace process."[121] Military officers and others in El Salvador refer to "forgetting" as a positive accomplishment.[122] A year after the Truth Commission's report was issued, even those who had opposed the early passage of an amnesty law showed little inclination to try to have it set aside.[123]

Although the Guatemalan truth commission accord was generally seen as far weaker than the Salvadoran Truth Commission provisions, Guatemala has thus far refrained from enacting a general amnesty. Guatemalan human rights groups united in the Alliance Against Impunity to try to ensure that no amnesty law would emerge from the negotiations. A National Reconciliation Law was passed on the heels of the final peace accords signed in December 1996. The Guatemalan law required courts to make individual decisions, and it excepts a number of crimes from its scope in partial recognition of the dictates of international law.[124] Moreover, two years after enactment of this law, no military officers had been granted amnesty. Guatemalan courts have proven so unreliable in prosecuting human rights crimes that an amnesty was arguably not necessary to protect perpetrators. The Historical Clarification Commission called for prosecution and punishment of crimes not eligible for amnesty, including genocide, torture, and forced disappearance, as well as those crimes not subject to prescription or not subject to amnesty according to Guatemalan or applicable international law.[125]

120. Instituto Universitario de Opinión Pública, Universidad Centroamericana José Simeón Cañas, Boletín de Prensa, Año VII, No. 2, July 14, 1993.

121. Author's interview with Foreign Minister Oscar Santamaría, July 20, 1994, San Salvador.

122. See, e.g., Tina Rosenberg, "What Did You Do in the War, Mama?" *New York Times Magazine,* February 7, 1999, 52, 93.

123. The issue arose in the context of the debate surrounding the election of the new Supreme Court. To try to assuage ARENA's fears that a court headed by Abraham Rodríguez, who had served on the Ad Hoc Commission, would seek to undo the amnesty law, FMLN leaders indicated that they would support a revised amnesty law were the court to declare the 1993 law unconstitutional. Should the law be found unconstitutional, the legislature could quickly pass a new amnesty law designed to pass constitutional muster.

124. Margaret Popkin, "Guatemala's National Reconciliation Law: Combating Impunity or Continuing It?" *Revista IIDH* 24 (1996): 173–84.

125. *Guatemala: Memory of Silence,* 58.

Both the timing and the scope of the Salvadoran amnesty distinguish it from amnesties granted in Uruguay, Argentina, and Chile. The amnesties in the Southern Cone did not extinguish civil liability, nor did they include crimes against judicial activity within their purview. In El Salvador the process of fact-finding was effectively curtailed by the far-reaching amnesty passed on the heels of the Truth Commission report. The Honduran Supreme Court found that a similar Honduran amnesty law required the courts to carry out investigations before determining whether a particular crime could be amnestied.[126]

In El Salvador, unlike the situation in Uruguay, the advisability of maintaining the amnesty was never the subject of a prolonged public debate with extensive citizen participation.[127] Nor did any exemplary trials take place, as in Argentina. In March 1998 the Argentine legislature made a symbolic statement by repealing, but not annulling, the exculpatory laws that had protected most members of the military from prosecution. In Chile the transitional government avoided placing further obstacles on the search for truth and justice by not passing an additional amnesty law.

As recent events in Argentina and Chile have demonstrated, demands for justice that have not been addressed are prone to resurface.[128] Because the vast majority of Salvadoran victims were *campesinos* without political clout or economic resources, and because the FMLN—transformed into a formidable political party—virtually abandoned this issue, Salvadoran victims found themselves with little political support. Nonetheless, five years after the Truth Commission report, there were some signs of public recognition that El Salvador owes a "debt to the past."[129]

The 1993 amnesty became front-page news in 1998 after former National Guardsmen convicted for the December 1980 murder of four U.S. churchwomen told representatives of the Lawyers Committee for Human Rights and a New York Times reporter that they had been acting on orders from

126. Corte Suprema de Justicia, República de Honduras, Amparo en Revisión, Caso 58–96, January 18, 1996.
127. For background on the referendum campaign that sought to overturn the Uruguayan amnesty law, see Americas Watch, *Challenging Impunity, The Ley de Caducidad and the Referendum Campaign in Uruguay* (1989).
128. See Margaret Popkin and Nehal Bhuta, "Latin American Amnesties in Comparative Perspective: Can the Past Be Buried?" *Carnegie Journal of Ethics and International Affairs* 13 (1999).
129. Father Rodolfo Cardenal, vice-rector of the Central American University, used this phrase in a March 1998 panel presentation marking five years since publication of the Truth Commission's report.

above. The four convicts, along with their sergeant, who had declined to talk, were the only people still incarcerated in El Salvador for human rights crimes committed during the war. Their statements led to debate about whether the 1993 amnesty barred further criminal investigation of those who ordered the killings. While not excluding the possibility of further investigations, President Armando Calderón Sol seconded his predecessor's preference to see the tragic past buried. The attorney general subsequently found that the case could not be reopened because of the expiration of El Salvador's ten-year statute of limitations for murder cases. In 1998 Salvadoran human rights groups presented the (new) Supreme Court's Constitutional Chamber with additional petitions challenging the constitutionality of the amnesty law.

The Truth Commission: An Overall Perspective

Because of the sweeping amnesty law so rapidly enacted and the failure to provide any redress for victims, it is easy to dismiss the Truth Commission's impact. Still, many Salvadorans understood that the commission's findings against key military officers played a crucial role in the larger effort to limit the power and role of the military, perhaps the most striking accomplishment of the peace process. Although the report did not constitute an official Salvadoran acknowledgment of the truth, it still must be considered an authoritative historical document, the value of which is not determined by the immediate acceptance or rejection of its findings. Unfortunately, the report is not required reading in Salvadoran schools. History does not have an important place in El Salvador today. Indeed, the country has no university history department.

The Truth Commission did an admirable job of describing certain illegal practices and identifying some of the people responsible for heinous crimes. The government's reaction and the hasty amnesty law truncated what should have been the beginning of a process. Political considerations under the guise of "reconciliation" and the need to reincorporate former combatants into civilian life were given greater importance than the rights of victims or society's need to address the past.[130] Participatory democracy requires

130. As Alejandro Garro comments on the "disguised amnesty laws" passed by the Alfonsín government and the sweeping pardons issued by his successor, "Burying past human rights

the active participation of civil society as well as politicians. The failure to address, even at a symbolic level, the losses of tens of thousands of people is likely to breed feelings of apathy, hopelessness, bitterness, cynicism, and exclusion. The scope and nature of the horrific violence that took place in El Salvador calls for exemplary justice in accordance with the rule of law and the principle that, under international norms and the Salvadoran constitution, certain kinds of conduct are never permissible, even in time of war. Unfortunately, seven years later, there was still no political will to undertake such an effort.

The Salvadoran government did not choose to establish an investigatory commission to find out the truth about past human rights abuses for which members of its armed forces had primary responsibility. Instead, the FMLN used its negotiating clout to insist that a commission be formed. As part of a UN-brokered negotiations process designed to end twelve years of civil war, government negotiators accepted the UN's proposal, apparently without fully appreciating its potential ramifications.[131] This lack of commitment to pursuing truth and justice has been evident in the official response to the report and its recommendations.

In his public response to the report, rather than advocating continued efforts to establish the complete truth, President Cristiani called for erasing, eliminating, and forgetting everything in the past.[132] One obvious lesson is that an official acknowledgment of past wrongdoing by state agents is unlikely to come from the same government responsible for many of those violations while it remains in power. This reality, coupled with the overly broad amnesty decree, limited the truth-telling effort. Still, the commission's report stands as a powerful indictment of the kinds of violations committed during the war and of the active and passive complicity of state institutions.

---

violations under the rug of 'national reconciliation' has not helped the process of instilling democratic values to the Argentine people. . . . Depriving the judiciary of the historic opportunity to pass judgment on past human rights abuses was not only constitutionally objectionable, but also, by creating a specter of impunity, it missed an historic opportunity for constructing Argentine democracy on strong foundations" ("Nine Years of Transition," 99–100).

131. One member of the government's negotiating team, David Escobar Galindo—a poet, lawyer, and university president, who did not serve in the government—states that the Truth Commission report was necessary and ultimately salutory, although he had numerous criticisms of the actual document and recommendations. Author's interviews March 23, 1993, and October 25, 1993, San Salvador.

132. Address to the nation, March 18, 1993; quoted in IACHR, El Salvador Report (1994), 70.

Nonetheless, as a consequence of the commission's findings, virtually no one admitted wrongdoing, and impunity remains among the most serious problems affecting human rights in El Salvador.[133]

The Salvadoran government has been eager to "turn the page" and put the "painful past behind us." In principle, it has accepted the notion that the military, the administration of justice, and the police must be radically transformed to prevent the recurrence of widespread abuses. After considerable delay, it accepted the premise that additional resources needed to be dedicated to the identification and eradication of illegal armed groups operating with impunity. Overall, implementation of Truth Commission recommendations was slow and selective, and it was plagued with difficulties and foot dragging.

Five years after issuance of the Truth Commission's report, many of its recommendations had not been implemented. Unquestionably, more effort has been made to implement the structural and institutional reforms proposed than to implement measures intended to impose administrative sanctions or ban individuals named in the report, or measures intended to contribute to national reconciliation.

Looking at how El Salvador has dealt with the past in comparative perspective, one is struck by the lack of visible societal demand for further truth and justice. In differing degrees, in Argentina, Chile, Guatemala, and South Africa, civil society has insisted that more be done to establish what happened to victims. The Salvadoran government and, to a lesser degree, the FMLN, the United States, and even the UN bear some responsibility for the choices in El Salvador. But it is also clear that civil society did not assume the role of protagonist with regard to the past.

At the end of the war, human rights groups called for justice but failed to develop a strategy for achieving it or maintaining the struggle in the face of the sweeping amnesty law. In part, this failure reflected the relative weakness of Salvadoran human rights groups and a general lack of technical resources. For the most part, Salvadoran human rights groups lacked the kind of technical capacity demonstrated by groups in countries such as Argentina, South Africa, and Guatemala. The very strength of the FMLN had inevitably impinged on the independence of some human rights groups and other actors in civil society, who were used to relying on the FMLN for leadership. The overwhelming presence of the UN did nothing to help Salvadoran NGOs

---

133. In this regard, see ONUSAL, 11th Human Rights Report, par. 6, 131.

address the past, instead reinforcing an unhealthy tendency toward dependence on international actors. The UN's failure to find ways to strengthen Salvadoran human rights NGOs, which it largely dismissed as politicized and lacking in technical expertise, did not help the situation. After the war, many capable young lawyers and human rights activists left human rights NGOs to move into positions in the justice system, which was undergoing dramatic reforms. Some also opted to work for international organizations and for the UN observers' mission (MINUGUA) in neighboring Guatemala. By comparison, working for human rights NGOs was not particularly prestigious.

The failure to establish a more complete truth has many consequences. Thousands of families do not know what happened to their relatives or even where their bodies are buried. This lack of knowledge leaves an open wound that is particularly difficult to heal. Many people who lived in communities that were devastated by human rights violations have found themselves unable to return because the horrific events and those responsible for them have not been brought to light. And of course, the failure to establish the truth leaves abundant opportunity for the Salvadoran inclination to trade in rumors. This situation was demonstrated in March 1997, days prior to elections for the Legislative Assembly and municipal governments, when former guerrilla leader Ana Guadalupe Martínez delivered a televised broadside against her former colleagues in the FMLN, accusing them of responsibility for a number of murders and other crimes committed during the war. While these accusations were rejected for their clear political motivation, they served as an uncomfortable reminder that so many crimes from that period remained to be clarified.[134]

Without in any way negating the report's profound significance and the effects that some of its recommendations may have had, it did not—and probably could not—fulfill the ambitious agenda established in the peace accords. In this respect, El Salvador offers an example to be avoided. The refusal to come to terms with the past, even in an exemplary fashion, or to provide any redress for victims and their families has not helped to end impunity, establish the rule of law, or promote reconciliation. Instead it has left victims and their relatives without recourse. Those who made the effort to tell their stories to the Truth Commission expected more—investigation of the fate of their relatives, identification of those responsible, and the possibility of prosecution and punishment of perpetrators or compensation for

134. See "Falsos Profetas de la Verdad," (El Salvador) *Proceso*, March 12, 1997, 749.

victims. While expectations were undoubtedly unrealistic, no real effort was made to protect victims' rights or ensure further efforts to establish the truth and achieve justice or undertake any symbolic measures.

It is far too soon to make a definitive judgment on the long-term effects of the Truth Commission report and other measures taken to overcome impunity in El Salvador. Certainly, the forced retirement of ranking military leaders named by the Ad Hoc Commission had an important symbolic significance. Likewise, the effort to place the military squarely under civilian rule and the creation of a new civilian police force are extremely important. Recognition of problems in the administration of justice, replacement of the Supreme Court, and an incipient judicial reform effort are also essential steps. But as ONUSAL's findings on continuing impunity and the Inter-American Commission's rulings indicated, they were not enough. And, as comparative perspective clearly shows, attempts to bury the past rarely succeed; demands for justice almost always reappear. Whether the effects of the Truth Commission report, the partial implementation of its recommendations, and the other measures established during the peace process will ultimately prove sufficient to overcome the long-standing heritage of impunity remains a crucial and unresolved question.

5

INSTITUTIONALIZING THE SAFEGUARDS
INCLUDED IN THE PEACE ACCORDS

The temporary bodies born of the peace accords ceased to exist after carrying out their specified missions. The UN Observer Mission, which so
dominated the terrain of human rights and peace accord compliance, was
gradually withdrawn. The original mission, ONUSAL, ended in April 1995,
after almost four years in the country. Progressively smaller units were left to
oversee outstanding issues in peace accord implementation through "verification" and "good offices" functions.[1] However, the UN found it difficult
to end its lengthy involvement in El Salvador. In the words of a former chief
of the mission, its mandate was "interpreted more broadly as time went on
to the point where toward the end the mission had practically become the

---

1. Some members of the Security Council believed that it was time for the UN to disengage
from El Salvador. The small team left after ONUSAL's departure was called the Mission of the
United Nations in El Salvador (MINUSAL); its (second six-month) mandate expired on April
30, 1996. Thereafter, the still smaller United Nations Office of Verification in El Salvador
(ONUV) operated from May 1 to December 31, 1996, and the Support Unit from January 1 to
June 30, 1997, both under the mandate of the General Assembly. For a description of the evolution of the UN operation in El Salvador, see Teresa Whitfield, "Staying the Course in El Sal-
vador," in *Honoring Human Rights: From Peace to Justice*, ed. Alice H. Henkin (Washington,
D.C.: Aspen Institute, 1998), 163–66.

engine of the process and was perceived as a factor in the governability of the country."[2]

The long-term success of the peace accords required the consolidation of the new institutions created to protect human rights and establish the rule of law. In contrast to the Truth Commission and the Ad Hoc Commission, the National Counsel for the Defense of Human Rights (PDDH) and the National Civilian Police (PNC) were established in the constitutional reforms and designed as permanent institutions with important roles in safeguarding human rights and overcoming impunity. Even with the UN's substantial presence and pressure, and with clear commitments in the peace accords, consolidating these institutions proved far more difficult than might have been anticipated. Inherent difficulties in building new institutions and creating domestic safeguards were compounded by corporate resistance, uneven political will to carry out reforms, and inconsistent international and domestic oversight.

The process of implementing the peace accords has demonstrated that reforms once enacted, no matter how well-intentioned, are unlikely to produce the intended results without substantial oversight of the implementation process. In the case of El Salvador, this meant the development of domestic oversight entities and capacity and, in the short to medium term, international oversight. The Human Rights Division of ONUSAL served as an oversight mechanism, pointing out many of the failings of the Salvadoran justice system and providing moral weight. Diagnosing the problems, however, was far easier than assisting Salvadoran institutions so that they could perform an oversight function, insist on compliance with their recommendations, and evaluate the success of implementation efforts.

The National Counsel for the Defense of Human Rights

(La Procuraduría para la Defensa de los Derechos Humanos–PDDH)

The "ombudsman" concept, a congressionally established oversight mechanism to ensure that government agencies treat citizens in accordance with law, developed first in Scandinavia. The Latin American ombudsman is a more recent creation, arising in a radically different context. In much of

---

2. Enrique ter Horst, "Some Lessons from the Field," paper presented to the First Nordic Peace-Keeping Mission Management Seminar, Stockholm, September 23–25, 1996, cited in Whitfield, "Staying the Course," 164.

Latin America, it has been designed to serve as a key human rights safeguard in the process of restoring or establishing new democratic governments. The Latin American institution is generally given authority to investigate and denounce official malfeasance or inaction. In countries like El Salvador, where government institutions have not been reliable and have often violated citizens' rights, the potential scope of work for a human rights ombudsman is enormous.

An effective ombudsman is likely to clash with government authorities; therefore, an adequate and protected budget becomes essential. In Central America, officeholders who have taken their role seriously and spoken out firmly in sensitive cases have found themselves converted into important political players. Thus, after Guatemalan president Jorge Serrano attempted a "self-coup" in 1993, Human Rights Ombudsman Ramiro de León Carpio was called on to serve out Serrano's term as president. De León Carpio was not affiliated with a political party and had gained substantial credibility as an effective ombudsman who had spoken out against government human rights violation.

Throughout Latin America, these new institutions have been assigned broad mandates, with oversight of a whole range of government actions and little possibility for enforcement. The effectiveness of the institution has depended greatly on the moral authority exerted by individual officeholders through resolutions and statements and on their ability to set appropriate priorities and obtain adequate funding. In many cases, the institutions themselves seem unclear about their role and priorities. Some have focused on human rights education and the rights of different identifiable and often marginalized groups (including prisoners, children, women, and indigenous populations), while others have emphasized development of their investigative capacity.

Mandated by the April 1991 constitutional reforms, the Salvadoran National Counsel for the Defense of Human Rights (PDDH) was slow to assume its myriad responsibilities, determine appropriate priorities, and establish necessary credibility. In part, these problems stemmed from ambiguities in the institution's constitutional mandate. Enabling legislation enlarged an already broad constitutional mandate by establishing deputy counsels for human rights, children, women, the environment, and the elderly. The institution was mandated to issue resolutions and recommendations but was not provided with any mechanism for enforcement. Given the magnitude of human rights problems in El Salvador and real budget constraints, donors initially urged the office to focus on the rights to life, liberty, and personal integrity.

The legislature's selection of the first National Counsel reflected partisan politics rather than concern for building a solid institution to safeguard human rights. Based on a political agreement between the ARENA and Christian Democratic parties, Carlos Mauricio Molina Fonseca, a Christian Democrat, was chosen for the post in February 1992. A former vice-minister of labor, Molina Fonseca had no previous human rights experience, and his staff had little prior experience in the field. The government was slow to provide the office with funding and did not back the institution wholeheartedly. Molina Fonseca avoided taking positions that might be seen as confrontational.

Pedro Nikken, the UN's independent expert on El Salvador and human rights advisor during the negotiations, expressed great concern about the institution's slow start. He noted that the new institution had "many departments but little activity."[3] He urged the PDDH to set priorities that would take into consideration its constitutional powers and the experience of similar entities in other countries, the situation in El Salvador, and its relationship with governmental and nongovernmental sectors.[4] He warned that the office needed to establish a strong presence as a "recourse for human rights violations" so that Salvadorans would not become skeptical and see it as another in a long line of weak entities established to protect citizens from abuses of power.[5] Nikken urged the government to take aggressive action to strengthen the new institution through the provision of needed physical, technical, and human resources, and he suggested that foreign experts could support this effort.

Despite Nikken's urging and the presence of ONUSAL's Human Rights Division in El Salvador at the time of the institution's founding, a close working relationship did not immediately develop. ONUSAL provided some training sessions on human rights and temporarily seconded a Salvadoran lawyer to work with the PDDH. The National Counsel did not embrace the suggestion that foreign experts could provide support and failed to build a solid relationship with domestic human rights groups. Salvadoran nongovernmental human rights groups deplored the institution's lack of activity and its failure to address key human rights concerns.[6]

3. Independent Expert's Report on the Situation of Human Rights in El Salvador, November 1992, par. 129.
4. Ibid., par. 273.
5. Ibid., par. 132.
6. At a September 1992 symposium in San Salvador on the role of Civil Society in the Peace Process, the head of the Central American University's Human Rights Institute publicly

Because the PDDH was designed to take on many of the verification and oversight functions temporarily being performed by ONUSAL's Human Rights Division, close cooperation and transfer of skills and experience was essential. Still, a July 1993 cooperation agreement did not lead to immediate collaboration. In his February 1994 report, Nikken specifically urged the Salvadoran government to take full advantage of ONUSAL's Human Rights Division, "an unprecedented deployment in the history of international protection of human rights."[7]

During 1994, faced with ONUSAL's anticipated departure, the two institutions finally began to work closely together. When the PDDH and ONUSAL began a new phase of close technical cooperation, the UN Secretary-General's Report emphasized that it would be "imperative" for the PDDH to give priority to consolidating investigations of human rights violations and noted that it was significant that the office was finally interested in receiving "the technical cooperation that ONUSAL has always stood ready to provide."[8]

During its last year in El Salvador, ONUSAL's Human Rights Division made the PDDH a priority, reflecting the UN's concern about the consequences of its departure and Salvadoran institutions' lack of preparation to take on an oversight role.[9] The UN Development Program (UNDP), which had channeled support to the PDDH from the outset, worked largely with European donors to devise programs to strengthen the institution. In August 1994, UNDP hired a lawyer from ONUSAL's Human Rights Division to oversee various technical assistance projects that were funded by European countries and Canada. The two UN agencies worked together to devise a strategy to provide continuing support to the PDDH after the departure of ONUSAL.

---

chastised the National Counsel. A representative of the nongovernmental Human Rights Commission, who was a member of the institution's Advisory Board, likewise expressed concern about the institution's slow progress. See, e.g., (El Salvador) *Proceso*, año 14, no. 596, January 26, 1994.

7. Informe del Experto Independiente, Professor Pedro Nikken, sobre la evolución de la situación de los derechos humanos en El Salvador, elaborado de conformidad con la resolución 1993/93 de la Comisión de Derechos Humanos y la decisión 1993/284 del Consejo Económico y Social, UN Doc. E/CN.4/1994/11, February 3, 1994, par. 151.

8. Report of the United Nations Secretary-General on the United Nations Observer Mission in El Salvador, UN Doc. S/1994/1000 (August 26, 1994), par. 44.

9. See Report of the Director of the Human Rights Division of ONUSAL covering the period from July 1 to September 30, 1994, UN Doc. A/49/585–S/1994/1220 (October 31, 1994) (ONUSAL, 12th Human Rights Report), pars. 23–24.

Beginning in July 1994, ONUSAL assigned legal and police officers to advise the National Counsel's offices on the acceptance, processing, and investigation of complaints. ONUSAL personnel assisted PDDH staff with the interpretation of international human rights norms and their practical application. This effort involved joint verification, which began in September 1994, and the gradual transfer of ONUSAL's caseload to the PDDH in preparation for the mission's eventual departure from El Salvador. Along with internal reforms supported by UNDP projects, these measures contributed to a significant increase in the number of rulings issued by the office.[10] By late 1994, the Director of ONUSAL's Human Rights Division pointed to positive results from increased cooperation and joint investigation of complaints.[11] However, the institution still lacked an effective follow-up mechanism to ensure that rulings were implemented. The Salvadoran entities to which recommendations were directed rarely, if ever, complied with the resolutions.

The decision to undertake a major cooperation effort came late in ONUSAL's tenure in El Salvador. In general, ONUSAL tended to dedicate more of its efforts to individual cases and problems and less to the more complex task of institution building.[12] The division was clearly better able to assist the National Counsel's office with a more solid methodology and accumulated experience after several years on the ground. Until July 1994, when mixed teams of legal and police officers were established, the UN mission suffered from difficulties caused by a lack of coordination between the Military and Police Divisions (brought in originally for peacekeeping purposes) and the Human Rights Division.[13] After ONUSAL's departure, the "somewhat strained" relations between MINUSAL and ONUV (the reduced, successor UN missions) and the director of the UNDP technical assistance projects complicated coordination of efforts to consolidate the institutional development of the PDDH.[14]

---

10. ONUSAL reported that during August and September alone, the National Counsel's office issued 47 rulings, compared with 27 rulings from January to July 1994 (ibid., par. 28). As of October 1994, the National Counsel's office had eight branches in the departments and was preparing to open two more.

11. Ibid., pars. 25–31.

12. For a thorough critique of ONUSAL's failure to give adequate priority to institution building, see Lawyers Committee for Human Rights, *Improvising History: A Critical Evaluation of the United Nations Observer Mission in El Salvador* (New York: Lawyers Committee for Human Rights, 1995), 107–18.

13. Whitfield, "Staying the Course," 164.

14. Ibid., 177.

Not until early 1995 could the PDDH provide national coverage, with fourteen branch offices open throughout the country. In March 1995 only 55 percent of those responding to a public opinion survey had heard of the National Counsel's office. Asked which institution best defended human rights at the time, respondents placed the National Counsel's office third, behind the National Civilian Police (PNC) and ONUSAL.[15]

The National Counsel's office achieved far greater recognition following the legislature's March 1995 selection of Victoria Marina Velásquez de Avilés, formerly Deputy National Counsel for Children's Rights, as the new National Counsel. In her first few days in office, Velásquez de Avilés issued a strong statement against reinstatement of the death penalty as well as a statement criticizing the PNC's conduct in violently breaking up a march of the war wounded. She also rejected as unqualified a proposed candidate for inspector general of the PNC.

Velásquez de Avilés quickly established a pattern of speaking out on important human rights issues and cases. The PDDH published resolutions, based on its investigations, disputing the findings of police investigations in several cases. These cases included the June 1994 murder of Ramón Mauricio García-Prieto, a young architect who was shot in front of his wife and infant son. The conservative and well-connected García-Prieto family insisted on a real investigation of the case.[16] Family members were followed and threatened. The investigation eventually led to a murder-for-hire ring in which some former police investigators were involved. Likewise, the National Counsel's investigation of the death of Adriano Vilanova, a university student, confirmed that the victim's death had resulted from a police beating and not a car accident or suicide as the police had maintained. The Salvadoran newspaper *El Diario de Hoy* published the National Counsel's findings, which coincided with its own investigative reports on the Vilanova case. The National Counsel also denounced the existence of a parallel investigative unit set up by the Minister of Public Security outside the PNC.[17]

Subsequent public opinion polls showed a significant increase in public confidence in the PDDH, which frequently found itself confronting the

15. "La opinion de los salvadoreños sobre la situación de los derechos humanos y los retos de la Procuradora," IUDOP Boletín de prensa, Año X, no. 3, March 30, 1995.

16. This case was highlighted in a 1997 article on justice in Central America. Douglas Farah, "Inefficient Court Systems Plague Central American Nations' Bid for Stability," *Washington Post*, August 1, 1997.

17. The results of these investigations were published in UNDP-funded pamphlets: Protección a los derechos humanos: El derecho a la vida, caso: Manuel Adriano Vilanova Velver, and caso: Ramón Mauricio García-Prieto Giralt (San Salvador: PNUD/PDDH, 1996).

Minister of Public Security and denouncing violations committed by the civilian police. An August 1996 opinion poll found that the PDDH had become the leading institution in defending human rights at the national level, named by 28.7 percent of respondents. However, when respondents were asked what institution best defends human rights at the local level, the National Counsel's percentage dropped and was easily surpassed by the PNC.[18]

By 1997 the majority of complaints presented to the National Counsel focused on police misconduct. Although the new National Civilian Police had several oversight mechanisms, including an inspector general, the two institutions did not coordinate. The PDDH did not refer cases of reported police abuses or misconduct to the inspector general so that the two institutions could together develop mechanisms to see that problems within the PNC were promptly addressed.

During this period the National Counsel successfully challenged the constitutionality of emergency anticrime legislation, which seriously undermined the rights of minors established in the Salvadoran constitution, the Convention on the Rights of the Child, and the new Juvenile Offenders Law. The PDDH relied principally on strong leadership and knowledgeable advisors within and outside the institution. Progress in institutional consolidation remained slow, including the elaboration and publication of resolutions and the development of an adequate mechanism to monitor compliance with resolutions. The PDDH had yet to develop the capacity to critique and propose legislative reforms to ensure compliance with international human rights standards.

The institution's new protagonism was rewarded with a 10 percent budget reduction in 1997, seriously hampering the National Counsel's efforts to strengthen the institution.

AID's judicial reform project was slow to support the PDDH. In neighboring Guatemala, the United States had provided substantial assistance to the ombudsman's office. AID officials in El Salvador found the institution ill-conceived, with a mandate that overlapped with other Salvadoran institutions and a need to establish appropriate priorities. While the UN shared AID's concern about the inadequate definition of the National Counsel's role, AID's position on this issue stood in sharp contrast to ONUSAL's belated efforts at constructive engagement.[19] AID officials found the institution's

18. The percentage dropped to 11.5 percent compared to 21.1 percent for the PNC. "Los salvadoreños opinan sobre el sistema de justicia y los derechos humanos," IUDOP, Boletín de Prensa, Año XI, no. 5, August 21, 1996.

19. AID contracted consultants to conduct an evaluation of the Ombudsman's Office in

mandate redundant with that of other Salvadoran institutions. Although the PDDH mandate definitely needed refinement, no other Salvadoran institution was assigned equivalent constitutional responsibility for guaranteeing respect for human rights. AID officials' comments about the office sometimes seemed to reflect a lack of understanding of the role the peace negotiators had envisioned for the office as a key human rights safeguard. Contrary to the views of some U.S. officials, the National Counsel's tasks were not ones that could be assumed by the Attorney General's office or by any human rights NGO. Notwithstanding its reservations, AID began to explore areas for cooperation during Velásquez de Avilés's tenure, looking for ways to strengthen the institution and provide training opportunities for staff.

Toward the end of Velásquez de Avilés's term as National Counsel, yet another public opinion survey found the percentage of Salvadorans who believed that the National Counsel's office best defended human rights at the national level had risen to 35.8 percent, compared to 11.6 percent for the PNC. This poll also asked those surveyed to evaluate the work of the National Counsel's office. Revealing a significant lack of understanding of the office's role, almost 10 percent of those surveyed asserted that the institution protected criminals. When asked where the National Counsel should focus more efforts during the next three years, almost half of respondents said that more emphasis should be given to protecting children's rights. By comparison, only 10.2 percent urged the institution to focus more on the protection of citizens against official abuses.[20] El Salvador ratified the Convention on the Rights of the Child in 1990. Sensitivity to the issue of children's rights increased greatly in postwar El Salvador, with the implementation of the new Juvenile Offenders Law and a number of NGOs increasingly active in this area.

Almost two thirds of those surveyed (63.3 percent) rated the office's performance as positive; a slightly higher percentage (more than two-thirds of respondents) evaluated positively the institution's work in investigating human rights violations. More than half of those polled favored the reelection

---

1993. See Development Associates, Inc., El Salvador: Evaluación de la Oficina del Procurador para la Defensa de los Derechos Humanos (November 23, 1993). This evaluation came on the heels of a UNDP evaluation that focused on the institution's constitutional design and enabling legislation (Enrique Bernales Ballasteros, Informe sobre la Procuraduría para la Defensa de los Derechos Humanos de El Salvador [September 29, 1993]).

20. "La opinión pública sobre los derechos humanos y los retos de la PDDH," IUDOP, Boletín de Prensa, Año XIII, no. 1, March 10, 1998.

of Velásquez de Avilés; less than a quarter opposed her continuation in office.

Despite the public's confidence in Velásquez de Avilés, the governing ARENA party would not countenance her reelection to a second three-year term. In March 1998, the political parties in the Assembly were unable to reach consensus to select a new National Counsel, which required a two-thirds majority vote. With presidential elections scheduled for March 1999, Velásquez de Avilés agreed to compete within the FMLN for the presidential nomination, as the candidate of an unusual coalition of party hard-liners and women's organizations. Although she enjoyed immense popularity, Velásquez de Avilés ultimately failed to win the nomination by a small (and contested) margin. Her venture into partisan politics unfortunately served to confirm the impression that the PDDH could easily serve as a springboard for opposition candidates for the presidency.

As the weeks wore on, the political parties in the Assembly were unable to reach an agreement, and no new National Counsel was named. In the meantime, Velásquez de Avilés's deputy, Eduardo Urquilla, served as interim National Counsel until the Assembly passed legislation specifically designed to prevent him from continuing to serve in that capacity. During his brief tenure, Urquilla signed a landmark resolution calling on the Salvadoran military and judicial authorities to undertake an investigation of the fate of children who disappeared in the course of military operations during the war. This resolution relied on international law to establish that the amnesty could not bar the investigation and prosecution of these cases.[21]

In July 1998 the political parties finally agreed to name a new National Counsel, Eduardo Antonio Peñate Polanco. An appellate judge with no experience in the human rights area, Peñate Polanco had a number of complaints pending against him in the Supreme Court and the PDDH for his failure to comply with due process requirements. The PDDH itself had found him responsible for violating due process guarantees. Human rights NGOs deplored the election of someone who not only lacked the credentials for the position but had himself been condemned by the institution he was to head and lacked the requisite moral solvency for the position.

Despite the leadership provided by Velásquez de Avilés, the institution was far from consolidated at the end of her tenure. Following the change in leadership in 1998, the National Counsel's office risked losing the public

21. Procuraduría para la Defensa de los Derechos Humanos, San Salvador, March 30, 1998, Caso SS-0449-96, reprinted in *En Búsqueda: Identidad – Justicia – Memoria* (San Salvador, May 1998); "PDDH pide investigación niños desaparecidos," *La Prensa Gráfica*, April 29, 1998.

confidence it had gained over the course of three years. The Salvadoran human rights NGO community warned that the new leadership could undermine the institution and deprive Salvadorans of what had been developing into an important instrument in the defense and protection of human rights. Reverting to wartime rhetoric, Peñate claimed that many PDDH employees were Communist Party stalwarts who constantly sought to destabilize the institution.[22] Salvadoran NGOs challenged Peñate's job performance as well as his qualifications. PDDH statistics for the first six months of his tenure showed a significant decrease in the institution's activities. In late 1999, a legislative commission began to investigate allegations of corruption and malfeasance to determine whether he should be removed from office. Several international donors suspended their assistance to the PDDH because of lack of confidence in Peñate's leadership. The legislature had shown itself incapable of setting aside partisanship to elect a National Counsel with strong credentials in the protection of human rights, instead resorting to a political compromise. Progress in consolidating the institution appeared to have stalled, with widespread concern that the gains made during Velásquez de Avilés's tenure would be lost.

The National Civilian Police (PNC)

The creation of the National Civilian Police was one of the greatest achievements of the peace accords. Painstakingly designed during the negotiations, the new civilian police was to replace the discredited militarized security forces with a completely new civilian-led force that would be effective and would respect human rights. The negotiators established equal quotas of former national police and FMLN combatants who would be allowed to join after screening, although the majority of the new force's members were to be drawn from the civilian population. International experts helped to plan and train the new police force. Despite the detailed accords on this issue, the wholly different philosophy underlying the new corps, and continuing international involvement, the new police encountered setbacks at every turn.[23] The tremendous difficulties that have arisen in consolidating this key

22. "Gracias a Dios, no pienso renunciar," *La Prensa Gráfica*, February 10, 1999.
23. For background on the civilian police, see Vickers and Spence et al., *Endgame: A Progress Report on Implementation of the Salvadoran Peace Accords*, December 3, 1992,

institution demonstrate the obstacles to implementing even those agreements
that were blueprinted in the accords.

Crises in the development of the civilian force stemmed from leadership
that often seemed to ignore the dictates of the peace accords and the PNC's
enabling legislation, continuing problems in recruitment and training,
attempts to create "parallel" police forces, and the failure to develop adequate internal discipline mechanisms. According to William Stanley, the
PNC and the Salvadoran Ministry of Public Security responded to challenges "in ways that threaten[ed] to return the PNC to patterns of institutional conduct reminiscent of its predecessors."[24] Recurrent episodes of
police violence marred the new institution's development.

The government undermined the terms of the peace accords by placing
former military personnel into the new force, including the wholesale incorporation of units slated to be disbanded. Beginning in late 1993, a military
officer appointed to direct PNC operations refused to allow ONUSAL police
to work with newly deployed units, despite an obvious need for additional
training. The new police faced an ongoing problem of insufficient resources
because of inadequate government funding and far less international assistance than anticipated. After the accords went into effect, the Salvadoran
government continued to channel additional resources to the National
Police, which was not completely phased out until December 1994. Despite
repeated requests, the UN was able to convince few foreign donors to provide funding for the establishment of the new force. Many donors view
police aid as too problematic.

The public responded very positively to the initial deployment of the civilian police, but complaints about police conduct increased with the growth of
the force.[25] Lack of knowledge of law and procedures were responsible for
many problems, but the UN and the National Counsel documented serious
abuses, including cases of torture and arbitrary executions. In July 1995 the
organized crime investigative unit (DICO) arrested four members of the
PNC, including the former head of the San Miguel office, for participation

---

10–20; William Stanley, *Risking Failure: The Problems and Promise of the New Civilian Police
in El Salvador* (Cambridge, Mass.: Hemisphere Initiatives, 1993); Charles Call, El Salvador
Peace Plan Update #3: Recent Setbacks in the Police Transition (Washington Office on Latin
America, February 1994); Gino Costa, *La Policía Nacional Civil de El Salvador (1990–1997)*
(San Salvador: UCA Editores, 1999); William Stanley, *Protectors or Perpetrators? The Institu-
tional Crisis of the Salvadoran Civilian Police* (Washington, D.C., and Cambridge, Mass.:
Washington Office on Latin America and Hemisphere Initiatives, 1996).

24. Stanley, *Protectors or Perpetrators?* iii.

25. See ONUSAL, 12th Human Rights Report, pars. 32–48.

in the Black Shadow (*Sombra Negra*) death squad, which had announced and carried out executions in the name of "social cleansing." Because of the widespread distrust of the judicial system, many Salvadorans actually supported the Black Shadow's actions.[26]

These problems were compounded by the uneven response to reported abuses and delays in establishing effective internal oversight mechanisms. The position of inspector general was not filled until October 1994; and the disciplinary, investigation, and control units were slow to establish adequate procedures. There was no effective coordination among the three internal disciplinary units within the PNC, much less with other state entities such as the National Counsel for the Defense of Human Rights and the Attorney General's office. ONUSAL deplored the "failure to observe the requisite rigor which ought to accompany internal disciplinary procedures in the police's early stages of existence."[27]

By September 1995 all political sectors in El Salvador had recognized the seriousness of the institutional problems facing the new police and the inadequacy of the institutional response. At the request of Salvadoran president Armando Calderón Sol, the reduced UN Mission, MINUSAL, prepared an evaluation and series of recommendations to address the principal problems in the public security sector. These far-reaching recommendations called for the elimination of irregular units (formed by the Minister of Security outside the PNC's structures); professionalizing the command structure; reinforcing internal discipline; reforming methods for handling social unrest to establish mechanisms for seeking the peaceful resolution of social conflicts; improved recruitment and training; and increasing civil society's input, including the creation of a politically pluralistic commission to advise the government on public security policy. The Salvadoran government was taken aback by the number and scope of the recommendations but eventually responded to many of them.

In January 1996 the government agreed to form the National Council on Public Security. Its members came from across the political spectrum. Although the Council was slow to begin work, over time it began to undertake some important tasks such as improving the statistical database on crime, information gathering, and enhancing capacity for professional and scientific investigation.

26. See Douglas Farah, "Tactics of New Death Squads Revive Fears in El Salvador," *Washington Post,* July 30, 1995, A21.
27. ONUSAL, 12th Human Rights Report, par. 43.

In the postwar years, Salvadoran authorities did not take full advantage of the professional and technical assistance available. The reluctance to capitalize on available assistance is often hard for outsiders to understand. A frustrated UN political officer, trying to understand how the Salvadorans could fail to take advantage of the expertise of ONUSAL's police contingent, wondered if he might feel the same way as the Salvadorans if his country were invaded by such a large UN mission. Certainly UN staff at times contributed to the problem by acting arrogantly, out of ignorance of local conditions or with insufficient consideration to Salvadoran sensibilities.

Poor donor coordination exacerbated some of the PNC's problems. At times U.S. assistance provided through the Justice Department's International Criminal Investigative Training Assistance Program (ICITAP) did not emphasize the same concerns raised by the UN mission. Likewise the Spanish National Police, who also provided major bilateral assistance to the new force, did not always share the UN's priorities. Thus, bilateral arrangements with donors could sometimes be used to undermine the UN's positions and recommendations aimed at long-term planning to ensure that the PNC reflected the model agreed to in the peace accords. This tension was nowhere clearer than in the realm of criminal investigation.

Virtually Nonexistent Criminal Investigation

With a few important exceptions, in the years immediately following the peace accords Salvadoran criminal justice continued to be characterized by inadequate—or nonexistent—criminal investigations. Human rights groups, which had long focused on the problem of impunity, increasingly focused on the need to improve criminal investigative capacity as a key component of police reform essential to ensure protection of human rights.

The problem is not a simple one. Traditional methods of investigation, which relied almost exclusively on confessions—routinely coerced—remained prevalent. Protecting the rights of suspects while obtaining admissible evidence requires different training, attitudes, and skills. The notion that criminal cases should be decided on the evidence and not on the basis of the economic and political power of the suspect—or the victim—is a revolutionary one.

At the same time that police were struggling to improve their technical skills and learn to act within the law, organized criminals had become far more sophisticated. In the postwar period, many were former military, paramilitary, and security force personnel. Some were former guerrillas. Soaring crime rates brought calls for tougher measures against criminals and complicated efforts to protect individual rights. In this difficult context, El Salvador and other countries in the region were seeking to improve their criminal investigative capacity and enhance protection of individual rights.

In postwar El Salvador, none of the Salvadoran authorities charged with responsibility for criminal investigations properly carried out its role. In an April 1993 report, ONUSAL's Human Rights Division deplored

> the absence of any policy governing the preservation of evidence relating to deaths or the taking of minimum care to ensure the safety of witnesses, and the improper handling of testimony; the failure to use proper technical means to establish the cause, manner and time of death; the failure to perform autopsies in a significant number of cases ... and the inefficiency of the judicial system and its auxiliary organs in identifying those responsible for deaths. This inability to investigate crimes is reflected in the failure of judges to show any initiative in taking the requisite legal steps in the early stages of the investigation; in the slow and delayed participation of the office of the Attorney General; in the meager or invalid evidence gathered for the purpose of establishing criminal liability; and in lenience in investigating cases involving military personnel or agents of the security forces.[28]

The Truth Commission was surprised to discover that Salvadoran authorities did not carry out thorough investigations even in cases in which the FMLN was thought to be at fault. This suggested that the problem went beyond political will, since the government had no problem in publicly assigning responsibility to the FMLN. Instead, it revealed a society unused to relying on objective evidence to prove responsibility—unused to relying on any evidence other than the defendant's confession and popular belief. The advantage of this system was that it left people free to believe what they chose and to take action accordingly. Professor Buergenthal has noted the difficulties posed to the Truth Commission by the Salvadoran practice of "trading in rumors":

> They were often passed on with such self-assurance and conviction that uninitiated foreigners could easily mistake them for the truth.

---

28. Report of the Director of the Human Rights Division of the United Nations Observer Mission in El Salvador (ONUSAL) up to 31 January 1993, UN Doc. A/47/912–S/25521, annex (April 5, 1993) (ONUSAL, Sixth Human Rights Report), par. 77.

The witness usually believed the rumor, and if we did not immediately accept the information as true, he or she would assume that we were protecting someone or that we were not serious about our investigation.[29]

These rumor-based convictions generally followed ideological lines and bore no consistent relationship to available evidence. Contrary theories of responsibility were rarely put to the test. Often there seemed to be little interest in trying to establish an objective or authoritative truth. This well-established pattern proved resistant to change. Even when scientific methods have been used to investigate crimes, investigation has usually been limited to the lowest links in the chain: those who planned and ordered crimes have rarely been identified.

The Unfortunate Legacy of the Special Investigative Unit

After the peace accords were signed, steps were taken to establish the new civilian police force. During this period Salvadorans, also under U.S. pressure to "civilianize" the Special Investigative Unit, debated whether to place the SIU under the jurisdiction of the Supreme Court or the Attorney General's office or to maintain it in the executive branch. The Supreme Court and CORELESAL, the Revisory Commission on Salvadoran Legislation, had concluded that the criminal investigation unit should be placed under the Supreme Court.[30] A 1991 evaluation of the U.S. judicial reform program commissioned by AID had concluded that the Supreme Court was not an appropriate venue. It noted that creating a "judicial police," as demanded by the Supreme Court, "could have the negative effect of making the judicial system more authoritarian, and not the police more democratic."[31]

29. Thomas Buergenthal, "The United Nations Truth Commission for El Salvador" *Vanderbilt Journal of Transnational Law* 27 (1994): 518.

30. As discussed *supra* at 66–67, CORELESAL itself was dominated by Supreme Court justices. See "Evaluación de la Comisión de Hechos Delictivos," December 7, 1989, published in CORELESAL—Informe, July–December 1989, Nos. 10–11; see also CORELESAL, "Anteproyecto y Exposición de Motivos de la Ley de Creación del Instituto Salvadoreño de Investigaciones Judiciales," reproducción por la Corte Suprema de Justicia en ocasión de la Conferencia sobre el tema "El Organismo de Investigación del Delito," held on June 18, 1991. When this conference took place, the constitutional reform agreed to at the negotiating table had given responsibility for criminal investigation to the Attorney General's office, not the Supreme Court.

31. Marcelo Sancinetti, Jorge A. Bacqué, and Marco A. Castro Alvarado, *Programa para una estrategia de reforma judicial de US AID* (San Salvador: Checchi and Company Consulting, Inc., 1991), 68.

Because of provisions included in the peace accords, the unit was never transferred to the Supreme Court. The peace accords gave the attorney general responsibility for directing criminal investigations but failed to define clearly what this responsibility entailed. The negotiations had produced no agreement to reform the Attorney General's office or to make the Salvadoran criminal justice system an adversarial one. In this context, experts from the United Nations Latin American Institute for the Prevention of Crime and the Treatment of Offenders (ILANUD) criticized the transfer of responsibility for investigations to the prosecutor's office as an "anomaly" and a "serious danger":

> This placement of the investigative police is only possible in a process that guarantees—in reality—the most absolute defense of the defendant from the first moment of detention and even before, with a public ministry with a long tradition of independence and professionalism, with a very well-organized public defense that promptly covers all the needs of legal attention; that is, with characteristics that by no means exist in El Salvador or in a good number of other countries in the region.[32]

The peace accords failed to spell out the fate of the SIU, allowing the unit to become the subject of a struggle between those who wanted to disband it and possibly incorporate some parts of it into the new civilian police, and those who wanted to transfer the unit to the Attorney General's office.[33] The Salvadoran government planned to rely on the SIU as the basis for the PNC's criminal investigative capability. As a result, no effort was made to train an entirely new investigative body within the PNC. Three years later, government negotiator David Escobar Galindo described this decision as a critical failure to prioritize building what should have been the backbone of the new PNC, its criminal investigative capacity.[34] This failure proved to have disastrous consequences.

The international actors most involved in police reform, the United Nations and the United States, sharply disagreed about the future of the SIU.

---

32. Eugenio R. Zaffaroni and Elias Carranza, "Informe de la Misión Científica para la Creación de una Nueva Policía Civil en El Salvador," undated manuscript on file with the author.
33. For a discussion of this dispute and related issues, see Popkin, *El Salvador's Negotiated Revolution* (New York: Lawyers Committee for Human Rights, 1993), 19–35.
34. Author's interview with David Escobar Galindo, San Salvador, April 1, 1995.

Despite overwhelming evidence to the contrary, U.S. personnel in El Salvador never admitted that the SIU—a product of the U.S. Administration of Justice project—was not an effective, independent investigative body. According to contemporary AID documents, the SIU was recognized in Central America and by the U.S. Department of Justice as "a highly competent criminal investigatory body."[35]

During the same period, UN Independent Expert Pedro Nikken and the (UN) Truth Commission called for the unit to be disbanded. According to Nikken, the SIU "has been perceived in some quarters as one of the causes, by reason of its lack of results at least, of the impunity with which violations of human rights have been committed."[36] Likewise, the Truth Commission concluded that it was "through [the SIU's] omissions that serious human rights violations ... were covered up."[37]

ONUSAL's Human Rights Division observed the SIU's actions over a period of time and found serious fault with the unit, documenting a number of cases in which the SIU failed to take necessary action.[38] The UN verification mission termed the lack of "a competent, independent body under civilian control capable of investigating crimes efficiently" as "one of the most glaring deficiencies of the criminal justice system." According to ONUSAL, "The [SIU] ... has not carried out this function satisfactorily, nor is it doing so now."[39] To cite one example, in October 1993 ONUSAL's Human Rights Division unsuccessfully urged the SIU to take steps to apprehend a suspect identified as the killer of an FMLN logistics expert. After the Director of ONUSAL's Human Rights Division personally visited the SIU to impress "upon the authorities the urgency of apprehending the suspect, since the information which ONUSAL had concerning his whereabouts would not be accurate indefinitely," steps were taken to carry out the arrest the following day. In the early morning hours, however, the suspect was found shot to death.[40]

35. AID Project Paper, "Judicial Reform II," Project No. 519–0376, September 1992, 3.

36. "Report on the Situation of Human Rights in El Salvador," prepared by the Independent Expert of the Commission on Human Rights in accordance with paragraph 12 of Commission resolution 1992/62 of 3 March 1992 and Economic and Social Council decision 1992/237 of 20 July 1992, UN Doc. A/47/596, November 13, 1992, par. 146.

37. *From Madness to Hope*, 184.

38. See, e.g., Report of the Director of the Human Rights Division of ONUSAL until June 30, 1992, A/46/955, S/24375, August 12, 1992 (ONUSAL, Fifth Human Rights Report), par. 41; ONUSAL, Sixth Human Rights Report, par. 67.

39. ONUSAL, Sixth Human Rights Report, par. 234.

40. Report of the Director of the Human Rights Division of the United Nations Observer Mission in El Salvador (ONUSAL) covering the period from 1 August to 31 October 1993, UN Doc. A/49/59, S/1994/47, January 18, 1994 (ONUSAL, Ninth Human Rights Report), pars. 28–29.

In its careful language, the UN noted that "basic standards of proper criminal investigation" were "being circumvented."[41]

While U.S. authorities espoused an officially "agnostic" position about the institutional framework for the SIU, they did favor maintaining it as a unit. Any failings of the SIU were relegated to the past.[42] U.S. authorities backed the SIU's former chief, Colonel Manuel Antonio Rivas, for a top position in the civilian police until the Truth Commission report described his role in actively suppressing and altering evidence in the Jesuit murder investigation.

The FMLN did not take a consistent position on the SIU. In December 1992 the FMLN signed an agreement with the Salvadoran government that allowed the SIU and the Executive Anti-Drug Trafficking Unit (UEA) to be incorporated into the PNC without any real review of investigators' records or retraining.

After its incorporation into the PNC, the SIU remained under its old leadership and equally ineffective. Investigations continued to proceed far too slowly, if at all, and no effort was made to coordinate with the Attorney General's office or the courts. The number of detectives in the unit was in any case insufficient to address the country's need for criminal investigation; the training and incorporation of PNC members progressed slowly.

U.S. personnel tended to focus narrowly on transmitting skills through training without looking at the results in terms of changed practices. A UN official commented that ICITAP in El Salvador was providing good technical training to the police, "but why don't they look at the results?" ICITAP trainers were often aware of the deficiencies of their trainees, but the program was set up not to be operational and inclined toward a narrow focus on training.

In an early 1995 review of PNC practices, ONUSAL found that the police initiated investigations in only 22 percent of cases reported to it. In the cases where an investigation was initiated, steps taken were minimal; generally limited to an inspection certificate, complainant's statement, and—at times— witness statements. ONUSAL found that "proceedings involving some kind of investigative activity by the PNC are practically non-existent."[43] The same ONUSAL study found that the PNC had carried out only 20 percent of the

---

41. Ibid., par. 31.

42. Author's interview with U.S. Embassy Legal Officer, San Salvador, October 1, 1993.

43. ONUSAL, Report of the Director of the Human Rights Division of the United Nations Observer Mission in El Salvador (ONUSAL), 1 October 1994 to 31 March 1995, UN Doc. A/49/888-S/1995/281, April 18, 1995 (ONUSAL, 13th Human Rights Report), par. 66.

judicial warrants for arrest issued.[44] The majority of PNC arrests were for petty offenses, such as drunkenness and disorderly conduct, suggesting that the PNC was not focusing its efforts on combating serious crime.

The much larger Executive Anti-Drug Trafficking Unit (UEA), which had been created by the U.S. Drug Enforcement Administration, proved to be a still greater problem. Like the SIU, the UEA was not mentioned in the peace accords and was also highly regarded by U.S. officials.[45] In October 1993, then Captain Oscar Peña Durán, who had headed the antinarcotics unit, was named as the PNC's Deputy Director for Operations.[46] The antinarcotics unit had developed a reputation for acting on its own without oversight or undue concern for legal restrictions.[47] Peña Durán proceeded to place his men in command positions throughout the PNC in plain violation of the PNC law and regulations.[48] He moved quickly to end the close working relationship between ONUSAL's Police Division and newly deployed PNC units.[49]

As in the case of the SIU, U.S. officials had difficulty acknowledging that an institution built entirely through U.S. assistance had serious defects. Nonetheless, after a few months it was evident to all, including U.S. officials who had originally recommended him, that Peña Durán was not an appropriate PNC leader.

44. Ibid, par. 43.

45. Charles Call, "El Salvador Peace Plan Update #3" (Washington Office on Latin America, February 4, 1994). In September 1993, 430 members of the antinarcotics unit were transferred to the PNC (11 had been rejected in a minimal screening process). Aside from the inadequate vetting procedures, the UN objected to the incorporation of approximately 70 anti-drug trafficking police who had joined the unit after the December 1992 agreement that allowed members of the unit to join the PNC. The SIU had less than 200 members when it was incorporated into the PNC.

46. Again, a September 1993 agreement between the government and the FMLN preceded his appointment. The agreement also permitted the entry into the PNC of certain former FMLN combatants who did not meet established requirements.

47. Call, "El Salvador Peace Plan Update #3," 3.

48. See Report of the Secretary-General on the UN Observer Mission in El Salvador, S/1994/561, May 11, 1994, par. 34: "ONUSAL has recently ascertained that many of the former sergeants of the Special Antinarcotics Unit enrolled in the National Civil Police as sub-inspectors are now responsible for criminal investigations in a number of delegations of the National Civil Police."

49. ONUSAL termed the government's decision not to request an extension of the technical assistance ONUSAL had been providing to the new civilian force "a self-defeating move" and noted that an increase in reported human rights violations by the new police had been accompanied by increased obstacles to ONUSAL verification activities, because police units had been instructed not to cooperate with the UN mission. See Report of the Secretary-General, May 11, 1994, par. 42(d).

After Peña Durán's May 1994 ouster, relations with ONUSAL were re-established and efforts undertaken to correct some of the problems within the PNC.[50] Still, former members of the two special units continued to cause problems. Resolving their status and undoing the damage caused by their wholesale incorporation into the PNC proved complex. When Salvadoran authorities belatedly agreed to implement UN recommendations to dismiss those who had been added to the unit in an irregular manner and require the remainder to undergo police academy training, the members of the two units refused to accept these terms. In early 1995, when the government announced that some members of the antidrug trafficking unit (DAN) would be discharged, their colleagues went on strike. They demanded reinstatement of those discharged, the exemption of all DAN agents from further training at the new police academy, and the granting of autonomy to the DAN. Ultimately, they opted to take severance pay and leave the PNC. In similar fashion, SIU members balked at the requirement that they go through police academy training and a thorough screening. In March 1995, after another strike, all but twenty members of the former SIU chose to leave with severance pay—but not before seriously damaging the credibility of the new force.

In early 1995 a witness identified a former SIU detective who had been incorporated into the PNC's Investigations Division (DIC) as one of several men involved in planning the October 1993 murder of FMLN leader Francisco Velis. Instead of arresting the suspect, even after a court order was issued, PNC officials allowed him to escape and flee the country. This incident raised serious doubts about the former National Police and SIU personnel involved in investigations. Not only did they fail to solve crimes and seemingly pervert investigations that might have uncovered military or police involvement, but some were apparently involved in the commission of serious crimes. As information about this incident came to light, the disastrous consequences of failing to heed the Truth Commission and ONUSAL recommendations became increasingly clear.

Between 1995 and 1998, the National Counsel for the Defense of Human Rights found that the DIC had on various occasions thwarted or diverted investigations in sensitive cases. The Minister of Public Security further confused the panorama by creating parallel structures, with no basis in the peace accords or the PNC law, to carry out sensitive investigations.

---

50. See Report of the Secretary-General on the United Nations Observer Mission in El Salvador, August 26, 1994, UN Doc. S/1994/1000.

The obstacles to creating a new criminal investigative capacity highlight the importance and sensitivity of who controls such an effort. Both the special narcotics unit and the SIU were linked to the military and to the United States. Neither the military nor the U.S. was eager to relinquish control, and neither was completely attuned to the requirements established in the peace accords.

Special Investigation of "Illegal Armed Groups": Death Squads and Organized Crime

Despite a marked improvement in the human rights situation in the postwar period, a series of FMLN leaders were killed or attacked in circumstances suggesting political motivation, and Salvadoran authorities remained ineffective in discovering the perpetrators. The SIU's notable lack of success in resolving these crimes led ONUSAL to call for the formation of an independent mechanism to ensure that investigations of extralegal or arbitrary executions would meet the requirements of "promptness, independence and efficiency."[51] The Salvadoran government initially rejected this recommendation, saying it preferred to work through existing channels because the country's institutional structure did "not allow for such bodies."[52] The government first formed a consultative mechanism, which proved inadequate, and then established an "Inter-Institutional Commission" which included representatives of the executive but failed to include the new National Counsel for the Defense of Human Rights, despite his office's broad constitutional powers to investigate human rights violations on a quasi-jurisdictional basis. The UN Secretary-General reported to the Security Council that the Inter-Institutional Commission "did not meet United Nations criteria for the investigation of summary executions."[53]

The Truth Commission had urged a further investigation of death squads, noting that "given the country's history, prevention is essential in this area." The commission called on the government to undertake an immediate and thorough investigation of "illegal armed groups," with the assistance of foreign police since the new civilian police would not yet be equal to such a task.[54]

51. See ONUSAL, Ninth Human Rights Report, par. 22.
52. ONUSAL, Report of the Director of the Human Rights Division of the United Nations Observer Mission in El Salvador up to 31 July 1993, UN Doc. A/47/1012, S/26416, September 15, 1993 (ONUSAL, Eighth Human Rights Report), par. 112(3).
53. Report of the Secretary-General on the United Nations Observer Mission in El Salvador, UN Doc. S/26790 (October 29, 1993), par. 11.
54. *From Madness to Hope*, 180.

It was only after two ranking FMLN leaders were killed in October 1993 that the Salvadoran government was willing to implement the Truth Commission's recommendation that it undertake a special investigation of illegal armed groups. On December 8, 1993, after considerable debate about its composition, UN Secretary-General Boutros-Ghali announced the formation of the "Joint Group for the Investigation of Politically Motivated Illegal Armed Groups," headed by two independent representatives of the Salvadoran government, the National Counsel for the Defense of Human Rights, and the Director of ONUSAL's Human Rights Division.[55]

With the help of an international staff, the Joint Group carried out an eight-month investigation.[56] Its mandate was limited to the period after the peace accords, and it failed to meet expectations that it would do what the Truth Commission had failed to do: list the civilians who had, in the past or more recently, financed the death squads. Still, the Joint Group officially recognized the existence of "illegal armed groups" responsible for summary executions, threats, and other acts of intimidation with political motivation. It also confirmed the link between existing groups and death squads active in earlier years. According to the Joint Group's report, these groups sought to destabilize the peace process. They favored the militarization of society, sought to ensure that the PNC would be ineffective, and generated fear in the population so that people would not join political parties or other entities perceived as threats to powerful political and economic interests.

The report found that violence in the postwar period had become more complex and sophisticated through links with organized crime—drug trafficking, money laundering, massive frauds, car theft, weapons trafficking, bank and armored car heists—that could finance politically motivated violence. The Joint Group recognized that these organized criminal structures flourished, thanks to the collaboration of some members of the armed forces and the PNC, members of the governing ARENA party, powerful individuals, and the judicial system, which continued to permit impunity. Through its investigations, the Joint Group was able to document the organization of rural networks that engaged in intimidation and criminal activity. These networks sometimes included elected officials and justices of the peace.

55. See letter dated December 7, 1993, from the Secretary-General Addressed to the President of the Security Council and Annex, "Principles for the Establishment of a Joint Group for the Investigation of Politically Motivated Illegal Armed Groups," UN Doc. S/26865 (December 11, 1993). The government had been reluctant to include the National Counsel for the Defense of Human Rights, which was excluded from the Inter-Institutional Commission.

56. The Report of the Joint Group for the Investigation of Politically Motivated Illegal Armed Groups in El Salvador was published on July 28, 1994. UN Doc. S/1994/989 (October 22, 1994). (Joint Group Report.)

The Joint Group called on the government to undertake a permanent effort to eradicate illegal armed groups. It called for the creation of a special unit within the PNC's Division of Criminal Investigation to deal with political violence and organized crime. Because of the special characteristics of politically motivated crime, the Joint Group recommended that the unit receive special training, adequate resources, and international technical and economic cooperation, and that members of this unit be carefully selected to guarantee necessary trust. The report emphasized the need for the Attorney General's office to assume its role of directing criminal investigations in collaboration with the PNC.

The Joint Group further called for a number of measures to promote reform of the judiciary. It urged the new Supreme Court to undertake a real purge of the judiciary, based on the evaluations of the National Judiciary Council. It called for special proceedings (within the framework of respect for legal due process and human rights) for cases with apparent political motivation or organized crime involvement and for special judges to hear those cases. Its other recommendations included passage of a temporary law to permit rewarding cooperative suspects and providing witness protection, and the establishment of permanent coordination mechanisms between the Attorney General's office and the PNC. The Joint Group also called for the National Counsel for the Defense of Human Rights to create a mechanism for technical verification (oversight) of investigation in crimes that appeared to be politically motivated. It provided guidelines for these kinds of investigations and stressed the importance of looking beyond those who carried out the actions—the last link in the chain—to those who gave the orders and planned the operations.

The Joint Group's findings were not well received by the government, yet efforts were eventually begun to implement at least some of the recommendations. A specially trained unit was formed in the PNC's Criminal Investigation Division. Slow to initiate work, largely because of bureaucratic delays in assigning foreign advisors to the unit, the organized crime investigative unit (DICO) was made up of carefully selected police who had not previously served in the PNC, SIU, or the FMLN. Criminal investigation remained a politically sensitive domain. Those unhappy with the reforms accused the unit of having FMLN ties, failed to provide needed resources, and interfered in its investigative efforts. The DIC (Investigations Division of the PNC) blocked investigations that led to its own members. Only after the 1996 scandal about the PNC's failure to detain a former SIU detective accused of involvement in the Velis killing, did the government accept the need to take additional measures to make criminal investigations effective. Unfortunately, these measures did not involve strengthening the DICO but relied instead on parallel structures outside the regular PNC command structure.

In July 1997, the UN Secretary-General noted that the model for the PNC developed in the peace accords had been subject to distortions, that criminal investigation by groups outside the institutional structure had "been fostered," and that the special organized crime investigative department (DICO) had been substantially weakened.[57]

The Supreme Court ultimately determined that the Salvadoran constitution would not allow the establishment of a special procedure for the appointment or designation of special judges to handle organized crime and politically motivated cases. The court also rejected the possibility of establishing special jurisdiction and protection for such cases.

The Criminal Procedure Code passed in 1996 included a legal basis for rewarding cooperative suspects with lenient treatment. Prosecutors are authorized to petition the court to forgo criminal prosecution or limit the charges when the defendant has made a decisive contribution to establishing the involvement of others in the same or a more serious crime.[58]

Some cases included in the Joint Group's report were later investigated by the PNC, with mixed results. The investigations of these cases, as well as subsequent cases in which some of the same perpetrators (including former members of the DIC) were shown to have been involved, left open the question of who was behind these crimes.

The Postwar Crime Wave

Even without unfortunate policy decisions, the PNC faced a formidable task as a new, untried police force confronting a postwar crime wave.[59] Faced with one of the world's highest per capita murder rates, the PNC was unable to investigate most homicides. According to statistics compiled by the National Council on Public Security, 6,792 homicides were reported to the

57. The Situation in Central America: Procedures for the Establishment of a Firm and Lasting Peace and Progress in Fashioning a Region of Peace, Freedom, Democracy, and Development: Assessment of the Peace Process in El Salvador, Report of the Secretary-General, UN Doc. A/51/917 (July 1, 1997), par. 9.
58. Código Procesal Penal (1996), article 20(2).
59. See, e.g., William Stanley and Charles T. Call, "Building a New Civilian Police Force in El Salvador," in K. Kumar, ed., Rebuilding Societies After Civil War: Critical Roles for International Assistance (Boulder and London: Lynne Rienner Publishers, 1997), 107–33.

Attorney General's office, but only 415 suspects were jailed on murder charges.[60] In 1997 the percentage of arrests to homicides improved slightly: 280 arrests for 3,926 homicides reported. A July 1998 public opinion survey found that only about two-thirds of murders were even reported to the appropriate authorities. Those who did report crimes (not just homicides) complained that in most cases (56 percent) the authorities had done nothing to solve the crime. Only 16.5 percent of respondents reported that their cases had been resolved.[61]

Frustrated with the PNC's perceived ineffectiveness in fighting crime, Salvadorans increasingly responded that people had the right to take justice into their own hands. A July 1998 public opinion survey found that more than half (52.5 percent) of those polled agreed that individuals had this right; only 40 percent disagreed. Even more disturbing was the finding that more than a third of those polled (36.8 percent) claimed to support the activities of illegal armed groups that engaged in social cleansing. Almost half of the Salvadorans polled said they would support the arming of neighborhood groups to defend themselves against crime. The poll's findings did not indicate an actual increase in crime compared with prior periods, but it suggested instead that the cumulative effect of a high crime rate and an ineffective state response was taking its toll on the citizenry, who were losing patience. In 1998 a new organization, "United Against Crime" (*Unidos contra la Delincuencia*), closely linked to the Salvadoran Chamber of Commerce, began calling for aggressive government measures to combat crime.

Despite the serious problems in developing the PNC's investigative capacity, the new force included many committed people and was seen in a very different light from its predecessors. The sheer number of crimes reported to the PNC reflected a substantial degree of trust in the institution. Public opinion surveys indicated that, at the local level, the PNC was considered the institution that best defended human rights. Unquestionably, PNC agents put their lives on the line. Over a five-year period (1993–98), 256 members of the new force had reportedly been killed, either in the line of duty or off duty. The rate of police fatalities in the first half of 1998 had

60. Cited in Asociación Pro-Búsqueda de Niñas y Niños Desaparecidos (Pro-Búsqueda), Fundación de Estudios para la Aplicación del Derecho (FESPAD), Instituto de Derechos Humanos de la Universidad Centroamericana José Simeón Cañas (IDHUCA), Oficina de Tutela Legal del Arzobispado de San Salvador (OTLA), Informe sobre la Situación Actual de los Derechos Humanos en El Salvador, presented to the Inter-American Commission on Human Rights, Washington, D.C., October 1998, 10.

61. IUDOP, "Los salvadoreños opinan sobre el problema de la delincuencia," Boletín, Año XIII, no. 3, August 13, 1998.

doubled (40 in slightly more than five months compared to an average of 42 agents per year in the preceding four years).[62] The new police force numbered 17,000 by the end of 1998.

Public opinion blamed the courts more than the police for the failure of the war against crime. The PNC attributed many of its failings in the effort to control crime to problems in the justice system and the law, particularly after the April 1998 implementation of the new Criminal Procedure and Penal Codes. Minister of Public Security Hugo Barrera blamed the new codes for tying the hands of police. Yet with or without the new codes, the police were clearly not up to the task. Luis Cardenal, president of the Chamber of Commerce and Industry and a member of the Public Security Council, insisted that the PNC needed to be modernized and reorganized to be more effective in fighting crime. He stressed the urgency of improving the professional skills of police assigned to criminal investigation. He also called for reevaluating the deployment of the police in light of crime statistics in different areas. The police still lacked necessary equipment and training as well as adequate oversight mechanisms.[63] The government had failed to develop, publicize, and implement a comprehensive anticrime strategy. Salvadoran authorities had done little to collect the guns and other weaponry left over from the war, restrict the possession of firearms, or address the socioeconomic conditions contributing to the crime wave.

The PNC has been undermined by military resistance to a civilian force, uneven civilian leadership, resource constraints, inadequate training and supervision, and difficulty in instilling a wholly different ethic and public perception of the role of police officers in a democratic society. In 1998 the DIC, in particular, remained understaffed, inadequately trained, and plagued by weaknesses in supervision and internal controls that contributed to continuing problems with corruption. Rather than confront the weaknesses in the PNC and the lack of comprehensive crime prevention strategies, Minister of Public Security Barrera preferred to blame the PNC's inability to control rampant crime on the new criminal justice legislation.

When Francisco Flores of the ARENA party assumed the presidency in June 1999, he made public security a top priority for his administration. He appointed a new minister of public security and police chief and announced a new crime prevention plan. He gave the Public Security Council, which had only a general advisory role during the Calderón Sol administration, a

---

62. "Un policía muerto por día en la última semana," *El Diario de Hoy*, June 13, 1998.

63. "Se necesita una reingeniería de la PNC dice Cardenal," *La Prensa Gráfica*, April 21, 1999.

specific role in shaping institutional reforms related to public security. While the recommendations of the prior council had never been implemented, the new administration expressed a commitment to putting them into effect. These included the creation of a system of computerized criminal statistics, the reform of the Division of Criminal Investigation, control mechanisms for public security entities, policies of social prevention of crime, and a proposed organic law for the public security branch.

In August 1999, former FMLN leader Salvador Samayoa, was given cabinet rank as the head of the new Public Security Council. Samayoa explained that President Calderón Sol had named the original council under pressure from the United Nations, not because he was convinced that it was important to have representatives of civil society involved in formulating and implementing the country's public security policy. He further noted that President Flores expressed greater belief in the need for social crime prevention measures and community policing.[64]

In the long term, consolidation of the PNC will necessitate the development of adequate internal and external domestic oversight mechanisms. The Flores administration placed all the PNC internal controls under the authority of its new PNC inspector general. From 1995 to 1998 the National Counsel for the Defense of Human Rights took on an external oversight role while Victoria Marina Velásquez de Avilés headed the office. Salvadoran NGOs, particularly the Human Rights Institute of the Central American University (IDHUCA), also played an important oversight role and worked closely with the National Counsel's office to document cases.

The Role of Salvadoran Nongovernmental Organizations (NGOs)

Nongovernmental human rights organizations in El Salvador played a crucial role during the war, denouncing human rights violations inside and outside the country and helping victims. Once the war ended, however, their roles became less clear. As discussed in connection with the Truth Commission's work, the human rights NGOs were largely excluded from the decisions about how to address past human rights violations and were unable to

---

64. Carlos Dada, "Vamos a trabajar para reformer la Ley de Armas," *La Prensa Gráfica*, August 27, 1999.

mount a successful challenge to the amnesty law. They also struggled to play a role in ensuring the effectiveness of the new institutions born of the peace accords.

Like their counterparts elsewhere in Latin America, the Salvadoran NGOs had difficulty finding their niche under significantly changed conditions. Suddenly they were called on to play a role in overseeing state institutions, to criticize and formulate proposed reforms, and to find new ways to work on behalf of their constituencies. To avoid becoming marginalized in the changed context, the NGOs needed to find new ways to insert themselves into the effort to guarantee human rights and the rule of law.

During the immediate postwar period, ONUSAL, with its massive presence, seemed to preempt the human rights field. Nor was ONUSAL's Human Rights Division particularly effective in working with the NGOs. It had an uneven and often unproductive relationship with Salvadoran human rights groups, which was plagued by misunderstandings on both sides. The human rights groups expected the UN to play a more forceful role in denouncing human rights violations and in supporting their work. Coordination was often minimal, and ONUSAL consultations with the NGOs were poorly timed. The Salvadoran groups found that the UN's diplomatic concerns led it to find human rights improvements and gloss over continuing violations. To Salvadoran NGO activists, much of ONUSAL's staff seemed either ignorant or arrogant. The UN found the human rights groups unduly critical of its work, slow to adjust to the new era of peace, and lacking in technical expertise. ONUSAL's "staff members were nervous about the political alignment of many of the NGOs and were struck by the poor technical capacity of many in the human rights organizations."[65] Still, in the waning months of ONUSAL's presence in the country, the Human Rights Division repeatedly emphasized the importance of the NGOs historically and in the current context, and provided useful training sessions for their staff. Unfortunately, this was a case of "too little, too late." According to Teresa Whitfield, "[T]he mission's inability to develop a more productive relationship with Salvadoran human rights NGOs remains one of its greatest failings. Above all, it was a waste of the important resource for institution building that the NGOs represented."[66]

The human rights groups continued to raise their voices on behalf of victims of human rights violations. The nongovernmental Human Rights

65. Whitfield, "Staying the Course," 177.
66. Ibid., 178; for a detailed account of the relationship between ONUSAL and the human rights NGOs, see Lawyers Committee, *Improvising History*, 93–102.

Commission (CDHES) was the only institution to present a proposal to implement the Truth Commission's recommendation to establish a reparations fund. The Central American University's Human Rights Institute (IDHUCA) was a constant critic of ONUSAL's Human Rights Division and the first National Counsel for the Defense of Human Rights, urging both to fulfill their mandates. During the tenure of National Counsel Victoria Velásquez de Avilés, IDHUCA worked closely with her office on the investigation of several high-profile murder cases in which police or former police were either implicated or had botched the investigation. Frustrated by the inadequacies of the Salvadoran investigation and constant harassment of the García-Prieto family, IDHUCA and the family presented a petition to the Inter-American Commission on Human Rights—one of the first to be filed about postwar human rights violations in El Salvador. The combined efforts of the National Counsel's office, IDHUCA, and the involvement of the IACHR led Salvadoran authorities to reopen the investigation to determine who else participated in and masterminded the crime.

After the war's end, one of the oldest Salvadoran human rights organizations, Socorro Jurídico Cristiano, founded by Archbishop Romero, closed its doors. A number of NGOs that had been active during the war, under the leadership of Tutela Legal, the Legal Aid Office of the Archdiocese, eventually joined forces with some of the newer groups in an effort to preserve historic memory. In 1998 they enlisted the support of San Salvador's mayor, elected the previous year on an FMLN ticket, and, in a downtown San Salvador park, laid the first stone of a future monument to the civilian victims of the war.

Some testimonies presented to the Truth Commission in 1992 mentioned children who had disappeared or been taken away during military operations. Although the Truth Commission was unable to address these cases, families whose children remained missing joined forces and eventually formed the Association in Search of Missing Children (*Asociación Pro-Búsqueda de Niñas y Niños Desaparecidos*). Through painstaking searches of orphanage and adoption records in El Salvador, as well as word of mouth, the association had succeeded in locating more than one hundred children by the end of 1999, with active files on hundreds of other cases.[67] The children were found in El Salvador, in a variety of European countries, and in the United States. Almost all the Salvadoran children have been eager to learn of their

---

67. See Tina Rosenberg, "What Did You Do in the War, Mama?" *New York Times Magazine*, February 7, 1999.

roots and at least visit their families of origin. In March 1998, the National Counsel for the Defense of Human Rights issued a resolution calling on the Salvadoran military and Salvadoran authorities to investigate these cases and prosecute those responsible.

Two NGOs formed in the late 1980s, the Salvadoran Institute for Legal Studies (IEJES) and the Foundation for the Study of Applied Law (FESPAD), played important roles in the transition period. These were not human rights organizations in the traditional sense; both had a track record of making proposals and contributing to the national discussion of different issues. IEJES involved itself in a broad range of issues, including some aspects of constitutional and electoral reform as well as community legal education. FESPAD focused on promoting popular legal education at all levels, improving community access to justice, particularly to defend social and economic rights, and presenting proposals for constitutional and legislative reform, notably in matters related to the judiciary. As new laws were approved, FESPAD offered training courses to private lawyers. In an innovative partnership, FESPAD worked closely with the advocacy training project of the Washington Office on Latin America to raise concerns about police accountability, both within the PNC and to NGOs and community groups. FESPAD also monitored implementation of the criminal justice reforms.

NGOs that focused on women's and children's rights took on new prominence in the postwar period. International donors were eager to support their work. NGOs formed to focus on women's issues played critical roles in the postwar years by advocating passage of the new Family Code and educating different sectors about its contents. The new Family Code and a new domestic violence law have, for the first time, made it possible for women to obtain restraining orders against their abusers. Domestic violence continues to be a major problem in El Salvador. Women's NGOs have played a key role in raising consciousness about domestic violence, winning approval of the new laws, and assisting women in using their protections. One of the women's NGOs encouraged mothers who were not receiving child support to organize as "*madres demandantes*" and insist that the State Counsel pursue "deadbeat dads." As a result of this initiative, the names of public officials who had not met their child support obligations were published in the newspapers. Other NGOs focused on children's rights, including the provisions of the new Juvenile Offenders Law.

During 1996 several human rights NGOs also became involved in a landmark effort to monitor conditions in off-shore manufacturing factories (*maquilas*), as part of an innovative agreement reached between the Gap, a U.S. clothing manufacturer, and the National Labor Committee, which focuses on workers' rights in overseas export production factories.

As Salvadoran human rights NGOs struggled to redefine their roles, they spread themselves thin with limited technical resources. Thus, although human rights NGOs began to explore important new initiatives in the years immediately following the peace accords, they were unable to establish the rights of family members to discover the truth about what happened to their relatives and obtain reparations. During the same period, when national institutions lacked the political will to carry out reforms and international leverage was lacking, the NGOs were unable to exert the necessary public pressure and develop constituencies for institutional reform.[68] Nonetheless and despite their technical limitations, particularly in the legal area, Salvadoran human rights NGOs continue to play a critical role in the postwar period.

68. Whitfield, "Staying the Course," 178.

6

JUSTICE REFORM IN THE POSTWAR YEARS

Five years after the peace accords were signed, UN Secretary-General Kofi Annan deplored "persistent deficiencies in the judicial system which have contributed to its lack of credibility with the general population."[1] Incompetent and corrupt judges remained on the job. Constitutional justice remained inefficient. The criminal justice system continued to operate slowly, exacerbating the problem of prisoners without sentences and prison conditions in general. Administrative functions remained concentrated in the Supreme Court, and an adequate judicial career structure had not been implemented.[2] Proposed reforms intended to address these and other deficiencies derived from negotiated constitutional reforms, from the U.S.-supported judicial reform effort, and from recommendations of the Truth Commission and ONUSAL's Human Rights Division. This chapter looks at advances in judicial reform as well as obstacles that hindered the implementation of many proposed reforms and their implications for building the rule of law.

During this period, both the United States and the United Nations played important and sometimes controversial roles. The San José Accord on

1. Report of the Secretary-General, July 1997, par. 22.
2. Ibid.

Human Rights mandated the UN mission to support the country's judicial authorities, monitor due process violations, and strengthen Salvadoran institutions entrusted with the protection of human rights. ONUSAL's Human Rights Division seemed well equipped to make a contribution in this area since it had a number of experienced South American lawyers on its staff who had experience with similar civil law systems. In December 1992 a Peruvian judge and law professor joined the UN mission to work on institution building and the administration of justice.

The mission's role in verifying the human rights situation—its casework—provided it with an unparalleled opportunity to understand how the legal system actually functioned and to diagnose its failings. Yet ONUSAL failed to make a significant contribution in this area. In its reports, UN experts cited international standards and principles as guidelines that should be applied to Salvadoran justice.[3] United Nations recommendations, including those of the Truth Commission, focused on two major areas: the judiciary (guaranteeing its independence, purging its ranks, and improving its quality) and criminal justice reform (improving due process protections and criminal investigations).

In 1993 the European Union provided a $500,000 grant to ONUSAL to train judges and police and to prepare training manuals for them. Little follow-up was provided to this effort because none of the three Salvadoran institutions involved assumed ownership of the initiative.[4] Trainers found that Salvadoran judges and police were ignorant not only of international human rights requirements but also of the dictates of the Salvadoran constitution and laws. Together with the PDDH, ONUSAL's Human Rights Division produced a practical handbook for Salvadoran judges and lawyers

3. The instruments cited by the UN included the International Covenant on Civil and Political Rights; the American Convention on Human Rights; the Body of Principles for the Protection of All Persons Under Any Form of Detention or Imprisonment, adopted by the General Assembly in its resolution 43/173 of December 9, 1988; Guidelines on the Role of Prosecutors adopted by the Eighth United Nations Congress on the Prevention of Crime and the Treatment of Offenders, held at Havana, Cuba, from 27 August to 7 September 1990 (A/CONF.144/28); Basic Principles on the Role of Lawyers, adopted by the Eighth United Nations Congress on the Prevention of Crime and the Treatment of Offenders; Model Protocol for a Legal Investigation of Extra-Legal, Arbitrary, and Summary Executions in Manual on the Effective Prevention and Investigation of Extra-Legal, Arbitrary, and Summary Executions, United Nations office at Vienna, Center for Social Development and Humanitarian Affairs, New York, 1991; Code of Conduct for Law Enforcement Officials, adopted by the General Assembly in its resolution 34/169.

4. See Lawyers Committee for Human Rights, *Improvising History: A Critical Evaluation of the United Nations Observer Mission in El Salvador* (New York: Lawyers Committee for Human Rights, 1995), 102–6.

on international instruments on civil and political rights. For the new civilian police, ONUSAL prepared a guide to the norms and procedures of the National Civilian Police and, once PNC leadership was amenable, met weekly with the PNC leaders to discuss violations by PNC agents.[5]

Because of Supreme Court President Gutiérrez Castro's poor relations with the UN mission, exacerbated by the Truth Commission's strong condemnation of him, ONUSAL's Human Rights Division had little possibility of engaging in substantive work with the judiciary until a new Supreme Court was named in July 1994.

Although AID's judicial reform efforts were under way long before the peace accords were signed, the peace process and the attention it focused on the need for judicial reform created a more "propitious climate for change."[6] The official agreement for "Judicial Reform II" was signed in September 1992 with the reform of Salvadoran criminal justice as its main focus. The project called for the development of a coordination of justice sector institutions, the Coordinating Commission for the Justice Sector (originally composed of the president of the Supreme Court, Minister of Justice, Attorney General, and Chief State Counsel).

The Judicial Reform II (JRII) project set an ambitious agenda designed to: (1) strengthen Salvadoran support to justice sector reform (through technical assistance, analytic studies, conferences, public education, observation visits, etc.); (2) expand the reform agenda by identifying, analyzing, and eliminating the legal and political barriers to improvement of respect for procedural guarantees, the equality of all citizens before the law, and access to justice (incorporating lawyers, law faculties, the private sector, political groups, and leaders in the analysis and identification of problems and the formulation of responses); and (3) strengthen the institutional capacity to carry out reforms. To facilitate the execution of the projection and improve coordination among justice sector institutions, the Technical Implementing Unit (*Unidad Técnica Ejecutora*) (UTE) was created under the Ministry of Justice. In 1993 the UTE prepared a five-year plan for the justice sector (*"Plan Quinquenal del Sector de Justicia"*), which described a series of ambitious goals for Judicial Reform II, including a substantial reduction in the backlog of criminal and civil cases and the number of pretrial detainees; legal reforms to enhance due process guarantees; and enhanced public

5. Ibid., 107

6. René Hernández Valiente, "Prologo" to Francisco Eliseo Ortiz Ruiz, *Diez Años de Reforma Judicial en El Salvador (1985–1995)*, (San Salvador: Fundación Friedrich Ebert, 1997), 14.

knowledge and understanding of the law, the role of justice sector institutions, and expectations that decisions will be made justly and in a timely fashion. The plan included specific objectives and dates by which they were to be achieved.[7]

Many in the governing ARENA party espoused a commitment to judicial reform, but their concerns were often more closely tied to the need for *seguridad jurídica* (a stable legal climate for foreign investment) than safeguards for individual rights. They understood the need to enhance judicial independence and overcome corrupt practices for economic and social development so that international investors would not fear arbitrary court decisions. Many also understood the importance of having a judiciary capable of ensuring that the other branches of government would comply with the constitution and laws. Nonetheless, outside the Ministry of Justice there was little support for strengthening the protection of individual rights in the face of a burgeoning crime rate.

Although draft legislation to replace the existing Criminal Procedures and Penal Codes was basically prepared, the leadership of the reform effort made a strategic decision to focus first on the passage and implementation of the new Family Code and Juvenile Offenders Law. At the same time, the project continued to work on criminal justice reform.

With $15 million allocated for JRII and extensive experience to build on from its prior effort, the U.S.-funded project was well situated to play a key role in promoting reforms. Because of problems encountered in implementing its earlier project, AID had begun working through an institutional contractor in late 1990. Most of the projects under JRII were implemented by the contractor under the leadership of Costa Rican lawyer Jorge Obando. The peace accords created a window of opportunity for carrying out fundamental reforms, yet much of the impetus in certain areas, including judicial reform, came from outside. Many of the reforms recommended by the Truth Commission came either from UN proposals during the negotiations or from ongoing efforts of the U.S.-funded criminal justice reform effort with its numerous (mostly Latin American) consultants. Reform efforts encountered institutional and political resistance, accusations that new laws had been manufactured by foreigners and were appropriate for conditions in Switzerland but not in crime-plagued El Salvador, and a generally poorly prepared legal community. Some key recommendations have never been heeded, while the implementation of others has been slow, inadequate, or

7. Ortiz Ruiz, *Diez Años de Reforma Judicial*, 83–88.

both. Nonetheless, some progress is now visible, including the enactment and implementation of a series of new codes.

The postwar years have shown that reforming the justice system and building the rule of law are enterprises fraught with difficulties even when substantial political will to carry out reforms exists and international assistance is available. In retrospect, many of the strategies employed raise questions for their apparent failure to address critical problems, poor coordination of efforts, and the failure to build a strong constituency for reform.

The Supreme Court and Judicial Governance

The holdover Supreme Court (1989–94) remained an obstacle to reform throughout its tenure. At times the insistence on the replacement of the Supreme Court may have seemed to prioritize changing people over reforming institutions. Yet the continued reign of Supreme Court president Gutiérrez Castro proved a major obstacle to institutional reform. He fought efforts to make the new Judiciary Council truly independent.[8] Furthermore, once the new Judiciary Council was in place, the Supreme Court repeatedly obstructed its work by refusing to allow it to replace the head of the Judicial Training School (a Gutiérrez Castro crony) and urging judges not to cooperate with its evaluation efforts. Despite pronouncements to the contrary, no serious effort to clean out the judiciary was undertaken.

The Supreme Court's hostility to the peace accords and to ONUSAL meant that the judiciary did not take advantage of ONUSAL's presence in the country. A framework agreement signed between the court and ONUSAL in 1993 yielded no concrete cooperation measures. Throughout Gutiérrez Castro's tenure, Dr. Juan Mateu Llort remained head of the Forensic Institute. In 1992 the Argentine Forensic Anthropology Team, in collaboration with the Forensic Institute, excavated one of the sites of the El Mozote massacre and found that the vast majority of the remains unearthed belonged to young children. As soon as the Argentines left the country,

8. The Supreme Court promptly presented proposed legislation that would have maintained its control over the Judiciary Council. After the Assembly designated a technical subcommission to prepare compromise enabling legislation for the new Judiciary Council, the Supreme Court's representative worked with ARENA's representative to limit the scope of reforms and retain considerable Supreme Court control. See Margaret Popkin, *El Salvador's Negotiated Revolution: Prospects for Legal Reform* (New York: Lawyers Committee for Human Rights, 1993), 11–15.

however, Dr. Llort announced that their work had actually proven that the dead at El Mozote were guerrilla combatants. ONUSAL noted that Dr. Llort gave "unsolicited opinions" and failed to carry out judicially ordered autopsies in a timely fashion.[9] Judicial appointments were also affected by the failure to replace the court.

Knowledgeable observers credit Gutiérrez Castro with having wielded his considerable power in the Assembly to prevent the approval of a constitutional reform proposed in April 1994 (to implement a Truth Commission recommendation) that would have taken away the Supreme Court's authority to name lower court judges and judicial employees. Gutiérrez Castro opposed some proposals to reform criminal procedures and sabotaged others by insisting on unworkable alternatives.

After a lengthy impasse and public recriminations on all sides, the Legislative Assembly unanimously elected a new Supreme Court in June 1994. The Truth Commission's condemnation of the prior court and the new constitutional formula for selecting the justices allowed the election of a court that represented a clear break from the past. The new justices reflected an unprecedented ideological pluralism, with the majority chosen for their professional merits rather than their identification with a particular political party. The new court claimed to take seriously its responsibility to confront many of the problems identified by the Truth Commission and ONUSAL— including purging the judiciary, addressing the problem of prisons crowded with pretrial detainees, and backlogs in case resolution.

Although the new Supreme Court moved too slowly for many, it cautiously took steps to begin a new era. The Constitutional Chamber began to issue some important rulings. Among these was a finding that a San Salvador municipal regulation limiting the time and place of public demonstrations violated the constitution. In some of its rulings, the court cited international human rights standards.

Despite important advances, problems within the judiciary continued to hamper efforts to build the rule of law. The new Supreme Court faced the thorny problem of improving a very mediocre judiciary and overcoming entrenched corruption and inefficiency. By the end of Chief Justice Domingo Méndez's three-year term in 1997, public opinion revealed widespread dissatisfaction with progress in reforming the administration of justice. An

9. See Report of the Director of the Human Rights Division of the United Nations Observer Mission in El Salvador (ONUSAL) covering the period from March 1 to June 30, 1994, UN Doc. A/49/281, S/1994/886 (July 28, 1994), pars. 71–74. (11th Human Rights Report.)

opinion survey carried out in 1996 found that more than fifty percent of those responding said they were totally dissatisfied or little satisfied with the way in which the Supreme Court had been functioning.[10]

Concentration of Attributes in the Supreme Court: Internal Independence of the Judiciary

In the postwar period, different Salvadoran institutions and the UN insisted that the powers of the Supreme Court should be limited to protect the internal independence of the judiciary. Reforms to ensure the external independence, or corporate autonomy, of the judicial branch were included in the peace accords. Despite these reforms, a 1996 poll found that 60 percent of those surveyed believed that Salvadoran judges were subject to political control.[11] Because efforts to enhance the internal independence of the judiciary were frustrated during the peace negotiations, the Supreme Court remained responsible for appointing and disciplining lower court judges and all judicial employees, licensing lawyers and notaries to practice, and supervising these professions.

Resistance to these kinds of changes is hardly unique to El Salvador. The Chilean Supreme Court in the postdictatorial era successfully thwarted attempts to establish a judicial council that would have included individuals outside the judiciary and would have played a significant role in judicial governance.[12]

The Truth Commission placed great emphasis on this theme: "One of the most glaring deficiencies which must be overcome in the Salvadoran judicial system is the tremendous concentration of functions in the Supreme Court of Justice, and in its President in particular, as the body which heads the judiciary."[13] The commission recommended the consideration of further constitutional reforms so that: (1) judges would not be appointed and removed by the Supreme Court but by an independent National Council of the Judiciary; (2) each judge would be responsible for administering his or her court's resources and would be accountable to the National Council of the Judiciary; and (3) an independent body and not the Supreme Court would

10. IUDOP, "Los salvadoreños opinan sobre el sistema de justicia y los derechos humanos," August 21, 1996.

11. Ibid.

12. See Comisión Andina, *Chile: Sistema Judicial y Derechos Humanos* (May 1995), 25–30.

13. *From Madness to Hope*, 181.

have responsibility for licensing lawyers and notaries and suspending or imposing sanctions on them.

ONUSAL's Human Rights Division attributed widespread due process violations principally to "the lack of independence of the judiciary, something which can only be overcome through urgent and essential constitutional reforms so as to change the Supreme Court's present vertical organization which constrains the independence of judges and magistrates and relativizes the freedom of judgement which they are supposed to have and to exercise in the fair administration of justice."[14] ONUSAL went so far as to say that the very success of the judicial reform rested on the elimination of this vertical structure:

> Without a truly independent judiciary, whose administrative structure does not compromise the judges' freedom and independence of judgement and the lawyers' action, the entire legal reform effort being promoted by the Ministry of Justice itself would be devoid of meaning. Modern legislation which provides basic guarantees of human rights cannot be effective if it is administered by a judiciary which has the power to influence the conduct of judges and lawyers either directly or indirectly.[15]

A 1994 ONUSAL survey found that more than one third of lower court judges listed pressure from their superiors as the main problem affecting their independence.[16]

Some U.S. officials suggested that the focus on this issue reflected the widespread antipathy to former Supreme Court President Gutiérrez Castro, who was widely held to have abused his power. Gutiérrez Castro's actions brought this issue to the forefront, but the problem was a structural one that prejudiced the independence of the judiciary and the legal profession regardless of who headed the Supreme Court.

The Truth Commission's recommendations for further constitutional reform did not meet with great receptivity. The government insisted that the issue of constitutional reform had been laid to rest during the 1991 Mexico negotiations; and with elections for the presidency, the legislature, and local governments taking place in March 1994, the pre-electoral period was not an appropriate time to consider further reforms. UN officials continued to

14. ONUSAL, 10th Human Rights Report, par. 75.
15. Ibid., par. 141.
16. ONUSAL, 12th Human Rights Report, par. 13.

insist on the importance of compliance with these binding recommendations and the need to initiate the reform process before the incumbent legislature left office so that the reforms might take effect before 1997. To take effect, constitutional reforms must be passed by one legislature and ratified by a two-thirds majority in the successor legislature. Salvadoran lawyers began to focus on the issue, and even the traditionally very conservative Lawyers Federation endorsed the concept of separating some administrative functions from the Supreme Court. Seeing their own interests potentially threatened by arbitrary Supreme Court actions, many conservative lawyers became convinced that it would be beneficial to limit the court's power over lower court judges and the legal profession.

Although President Cristiani never dropped his public opposition to the reforms, he authorized the Ministry of Justice to carry out a technical study and propose reforms to be presented to the Assembly after the March 1994 elections. Influential members of the business community with leadership positions in the ARENA party saw the importance of an independent judiciary and also wanted to take advantage of the call for constitutional reform to promote other reforms affecting economic interests. COPAZ, the coordinating body established to oversee implementation of the peace accords, advised the legislature that it favored a constitutional reform that would transfer responsibility for naming and dismissing judges from the Supreme Court to the National Council on the Judiciary and another that would transfer responsibility for licensing and disciplining the legal profession to a professional oversight body.[17]

Despite this apparently overwhelming consensus, the legislature failed to approve the proposed reforms to remove administrative responsibility for the lower courts from the Supreme Court. Several factors contributed to thwarting the reform effort. The reforms were introduced into the legislature only days before the end of its term. Dozens of other proposals were also presented, shifting some legislators' attention away from the judiciary. Knowledgeable observers also credited former Supreme Court president Gutiérrez Castro and the former Assembly president with using their considerable influence within the ARENA party to prevent passage of these reforms. The only potential change in the Supreme Court's power would have come from a reform to end its oversight of the legal profession. A new National Council on Lawyers and Notaries was to be assigned this function.[18]

17. Letter from COPAZ to the leadership of the Legislative Assembly, April 6, 1994. The content of this letter was reprinted in *La Prensa Gráfica* of April 14, 1994.
18. Salvadoran Legislative Assembly, Acuerdo de Reformas Constitucionales, April 29, 1994.

Members of the Supreme Court and the Legislative Assembly maintained that some of the reforms passed were ill-conceived, while others suffered from technical defects. After considerable debate and pressure from the UN, the successor (1994–97) legislature finally acted on the reforms, declining to ratify a number of those passed by its predecessor. Some of the reforms passed in 1994 were reformulated to reflect technical or substantive changes. To become part of the constitution, these would need to be ratified by the 1997–2000 Assembly. The reform designed to shift disciplinary power over lawyers to a new body was among those reformulated.

The 1994–1997 legislature again chose not to amend the constitution to transfer disciplinary powers over the judiciary from the Supreme Court to the Judiciary Council. Thus, although important sectors of the Salvadoran legal community, international experts, and the UN had identified this issue as critical to the independence of the judiciary, Salvadoran legislators failed to address it. The legal profession became increasingly conscious of the need for these reforms, but legislators remained susceptible to the machinations of the forces opposed to them. The issue of judicial governance had not been resolved and remained a pressing problem despite the improved image of the Supreme Court.

The National Judiciary Council

Through the peace accords, El Salvador opted for the establishment of an independent judiciary council as a mechanism to improve the independence and quality of the judiciary. In this respect, the peace accords sought to improve on a concept already enshrined in the 1983 constitution. Enabling legislation finally passed in 1989 ensured that the Supreme Court would have absolute control over the Judiciary Council.[19] The 1991 constitutional reforms established that the council would be independent and sought to broaden its composition and mandate. The council was given responsibility for proposing candidates for the Supreme Court, appellate and trial courts, and justices of the peace. After considerable disagreement and protracted negotiations, the Assembly passed compromise legislation to implement the constitutional reform in December 1992.[20] While the new law was a

19. See Popkin, *Prospects for Legal Reform*, 9.
20. Ley del Consejo Nacional de la Judicatura, Decree 414, D.O., Tomo No. 318, January 13, 1993. For a more detailed description of the background of this legislation and the debate about the Judiciary Council's role, see Popkin, *Prospects for Legal Reform*, 9–17.

significant advance over the 1989 legislation, it did not fully guarantee the independence of the council. The Judiciary Council was to be composed of eleven members who would represent the Supreme Court, appellate magistrates, first instance judges, practicing lawyers, law professors, and the Public Ministry. Council members were to be selected by a two-thirds vote of the Assembly, which would choose from slates of three candidates. The council was also given responsibility for evaluating the performance of judges at all levels except the Supreme Court. The council's evaluations were to be used by the Supreme Court in deciding on promotions, disciplinary measures, and dismissal.

In recent years countries throughout Latin America have been struggling to determine how best to administer judicial governance. El Salvador was one of only three Latin American countries to have established an independent judiciary council to administer the judicial career (the others were Colombia and Paraguay). Some countries relied on bodies attached to the Supreme Court, while in many others the Supreme Court retained full responsibility for judicial administration.[21] The solution proposed by the Justice Strengthening Commission in Guatemala, mandated by the peace accords, would create a permanent tribunal, made up of a mixture of appellate and lower-court judges, to look into complaints against judges.[22]

In discussing judicial councils in Europe and Latin America, Professor Zaffaroni noted that most of the Latin American councils are "deceptive councils" (*consejos engañosos*) primarily because their composition does not democratically represent the judiciary or because of limitations in their mandate. Zaffaroni defined three stages in the development of judicial selection methods in the continental European tradition. In the "arbitrary/empirical" stage, judges were appointed according to the whims of politicians responsible for their selection. Since the end of the nineteenth century, European judges have been chosen on a competitive basis still rare in Latin America. Democratic judiciaries (*magistraturas democráticas de derecho*) emerged in Europe after World War II. Because their judiciaries had been complicit in the horrors of World War II and the Holocaust, Europeans were forced to recognize that an undemocratic judiciary poses a threat to democracy.

21. Jorge Obando, "Reform of the Justice Sector," in *Governance and Democratic Development in Latin America and the Caribbean* (New York: UN Development Program [1997]), 124.
22. Comisión de Fortalecimiento de la Justicia, *Una Nueva Justicia para la Paz: Resumen Ejecutivo del Informe Final de la Comisión de Fortalecimiento de la Justicia* (Guatemala, April 1998), 35.

Finally, in the wake of World War II (and in the 1970s after the end of fascist rule in Spain and Portugal), two institutions were adopted in Europe: constitutional courts and judicial councils designed to govern the entire judiciary.[23]

Not all those involved in judicial reform efforts in El Salvador agreed that the Judiciary Council should be given responsibility for judicial governance. AID's program manager in El Salvador argued that the council was not an appropriate body to take on all the administrative functions of the judicial system.[24] She maintained that transferring responsibility to the Judiciary Council would not eliminate politics and favoritism from decision making and that actions of the new council reinforced this view. She attributed most of the pressure for these changes to the UN, the United States, and other international players. While these criticisms were well founded, they failed to address the underlying problem resulting from Supreme Court responsibility for both functions. The council as constituted *was* relatively weak. This did not necessarily mean that the concept was erroneous, but that the mandate and composition of the council needed to be strengthened.[25] It would be a mistake to think, however, that shifting responsibility for judicial governance to the Judiciary Council would automatically guarantee judicial independence and accountability.

In a 1993 report, ONUSAL criticized the law governing the Judiciary Council as inadequate to guarantee its independence. It cited the need to give the council budgetary independence from the Supreme Court and noted that procedures for selecting council members to represent different sectors were not adequately regulated. For example, the legislature selected representatives of appellate and first instance judges from a Supreme Court list of those with most seniority rather than a democratic election by the judges and magistrates themselves. ONUSAL recommended that members of the council instead be selected directly by the institutional or social sector they represented. It called for further constitutional reforms so that the Judiciary Council, rather than the Supreme Court and the Legislative Assembly, would be responsible both for selecting and appointing magistrates and judges.[26]

23. Eugenio Raúl Zaffaroni, "Dimensión política de un poder judicial democrático," Comisión Andina de Juristas, Boletín no. 37 (June 1993).

24. Linn Hammergren, "El Salvador's National Judicial Council," paper presented at the First Global Rule of Law Conference sponsored by the National Center for State Courts and the U.S. Agency for International Development, Washington, D.C., July 13–15, 1994.

25. Zaffaroni, "Dimensión política," 21, 31.

26. ONUSAL, Sixth Human Rights Report, par. 224.

In this area, as in several others, the UN might be charged with having attempted to impose its own views. Valid arguments exist for and against entrusting the Judiciary Council with the entire judicial appointment process. A mixed process, where one institution nominates and another selects, also has its adherents. A review of judicial governance in Latin America and Europe suggests many possible configurations and the need to improve most of them. Experience suggests that no model will guarantee judicial independence and accountability in all contexts.

Given the lackluster performance of the new Judiciary Council, resistance to entrusting it with additional powers was understandable. In 1995 the Supreme Court viewed the council as unprepared to take on all those responsibilities.[27] In subsequent years, the council has shown greater capacity to take on increased responsibility. Former CNJ head Jorge Eduardo Tenorio was elected Chief Justice of the Supreme Court in 1997. He vowed to turn over additional responsibilities to the Judiciary Council. Reforms to make this possible were again under discussion. The council itself proposed reforms so that the Supreme Court would no longer have representation on it. A reformed CNJ law, passed in January 1999 over the objections of the judiciary, excluded all representatives of the judiciary from the Judiciary Council and reduced its membership from eleven to six.[28] Judges protested their exclusion from the council and challenged the constitutionality of the new law.

Moving toward a professionally competent, accountable, and functionally independent judiciary is an essential precondition for the success of other justice system reforms. The pertinent question for international actors was how they could assist Salvadorans in taking advantage of the opening afforded by the peace process to move toward the goal of better judicial selection and enhanced independence of the judiciary. The constitution had been reformed and the National Judiciary Council given a greater role in the selection of judges. The council's capacity needed to be improved and the Career Judicial Service Law revised to establish objective criteria for the selection and promotion of judges. International donors could have placed greater emphasis on the need for advances in these areas to ensure the necessary underpinnings for a more independent and professional judiciary. The complexity of these issues suggests the need for a thorough, broad-based,

27. Author's interview with René Hernández Valiente, magistrate of the Constitutional Chamber, vice president of the Court, San Salvador, March 30, 1995.
28. Legislative Decree No. 536, January 27, 1999, published in *Diario Oficial* No. 30, Tomo 342, February 12, 1999.

and honest Salvadoran study of different options for judicial governance to help to develop an effective system that would guarantee the independence of the Salvadoran judiciary.

Appropriate legal reforms require a legislative branch with some under-standing of the issues at stake. Otherwise, legislatures may refuse to pass legislation after years of work to prepare it or, as in El Salvador, pass legis-lation without seriously considering its appropriateness and potential alter-natives. Thus, in a ten-year period, the Salvadoran legislature passed three quite different enabling laws for the National Judiciary Council. The first provided for complete Supreme Court domination, the second included limited judicial branch participation, and the third eliminated the judiciary from the council. Since many countries are struggling with issues of judicial independence, judicial governance, and the composition and role of judiciary councils, Salvadorans might have benefited from discussions with experts who have observed how different models function for judicial selection, evaluation of judges, discipline, and generally supervising the judicial career. International donors might have aided this process by, for example, organiz-ing events at which speakers shared the lessons learned from experience with other judiciary councils.[29]

Evaluation of Judges and Cleaning Out the Judiciary

One of the most frequently cited obstacles to building the rule of law in El Salvador continues to be the unreliability of the judges themselves. In his five-year assessment of the peace process, the UN Secretary-General empha-sized this point:

> [T]he greatest failing in [the administration of justice] is the lack of efficacy in the process of vetting judges and officials who are dishon-est, incompetent or whose motivation has failed them. The Supreme Court of Justice and the National Council of the Judiciary have evaluated judges in a manner and at a pace which have not proved adequate to the gravity of the situation. The inability to make more substantial and bold progress in this endeavour represents a failure to comply with an indispensable condition for the structuring of a

29. See Linn Hammergren, "Fifteen Years of Judicial Reform in Latin America: Where We Are and Why We Haven't Made More Progress." http://darkwing.uoregon.edu/~caguirre/ hammergren.htm.

system which, together with an efficient police, would be capable of eradicating impunity and guaranteeing justice.[30]

The peace accords included neither a mechanism nor a timetable for cleaning out the judiciary. Well aware of the judiciary's poor reputation, the interparty commission set up during the peace negotiations had called for an evaluation process.[31] The constitutional reforms establishing the National Council of the Judiciary gave the new body responsibility for evaluating judges but no authority to take action based on those evaluations. This responsibility was still entrusted to the Supreme Court.

The Truth Commission, ONUSAL, and the Joint Group (see discussion below) all identified cleaning out the judiciary as critical to improving the administration of justice and respect for human rights. Cognizant that the peace accords had not addressed this issue, the Truth Commission called for reforming the Career Judicial Service Act to empower the Judiciary Council to carry out rigorous evaluations of judges so that only those who "have demonstrated judicial aptitude, efficiency and concern for human rights and offer every guarantee of independence, judicial discretion, honesty and impartiality in their actions may remain in the career judicial service."[32]

While the National Council of the Judiciary was not given authority to oversee the judiciary, new enabling legislation made the council responsible for carrying out evaluations of all lower court judges at least once a year or at the Supreme Court's request.[33] The evaluation was to focus on case management and judicial administration. However, ONUSAL pointed to "glaring omissions" related to the failure to take into account quality (as well as quantity) factors, professional qualifications, and concern for the human rights of the accused and victims.[34] After completing the evaluation, the Judiciary Council delivered its report to the Supreme Court, which, other

30. Report of the Secretary-General, July 1, 1997, par. 23.

31. Comisión Interpartidaria, Subcomisión de la administración de justicia, Primer Informe de la subcomisión de la administración de justicia, San Salvador, June 6, 1990, 6: "Because of the corruption and serious deficiencies in the administration of justice in the Judicial Branch, it is indispensable to proceed to review the actions of each one of the judges and magistrates and confirm in their posts only those who truly have judicial vocation surrounded by the guarantees of independence, judicial criteria, honesty and impartiality in their actions."

32. *From Madness to Hope*, 177.

33. Ley del Consejo Nacional de la Judicatura, Decree 414, D.O., Tomo No. 318, January 13, 1993, article 33. This provision bore considerable resemblance to provisions in the original legislation proposed by the Supreme Court in 1984. See CORELESAL, *Consejo Nacional de la Judicatura,* San Salvador, June 1988, 271ff.

34. ONUSAL, Sixth Human Rights Report, par. 226.

factors being equal, was to rely on the evaluations to determine promotions and take appropriate measures when the council's evaluations showed that a magistrate or judge's actions merited dismissal.[35]

The Judiciary Council's first evaluation met with resistance from the Supreme Court and judges who questioned the qualifications of the evaluators. Once the council's evaluations became public, judges protested that they had been denied the opportunity to defend themselves. In late 1994, the head of ONUSAL touched off a diplomatic incident when he described some judges on an ONUSAL list of forty-eight judges presented to the Supreme Court as "corrupt and shameless."[36] The court took umbrage, as did President Calderón Sol, while ONUSAL emphasized that it was only providing information that had been reported to its offices: how the data was to be used remained for the court to determine. The vice president of the Supreme Court maintained that most (30 of 48) cases listed by ONUSAL lacked any foundation.[37] The Salvadoran Lawyers Federation entered the fray with a petition to the Supreme Court arguing that the Judiciary Council's involvement in the evaluation process violated the Salvadoran constitution, which grants the Supreme Court exclusive authority over the lower courts.

The net effect of all the publicity was to increase public consciousness about the need to clean out the judiciary at the same time that judicial sensitivity to outside—particularly foreign—criticism of its conduct reached new heights. The Supreme Court insisted on the need to move slowly and ensure that accused judges were afforded adequate due process protections. In April 1995 the court formed an investigative division to look into charges of malfeasance and corruption. Under the new system, the Judiciary Council's findings from its evaluations were to be transmitted to the Supreme Court's Investigative Division for review and to allow judges accused of wrongdoing to present their defense.

In May 1997, near the end of Chief Justice Domingo Méndez's three-year term, the Supreme Court had removed a total of thirty-one judges (two were appellate magistrates, the remainder justices of the peace and trial court judges), while sanctioning a somewhat larger number with suspensions or transfers. In only one case was corruption cited as the reason for the action. The most commonly cited infractions were inexcusable ignorance, incapacity, and negligence.[38]

---

35. Ley del Consejo Nacional de la Judicatura, article 37.
36. *La Prensa Gráfica*, November 3, 1994.
37. Author's interview with René Hernández Valiente, San Salvador, March 30, 1995.
38. J. Michael Dodson and Donald W. Jackson, "Re-inventing the Rule of Law: Human Rights in El Salvador," *Democratization* 4 (Winter 1997): 110, 122.

Given the numbers involved—in 1995, 320 justices of the peace, 120 first instance judges, and 80 second instance magistrates—many observers faulted the Supreme Court for not acting more aggressively. Lower court judges nonetheless felt themselves under attack, especially when unofficial versions of the Judiciary Council's findings appeared in the press. Others pointed to the lack of qualified replacements available and stressed the need to improve the judiciary as a whole. The situation was not one in which simply weeding out a few rotten apples would resolve the judiciary's serious deficiencies.

Just as important as having a system for judicial vetting is the kind of evaluation system created and how it is implemented. The Chilean Supreme Court, for example, used its disciplinary power over lower court judges as a means to control them. Judges who applied criteria different from those established by the Supreme Court were given poor ratings. While the court remained under the domination of Pinochet appointees, efforts to introduce human rights criteria were largely stifled.

Thus, while it is fair to criticize the Supreme Court for its slowness in cleaning out the judiciary, such criticisms must be tempered by the need to carry out evaluations in a manner that does not further compromise judicial independence. In 1997 the Association of Women Judges indicated that unhappy litigants were using complaints to the Supreme Court as a means of attacking judges who had ruled against them. The judges felt themselves vulnerable to such attacks, particularly when the complaining party was a powerful figure or friend of Supreme Court justices. The court did not appear to have developed an effective mechanism to quickly weed out meritless charges brought to try to reverse unfavorable decisions. As long as the court remains directly responsible for judicial discipline and tenure, judges may find themselves in this awkward situation.

Respecting the constitutionally guaranteed corporate autonomy of the judiciary inevitably complicates the goal of cleaning out the judiciary or institutionalizing some kind of judicial accountability. During the Salvadoran peace process, the negotiators were well aware that the Supreme Court president, who headed the judiciary, would not have accepted any agreement that compromised its independence. The executive could commit the military and security forces to drastic changes precisely because of the president's role as commander-in-chief. The military itself was represented at the negotiating table. The military is traditionally a rigidly hierarchical institution, which should be subservient to the executive, not independent. Military officers serve in their commands until they are transferred or removed from their positions. They are, at least theoretically, subject to the decisions of the executive. This fundamental distinction explains why a special commission named by the executive could not review the records of individual judges as the Ad Hoc Commission did with military officers. Ignoring this distinction, in early 1997 the Public Security Council recommended the establishment of an "Ad Hoc" Commission for Judges. Legislators from across the political spectrum quickly rejected the idea.

The challenge remains, however, to develop effective mechanisms to remove from the judiciary those who are corrupt, ignorant, and abusive without undermining the necessary independence of the judiciary: to establish judicial accountability. According to Jorge Correa Sutil, the "challenge ... is to ensure the maximum independence of the judiciary, so long as it coordinates with other branches of government, ... is attuned to societal requirements, and operates with utmost transparency."[39] Judicial accountability goes beyond appointment, discipline, and removal mechanisms. It also involves the transparency of judicial processes, enabling and obliging judges to give reasoned justifications for their decisions and facilitating increased public knowledge and criticism of the judiciary's work.

Judicial Training and Selection

International experts working with ONUSAL were appalled by the professional level of judges in general. They found many judges unable to analyze cases and apply relevant law, unfamiliar with human rights norms and, to their dismay, provisions of the Salvadoran constitution. In this regard, the situation in El Salvador seemed far worse than that in many other Latin American countries where legal education and traditions had been stronger. Judicial decisions, like those in many Latin American countries, often adopted a literalist approach, with judges seeing themselves as merely enforcing the law. This view of a judge's role leads to ritualistic formalism, bureaucratic behavior, passivity, and renouncing the possibility of giving direction to the law. Salvadoran judges reflected many of the traits found in other judiciaries organized on an authoritarian model with a "trained resistance to change."[40]

The peace accords established that justices of the peace should, wherever possible, be lawyers and that candidates were to be nominated by the National Judiciary Council. Because justices of the peace had traditionally

39. Jorge Correa Sutil, "Modernization, Democratization, and Judicial Systems," in *Justice Delayed*, ed. Edmundo Jarquín and Fernando Carrillo (Washington, D.C.: Inter-American Development Bank, 1998), 106.
40. Luis Pásara, "Judicial Reform and Civil Society," in *Justice Delayed*, ed. Edmundo Jarquín and Fernando Carrillo (Washington, D.C.: Inter-American Development Bank, 1998), 88.

been appointed based on political party patronage criteria with little consideration for professional qualifications, this reform called for their wholesale replacement. After lengthy delays, new justices of the peace were appointed throughout the country. The replacement of these judges has yielded some positive results. According to ONUSAL observers, the new judges were generally more interested in acquiring professional skills and fulfilling their duties. Some foreign observers have questioned the decision to require judges with formal legal training for these posts rather than giving priority to respected citizens of a given locale. While in theory local justices of the peace may be preferable, in Salvadoran practice they had protected the interests of the powerful in their communities.

The peace accords highlighted the need for a new career judicial service law to regulate entry into the profession as well as advancement and supervision, so that training at the Judicial School would be mandatory and that merit, rather than favoritism, would be the basis for entry and advancement. A reformed law proposed by the Supreme Court was passed in the wake of the accords, but it did not substantially change past practices. In early 1993, in its Sixth Human Rights Report, ONUSAL noted that "no clear criteria have been established to ensure that selection procedures are basically uniform and that they are not so vague that they can be manipulated."[41] A year later ONUSAL reiterated its observations and urged that the new Career Judicial Service Act also establish the kind of training to be given by the Judicial Training School so that it could fulfill the objective established in the peace agreements of "promoting continuous improvement in the professional standard of judges and other judicial officials."[42]

According to the UN, "integral and sustained" training for judges, firmly anchored in international human rights norms, differed from training courses being offered in El Salvador. In late 1994, warning of the danger that old vices were likely to reappear, Diego García-Sayán, the outgoing head of ONUSAL's Human Rights Division, explained that the kind of training needed "goes far beyond lectures and specialization courses as it means working on the basic conception of what it means to be a judge or prosecutor in a democratic State."[43] The U.S. AID judicial reform project was sponsoring virtually all the judicial training in El Salvador at the time. The National Judiciary Council was slow to assume responsibility for the Judicial Training School. Instead, throughout 1995 AID's institutional contractor continued to provide

41. ONUSAL, Sixth Human Rights Report, par. 232.
42. ONUSAL, Tenth Human Rights Report, par. 93.
43. Evaluación de la situación de los derechos humanos, November 11, 1994 (evaluating progress over the more than two years of García-Sayán's leadership).

all resources necessary to run the school. Implicitly criticizing the U.S.-supported efforts, ONUSAL seemed to argue that more basic training was needed to overcome the weaknesses detected during their training effort.

In the postwar period, the poor quality of the judiciary could no longer be blamed on poor pay. Remuneration for judges rose substantially as a result of the constitutional amendment setting aside 6 percent of the national budget for the judiciary. In 1996 monthly judicial salaries ranged between $1,100 and $1,500 per month; Supreme Court justices earned $2,000 per month. By way of comparison, prosecutors earned from $500 to $700 per month, the attorney general received $1,500, and public defenders earned still less. With one judge for every 10,965 inhabitants (492 in all), El Salvador had one of the most favorable proportions of judges to citizens in any Central American country.[44] Although the judiciary continued to argue that it needed more money, its failings in the postwar period could no longer be attributed to an insufficient budget. Judicial salaries compared favorably to those of others in the legal profession and were comparable to those in Costa Rica. The peace negotiators' decision to set aside in the constitution 6 percent of the national budget for the judiciary and nothing for the institutions that make up the Public Ministry created an enormous imbalance in resources. In 1996 the Attorney General's office received some .02 percent of the national budget.

The mediocre performance of many Salvadoran judges and lawyers reflects a tradition of poor legal training. Serious initiatives to improve law schools, as well as postgraduate training for law professors and judges, were urgently needed. Given the difficulty of changing established practices, emphasizing training of new professionals who would be more likely to be open to new ideas became essential. Unfortunately, no programs were initiated in the law schools between 1993 and 1997. Between 1991 and 1993, AID had undertaken an effort to support curriculum reform and the preparation of new manuals of constitutional, criminal, family, and commercial law. Some twenty-five institutions offered law degrees, but the quality of most programs was notoriously poor. Even the better law faculties relied almost exclusively on part-time professors, practitioners who were contracted to teach a class. Legal education was beyond the scope of the peace accords, but it needed to be radically improved if the justice system was to be transformed. Without significant improvements in this area, cleaning out the judiciary would have a limited effect.

44. Arthur Mudge et al., *Reforma Judicial II Evaluación, Informe Final, Reforma Judicial II*, Project No. 519–0376 (Washington, D.C.: Management Systems International, January 1997), 2.

The Role of the Attorney General's Office

The public prosecutors' office faced the great challenge of taking on a key substantive role in fighting crime and ensuring the legality of the judicial process. Traditionally a weak and extraneous institution in a fundamentally inquisitorial system, the Attorney General's office, part of the Public Ministry, was ill-prepared for its new role. While assigning the Attorney General's office primary responsibility for criminal investigation, the peace accords had failed to introduce reforms of the institution or guarantee it greater resources. During the peace negotiations, proposals had included the Public Ministry within the 6 percent to be set aside for the judiciary; however, the peace accords referred only to the judicial branch. A proposed April 1994 constitutional reform that was rejected by the subsequent legislature would have allocated one third of that 6 percent (2 percent of the national budget) to the Public Ministry.

Unfortunately, the Attorney General's office was both unprepared for, and afraid of, its new relationship with the police. Unsurprisingly, the new police force was reluctant to recognize the prosecutors' new role. The weakness of the institution permitted the police to continue to act independently. Despite reforms stemming from the peace accords that give the Attorney General's office control over police investigations, long tradition dictated that police themselves directed investigations and decided what evidence to use. In early 1995 an ONUSAL study of PNC practices revealed that none of the units observed by ONUSAL even notified the Attorney General's office of their actions, a situation ONUSAL found "alarming."[45] Prosecutors rarely ventured out to crime scenes to oversee initial investigations.

In the postwar years, AID's reform effort focused training efforts on this institution and found it poorly organized, with inadequate supervision and leadership, no specialization either geographically or by type of crime, and without a system of coordination. No systems had been developed to organize case information and tracking. Prosecutors lacked job security and commitment to their mission.

Given the very serious inadequacies of the Attorney General's office, training could only be expected to produce limited results. The limited academic background of most prosecutors, the majority of whom were not law school graduates, further reduced the potential effectiveness of training. Still, according to the team that evaluated AID's Judicial Reform II project

45. ONUSAL, 13th Human Rights Report, par. 43.

in 1996, Checchi's consultants had achieved some important advances in changing the institutional mentality through a combination of training and institutional reforms. The evaluators felt that the long-term consultants brought in by Checchi had helped significantly through the successful use of case studies and by encouraging the institution to take key steps in the areas of reorganization, delegation, and reduction in micromanagement from above.[46] While some prosecutors appeared to be playing a more active role, the institution was far from consolidated. Prosecutors still earned approximately half the salary of judges and suffered from a lack of computers, telephones, and radios.

With the enactment of the new Criminal Procedure Code in December 1996, strengthening the Attorney General's office became a national priority, since the new code assigned major responsibility for criminal investigation and prosecution to that office. In 1996 the UN, through UNDP, also implemented a project to train prosecutors in sensitive criminal investigation techniques.

By early 1998, as the new code was being implemented, the prosecutor's office had begun to show important signs of independence. The prosecutor's office brought criminal charges against police investigators who were alleged to have carried out a sham investigation of the murder of radio newsannouncer Lorena Saravía, purportedly to protect those responsible for the murder. Still, the massive transformation called for by the new code overwhelmed the limited resources of the institution. Twenty prosecutors resigned in the first few weeks after the new codes went into effect, many opting for better-paid positions in the judiciary. As an institution that had not been overhauled through the peace accords, and with limited material and human resources, the Attorney General's office faced an uphill battle to carry out its key role in the new criminal justice system.

Protecting Individual Rights: Criminal Justice Reform

In El Salvador, as in other countries in Latin America, an emphasis on the protection of individual rights has often been blamed for high crime rates and the quick release of criminal suspects. Faced with very serious crime waves, postwar El Salvador and Guatemala have faced the thorny task of

---

46. Mudge et al., *Reforma Judicial II Evaluación,* 41–43.

effectively combating crime while new protections for individual rights are being implemented. Debates about the need to control crime inevitably seem to focus first on laws rather than crime prevention, controlling access to firearms, improving police training and deployment, or the socioeconomic factors responsible for high crime rates.

Many of those involved in criminal justice reform in Latin America have emphasized that democratic consolidation requires ensuring procedural fairness to the innocent and the guilty in addition to procedural efficiency in law enforcement against criminals.[47] Obtaining convictions at the cost of sacrificing fundamental rights can only undermine efforts to consolidate democracy.

In its renewed effort, which began in 1991, the AID judicial reform project emphasized criminal justice reform and the protection of individual rights. The draft legislation prepared under the auspices of the AID project sought to establish procedural safeguards against police and judicial abuses. The proposed reforms were designed to move away from the written, inquisitorial system, toward more adversarial, oral proceedings that would improve efficiency and transparency.

The ATJ, the law reform unit of the Ministry of Justice, proposed a series of immediate, urgent reforms, which fared poorly in terms of winning legislative approval in part because of opposition from the Supreme Court. President Cristiani's second justice minister, René Hernández Valiente, became convinced of the need for far-reaching legal reform with a strong emphasis on protecting individual rights.[48] The justice minister, President Cristiani, and others from the "modernizing sector" of the ARENA party maintained that judicial reform was necessary to promote foreign investment in the country as well as for democratic consolidation. Under Hernández Valiente's leadership and the direction of AID's contractor, teams of Salvadoran lawyers working with consultants from other Ibero-American countries prepared draft legislation to replace the Criminal Procedure and Penal Codes, as well as a Sentencing Law. During this period a new Family Code was finalized, and a Juvenile Offenders Law was prepared (the latter largely under UNICEF auspices).

47. Alejandro M. Garro, "Nine Years of Transition to Democracy in Argentina," *Columbia Journal of Transnational Law* 31 (1993): 33.
48. See René Hernández Valiente, "Justice in Central America in the Nineties," in *Justice and Development in Latin America and the Caribbean,* Seminar sponsored by the Inter-American Development Bank, San José, Costa Rica, Feb. 4–6, 1993 (Washington, D.C.: Inter-American Development Bank, 1994).

The period between 1991 and 1993 were dynamic years for the AID-funded judicial reform effort, since analyses of the system's defects led to drafts of proposed legislation and increased discussion of the issues with nongovernmental sectors. This work was thoroughly grounded in international human rights principles. It also relied on an Inter-American Human Rights Institute–sponsored study of criminal justice legislation throughout Latin America.[49]

Still, the judicial reform project remained primarily a governmental effort. Although AID now acknowledged the need to build societal support for judicial reform, only limited initiatives were undertaken. The Salvadoran bar associations, joined together in the Federation of Salvadoran Bar Associations, were a conservative and nonrepresentative group. (Bar membership was not obligatory, and the associations functioned largely as social clubs.) The one exception was the Center for Juridical Studies (CEJ), which addressed legal issues in a serious way and made several important proposals for reform of the governance of the judicial branch. The late 1980s saw the birth of two Salvadoran nongovernmental organizations that focused on justice issues and played an important role in promoting discussion of legal reform.[50] It was not until the peace process was well under way that nongovernmental organizations identified with the left were formally included in discussions of proposed reforms. These belated outreach efforts were spurred in large measure by foreign consultants brought in by AID's institutional contractor. These consultants understood the importance of engaging a range of actors in any successful judicial reform effort.

One unanticipated but important contribution of the foreign consultants, notably Alberto Binder of Argentina, was their own initiative to encourage law students to play an active role in the reform effort. Some students at the University of El Salvador were receptive and planned well-attended student conferences to discuss issues related to criminal justice reform and human rights. Students who worked with Binder also formed a center for the study of criminal law (CEPES), linked to existing centers in Argentina and

49. Eugenio Zaffaroni, *Sistemas penales y derechos humanos en América Latina* (San José, Costa Rica: Inter-American Institute for Human Rights, 1986). The Zaffaroni study, along with the Model Criminal Procedure Code for Ibero-America, drafted by another Argentine, Julio B. Maier, have influenced recent criminal justice reform throughout Latin America.

50. CESPAD, the Center for Studies of the Application of Law, was founded in 1988 and has played an active role in educating the public about legal issues and the need for fundamental legal and constitutional reform. IEJES, the Salvadoran Institute for Legal Studies, was formed in 1987 and, over several years, held many fora to promote discussion of a wide variety of legal and social issues.

Guatemala, under the auspices of FESPAD. CEPES and FESPAD played an important role in supporting the reform effort and educating the legal community about the reforms.

Another factor that contributed to creating a climate for reform was an editorial change at *La Prensa Gráfica*, one of the country's two leading newspapers. This traditionally conservative daily took up an editorial line that favored the peace process and the judicial reform effort. *La Prensa Gráfica* endorsed the peace process, the need for fundamental reforms, and a judicial system capable of protecting individual rights.[51]

Despite this relatively favorable climate, ONUSAL and the AID project failed to develop an effective working relationship in support of justice reform. This situation led to duplication of efforts instead of what could have been a productive coordination. The UN to a large extent failed to find effective ways to contribute to AID's substantial justice reform effort, instead undertaking parallel initiatives with insufficient coordination; while AID failed to take advantage of ONUSAL's greater contact with national reality. AID staff often did not take ONUSAL recommendations as constructive criticism, although they recognized that ONUSAL at times exerted an important moral force in favor of reform. ONUSAL staff were also dubious about AID's efforts, largely because of their knowledge of its historical role in the region. AID's consultants, many of whom were well known in the Latin American human rights movement, helped to overcome these preconceptions.

Throughout this period, high-profile cases continued to demonstrate the failings of the justice system and its susceptibility to military and other powerful pressures. The Jesuit murder investigation and trial (in September 1991) highlighted many weaknesses in the Salvadoran legal system, which were pointed out by international observers, many of whom came from other Latin American countries and Spain. Their observations indicated that the Salvadoran criminal justice system was notably deficient, even in comparison to other Latin American systems. Other prominent cases illustrated the incapacity of the legal system to carry out effective investigations, protect the rights of suspects, or convict those responsible for serious crimes.

An army major accused in 1989 of ordering the killing of ten civilian captives during a military operation in San Sebastian was never brought to trial.[52] He had reportedly threatened to testify that he had been following

51. This change in editorial policy was largely attributed to David Escobar Galindo, a member of the government's negotiating team who is a university president, poet, and leading intellectual.

52. In 1993, after the Truth Commission issued its report, he was granted amnesty.

orders from higher ranking officers. Shortly after the Jesuit murder trial, a jury acquitted thirteen former civil defense members for a series of murders that took place in the jurisdiction of Armenia in 1981, even though one actually confessed his involvement in court. A strong military presence around the courtroom and intimidation of the jurors appeared to have accounted for the verdicts. The kidnapping-for-profit case, in which powerful defendants won their freedom through the justice system's collusion, was key in illustrating the need for profound reform. In that case, the victims were themselves wealthy businessmen who belonged to the ARENA party. While these cases highlighted a deficient justice system, they fundamentally revealed an entrenched system of impunity with which the justice system, willingly or unwillingly, complied.

At the same time that military defendants continued to avoid conviction, others accused of political murders could be held for lengthy periods without any credible evidence against them. In one highly publicized case, a university student was held for more than three years on charges of murdering two right-wing ideologues. The only evidence linking Adolfo Aguilar Payés to the crimes was an extrajudicial confession that contradicted established facts in the case, such as the time of the killing and the type of vehicle involved. The original prosecutor on the case had urged dismissal of the charges, based on the lack of credible evidence. In what was seen as a clearly political decision by the judiciary, the judge, the appellate court, and the Supreme Court all agreed that the defendant should nonetheless stand trial. A jury trial finally took place after the defendant had engaged in a lengthy hunger strike resulting in his hospitalization and after the new National Counsel for the Defense of Human Rights had publicly chastised the judge for delaying the trial. The prosecution argued that the defendant should be convicted because military officers had been convicted the year before for killing the Jesuits. Following this logic, it was only fair to convict someone for the murder of a right-winger. Perhaps surprisingly in this context, the jury ultimately voted for acquittal.

As these cases suggest, the problems confronting the judiciary at the end of the war went far beyond the need for legal reforms. Its independence compromised and subject to political and military manipulation, the criminal justice system needed a major overhaul.

The proposed reforms encountered substantial resistance. After years of UN insistence that the criminal justice reforms were essential to the peace process, the legislature finally enacted the new Criminal Procedure Code in December 1996 and the Penal Code in April 1997. Both laws entered into effect in April 1998, and both, within the first few months, encountered multiple objections and demands for reform. While it would be premature to try to evaluate the effectiveness of the new laws, it may be useful to review some of the key issues and debates, most of which were aired during the five years leading up to the enactment of these laws.

Inadequate preparation of the terrain for reform as well as a highly formalistic legal system; institutional resistance; poorly trained police, judges, prosecutors, and defense attorneys; and a lack of societal commitment to reform led to problems in implementing the few reforms approved before 1996 and resistance to enacting others.

Although an agreement to undertake criminal justice reform was not included in the peace accords, the Truth Commission's recommendations explicitly endorsed the AID-sponsored effort to reform Salvadoran criminal justice carried out under the Ministry of Justice. Thus, approval of the Criminal Procedure and Penal Codes became an aspect of compliance with the peace accords, subject to UN oversight. Given the highly negative official reaction to the Truth Commission's report, then Minister of Justice Hernández Valiente, interviewed shortly after the report's release, suggested that the Truth Commission's embrace of his ministry's efforts might have done more harm than good. Over time, however, it became clear that the UN's ability to verify compliance with the Truth Commission recommendations provided an important impetus for ultimately enacting the reforms.

The difficult path to winning legislative approval and the effective campaign against the new criminal justice legislation suggest that other steps might have been helpful to try to develop a more solid consensus in favor of the reforms. It was not until 1996—five years after the Sancinetti team's evaluation—that AID arranged for an outside evaluation of the JRII project. An ongoing evaluation process might have suggested modifications in the JRII plan to win broader support.

A 1996 evaluation of JRII found that "consultations" with different sectors about the proposed reforms tended to be expositions with little opportunity for genuine discussion or input. Nor did most of those consulted make much effort to have input into the process, seeing it as belonging to the ATJ and foreign consultants. A law school dean interviewed in 1994 explained that since the code reform effort belonged to the AID project, there was no reason for the law school to become involved. The project made no real effort to bring in key sectors of civil society, such as the private sector and NGOs. One can also question the extent to which this would have been feasible, given that the private sector was hardly likely to endorse

reforms seen as offering excessive guarantees to criminal suspects. The evaluation team found that the project relied excessively on foreign consultants
and that many of the Salvadorans involved were relatively young.[53]

The UN designated the passage of the criminal justice legislation a key
outstanding commitment from the peace accords and played an essential
role in pushing the legislature to act on the codes. An emerging consensus
among political elites in favor of passage of the codes was suddenly threatened, however, when the Legislative Assembly passed draconian "emergency anticrime" legislation in March 1996.[54] This temporary legislation
threatened to derail the effort to pass the new Criminal Procedure and Penal
Codes, since the emergency law gave police a freer hand in law enforcement
and limited suspects' rights. It was passed in the wake of organized protests
against crime in eastern El Salvador and claimed to respond to public clamor
about juvenile delinquency. New juvenile justice legislation that had gone
into effect in 1994 had been publicly decried as soft on juvenile delinquents
because it favored alternative sentences or treatments over incarceration.
The emergency legislation made preventive detention and incarceration the
rule and was applicable to minors between the ages of fourteen and eighteen.
Manipulation of the media hid the reality that juveniles in El Salvador were
responsible for a relatively small proportion of serious crimes and that the
new juvenile justice system was actually functioning with far greater efficiency than the traditional criminal justice structures.[55]

The passage of this emergency legislation and a proposed (but never
passed) "Social Defense Law," which would have authorized the preventive
detention of deportees accused of crimes in the United States and of HIV-
positive persons, presented the reform effort with its most serious crisis. A
public opinion survey conducted in May 1996 found that 83.1 percent of
those polled believed that the emergency law was necessary to combat
crime.[56] Curiously, despite this show of support for the law, the majority of
those polled attributed the high crime rate to economic conditions and did
not believe that the emergency law would be successful in reducing crime.

The successful manipulation of public opinion in favor of the emergency
law and against the reforms made it clear that those involved in the reform

53. Mudge et al., *Reforma Judicial II Evaluación,* 19.

54. The Temporary Emergency Law Against Delinquency and Organized Crime, Decree
668, was passed on March 19, 1996, *Diario Oficial,* Tomo 330, No. 58, March 22, 1996.

55. See generally, Sneider Rivera, *La Nueva Justicia Penal Juvenil, La Experiencia de El
Salvador* (San Salvador: Corte Suprema de Justicia, FESPAD, UNICEF et al., 1998).

56. Public Opinion Institute (IUDOP), Central American University José Siméon Cañas,
Boletín de prensa, Año XI, no. 2, May 22, 1996, "Los salvadoreños opinan sobre la delincuencia común y la ley de emergencia."

process had failed to build a constituency for reform. The public had little understanding of the reforms already in effect or the goals of the proposed codes. Still, important sectors of Salvadoran society publicly argued that the emergency law not only violated the constitution and applicable international law but also that it was an ill-conceived effort to address crime exclusively through repressive laws rather than an overall government policy. Supreme Court magistrate René Hernández Valiente, who as Minister of Justice had been intimately involved in the creation of the new codes, spoke out publicly against the anticrime policy reflected in the emergency legislation. In addition to important public pronouncements against the law, several interested parties presented petitions to the Supreme Court challenging the constitutionality of different aspects of the law. In an unprecedented and positive development, two of the more substantive challenges were presented by a group of young public defenders, who acted without the official sanction of their institution, and by the National Counsel for the Defense of Human Rights. When the Juvenile Offenders Law went into effect in 1995, a unit of public defenders was assigned to work exclusively on cases under this law and developed experience in a wholly new process with oral procedures. Members of this unit, with assistance from consultants working with the AID project, prepared a serious constitutional challenge to the emergency anticrime legislation passed in March 1996.

Within the year, the Criminal Procedure and Penal Codes were approved and the Supreme Court had declared the most questionable aspects of the emergency law unconstitutional. Before the new codes were approved, some key provisions underwent serious revisions, but the overall thrust of the legislation remained the same.

The following sections look at how some of the key issues first raised as partial reform proposals fared during this period (roughly 1991–96). This discussion provides insights into the resistance to reform, questionable strategies, and how the process ultimately advanced.

The Extrajudicial Confession

Perhaps the most controversial of proposals for urgent reforms presented in 1991 would have prohibited the use of the extrajudicial confession.[57] The legislature failed to take up this proposed reform, which engendered

---

57. See Ministerio de Justicia, Dirección General de Asistencia Técnico Jurídica, *La Confesión Extra-judicial* (San Salvador: Ministerio de Justicia, 1993). Although this proposal was not published until 1993, it was circulated for discussion in 1991.

particular resistance because of the strong tradition of police reliance on confessions.

Opponents of this reform objected that the police lacked the capacity to obtain other kinds of evidence. Argentine Judge Leopoldo Schiffrin, an AID consultant, rejected the notion that the extrajudicial confession must retain evidentiary value until police can rely on scientific evidence.[58] He noted that even without the extrajudicial confession, satisfactory results can be obtained by police who dedicate themselves to collecting evidence and judges who immediately interrogate defendants. Moreover, the Salvadoran argument was circular: as long as they could rely on extrajudicial confessions, the police had no incentive to take other kinds of evidence seriously and were unlikely to learn scientific methods.

In October 1992, prominent Salvadoran jurist José María Méndez presented the Supreme Court with a challenge to the constitutionality of the extrajudicial confession. The court, however, did not respond.

In its March 1993 report, the Truth Commission called for abolition of the extrajudicial confession.[59] The draft Criminal Procedure Code circulated for public comment by the ATJ in 1993 would have prohibited the police from interrogating suspects about suspected criminal acts.[60] Any suspect's statement to the police that contained an express or implied confession to the acts charged and evidence obtained based on such a statement would have been "absolutely null" and could not have been used in the proceedings. Following the Argentine model, the widespread danger of police coercion was thought to justify the exclusion of evidence of any direct or indirect confession, regardless of the circumstances under which it was rendered. In short, the draft legislation would have completely prohibited the use of extrajudicial confessions. Such a prohibition goes far beyond U.S. law, which only tries to ensure that confessions to police are "voluntary." U.S. police rely heavily on "voluntary" confessions and information provided by suspects themselves before they consult with counsel, often because suspects, despite having been advised of their right to remain silent and to have counsel, have been led to believe that they may win a better deal by cooperating.[61]

58. Williams et al., "Análisis de Identificación de Areas de Reforma Legal y Constitucional" (San Salvador: Checchi and Company Consulting, Inc.), presented to USAID El Salvador, June 1991, 50.

59. *From Madness to Hope*, 181.

60. Anteproyecto del Código Procesal Penal, article 247.

61. Peter Carlson, "You Have the Right to Remain Silent . . . ," *Washington Post Magazine*, September 13, 1998, W06.

In April 1994, with ratification of the Criminal Procedure Code pending, the outgoing legislature adopted a series of constitutional reforms, some of which had been suggested by the Truth Commission. To become part of the constitution, these reforms needed to be ratified by a two-thirds vote of the successor legislature. One of the proposed amendments would have established that extrajudicial confessions could not be considered legal evidence.[62] The powerful National Association of Private Enterprise (ANEP) sent a letter to President Calderón Sol in late 1994 urging that the extrajudicial confession be maintained as legal evidence at least in proceedings for kidnappings, extortion, and drug-related crimes.[63] Instead of ratifying the constitutional reform passed by its predecessor, the (1994–97) legislature passed a different reform that would permit the extrajudicial confession to serve as evidence if defense counsel were present when it was taken.

The draft code's rejection of extrajudicial confessions was directly challenged in early 1996, when the legislature precipitously passed the Emergency Anti-Crime Law. This legislation appeared to sanction the use of extrajudicial confessions.

Not surprisingly, the evidentiary value of the extrajudicial confession was hotly debated in the days leading up to passage of the Criminal Procedure Code. The final compromise permitted confessions made to police to be considered evidence if they are made in the presence of defense counsel, are consistent with other evidence in the case, and are not obtained through physical or moral coercion.[64]

The Right to Defense

The first significant criminal justice reform actually passed and implemented in the postwar period greatly increased protection of defendants' rights by requiring that they be provided immediate access to a lawyer. The difficulties encountered in implementing this legislation and the resistance to it provide important lessons for legal reform efforts.

Unexpectedly, in May 1992 the legislature approved a public defense law

62. Asamblea Legislativa, Acuerdo de Reformas Constitucionales, article 2 (reforming constitution, article 12), April 29, 1994.

63. Letter from Roberto Vilanova to President Armando Calderón Sol, September 29, 1994, on file with the author (Vilanova letter.) This letter harked back to the reforms enacted in 1987, which established special procedures for the cases involving these crimes in order to make convictions more likely. See discussion *supra* at 74.

64. Código Procesal Penal (1996), article 222.

proposed by the ATJ law reform unit. The new law was designed to implement article 12 of the Salvadoran constitution by guaranteeing the right to
representation by counsel from the time of police detention.[65] If the suspect
or her relatives failed to name counsel, she was to be represented by a public
defender or appointed counsel.[66] This provision prohibited judges from
using evidence obtained in violation of the guarantees provided and decreed
that judicial proceedings based directly on illegally obtained police evidence
would be declared null.

Police were charged with the responsibility for contacting the Public Defenders' Office of the State Counsel (*Procuraduría General de la República*)
or, if no public defender were available, asking the local judge to appoint
counsel.[67] The reform authorized counsel to meet privately with their clients
before they were required to make any formal statement and to be present
when a statement was taken.[68]

The new law established a sanction of three to eight years in prison for
those who failed to respect defendants' rights.[69] It provided what was reportedly the continent's strictest guarantees of defense from the time of detention.[70] Not surprisingly, the law proved difficult to implement. A number of
ONUSAL legal officers expressed doubts about the Salvadoran legal system's
ability to adapt to such an "advanced" law. Unprepared for passage of the
law, Salvadoran authorities failed to take steps to make its provisions known.

When the law went into effect, the State Counsel had 108 public defenders to cover the entire country.[71] Although not a huge number, this number
was more than could be found in most Latin American countries at the time.
Working to capacity and adequately distributed, this might have been a
sufficient number. However, in some areas of the country, public defenders

65. Legislative Decree No. 238, May 6, 1992, which entered into effect in August 1992.
66. Código Procesal Penal (1973), reformed article 46, section 3.
67. Ibid., article 62.
68. Ibid., article 66. A prohibition against night-time detentions was included in the San
José Human Rights Agreement of July 26, 1990, article 2(d).
69. Código Penal (1973), reformed article 24.
70. The federal criminal procedure code enacted in Argentina in 1992 required police to
make a detainee available for judicial questioning within six hours of detention (Cód. Proc.
Pen., art. 286). Police officers were only permitted to question a suspect to establish his or her
identity (Cód. Proc. Pen., art. 184). Breaking from Argentine tradition, the new law authorizes
defense counsel to meet with and assist a detainee held incommunicado before judicial questioning. See Garro, "Nine Years of Transition," 44, n. 135.
71. The public defender unit attached to El Salvador's Public Ministry preceded the peace
accords. In February 1993 responsibility for funding this office was transferred from AID to the
government of El Salvador.

were not available to respond quickly to calls from the police. In these same areas, there were virtually no lawyers practicing criminal defense. Compounding the problem, judges or justices of the peace had to be located so that defense counsel could be appointed. Outside the capital, judges worked half-days, and many justices of the peace spent little time in their offices.

Even when defense attorneys were available, the quality of defense was a serious issue. ONUSAL found that many public defenders did very little to represent their clients. On a number of occasions, ONUSAL legal observers found themselves advocating for defendants because counsel failed to take necessary steps.[72] Appointed counsel received no compensation from the state. Lawyers who refused to accept cases could be fined, but the quality of representation was not guaranteed. This is hardly a problem unique to El Salvador, yet indigent Salvadoran defendants seemed to be wholly without recourse for counsel's failure to provide effective representation.[73]

In the immediate postwar years, the public defenders office was described by those who worked with the AID program as "awful, poorly organized, and unmotivated."[74] Public defenders, some of whom were genuinely committed to their task, lacked institutional support, career incentives, and job security. In general, public defenders lacked a sense of mission and minimally fulfilled their duties. They were underutilized and rarely showed initiative. Because they had no employment guarantees, defenders were unlikely to question authority or arbitrary rules, such as a prohibition against representing suspects accused of rape. The economic situation of the State Counsel's office was precarious and was compounded by a lack of government support when the State Counsel was not a member of the governing party. Faced with inadequate salaries, defenders routinely engaged in professional work outside the institution. One AID consultant noted that the State Counsel's office as a whole was in such a state of neglect that any donation simply disappeared. In these circumstances, training was unlikely to result in changed practices.

The establishment of a public defenders office was a necessary and positive step, but making the institution an effective one proved a major challenge.

---

72. See, e.g., Popkin, *Prospects for Legal Reform*, 40.

73. For related problems with court-appointed lawyers in the United States, see "Lawyers for the New York Poor: A Program with No Monitor," *New York Times*, May 23, 1994, 1; Stephen B. Bright, "Counsel for the Poor: The Death Sentence Not for the Worst Crime but for the Worst Lawyer," *Yale Law Journal* 103 (1994): 1835–83.

74. This analysis is based primarily on interviews with consultants by Checchi and Company to work on the AID-sponsored judicial reform effort, San Salvador, April 15, 1995. Some of these observations were confirmed by members of ONUSAL's Human Rights Division.

Unless the institution was transformed into a more efficient and dynamic protector of defendants' rights, training courses for public defenders could only yield minimal results. Such a transformation required improved employment conditions with an adequate promotion system, supervision of efficiency and workload, and a system to keep track of case distribution and ensure that defenders visited their incarcerated clients. The office also needed to be decentralized, with a more rational geographical distribution of resources, so that it could provide adequate national coverage. Most important, public defenders needed to have a genuine commitment to their task.

In practice, police complained that defense counsel routinely instructed their clients not to make statements, thus complicating their work. Two years after this law went into effect, a 1994 ONUSAL opinion survey among first instance judges and justices of the peace found their biggest problem to be "their working relationship with the office of the Chief State Counsel," that is, public defenders.[75] In many cases, no lawyer appeared or was appointed.

Determining standards for declaring proceedings null based on failure to comply with the defense law proved particularly difficult. Judges received conflicting instructions from consultants working with AID's judicial reform effort, the Supreme Court, and ONUSAL. Sophisticated defendants and corrupt judges were able to use this provision as a technical hook to win release of defendants when important interests—or money—were at stake. Private enterprise united in ANEP urged the repeal of this provision.[76] Responding to mounting criticism, the Supreme Court endorsed a proposal that would annul only the specific procedural act and its consequences rather than the entire proceeding.[77]

The problems encountered in implementing the public defense law highlighted the failure to create consciousness about the need for, and intent of, legislation designed to protect individual rights. This law was not widely known or debated before its passage. Since the law went into effect just months before the new civilian police force was initially deployed, a real opening existed to incorporate training about the new law into police training courses. The judiciary's reaction to the law highlighted the need for training judges so that they could understand the need to protect defendants'

75. ONUSAL, 12th Human Rights Report, par. 14.
76. See Vilanova letter, September 29, 1994.
77. Author's interview with René Hernández Valiente, vice president of the Supreme Court, San Salvador, March 30, 1995.

rights and apply the law responsibly. Implementation of the law focused attention on the lack of defense attorneys available in many areas of the country and the poor quality of defense provided. Without competent defense counsel available, the guarantee of the right to defense becomes meaningless.

The law was passed without giving adequate consideration to the realities of the Salvadoran legal system and the need to take measures to assure that competent defense counsel are available to all suspects. On the other hand, passage of the law brought the need for competent public defenders on a national scale to the fore. Some judicial reform proponents argue that no country will ever be prepared for these kinds of changes and that the destabilizing effects of reforms are necessary to provoke needed changes. The risk, however, is that the law will either not be adequately enforced because of the difficulty of obtaining defense counsel on short notice or that it will simply be repealed.

The draft Criminal Procedure Code would have absolutely barred police from questioning suspects about the acts under investigation. Before passage of the code, this section was modified so that suspects could be questioned after they had a chance to consult with counsel. The Criminal Procedure Code passed in 1996 establishes the right to defense counsel from the time of detention. If the suspect does not name a lawyer, a public defender must be provided within twelve hours of the detention. Suspects may not be questioned unless they have a lawyer present, and they should meet with counsel before answering any questions.[78]

The new law relies heavily on the public defenders' office, which has been expanded in an effort to cover the increased demand. By the time the new Criminal Procedure Code went into effect, concentrated training of public defenders had begun to show results as public defenders were better prepared to work with the new legislation than their colleagues in the private bar.[79]

Pretrial Detention

Overcrowded prisons were a major factor in a series of prison disturbances and bloody riots in the postwar period. Prisoners were routinely incarcerated for lengthy periods of time before their cases were resolved. Most of those incarcerated belonged to the least favored social strata and lacked the economic resources for a timely and effective defense.

78. Código Procesal Penal (1996), article 242.
79. Interview with Jaime Martínez, director of CEPES, San Salvador, August 25, 1998.

Although the prison situation deteriorated dramatically in the years after the war's end, the large percentage of unsentenced prisoners was a long-standing problem. In 1990 CORELESAL found that approximately 90 percent of those in prison had not been convicted.[80] A temporary law passed to ameliorate this problem required the release of prisoners who had been held longer than the period allowed by law.[81] In the course of a year, 448 prisoners had been released under this law, less than 10 percent of the prison population. Intended to reduce prison overcrowding as well as address delays in the courts, this measure failed to resolve either problem.[82]

Two years later the statistics remained very much the same: only 531 of a total prison population of 5,286 were serving sentences.[83] According to 1994 statistics, 80 percent of inmates (1,191 out of 5,976) were still awaiting trial.[84] The total number of prisoners continued to grow.

By 1994 the prison situation had become so explosive that ONUSAL recommended the declaration of an emergency situation in the penitentiary system and made a number of suggestions to different institutions involved with the administration of justice to address the crisis. For example, ONUSAL recommended that the Supreme Court issue general instructions to criminal court judges to review all cases with incarcerated defendants.[85] In 1994 the average instruction period lasted 555 days.[86]

The Criminal Chamber of the new Supreme Court began to address this problem through a systematic effort to review the cases of prisoners awaiting trial. As of March 1995, the court claimed to have reduced the number of pretrial detainees to 65 percent of the total.[87] A few months later, however, the situation had again deteriorated to the earlier level of 80 percent, apparently because of increasing detentions by the new police. The prison population, which had hovered around 5,000 for several years, climbed to 7,200 in July 1995.

80. CORELESAL, Problematica de la administración de justicia en El Salvador, December 1990, 117–18.

81. Emergency act to resolve the problem of unconvicted prisoners, Decree No. 769, April 25, 1991.

82. ONUSAL, Report of the Director of the Human Rights Division for the period from 1 January to 30 April 1992, UN Doc. A/46/935, S/24066 (June 5, 1992) (Fourth Human Rights Report).

83. Ibid., par. 32.

84. ONUSAL, 12th Human Rights Report, par. 52.

85. Ibid., par. 54.

86. Interview with consultants, Checchi and Company, San Salvador, April 5, 1995.

87. Interview with Gustave Torres, magistrate, Criminal Chamber of the Supreme Court, San Salvador, April 4, 1995.

The new Supreme Court addressed the issue of pretrial detention when it granted a habeas corpus petition on behalf of former FMLN commander Joaquín Villalobos.[88] A majority of the magistrates in the Constitutional Chamber ruled that since international treaties ratified by El Salvador preclude the automatic imposition of pretrial detention, preventive detention must be based on a specific judicial determination of its necessity in each case.[89] This ruling led to an effort to pass an immediate reform that would make preventive detention the exception in all cases involving potential sentences of less than eight years. The draft legislation would have made it possible to appeal a judge's decision and incorporate new noncustodial precautionary measures that could be combined with release from custody. The draft Criminal Procedure Code went still further by making preventive detention in all cases the exception rather than the rule and providing an array of alternatives to incarceration. Pretrial detention would have been limited to cases where there was a real danger of flight or where the defendant's freedom could prevent completion of an investigative step.

However, the emergency anticrime legislation enacted in 1996 reaffirmed the traditional Salvadoran approach that favored pretrial detention, thus undercutting the provisions of the Juvenile Offenders Law and the proposed Criminal Procedure Code. Before its passage, the new Criminal Procedure Code was altered so that provisional detention is the norm for those accused of crimes with a maximum sentence greater than three years, although judges were authorized to order alternatives to detention in certain circumstances. Judges may order the detention of those accused of less serious crimes, based on the circumstances of the crime, the social alarm it caused or the frequency with which similar crimes are committed, or if the defendant has already been given an alternative to incarceration.[90]

Separating Instruction Judges from Sentencing Judges

Until the new codes went into effect in 1998, a single judge continued to preside over the instruction and plenary phases of trials. Thus the same judge could decree the provisional detention of a suspect, elevate the case to trial, preside at trial, and ultimately sentence a defendant accused of nonjury crimes or found guilty by a jury.

---

88. Case of Joaquín Villalobos Huezo, Constitutional Chamber of the Supreme Court of Justice, November 17, 1994; reprinted in *Foro Judicial* (San Salvador: FESPAD, December 1994).

89. In reaching its ruling, the Supreme Court relied on article 144 of the Salvadoran constitution, which gives international treaties precedence over domestic laws.

90. Código Procesal Penal (1996), articles 292–94.

The renewed AID-funded law reform effort identified this as a priority for reform and prepared proposed legislation in 1992 to separate investigative and sentencing judges. By 1992 a number of Latin American countries had already accomplished this.[91]

The ATJ proposed converting existing criminal courts into sentencing courts and creating new instructional courts based on a statistical study of actual needs. The Ministry of Justice had specifically rejected an earlier proposal that would have transferred the instruction responsibilities to justices of the peace.[92] The background for the legislation noted that the crucial role entrusted to instruction judges required maturity, knowledge, and experience beyond that required of justices of the peace. Moreover, converting each justice of the peace court to an instructional court would have required resources—qualified personnel, an adequate locale, typewriters, telephones, radios, transportation, and a place to hold detainees. Instead of arbitrarily converting all 305 justices of the peace into instructional judges, the ATJ called for empirical studies of actual needs so that it could then propose a geographic distribution of instructional courts based on population density, the number of criminal cases in the area, and the optimal utilization of personnel and infrastructure. The law reform unit calculated that less than 100 instruction judges were actually needed on a national basis.

Supreme Court President Gutiérrez Castro, who opposed many reform initiatives of the AID project, endorsed the concept of separating the two functions but insisted that all justices of the peace be converted into investigating judges and that a prosecutor and public defender be assigned to each of their 305 courts. Although the AID project and the Ministry of Justice knew that this was an unworkable proposal, they did not oppose it, and the Assembly approved the reform proposed by Gutiérrez Castro.

Because the law passed required that a prosecutor and a defender be assigned to each justice of the peace—a change that far exceeded the resources of these institutions—implementation of the law was repeatedly postponed. In December 1994 the law that would have converted justices of the peace into instruction judges was derogated without ever having been

91. These included Argentina, Costa Rica, Ecuador, Perú, Dominican Republic, and Guatemala. Colombia, Mexico, Panama, and most recently, Guatemala, entrust the instruction phase to the Public Ministry (prosecution). When the prosecution is responsible for the instruction, the instruction judges take on an oversight function and are responsible for the intermediate phase of the proceedings.

92. Ministerio de Justicia, Dirección General de Asistencia Técnico Jurídica, Separación de las Funciones de Juez Instructor y Juez de Sentencia, Reformas al Código Procesal Penal y a la Ley Organica Judicial (Ediciones Ultimo Decenio), May 1993.

implemented. No interim measures were undertaken to separate the instruction phase from the sentencing phase.

The passage of this law raised questions about Salvadoran commitment to implement necessary reforms. Well aware of the problem, the Ministry of Justice and AID-sponsored reform effort failed to make a public issue of the impracticality of the Supreme Court proposal. Nor did this acquiescence to the Supreme Court president yield cooperation from him on other fronts. Instead, it seems to have been intended to produce exactly the result achieved: to obstruct and delay the process of change.

Under the new Criminal Procedure Code, first instance judges are divided between investigating judges (*jueces de instrucción*) and sentencing judges (*jueces de sentencia*), with clearly delineated roles. Sentencing tribunals are normally made up of three judges. In the limited number of cases that are still to be heard by juries, a sentencing judge presides.

The New Criminal Procedure and Penal Codes

In October 1994 the UN described the delay in enacting key legal reforms as "the biggest obstacle to the process of institution-building." The legislative bottleneck became so severe that ONUSAL termed this "unaccountable delay ... one of the main hurdles to improving the administration of justice and machinery for protecting human rights in El Salvador."[93] Despite the wealth of proposals for "urgent partial reforms" prepared by the Justice Ministry's law reform unit and the repeated urging of ONUSAL and the Truth Commission's recommendation, review of existing proposals was slow and legislative approval slower still.

The ATJ circulated the draft Criminal Procedure Code for comments in 1993. The Ministry of Justice submitted the proposed legislation to the Assembly in May 1994. In early 1995, with substantial assistance from AID's judicial reform project, the Assembly's Commission on Legislation undertook an intensive effort to review the proposed codes. Legislators attended seminars, and some visited Costa Rica and Spain to learn more about the issues involved. The legislators on the commission claimed to be convinced of the importance of approving the legislation, but assurances that the codes would be approved by the end of April 1995 went unfulfilled. Some groups and individuals voiced disagreement with a number of the proposed reforms. The September 1994 communication from ANEP to President

93. ONUSAL, 12th Report on Human Rights, par. 18, 113.

Calderón Sol urged the retention of special procedures enacted in the 1980s to facilitate prosecutions for kidnapping, extortion, and drug-related crimes as well as certain presumptions of guilt. This letter further called for maintaining the extrajudicial confession as evidence for these crimes.

These specific concerns reflected a broader concern among the private enterprise sector and some parts of the government that the reforms were inappropriate because of their emphasis on protection of individual rights in the face of a serious crime wave. They also indicated a continued desire to maintain special procedures to enhance the possibility of conviction for crimes of particular concern to the economic elite.

In 1995 and 1996, as public anxiety about the postwar crime wave grew, concerns about prison overcrowding and abuses of detainees seemed less urgent. Passage of emergency anticrime legislation, parts of which flatly contradicted the *garantista* precepts of the proposed Criminal Procedure Code, created new obstacles to approval of the codes. The UN exerted its considerable weight to push for approval of the codes, viewing this step as one of the key pending commitments from the peace accords. MINUSAL and UTE staff worked with legislators reviewing the codes until they were barred from the discussions by ARENA legislators in 1996.[94] Legislators opted to change some important provisions of the Criminal Procedure Code to, for example, maintain the possibility of using extrajudicial confessions. Still, when the code was approved in December 1996, following a final push by UN envoy Alvaro de Soto, it had not been substantially modified.

The initial reaction to the codes in the days after they went into effect in April 1998 suggested that legislators should have dedicated more time to reviewing their provisions and consulting with the different operators in the justice system to see which aspects might negatively affect their work. Although the draft codes had been in circulation for three years prior to their approval by the Assembly, very little serious review had taken place. ANEP and others focused on a few provisions and were successful in winning some changes. But the Ministry of Public Security and the National Civilian Police (PNC), both of which reacted with outrage to the new provisions, apparently had not undertaken a thorough analysis of the codes during those three years.

As soon as the new codes went into effect, Public Security Minister Hugo Barrera began calling for reforms to give the police greater freedom of

---

94. Teresa Whitfield, "Staying the Course in El Salvador," in *Honoring Human Rights*, ed. Alice H. Henkin (Washington, D.C.: Aspen Institute, 1998), 174.

action. In particular, police complained of restrictions on their ability to carry out searches. Barrera blamed the high crime rate on the new laws and claimed that many hardened criminals were being released pursuant to the new legislation. Many Salvadorans actually believed that the new laws prevented the police from taking any action without a judicial order, even to stop the commission of a murder in their presence. Police statistics reflected a 50 percent decrease in detentions of suspects from 1997 to 1998, when the new codes entered into effect.[95] Official statistics showed a substantial decrease in arrests following implementation of the new codes. Much of this decrease reflected the conversion of many minor crimes into violations subject to fine. The number of suspects arrested for murder actually increased in 1998 (from 690 in 1997 to 763 in 1998), although the number of murders recorded also increased (from 1,747 to 2,470).[96] The director of the PNC criticized judicial decisions to grant alternatives to incarceration: "[Criminals] can easily benefit from alternative measures, at times totally absurd ones, which the law allows."[97]

In general terms, the new codes provided the framework for a modern criminal system designed to ensure that criminal justice would be independent, speedy, transparent, and respectful of due process guarantees and fundamental rights. The Criminal Procedure Code created a far more adversarial process, with greater responsibility vested in the prosecutor's office. In addition to directing police investigations, prosecutors were responsible for preparing a document requesting a particular disposition of the case. The prosecution could recommend the initiation of formal proceedings with or without pretrial detention of the accused, the rejection or dismissal of the complaint, that prosecution not be undertaken for one of the specific reasons set forth by law, conditional suspension of the proceedings, abbreviated proceedings when the penalty sought does not exceed one year in prison, or conciliation.[98]

Broad prosecutorial discretion is traditionally considered repugnant to a civil law system. Under the new code, prosecutors are vested with unprecedented authority to recommend that cases not be prosecuted. Allowing prosecutorial discretion is meant to permit the prosecution to devote limited resources to proceeding against significant and meritorious cases, yet it can

95. "Códigos redujeron detenciones en 1998," *La Prensa Gráfica*, January 5, 1999.
96. Ibid.
97. "Policía critica códigos que permiten liberar a criminales," *La Prensa Gráfica*, January 5, 1999.
98. Código Procesal Penal, article 248.

open the door to arbitrary decisions. Under the new code, the prosecutor and the instruction judge must both agree to the exercise of the court's discretion not to prosecute.[99] Prosecutors can apply the principle of "opportunity" to request the judge's agreement to forgo prosecution in whole or in part under the following circumstances: because the insignificance of the act or the minimal role of the accused does not affect the public interest; when the accused did everything possible to prevent the commission of the crime or contributed decisively to the identification of others involved; when the accused suffered serious physical or moral harm because of the act; when the penalty for the alleged infraction lacks importance in view of the punishment already imposed or expected for other infractions or likely to be imposed in proceedings under way outside the country. A judge can also apply these criteria on her own initiative, but must have the agreement of the prosecutor.[100]

The new code abandons the inquisitorial system that vested in a single magistrate the power to investigate, charge, conduct the instruction and plenary phases of the proceedings, and finally sentence. Instead, the prosecution is given a much greater role, and the judge who oversees the instruction cannot be the sentencing judge. The maximum length of instruction is six months, after which an appellate court can, in exceptional cases, grant one extension that cannot exceed six months.[101] The presiding judge is to look for possibilities for conciliation between the parties. In the months following implementation of the codes, approximately 10 percent of cases were being resolved through conciliation. Concerns were raised that some of these agreements might have been the product of intimidation.

For this more adversarial system to function effectively, both the prosecution and the defense must play a strong and active role. Strengthening these roles requires not only an enormous commitment of resources but also a radical change in conceptions about them. Mechanisms must be developed to ensure that indigent defendants receive adequate representation and that powerful defendants are effectively prosecuted. The locus of corruption may shift from the courts to the prosecution and police, but the temptation to resolve disputes through financial means will not disappear. Public hearings in which both parties have ample opportunity to establish what evidence does or does not exist are essential safeguards against back-room deals.

99. Ibid, article 20.
100. Ibid.
101. Ibid., articles 274–75.

The code includes a number of provisions to protect the rights of defendants and of victims, who are entitled to participate in the proceedings and be heard in court. Private prosecution of cases is extended to any citizen or association of citizens when public officials have committed crimes by abusing their authority, or when crimes imply a serious and direct violation of fundamental human rights.[102]

The reforms convert the traditional written proceedings into an almost entirely oral process, from a preliminary hearing before a justice of the peace to a trial. Salvadorans had limited prior experience with oral proceedings following their introduction in the Family Code (1993) and the Juvenile Offenders Law (1995).

An instruction judge presides over the investigative phase of the case. In proceedings for crimes with less than a three-year maximum penalty, an abbreviated procedure is available for defendants who choose to admit guilt. In such cases, the judge is barred from imposing a sentence greater than that proposed by the prosecutor.

The new code maintains a jury system but strictly limits the cases in which juries will be used.[103] Under the new oral proceedings, jurors are to hear the concentrated presentation of evidence. Nonjury cases (including murder, robbery, extortion, fraud, kidnapping, sex crimes, crimes requiring private action such as rape and wounding, white collar crimes, crimes against the environment, and drug trafficking) are heard by a three-judge sentencing court. The new Penal Code includes crimes such as torture, forced disappearance, and violations of the laws of war. It recognizes, prospectively, that these are not subject to a statute of limitations.

In the weeks following implementation of the new codes, several notorious prisoners won release once their sentences were recalculated pursuant to article 48 of the new Penal Code, which was designed to address the excessive periods many defendants had spent in pretrial detention and to reduce the overall prison population. This provision gave prisoners two days of credit toward their sentence for each day of pretrial detention that exceeded six months, and three days of credit for each day that exceeded one year. Shortly after the codes went into effect, the Salvadoran (and international) public saw three of the five former National Guardsmen convicted for killing and raping four U.S. churchwomen in 1980 walk out of prison after

---

102. Ibid., article 95. Private prosecution is also authorized in crimes against the exercise of the right to vote or when crimes affect diffuse general interests.
103. Ibid., article 53.

serving seventeen years of their thirty-year sentences. Even more disturbing to the economic elite in El Salvador, former National Guard lieutenant Rodolfo Isidro López Sibrián, convicted for his role in a kidnapping-for-profit ring, also won release after serving twelve years of a thirty-year sentence, thanks to article 48.

Had different sectors of Salvador society seriously studied the proposed codes during the three years before they became law, most of the articles that have proven particularly controversial in practice could have been identified and modified. The potential effect of article 48 was quite apparent, yet none of the groups so outraged by its effects suggested modifying its terms so that the new calculation would not be used to free those convicted of particularly serious crimes. As a Salvadoran editorial put it, "Now the Legislative Commission of the Assembly has said that it is already reviewing the new legislation. To err is doubtless human, and to correct shows wisdom. But why in our country are things always done after the fact? Wasn't it obvious, from the time the codes were drafted, that something like this would soon happen? Weren't [the codes] reviewed and approved by the full Assembly?"[104]

One year after the new codes went into effect, the Coordinating Committee for the Justice Sector (composed of the Supreme Court president, attorney general, minister of justice, president of the judiciary council, and the state counsel) reported improvements in efficiency in handling cases, coordination among justice sector institutions, and citizen access to justice. Nationwide, the Supreme Court reported that the new sentencing courts had handed down ninety-nine convictions, which represented a 50 percent conviction rate at trial.[105] The increased rate of convictions, which is not necessarily indicative of a more reliable system, did not reflect any improvement in the effectiveness of criminal investigation, however. A study released by FUSADES (the Salvadoran Foundation for Economic and Social Development) in April 1999, found that suspects were arrested in only 6 to 8 percent of murder cases.[106]

Some critics recognized that the codes had made justice more efficient but argued that they failed to protect citizens' rights and coddled criminals. Minister of Public Security Hugo Barrera claimed that the codes were "the principal problem in public security, because they provide excessive protections

104. "La Justicia y los Nuevos Códigos Penales," *El Faro* (newspaper on Internet), July 3, 1998.

105. "Funcionarios presentan la 'cara' oficial de los Códigos," *La Prensa Gráfica*, April 20, 1999.

106. "Justicia de El Salvador reprobada," *La Prensa Gráfica*, April 21, 1999.

to criminals."[107] National Civilian Police chief Rodrigo Avila maintained that crime had increased because of the new codes and their elimination of certain crimes, such as receiving stolen property. He reportedly attributed 40 percent of crimes to inadequate legal provisions."[108] Barrera also criticized the Juvenile Offenders Law because of its extensive alternative sentencing provisions. Nonetheless, official statistics reflected a slight decrease in juvenile crime since the law went into effect in 1995. Implementation of the Juvenile Offenders Law had led to the creation of a series of new programs for diversion and rehabilitation of juvenile offenders.

The difficulties inherent in implementing a radically new system of criminal justice were exacerbated by the forceful criticism of the minister of public security, the police, and the private sector. The media have given great play to the criticisms of the new codes. Reforms were quickly proposed by the private enterprise sector and enacted to increase prison terms and give police greater freedom of action. Approval of the new codes is plainly only the beginning—and a beginning fraught with challenges—of creating a criminal justice system that respects individual rights and that is efficient and transparent.

El Salvador's homicide rate is among the highest in Latin America, and Salvadorans voiced more concern about insecurity in 1998 than they did during the war years. Because crime is so prevalent in postwar El Salvador, the transformation of the justice system is only likely to succeed and be accepted if it is accompanied by a comprehensive effort to prevent and fight crime. Otherwise, the criminal justice reforms risk becoming the scapegoat for the country's inability to control rampant criminal activity.

107. "Auge delincuencial por nuevas leyes: Barrera," *La Prensa Gráfica*, April 19, 1999.
108. "Urgen reformar códigos," *El Diario de Hoy*, April 20, 1999.

7

LESSONS FROM THE SALVADORAN EXPERIENCE

The Role of International Actors and Civil Society in Building the Rule of Law and Establishing Accountability

As the preceding chapters document, the Salvadoran peace process benefited from enormous international involvement, in part attributable to El Salvador's inflated importance during the waning years of the Cold War. Between 1992 and 1995, international donors provided El Salvador with some $400 million per year in loans and grants toward the implementation of the peace accords.[1] First the UN Security Council and then the General Assembly authorized a long-term and extensive UN presence to provide verification and good offices for the implementation of the peace accords. Yet despite this far-reaching international involvement and the overall success of the peace process, progress in establishing accountability, providing reparations to those who suffered the brunt of the war, and building the rule of law seems meager and grudging.

Hundreds of millions of dollars are now being poured into justice reform in Latin America, thanks to the increasing involvement of multilateral and

---

1. James K. Boyce, "Movilización de recursos externos," in James K. Boyce, Coordinator, *Ajuste Hacia la Paz: La política económica y la reconstrucción de posguerra en El Salvador* (San Salvador: UNDP, 1995), 98–99. This study notes the Salvadoran government's expectation that the implementation of the peace accords would be financed by the international community and its reluctance to marshal its own resources.

bilateral donors who have recognized that an effective, independent, and accessible justice system is essential to ensure that peace and development will be sustainable. In El Salvador, for example, the Inter-American Development Bank recently launched a $27.3 million project. Between 1993 and 1998, the United States provided El Salvador with almost $41 million in rule of law funding, making it the third largest recipient in the world during that period.[2]

The Salvadoran experience raises the question of how international support can be most effective and whether excessive or inappropriate international involvement can actually inhibit progress in some areas. International donors can provide crucial assistance, but they cannot and should not replace societal processes. The enormous international involvement in El Salvador was not matched by a corresponding role for civil society in setting an overall agenda for reform, defining priorities, or choosing the measures that would be undertaken. Seven years after the peace accords, and with the added perspective of developments in other countries that have faced similar issues, some important lessons can be gleaned from the Salvadoran experience.

The international community can play an important role in establishing the truth about, and accountability for, serious international crimes, but it can play only a limited role in promoting national reconciliation. In recent years the international community has taken on a growing role in establishing accountability for crimes against humanity and war crimes—a role that it had eschewed since Nuremberg. The Genocide Convention of 1948[3] and the Torture Convention of 1984[4] established that these crimes are subject to universal jurisdiction, but deferring to sovereignty claims, national courts had been reluctant to exercise this jurisdiction. European countries sometimes found a jurisdictional basis to initiate prosecutions of former Latin American dictators and military commanders for human rights crimes, often when the victims were citizens of that European country. These proceedings were limited, however, by the defendants' absence from the jurisdiction.

2. U.S. General Accounting Office, *Foreign Assistance: Rule of Law Funding Worldwide for Fiscal Years 1993–98,* June 1999, GAO/NSIAD–99–158. $27.9 million of the total was allocated for criminal justice and law enforcement. Only Haiti and Russia received larger amounts of rule of law funding in these years.

3. Convention on the Prevention and Punishment of the Crime of Genocide, adopted December 9, 1948, *entered into force* January 12, 1951, 78 U.N.T.S. 277.

4. Convention Against Torture and Other Cruel, Inhuman, or Degrading Treatment or Punishment, adopted December 10, 1984, *entered into force* June 26, 1987, G.A.Res. 39/46, 39 UN GAOR Supp. (No. 51), 197, UN Doc. A/39/51 (1984).

Spanish prosecutions of Argentine and Chilean officers for crimes committed in Latin America have opened new possibilities for holding perpetrators of atrocities accountable. In October 1998, British authorities arrested former Chilean dictator Augusto Pinochet in London, based on an extradition request from a Spanish court seeking to try him for crimes committed during his rule. Spanish Judge Baltasar Garzón alleged universal jurisdiction in the case against Pinochet, whom he charged with genocide, torture, and other crimes against humanity. The British Law Lords ruled in March 1999 that Pinochet had no immunity from prosecution that would prevent his extradition to Spain to face charges of torture for acts that took place after provisions of the Torture Convention were enacted into law in the United Kingdom in 1988.[5] European criminal proceedings are already limiting the travel plans of many individuals implicated in serious human rights violations. Civil actions have been successfully litigated in the United States against torturers from various countries and have resulted in generally unenforceable default judgments.[6] These too have constrained the travel and residence plans of former rulers and military officers.

The attempt to extradite Pinochet for trial in Spain sent shock waves through Latin America. The Salvadoran reaction to Pinochet's arrest was strong and polarized. Some saw an opportunity to pursue perpetrators who had been protected from justice in El Salvador. David Escobar Galindo, who served on the Salvadoran government's negotiating team, warned that trying Pinochet at this stage would reopen the past, with incalculable consequences for the Chilean transition process.[7] An editorial in *La Prensa Gráfica* insisted that leaving behind the violence generated by Cold War confrontations required the sacrifice of "forgiving and forgetting." Echoing Escobar Galindo's sentiments, the newspaper opined that the movement for international justice for crimes against humanity could be very beneficial in the future, so that henceforth, "no one escapes the long arm of justice."[8] The editorial then sought to distinguish Pinochet's situation from the Salvadoran negotiated solution "without winners or losers." It asserted that the Truth Commission's very clear and courageous, albeit controversial report had allowed a peaceful transition. Yet as the IACHR stated in its 1999 decisions on El Salvador's

5. The Convention was incorporated into the law of the United Kingdom by section 134 of the Criminal Justice Act 1988.
6. Beth Stephens and Michael Ratner, *International Human Rights Litigation in U.S. Courts* (Ardsley: Transnational Publishers, 1996).
7. David Escobar Galindo, "Las lecciones del caso Pinochet," *El Faro*, November 1998.
8. "La tentación del pasado," *La Prensa Gráfica*, November 1998.

amnesty, the Truth Commission's work did not fulfill El Salvador's obligation to determine the truth about past human rights violations and bring those responsible to justice.

Universal jurisdiction is crucial precisely because countries undergoing democratic transitions or emerging from armed conflicts are rarely in a position to hold perpetrators accountable. Before relinquishing power or signing a negotiated agreement, those responsible for atrocities often exact compromises by persuading others that this is the price of a peaceful transition. But should the international community have to respect this type of compromise? The requirements of international law are clearly not meant to be optional, allowing each country to decide whether to honor them and whether other countries must accept that country's decision. If these precepts are indeed universal, all those who violate them must run the risk that they will be held accountable. Otherwise, the widely held conviction that war or subversion justifies actions outside the law—even atrocities—will never be challenged. Pinochet's arrest suggests that other countries may begin to assert universal jurisdiction when the country where the crimes against humanity were committed abdicates its responsibilities under international law. Developments in Chile in the year since Pinochet's arrest suggest that the exercise of universal jurisdiction may also help to embolden domestic courts.

While many Latin Americans express a preference for an international criminal tribunal rather than the exercise of universal jurisdiction by courts in other countries, this alternative remains theoretical, at least until the International Criminal Court (ICC) is actually established. The ICC will exercise jurisdiction over a limited number of crimes and will not have jurisdiction over crimes committed before it goes into effect.[9]

In the 1990s, for the first time since Nuremberg, the international community established ad hoc tribunals to try those accused of committing genocide, war crimes, and crimes against humanity in the former Yugoslavia and in Rwanda. These international efforts have proven crucial in preserving evidence, demonstrating that the international community will hold violators of internationally recognized crimes accountable, advancing the interpretation of international humanitarian law, prosecuting some war criminals, and assuaging the international community's need to do something—often after the worst of the killing has ended. But they cannot substitute for a societal process of coming to terms with atrocities of the past. Unfortunately,

9. Rome Statute of the International Criminal Court, adopted by the United Nations Diplomatic Conference of Plenipotentiaries on the Establishment of an International Criminal Court on July 17, 1998.

the proceedings of international tribunals may have minimal impact inside the country where the violations took place. While the South African public could closely follow the Truth and Reconciliation Commission's public hearings and Argentines observed the trials of the generals, the proceedings of the international tribunals for the former Yugoslavia and Rwanda have not been accessible to most people in Bosnia or Rwanda.

The Salvadoran, Haitian, and Guatemalan experiences with truth commissions have likewise shown that the international community can provide crucial assistance in establishing the global truth about patterns of violations and the facts in illustrative cases. Because international investigators are less likely to be identified with either party to the conflict, witnesses may feel more comfortable providing information to them. International experts may also bring experience in data analysis and the application of internationally recognized standards, both of which are essential to construct an objective picture of what happened. In some situations, it may be easier for a foreigner to stand up and describe state responsibility for unspeakable acts. Thus, in presenting the Guatemalan Historical Clarification Commission's conclusions and recommendations, it was Professor Christian Tomuschat, the German international law expert who coordinated the commission, who gave the most powerful indictment of the atrocities committed by the Guatemalan military. He also singled out the United States for its role in supporting military and security force structures that committed violations.

International investigators trained in forensic anthropology may be able to assist by unearthing mass graves, identifying the victims, and determining the manner of their death. Experienced investigators have also assisted in uncovering and preserving other evidence and in interviewing witnesses — often taking special precautions to ensure their safety. At the evidentiary and due process levels, international investigations and prosecutions plainly have resources available to them that few domestic justice systems could hope to rival, particularly those in countries emerging from armed conflict.

International pressure may be essential, as it was in El Salvador, to ensure compliance with the recommendations of temporary bodies such as the Truth and Ad Hoc Commissions. But beyond assistance in fact-finding and pressure for compliance with specific recommendations, international actors have a limited ability to encourage countries to address the abuses of the past. The international community has yet to take a strong and consistent stand against the issuance of broad amnesties meant to benefit those responsible for crimes against humanity or serious violations of human rights. In part, an element of realpolitik enters in. Thus, the United States has been reluctant to condemn those it sees playing a generally positive role in the region or in their country. In some cases, perpetrators of crimes against humanity have later been instrumental in facilitating transitions to democracy, negotiating peace agreements, or ensuring regional stability. Still, the Dayton Accords demonstrated that it is possible to negotiate a peace accord without a promise of amnesty, although the failure of NATO troops to arrest notorious war criminals suggests to some a tacit understanding. And in Guatemala the amnesty provisions approved in the wake of the peace accords were drafted with technical assistance from the UN and included some of the international law limitations regarding the kinds of crimes subject to amnesty.

By stating clearly that international law calls for the prosecution of those responsible for crimes against humanity and war crimes, international actors could establish that decisions to forgo prosecution or to enact broad amnesties without establishing accountability will violate international law. The United Nations and other international bodies involved in peace negotiations should be clear and consistent about international law requirements. In the Americas, they should also rely on Inter-American jurisprudence and recent treaties that have placed specific obligations on states to investigate and prosecute those responsible for torture, [10] forced disappearances,[11] and violence against women.[12] It can encourage governments and, where appropriate, insurgencies or other nonstate actors to undertake efforts to find out what happened to individual victims. In certain cases, foreign governments, notably the United States, may have relevant documentation that can be declassified and provided to those investigating the past. In some cases, the role of international actors in supporting a party to the conflict may make them reluctant to have the full extent of their own responsibility investigated or to demand that prosecutions of their erstwhile allies be carried out.

The international community can play a valuable role in providing examples of what has been done elsewhere through opportunities for interchange

10. The Inter-American Convention to Prevent and Punish Torture, December 9, 1985, OAS Treaty series No. 67, OAS Doc. OEA/Ser.A/42 (SEPF), in force since 1987.

11. The Inter-American Convention on Forced Disappearance of Persons, June 9, 1994, OAS Doc. OEA/Ser.P AG/doc.3114/94 rev. 1, reprinted in 33 I.L.M. 1529 (1994), in force since 1996.

12. The Inter-American Convention on the Prevention, Punishment, and Eradication of Violence Against Women, June 9, 1994, reprinted in Inter-American Commission on Human Rights, *Basic Documents Pertaining to Human Rights in the Inter-American System (Updated to May 1996)*, 85, OAS Doc. OEA/Ser.L./V/II.92, doc. 31, rev. 3 (1996).

Douglass Cassel has proposed guidelines on amnesties for serious violations of human rights in the Americas, for use by diplomats and officials of the UN, the OAS, the U.S. government, and other governments involved in peace negotiations. See *Law and Contemporary Problems* 59 (1996): 197, 228.

with key players in and outside government who have been involved in, or have closely observed, these processes and for frank discussions about the strengths and weaknesses of different choices. Presentations by individuals who worked on a truth commission should be complemented by informed discussions of different options and their actual, not just theoretical, impact.

Temporary commissions and other entities needed to make the transition from an armed conflict to peace or from an authoritarian regime to a democratic one should not become substitutes for state institutions' responsibilities to guarantee human rights. The potential role of a temporary international commission formed in the wake of a negotiated peace agreement should be distinguished from other longer term measures that a society must undertake if it is to restore the dignity of the victims, recognize the harm done to them, provide an opportunity for material and moral reparations, and create a basis for reconciliation.

The challenge for these temporary bodies, often composed largely of foreigners, is to help state institutions assume their responsibilities rather than inadvertently encourage them to ignore them because they were addressed by the special commission. The goal of a temporary commission should be to facilitate a longer term societal process, not to become a substitute for that process. This is a tricky issue, since temporary bodies born of the peace accords fulfilled roles that Salvadoran institutions were not equipped or willing to assume. The follow-up to the Chilean truth commission is revealing in this regard: a successor foundation was established to continue the commission's work and address the issue of reparations, while considerable evidence gathered by the commission was turned over to the courts. National entities seem to be better suited to such tasks as delving into the individual circumstances of victims and their families as well as devising creative and appropriate methods of compensation. The Guatemalan commission, well aware of the Salvadoran precedent, stressed the need to establish follow-up mechanisms for such tasks as providing reparations, searching for the disappeared, locating children forcibly separated from their families, and overseeing implementation of the commission's recommendations. It also called for the prosecution of those crimes not subject to amnesty under the National Reconciliation Law. In El Salvador, the UN Truth Commission did not call for such mechanisms or encourage prosecutions.

For commissions to be successful in having state institutions continue their work or undertake specific reforms or actions, a government must effectively adopt the commission's findings and accept state responsibility—a less likely scenario when the commission is a wholly international enterprise. Only because the Salvadoran peace accords made the recommendations of the

Truth Commission binding on the parties, was the UN able to exert pressure and force compliance with a number of recommendations. Domestic follow-up that was not forthcoming would have been needed to attempt to investigate the thousands of cases that the Truth Commission could not address in its limited existence.

Role of Civil Society in Establishing Accountability and Promoting Reconciliation

National groups can also play a key role in establishing accountability and promoting reconciliation. In this regard, Guatemala contrasts sharply with El Salvador. Guatemalan NGOs joined together in the Alliance Against Impunity to prevent passage of a broad amnesty law. While they objected strongly to the terms of the National Reconciliation Law (NRL) passed in December 1996, the NRL's provisions in part reflect an understanding of international law limitations on amnesties. Through 1998, the Guatemalan judiciary had not granted amnesty to anyone accused of a serious human rights violation. The mandate of the Guatemalan Historical Clarification Commission (HCC) was in many ways weaker than its Salvadoran counterpart. Yet Guatemalan involvement in the process was much greater. Even before the HCC began its work, Guatemalan NGOs had begun an extensive process of collecting testimonies and encouraging those who had not been able to speak out to do so. Both Guatemalans and foreigners who had worked with Guatemalan NGOs were called on to assist the HCC. The commission's surprisingly strong report reflects the crucial contributions of NGOs.

Establishing the truth, seeking justice, and providing material or moral reparations as a basis for reconciliation require political will and an organized civil society. The international community cannot create either of these, but it can provide support to NGOs so that they can increase their capacity to play a role in peace process implementation by developing their oversight capacity and supporting creative initiatives to contribute to the reconciliation process and influence state policies.

The Challenge of Building the Rule of Law

In addition to addressing past human rights abuses, negotiated transitions now routinely include judicial reform as an agenda topic. A negotiations process to end a period of armed conflict represents a unique opportunity to place judicial reform on the national agenda and make it part of a global effort to create more democratic institutions. Furthermore, a UN human rights mission that may follow the negotiations provides unparalleled opportunities to diagnose a system's ills and have international technical assistance available to assist in overcoming them. Nonetheless, the parties to peace negotiations are unlikely to be particularly well suited to the complex task of building the rule of law, which involves normative, cultural, and institutional changes. These limitations can be addressed, at least in part, by including broad sectors of civil society in the process of formulating proposals. Many of the elements considered necessary to guarantee judicial independence—a guaranteed percentage of the national budget, changes in the judicial appointments and disciplinary system, and improved judicial training—were included in the Salvadoran peace accords. However, the reforms agreed to were not based on a broad national consensus or involvement of the justice sector in the discussion, and implementation encountered many obstacles.

Justice reform in postwar El Salvador was, in the words of the UN, a "test case" for the international community. El Salvador had the benefit of a negotiated agreement between an elected government and a representative insurgency as well as enormous international involvement, particularly of the UN and the United States. This "best-case" scenario can mask the problems resulting from a lack of Salvadoran ownership of the process and the top-down approach. Despite their shortcomings, peace negotiations can provide a unique opportunity to initiate a comprehensive, broad-based judicial reform process and to introduce constitutional reforms, for example, to enhance the independence of the judiciary, make habeas corpus protections effective, or improve protections of individual rights. Yet it would be a mistake to view the peace agreements as resolving all the outstanding issues in the justice system. At best, they are likely to establish the conditions that would allow for resolution of outstanding problems.

If anything is clear from the Salvadoran experience, it is that changing entrenched attitudes and practices is far more difficult than outside actors tend to appreciate. Change in a country such as El Salvador requires changing attitudes of the populace, those in the justice sector, and those with political power; involving different operators in the justice sector and civil society groups in a reform effort; a great deal of training and retraining based on internationally accepted standards incorporated into domestic law and practice; follow-up and oversight; and long-term international involvement. The public needs to see actual improvements in protecting rights, adjudicating disputes, and controlling crime. Otherwise, past practices tend to reassert themselves. Despite all the attention given to judicial reform in recent years, we still do not fully understand the process by which a society changes its judicial and police practices. Some changes will necessarily take a longer time because they require training a new generation of lawyers, but immediate changes are necessary to ensure that the process of democratic consolidation will continue.

The obstacles to building the rule of law are far greater in countries such as El Salvador, Haiti, and Guatemala than in countries that have stronger legal frameworks and legal education, even if these have been perverted by an authoritarian regime. Yet the international community is likely to be called on to play a larger role in countries with weaker or more damaged institutional structures. If the problem in El Salvador were primarily one of overcoming problems created by the war, the transformation called for would be less daunting. As Fernando Carrillo has put it, judicial reform in many Latin American countries is starting at what resembles "the first day of creation" rather than a process of "regaining lost opportunities."[13]

Given this reality, it is a mistake to think that the necessary transformation can take place over the lifetime of one or several justice reform projects. What is called for is a massive undertaking that will require many years of support and dedicated efforts. As international experts involved in judicial reform projects have increasingly recognized, reforms can only succeed if the impetus for them comes from within a country: "Needs cannot and should not be made up."[14] Donor-funded judicial reform projects need to avoid both the reality and the perception that "objectives, components, consultants and conditions are imposed" from outside.[15]

In this context, it is crucial that donor-supported projects help to initiate what must ultimately be a societal process and that projects be designed in such a way that their effects do not simply disappear when funding comes to an end. While international assistance can be helpful in assessing the current state and needs of the judiciary, there is little evidence in quantitative and qualitative terms that quickly implemented, makeshift solutions can have a positive impact on what ultimately needs to be a long-term societal process.

    13. Fernando Carrillo, "The Inter-American Development Bank," in *Justice Delayed: Judicial Reform in Latin America,* ed. Edmundo Jarquín and Fernando Carrillo (Washington, D.C.: Inter-American Development Bank, 1998), 149.
    14. Jorge Obando, "Reform of the Justice Sector," in *Governance and Democratic Development in Latin America and the Caribbean* (New York: UN Development Program, 1997), 117.
    15. Ibid., 120.

Short-term training—the favored method in these situations—can only yield limited results. One sobering lesson from El Salvador is that international actors tend to underestimate resistance to the profound changes needed to build the rule of law.

As the UN's massive presence in El Salvador drew to a close, there was a sense that more could have been done. The years after the peace agreements were signed constituted an unprecedented opportunity for fundamental change in the country and for international assistance. ONUSAL was slow to initiate institution-building efforts and made little effort to work with NGOs. On the other hand, Salvadoran institutions failed to capitalize on the technical assistance available. In part this may reflect the failure of international institutions to make a serious effort to offer their services in ways that would not be seen as impinging on Salvadoran sovereignty. Nonetheless, the institutional reluctance to accept foreign technical and professional assistance seemed to reflect a widespread resistance to changing the status quo. It has become a truism that no amount of international assistance will produce changes if the requisite political will to implement reforms does not exist.

Unlike ONUSAL, the UN observers' mission in Guatemala, MINUGUA, sought to combine institution building and human rights verification from the outset. At times this led to tensions within the mission because of the varying perspectives of UN investigators working with Guatemalan law enforcement personnel as they investigated human rights crimes and human rights observers verifying shortcomings in the same investigations. On the whole, however, the two functions were seen as complementary. The observations of human rights observers helped determine priorities for institutional strengthening.

In Guatemala the UN established a coordination between MINUGUA and UNDP based on the experience of other missions that had lacked effective coordination with permanent UN agencies as well as adequate plans to continue institution-building activities after the end of the temporary mission. MINUGUA's activities in institution building necessarily amounted to "strategic inputs" rather than a "comprehensive overhaul of the justice system."[16] MINUGUA gave priority to working with the public prosecutor's office, which was in the process of assuming a leading role in criminal investigations and prosecutions. It offered assistance in reorganizing the institution, training in the new Criminal Procedure Code, developing investigation

---

16. Leonardo Franco and Jared Kotler, "Combining Institution Building and Human Rights Verification in Guatemala: The Challenge of Buying In Without Selling Out," in *Honoring Human Rights,* ed. Alice H. Henkin (Washington, D.C.: Aspen Institute, 1998), 61.

strategies, implementing policies to improve the professional skills of personnel, and establishing an internal disciplinary system. MINUGUA also helped
design an overall criminal policy and improve coordination with the police.[17]

Other Guatemalan institutions were less receptive to MINUGUA's involvement. The Guatemalan government had opted for a bilateral assistance
arrangement with Spain for the National Civilian Police, and the Supreme
Court was a "reluctant partner." As it focused on institution building,
MINUGUA found that expectations for reform were often unrealistic and
that Guatemalan institutions had a limited capacity to absorb international
assistance.[18] Technical assistance could have only a limited impact on institutions plagued by structural problems such as insufficient resources and
skilled staff, and lacking objective standards and effective mechanisms for
evaluation and supervision. Despite the successful completion of training
activities, it was difficult to determine whether training was having any
noticeable impact on institutional behavior. To be successful, institution
building must set in motion a long-term comprehensive reform of the justice
system. With this in mind, MINUGUA concluded that temporary missions
should emphasize sustainability, which requires building national capacity
to sustain reforms.

Working closely with national counterparts, international actors should
establish strategic priorities because of shrinking resources and the need to
implement some fundamental reforms during the window of opportunity
after the peace settlement (or transition) that will provide impetus and a
framework for further reforms. Donors should speak out about actions that
undermine the letter or spirit of the peace accords or that contradict international human rights norms.

Promoting the Rule of Law When a Government Lacks Commitment to Reform

Unfortunately, the availability of funding often does not coincide with a
country's readiness to undertake major reform efforts. U.S. funding is politically driven and is made available at critical moments for U.S. policy—for
example, El Salvador in 1984 and Haiti in 1994–95. Thus, the dollars are
available and must be allocated, but the counterparts may have a very limited

17. Ibid., 56.
18. Ibid., 61–62.

ability to absorb the assistance and may actually be resistant to change. Regardless of their capacity to carry out reforms, however, leaders of the judicial and executive branches rarely turn down offers of additional resources.

A difficult question is whether money should be provided for judicial reform in the kind of situation existing in El Salvador or Guatemala during the 1980s. Human rights groups object that this kind of aid legitimizes regimes that continue to violate human rights at the same time that it fails to introduce any substantive improvements because those in power are not seriously committed to reform. Yet these programs had some positive effects, although hardly enough to justify the millions of dollars expended. Lawyers and judges trained under the U.S.-funded program in Guatemala credit the program with opening their eyes about human rights standards and prosecutorial methods. Salvadorans cite fewer positive effects of training, which began later, but note that the work carried out by CORELESAL provided valuable groundwork for subsequent, more serious law reform efforts. They also note that because there was no indigenous judicial reform effort, the U.S.-funded project heightened consciousness—albeit in limited circles—about the need for reform. Unfortunately, however, the AOJ project failed to address the institutional, political, and attitudinal changes necessary for fundamental, sustainable reform.[19] Nor did it tackle such key issues as judicial independence.

When a government is not committed to reform, creative programs can be devised to support those who are likely to be interested in reform. This requires that donors make an honest evaluation of the groups and individuals actually or potentially interested in judicial reform. Donors can target sectors and issues likely to increase demand for reform and prepare people and groups for participation in a reform effort once political conditions permit. Although civil society organizations are likely to have been weakened by repression, donors can provide funding to nongovernmental organizations to carry out training, research efforts, and education to build a consciousness of the need for fundamental reform. The international community can help to legitimize civil society efforts, which should eventually contribute to institutional reform.[20] In countries that have established a human

19. U.S. General Accounting Office, *Foreign Assistance: Promoting Judicial Reform to Strengthen Democracies*, GAO/NSIAD–93–149 (September 1993).

20. See, e.g., Carlos Dada, "Vamos a trabajar para reformar la ley de Armas," *La Prensa Gráfica*, August 27, 1999.

rights ombudsman or other independent entity designed to oversee the human rights situation, donors may be able to work with and strengthen these institutions.[21] In all cases, donors should insist on open and transparent processes.

When political will to undertake reforms does not exist, donors can still provide valuable opportunities for interchange with individuals involved in reform efforts in other countries. Such contacts serve to break down isolation and plant seeds that may bear fruit years later. Foreign consultants can provide new ideas, bibliography, and links to groups in other countries faced with similar challenges. Donors can provide access to essential documents, codes, and legal analysis (often extremely scarce), as well as information about developments in other countries in the region (or with similar legal systems). Individuals in a country engaged in civil war or under an authoritarian regime may find themselves unusually isolated from developments taking place in the region. Opportunities for contact with colleagues in other countries can help break down this isolation and make it easier to reach a consensus about a comprehensive strategy for reform, the most fundamental problems to be addressed, and the pros and cons of different strategies. Donors can also fund conferences or provide opportunities for interchange designed to promote discussion of alternative reform strategies or solutions to particular problems. Through the Internet, contacts can easily be maintained and expanded.

Efforts to improve law schools and judicial training schools take on great importance in the long-term process of training a new generation of lawyers and judges with an entirely different mentality. Donors can help with the development of new curricula that include, for example, the study of legal ethics and human rights, and the introduction or improvement of clinical programs. Donors may be able to provide information about, and funding for, valuable opportunities available to students and graduates (including international moot court competitions and programs for study abroad).

Diagnostic efforts can begin to identify obstacles to the independence of judges, key problems in the criminal justice system, sources of delay, and arbitrary actions. Donors can suggest that NGOs interested in women's rights, for example, undertake to diagnose gender-based discrimination in

21. The Government Human Rights Commission in El Salvador received considerable AID funding but enjoyed neither independence, authority, nor credibility. Under the executive branch, the human rights commission sought to better the government's human rights image, focused on FMLN abuses and acts of sabotage, and monitored the flow of prisoners accused of political crimes.

existing laws and practices, and propose appropriate changes. Debate about potential reform can also be encouraged through the media. Donors can also support efforts to improve access to justice through legal aid services or law school clinics. Successful efforts of this kind are likely to increase demand for reform of the system as well as serve a public education function. They can encourage studies of other steps necessary to improve access to justice (e.g., waiving court fees, establishing or strengthening public defender programs).

International donors should avoid viewing judicial reform efforts as substitutes for military reform, civilian control over the military, or other efforts to overcome impunity. A judicial reform effort should be part of a broader effort to consolidate democracy and overcome a tradition of impunity for privileged sectors. By itself, no amount of judicial reform will put an end to impunity. Progress on high-profile, sensitive cases inevitably reflects the political will—or more often, lack thereof —to confront the military or other powerful interests. Careful conditioning of assistance should be used to ensure that a government is committed to reform and that foreign assistance is not simply used to legitimate a government that fails to undertake essential institutional reforms and effective measures to improve its human rights performance. A judicial reform effort needs to be highly cognizant of the overall political climate, while developing methods to evaluate what the project itself has set out to achieve.

Reform Efforts Reflecting a National Consensus

Donors should encourage counterparts to carry out thorough diagnostic studies that will lead to comprehensive strategies. Judicial reform advocates have developed a laundry list of basic elements for reform, such as guaranteeing the judiciary a percentage of the national budget, improved selection and disciplinary systems, better court administration through case management and court management reforms, procedural reforms, alternative dispute resolution mechanisms, improving access to justice, and legal education and training programs.[22]

In recent years, Latin American reformers have embraced the adversarial system and introduced oral proceedings. The corollary to the adversarial system, a developed system of plea bargaining, has met with less acceptance.

22. Maria Dakolias, *The Judicial Sector in Latin America and the Caribbean: Elements of Reform*, Technical Paper no. 319 (Washington, D.C.: World Bank, 1996), 7.

While the experiences of other countries can be very helpful, donors need to avoid prescribing particular solutions or making assumptions about needs and priorities. Carrying out diagnostic studies with broad-based participation should ensure the identification of critical problems to be addressed by the project, allow opposition to surface early so that it can be adequately addressed, and contribute to the development of a social base for reform.[23] Close contact with national reality should ensure that reforms proposed are not outside the realm of possibility or inappropriate to the national reality. Thus, reform efforts need to take into account public concerns about crime and the capacity to absorb changes, but they should not allow these concerns to be used to preclude essential reforms to protect individual rights.

Donors can also encourage the formation of coordinating bodies to support reform that include representatives of key sectors of the population. Official coordinating bodies are essential to determining priorities and sequencing in the implementation of long-term, comprehensive strategies. States need to assume responsibility for identifying problems in the justice sector, and for proposing and implementing solutions. In El Salvador, the United States pushed for the creation of a justice sector coordination and the *Unidad Técnica Ejecutiva* (UTE), neither of which included any nongovernmental participation. In their early years, these official bodies showed little dynamism and did not actively engage donors to establish priorities and avoid duplication of efforts. To build a broader consensus, efforts to design and develop judicial reform projects should include representatives of the legal community and civil society in general.

In contrast, in Guatemala the 1996 peace accords called for the president to create a "Justice Strengthening Commission."[24] The commission was composed of three Supreme Court justices, one appellate justice, the former president of a lawyer's association (and former cabinet minister), an advisor to the private enterprise coordination (CACIF), the president of an NGO that works on justice issues, two law school deans, a legal advisor to Mayan organizations, the director of the National Civilian Police, and an advisor to the Public Ministry. The commission was given a six-month mandate to engage in broad discussions aimed at producing a report and recommendations that could be rapidly implemented. The UN observers' mission in

23. Patrick J. Gavigan, *Halfway to Reform: The World Bank and the Venezuelan Justice System* (New York: Lawyers Committee for Human Rights and Venezuelan Program for Human Rights Education and Action, 1996), 115–16.

24. See Agreement on Strengthening Civil Power and the Role of the Army in a Democratic Society, September 19, 1996.

Guatemala, MINUGUA, was available to advise the commission, whose agenda included, but was not limited to, the issues of modernization, access to justice, improving efficiency, and professional excellence. The commission held ten public meetings (four in the capital and six elsewhere in the country) with representatives of governmental, Mayan, women's and human rights organizations, research and educational institutions, professional organizations, unions, and other groups concerned with justice in Guatemala.[25] Its final report included a series of observations and recommendations.

Ideally, an effort to build the rule of law should be a national effort that plays a crucial role in the larger effort to ensure a firm and lasting peace (in the case of countries emerging from a period of armed conflict). Ownership of a judicial reform project by a single institution or political party is likely to doom the effort to failure. Similarly, a project sponsored by a single donor is likely to fail. Donors can try to depoliticize assistance by routing funds through intermediaries and involving Europeans, who also may have the advantage of having legal systems more akin to those in Latin America. Donors should establish mechanisms to coordinate their efforts in order to avoid haphazard, inconsistent, or duplicative efforts. Competition among donors to control reform initiatives inevitably complicates reform processes.

In recent years, the shape of donor involvement has been evolving. The UNDP, the World Bank, and the Inter-American Development Bank (IDB) have become increasingly involved in judicial reform, which is now understood as crucial to sustainable development, the consolidation of democracy, and a stable environment for investment. The World Bank, for example, has concluded that reform programs should "address the political, economic and legal causes at the root of an inefficient and inequitable judiciary."[26] Within each institution, concerns have been raised about their involvement in this politically sensitive area, particularly as the IDB and UNDP plan or undertake projects related to criminal justice and human rights. (World Bank policy has precluded its involvement in this sphere.)

The technical capacity of these institutions is not in question. Moreover, as a number of publications now attest, these institutions have now incorporated many of the lessons learned about international assistance in justice reform. Unfortunately, these lessons are not always put into practice. Donors have continued to repeat similar mistakes in different countries, suggesting that important lessons learned are not always incorporated into

25. Comisión de Fortalecimiento de la Justicia, *Una Nueva Justicia para la Paz,* Guatemala, April 1998.
26. Dakolias, *Elements of Reform,* 7.

planning and implementation of judicial reform projects. Even projects that begin by recognizing the lessons of past experience need to develop adequate oversight mechanisms to keep their efforts on track and be prepared to mobilize political pressure when projects are derailed. When donors announce that they will be initiating a multimillion-dollar project in a country *before* doing a needs assessment, they run the risk of encouraging unnecessary or impractical projects.

Carefully selected foreign consultants can play a key role in providing expertise. It was unreasonable to expect that Salvadoran solutions that effectively guarantee individual rights would emerge unassisted, given the country's history and limited legal resources. One of the challenges to donor-supported reform efforts is to help build a domestic capacity to spearhead the reform effort, relying on foreign consultants for technical assistance but driving the effort—and establishing the agenda—from within. With this in mind, key contributions can be those that allow individuals and groups within a country to develop understanding and skills for the long haul.

Evaluating the Success of Justice Reform Efforts

In the early years of AID's judicial reform efforts in El Salvador, U.S. officials seemed to have little interest in a serious evaluation of the project. With political concerns in Washington driving the project, its purported goals were of little importance. But because of the complexity of justice reform and the resistance changes are likely to encounter, ongoing evaluation processes are essential.

Had the United States wanted to assess whether its efforts were contributing to the improvement of criminal justice, it might have tried to determine whether police, prosecutors, and judges were following procedures that complied with Salvadoran law and international standards in areas such as investigations, prosecutions, treatment of detainees, access to counsel, compliance with time periods, and quality of judicial resolutions. The U.S. project could have given priority to the establishment of oversight mechanisms at the national and local level so that civil society could become involved in monitoring the performance of the different actors in the justice system. It should certainly have looked at the kinds of law reforms proposed and approved as well as the adequacy of their implementation. In recent years, public opinion surveys have been used as indicators. Public opinion is unlikely to reflect improvements in judicial processes immediately, however. Targeted surveys or focus groups may be more effective in evaluating a project's effectiveness.

If criteria for project assessment are based on statistics that do not involve a human rights component, they may ignore or correlate negatively with the inclusion of procedural safeguards.[27] For example, using the number of convictions achieved as a way to evaluate the performance of prosecutors can be highly problematic. Evaluations of prosecutors could also take into account other factors, such as efficiency in handling caseloads (dismissals as well as prosecutions), legal analysis and drafting, and the lack of judicial rebuke and citizen complaint.[28]

In evaluating training, projects have often cited the number of training sessions held as an indicator of success. Yet many trainees willingly attend seminars but do not incorporate what they have been taught into their work. To make training effective, projects must be able to assess needs before training and impact afterward. Impact assessment can involve on-the-job follow-up or mechanisms that, for example, require participants to submit a subsequent resolution (in the case of judges) or brief (in the case of lawyers and prosecutors) that reflects what they learned in the seminar. Effective oversight mechanisms should be able to gauge whether judges are issuing decisions on a more timely basis or whether citizen complaints about abusive police practices are decreasing.

When funding is provided to state institutions or others, foreign actors need to maintain sufficient distance from those institutions so that they can engage in stocktaking exercises and honestly evaluate whether project objectives are being furthered. Although outside evaluations are necessary, project evaluation should be ongoing, rather than waiting for an outside evaluator to come and tell those involved in a project that its efforts are not producing and are unlikely to produce the intended results. An assessment of project progress cannot be made on a purely technical level. A political component should look, for example, at a country's progress in overcoming military impunity and holding police accountable for abuses.

International human rights standards provide essential guideposts to determine whether reforms are likely to contribute to the establishment of the rule of law. During the 1980s in El Salvador, AID personnel at times dismissed as "politicized" those using international human rights norms to

27. Proposed categories to be measured include the conviction rate, rate of judicial acceptance of investigative results, percentage of cases taken to judgment, average length of proceedings, and number of cases in which defense counsel represent the accused. These criteria are solely quantitative and allow no consideration of fairness and compliance with international norms.

28. John H. Langbein, "Land Without Plea Bargaining: How Germans Do It," *Michigan Law Review* 78 (1979–80): 217.

critique the Salvadoran justice system. In recent years, however, AID has looked to these norms to ensure that constitutions and laws conform to human rights standards, including instruments that the United States has not ratified.[29]

In countries where the United States has had less at stake politically, program evaluations have led to decisions to suspend or limit the scope of judicial reform funding because sufficient political will did not exist. AID made such determinations in Guatemala in 1991[30] and in Peru in 1994. In Guatemala the conditions for renewing assistance included passage of a new Criminal Procedure Code and the reorganization of the Attorney General's office. AID's willingness in these cases to review existing programs to determine whether goals were being met and human rights concerns addressed was positive. Yet this type of review does not seem to have become institutionalized.

The Challenges Ahead

International donors will continue to play crucial but diminishing roles in countries such as El Salvador, but societal expectations must also change. Somehow Salvadorans must come to understand that the rule of law applies and that disputes should no longer be resolved on the basis of the relative power of the contenders.

For democracy to succeed, the transformations required must be assumed not only by state institutions and politicians but by the population as a whole, including those who were excluded from participation and victimized under the prior arrangement. An integral part of changing attitudes involves providing some kind of real or symbolic reparation to those who suffered the consequences of the acts of violence that occurred during the war. This task is immense and is complicated by the failure to address the situation of tens of thousands of victims of the war—parents who lost children, children who

29. See Center for Democracy and Governance, Bureau for Global Programs, Field Support, and Research, U.S. Agency for International Development, *Handbook of Democracy and Governance Program Indicators* (Washington, D.C.: Management Systems International, 1998) 19, 27. Among the international instruments cited are the International Covenant on Social, Economic, and Cultural Rights, the Convention on the Elimination of All Forms of Discrimination Against Women (CEDAW), the European Convention for the Protection of Human Rights and Fundamental Freedoms, the American Convention on Human Rights, and the African [Banjul] Charter on Human and Peoples' Rights.

30. See USAID/Guatemala, Stocktaking of 1986–1991, Administration of Justice Program (October 1991).

lost parents, spouses who lost spouses. Only time will tell how serious the consequences of these failures will be.

Despite all the setbacks and problems detailed here, the Salvadoran peace process remains an example for the world. The peace agreements created a window of opportunity, but that opening was of finite duration. Failure to take advantage of it to make substantial progress toward consolidating democratic institutions and the rule of law, while building adequate domestic safeguards against abuses leaves open the possibility of past practices reasserting themselves. El Salvador still risks accomplishing only an incomplete transformation, which could leave some gains reversible and many reforms either never approved or, at best, inadequately implemented.

The obstacles are real: erratic political will, an enormous need for technical and economic resources, weak or incipient state institutions charged with safeguarding human rights, the tendency for old vices to reassert themselves in new forms, the lack of adequate oversight mechanisms within institutions, a weak civil society, and enormous economic exclusion. Constant vigilance is necessary, and this will no longer come from the UN. Domestic oversight mechanisms must become equal to the task.

One of the greatest challenges confronting El Salvador as the century begins is addressing the country's unprecedented crime wave. The postwar Salvadoran state is no longer responsible for massive human rights violations, but it remains incapable of controlling common crime and ensuring a modicum of security to the populace. Eight years after the peace accords were signed, Salvadorans claimed to live in greater fear than they did during the war. Criminal bands, often composed of ex-soldiers or former guerrillas, operated with virtual impunity because people were afraid to denounce them to the authorities. While this situation is particularly acute in El Salvador, other countries emerging from armed conflicts or authoritarian rule, including South Africa and Guatemala, are experiencing similar crime waves that also threaten democratic gains. Weak justice systems and inexperienced police are called on to confront levels of crime and heavy weaponry that would test the most established and reliable justice system. Lacking confidence in state institutions, the citizenry calls for tougher, more authoritarian measures and sometimes may even take the law into its own hands. The international community will need to draw on all its creativity to assist countries to combat this threat to postconflict societies. As in other areas, donors can provide critical opportunities to share experiences and ideas. One critical area for donor assistance is the development of targeted crime prevention initiatives. Above all, they should emphasize the need to address the crime problem on all fronts. This means long-term solutions to address the socioeconomic causes of crime; to limit the possession of firearms; to strengthen the justice system so that it is efficient, independent, accountable, and protective of individual rights; and to professionalize the police to make it capable of combating crime without violating citizens' rights. Without comprehensive anticrime policies consistent with democratic values, countries risk returning to authoritarian models and abandoning key democratic reforms.

The challenges ahead remain enormous as El Salvador and other countries that have found the resources to end years of bitter conflict must now use all their creativity to find ways to overcome impunity and consolidate the rule of law.

BIBLIOGRAPHY

Books, Chapters, Articles

Abregú, Martín. "La tutela judicial del derecho a la verdad en la Argentina." *Revista IIDH* 24 (1996).

Acuña, Carlos H., and Catalina Smulovitz. "Guarding the Guardians in Argentina: Some Lessons About the Risks and Benefits of Empowering the Courts." In *Transitional Justice and the Rule of Law in New Democracies,* ed. James McAdams (Notre Dame: University of Notre Dame Press, 1997).

Alvarez, José E. "Promoting the 'Rule of Law' in Latin America: Problems and Prospects." *George Washington Journal of International Law and Economics* 25 (1991).

Americas Watch. *El Salvador's Decade of Terror.* New Haven: Yale University Press, 1991.

Anderson, Kenneth H. "Action Specific Human Rights Legislation for El Salvador." *Harvard Journal of Legislation* 22 (1985).

Anderson, Thomas P. *Matanza: El Salvador's Communist Revolt of 1932.* Lincoln: University of Nebraska Press, 1971.

Aristide, Bertrand. "The Role of the Judiciary in the Transition to Democracy." In *Transition to Democracy in Latin America: the Role of the Judiciary,* ed. Irwin P. Stotzky. Boulder: Westview Press, 1993.

Armstrong, Robert, and Janet Shenk. *The Face of Revolution.* Boston: South End Press, 1982.

Arnson, Cynthia. *Crossroads: Congress, the President, and Central America 1976–1993,* 2d ed. University Park: Pennsylvania State University Press, 1993.

Ash, Timothy Garton. "The Truth About Dictatorship." *New York Review of Books* 45 (February 19, 1998): 35.

Baloyra, Enrique. *El Salvador in Transition.* Chapel Hill: University of North Carolina Press, 1982.

Binder, Alberto M. *Justicia Penal y Estado de Derecho.* Buenos Aires: Ad-Hoc, SRL, 1993.

Bonner, Raymond. *Weakness and Deceit: U.S. Policy and El Salvador.* New York: Times Books, 1984.

Boutros-Ghali, Boutros. *An Agenda for Peace.* New York: United Nations, 1992.

Bright, Stephen B. "Counsel for the Poor: The Death Sentence Not for the Worst Crime but for the Worst Lawyer." *Yale Law Journal* 103 (1994): 1835.

Brody, Reed. "The United Nations and Human Rights in El Salvador's 'Negotiated Revolution.'" *Harvard Human Rights Journal* 8 (Spring 1995): 153.

Browning, David. *El Salvador, Landscape and Society.* London: Clarendon/Oxford University Press, 1971.

Buergenthal, Thomas. "The United Nations Truth Commission for El Salvador." *Vanderbilt Journal of Transnational Law* 27 (1994): 497.

Byrne, Hugh. *El Salvador's Civil War: A Study of Revolution.* Boulder and London: Lynne Rienner Publishers, 1996.

Carlson, Peter. "You Have the Right to Remain Silent ..." *Washington Post Magazine,* September 13, 1998, W06.

Carothers, Thomas. *In the Name of Democracy: U.S. Policy Toward Latin America in the Reagan Years.* Berkeley and Los Angeles: University of California Press, 1991.

———. "The Rule of Law Revival." *Foreign Affairs* 77 (1998): 2.

Carrillo, Fernando. "The Inter-American Development Bank." In *Justice Delayed: Judicial Reform in Latin America,* ed. Edmundo Jarquín and Fernando Carrillo. Washington, D.C.: Inter-American Development Bank, 1998.

Cassel, Douglass. "Lessons from the Americas: Guidelines for International Response to Amnesties for Atrocities." *Law and Contemporary Problems* 59 (1996): 4.

———. "International Truth Commissions and Justice." *Aspen Institute Quarterly* 5 (1993): 69.

Correa Sutil, Jorge. "Dealing with Past Human Rights Violations: The Chilean Case After Dictatorship." *Notre Dame Law Review* 67 (1992): 1455.

———. "The Judiciary and the Political System in Chile: The Dilemmas of Judicial Independence During the Transition to Democracy." In *Transition to Democracy in Latin America: The Role of the Judiciary,* ed. Irwin P. Stotzky. Boulder: Westview Press, 1993.

———. "Modernization, Democratization, and Judicial Systems." In *Justice Delayed: Judicial Reform in Latin America,* ed. Edmundo Jarquín and Fernando Carrillo. Washington, D.C.: Inter-American Development Bank, 1998.

———. " 'No Victorious Army Has Ever Been Prosecuted ...': The Unsettled Story of Transitional Justice in Chile." In *Transitional Justice and the Rule of Law in New Democracies,* ed. James McAdams. Notre Dame: University of Notre Dame Press, 1997.

Costa, Gino. *La Policía Nacional Civil de El Salvador* (1990–1997) San Salvador: UCA Editores, 1999.

Crawford, Kathryn Lee. "Due Obedience and the Rights of Victims: Argentina's Transition to Democracy." *Human Rights Quarterly* 12 (1990): 17.

Crepeau, François. "Rapport d'un observateur international dans l'affaire du meurtre des Jesuites a la Universidad Centroamericana de San Salvador." *McGill Law Journal* 37 (1992).

Crocker, David A. "Reckoning with Past Wrongs: A Normative Framework." *Ethics and International Affairs* 13 (1999).

Dakolias, Maria. *The Judicial Sector in Latin America and the Caribbean: Elements of Reform.* Technical Paper no. 319. Washington, D.C.: World Bank, 1996.

———. "A Strategy for Judicial Reform: The Experience in Latin America." *Virginia Journal of International Law* 36 (1995): 1, 167–231.

Danner, Mark. *The Massacre at El Mozote.* New York: Vantage Books, 1994.

"El Decreto 507, una Monstruosidad Jurídica." *Estudios Centroamericanos.* San Salvador (January–February 1981), reprinted in Universidad Centroamericana José Simeón Cañas, Instituto de Derechos Humanos. *Recopilación de Trabajos Publicados en la Revista Estudios Centroamericanos (ECA), Volumen II: Comentarios y Documentos.* San Salvador: 1986.

"La Derogatoria de la Ley de Defensa y Garantia del Orden Público." *Estudios Centroamericanos.* San Salvador (April 1979).

DeWind, A. W., and S. L. Kass. "Justice in El Salvador: Report of a Mission of Inquiry of the Association of the Bar of the City of New York." *Recordings of the Association of the Bar of the City of New York* 38 (1983).

Diamond, Larry, Juan Linz, and Seymour Martin Lipset, eds. *Democracy in Developing Countries: Latin America.* Boulder: Lynne Rienner Publishers, 1989.

Dodson, J. Michael, and Donald W. Jackson. "Re-inventing the Rule of Law: Human Rights in El Salvador." *Democratization* 4 (Winter 1997): 4.

Doggett, Martha. *Death Foretold: The Jesuit Murders in El Salvador.* Washington, D.C.: Georgetown University Press, 1993.

———. *Underwriting Injustice: AID and El Salvador's Judicial Reform Program.* New York: Lawyers Committee for Human Rights, 1989.

Los Escuadrones de la Muerte en El Salvador. San Salvador: Editorial Jaragua, 1994.

Fiss, Owen. "The Limits of Judicial Independence." *University of Miami Inter-American Law Review* 25 (1993).

———. "The Right Degree of Independence." In *Transition to Democracy in Latin America: The Role of the Judiciary,* ed. Irwin P. Stotzky. Boulder: Westview Press, 1993.

Franco, Leonardo, and Jared Kotler. "Combining Institution Building and Human Rights Verification in Guatemala: The Challenge of Buying In Without Selling Out." In *Honoring Human Rights: From Peace to Justice,* ed. Alice H. Henkin. Washington, D.C.: Aspen Institute, 1998.

Fuentes Hernández, Alfredo, ed. *Reforma Judicial en América Latina: Una tarea inconclusa.* Santa Fe de Bogotá: Corporación Excelencia en la Justicia, 1999.

Galindo, Francisco Bertrand, José Albino Tinetti, Silvia Lizette Kuri de Mendoza, and María Elena Orellana. *Manual de Derecho Constitucional.* San Salvador: Centro de Investigación y Capacitación, Proyecto de Reforma Judicial, 1992.

García-Sayán, Diego. "The Experience of ONUSAL in El Salvador." In *Honoring Human Rights and Keeping the Peace: Lessons from El Salvador, Cambodia and Haiti,* ed. Alice H. Henkin. Washington, D.C.: Aspen Institute, 1995.

Gardner, James A. *Legal Imperialism: American Lawyers and Foreign Aid in Latin America.* Madison: University of Wisconsin Press, 1980.

Garro, Alejandro M. "Nine Years of Transition to Democracy in Argentina: Partial Failure or Qualified Success?" *Columbia Journal of Transnational Law* 31 (1993).

———. "The Role of the Argentine Judiciary in Controlling Governmental Action Under a State of Siege." *Human Rights Law Journal* 4 (1983).

Garro, Alejandro M., and Henry Dahl. "Legal Accountability for Human Rights Violations in Argentina: One Step Forward and Two Steps Backward." *Human Rights Law Journal* 8 (1987): 283.

Gavigan, Patrick J. *Halfway to Reform: The World Bank and the Venezuelan Justice System*. New York: Lawyers Committee for Human Rights and Venezuelan Program for Human Rights Education and Action, 1996.

Goldman, Robert K. "International Law and Amnesty Laws." *Human Rights Internet Reporter* 12 (1988): 9.

———. "Report to the Lawyers Committee for Human Rights on the Jesuit Murder Trial." Appendix C to *Death Foretold: The Jesuit Murders in El Salvador*, Martha Doggett. Washington, D.C.: Georgetown University Press, 1993.

Guidos Véjar, Rafael. *El Ascenso del Militarismo en El Salvador*, 4th ed. San Salvador: UCA Editores, 1980.

Haggarty, Richard A., ed. *El Salvador: A Country Study*. Washington, D.C.: Federal Research Division, Library of Congress, 1990.

Hammergren, Linn. *The Politics of Justice and Justice Reform in Latin America: The Peruvian Case in Comparative Perspective*. Boulder, Colo.: Westview Press, 1998.

Hayner, Priscilla B. "Fifteen Truth Commissions—1974 to 1994: A Comparative Study." *Human Rights Quarterly* 16 (1994): 597.

———. *Unspeakable Truths: Confronting State Terror and Atrocity*. New York: Routledge, 2000.

Henkin, Alice H., ed. *State Crimes: Punishment or Pardon*. Washington, D.C.: Aspen Institute, 1989.

———, ed. *Honoring Human Rights and Keeping the Peace: Lessons from El Salvador, Cambodia, and Haiti*. Washington, D.C.: Aspen Institute, 1995.

———, ed. *Honoring Human Rights: From Peace to Justice*. Washington, D.C.: Aspen Institute, 1998.

Holiday, David, and William Stanley. "Building the Peace: Preliminary Lessons from El Salvador." *Journal of International Affairs* 46 (1993): 415.

Inter-American Development Bank. *Justice and Development in Latin America and the Caribbean*. Seminar sponsored by the Inter-American Development Bank, San José, Costa Rica, February 4–6, 1993. Washington, D.C.: Inter-American Development Bank, 1994.

Jarquín, Edmundo, and Fernando Carrillo, eds. *Justice Delayed: Judicial Reform in Latin America*. Washington, D.C.: Inter-American Development Bank, 1998.

Johnstone, Ian. *Rights and Reconciliation: United Nations Strategies in El Salvador*. Boulder and London: Lynne Rienner Publishers, 1995.

Karl, Terry Lynn. "El Salvador's Negotiated Revolution." *Foreign Affairs* 71 (1992): 147.

Kaye, Mike. "The Role of Truth Commissions in the Search for Justice, Reconciliation, and Democratisation: The Salvadorean and Honduran Cases." *Journal of Latin American Studies* 29 (1997).

Kritz, Neil J., ed. *Transitional Justice: How Emerging Democracies Reckon with Former Regimes*. Washington, D.C.: United States Institute of Peace, 1995.

Krog, Antjie, and Charlayne Hunter-Gault. *Country of My Skull: Guilt, Sorrow, and the Limits of Forgiveness in the New South Africa*. New York: Times Books, 1999.

Langbein, John H. "Land Without Plea Bargaining: How Germans Do It." *Michigan Law Review* 78 (1979–80).

Lawyers Committee for Human Rights. *Improvising History: A Critical Evaluation of the United Nations Observer Mission in El Salvador*. New York: Lawyers Committee for Human Rights, 1995.

LeoGrande, William M. *Our Own Backyard: The United States in Central America, 1977–1992*. Chapel Hill and London: University of North Carolina Press, 1998.

Malamud-Goti, Jaime. *Game Without End: State Terror and the Politics of Justice*. Norman and London: University of Oklahoma Press, 1996.

———. "Human Rights Abuses in Fledgling Democracies: The Role of Discretion." In *Transition to Democracy in Latin America: The Role of the Judiciary*, ed. Irwin P. Stotzky. Boulder: Westview Press, 1993.

———. "Punishment and a Rights-Based Democracy." *Criminal Justice Ethics* (Summer–Fall 1991).

———. "Transitional Governments in the Breach: Why Punish State Criminals?" *Human Rights Quarterly* 12 (1990): 1.

———. "Trying Violators of Human Rights: The Dilemma of Transitional Democratic Governments." In *State Crimes, Punishment or Pardon*. Washington, D.C.: Aspen Institute, 1989.

Martínez, Ana Guadalupe. *Las Cárceles Clandestinas de El Salvador*. San Salvador: UCA Editores, 1992.

McAdams, James A., ed. *Transitional Justice and the Rule of Law in New Democracies*. Notre Dame: University of Notre Dame Press, 1997.

McClintock, Michael. *The American Connection*, Vol. 1: *State Terror and Popular Resistance in El Salvador*. London: Zed, 1985.

Méndez, Juan E. "Accountability for Past Abuses." *Human Rights Quarterly* 19 (1997): 2.

Méndez, Juan E., Guillermo O'Donnell, and Paulo Sérgio Pinheiro, eds. *The (Un)Rule of Law and the Underprivileged in Latin America*. Notre Dame: University of Notre Dame Press, 1999.

Menéndez, Isidro, Presbítero, Doctor y Licenciado. *Recopilación de Leyes de El Salvador*. Guatemala: Imprenta de L. Luna, plazuela del Sagrario, Libro 4.

Mignone, Emilio F., et al. "Dictatorship on Trial: Prosecution of Human Rights Violations in Argentina." *Yale Journal of International Law* 10 (1984): 118.

Minow, Martha. *Between Vengeance and Forgiveness: Facing History After Genocide and Mass Violence*. Boston: Beacon Press, 1998.

Montgomery, Tommie Sue. *Revolution in El Salvador: Origins and Evolution*. Boulder: Westview Press, 1982.

Neier, Aryeh. *War Crimes: Brutality, Genocide and the Struggle for Justice*. New York: Times Books, 1998.

———. "What Should Be Done About the Guilty?" *New York Review of Books* 32 (February 1, 1990).

Nino, Carlos Santiago. "Human Rights in Context: The Case of Argentina." *Yale Law Journal* 100 (1991): 2619.

———. "The Human Rights Policy of the Argentine Constitutional Government: A Reply." *Yale Journal of International Law* 11 (1985): 217.

"La Nueva Corte Suprema de Justicia y los Reos Políticos." *Estudios Centroamericanos*. San Salvador (August 1982).

O'Donnell, Guillermo, Philippe Schmitter, and Laurence Whitehead. *Transitions from Authoritarian Rule*. Baltimore: Johns Hopkins University Press, 1986.

Oficina de Derechos Humanos del Arzobispado de Guatemala. *Guatemala: Never Again*. Maryknoll: Orbis Books, 1999.

Orentlicher, Diane F. "Addressing Gross Human Rights Abuses: Punishment and Victim Compensation." In *Human Rights: An Agenda for the Next Century,*

Studies in Transnational Legal Studies, No. 26, ed. Louis Henkin and John Lawrence Hargrove. Washington, D.C.: American Society of International Law, 1994.

——. "The Role of the Prosecutor in the Transition to Democracy in Latin America." In *Transition to Democracy in Latin America: The Role of the Judiciary,* ed. Irwin P. Stotzky. Boulder: Westview Press, 1993.

——. "Settling Accounts: The Duty to Prosecute Human Rights Violations of a Prior Regime." *Yale Law Review* 100 (1991): 2537.

——. "A Reply to Professor Nino." *Yale Law Journal* 100 (1991): 2641.

Ortiz Ruiz, Francisco Eliseo. *Diez Años de Reforma Judicial en El Salvador (1985–1995): Aproximación a un Diagnóstico.* San Salvador: Fundación Friedrich Ebert, 1997.

Osiel, Mark. *Mass Atrocity, Collective Memory, and the Law.* New Brunswick: Transaction Books, 1997.

Pásara, Luis. "Judicial Reform and Civil Society." In *Justice Delayed: Judicial Reform in Latin America,* ed. Edmundo Jarquín and Fernando Carrillo. Washington, D.C.: Inter-American Development Bank, 1998.

Pasqualucci, Jo M. "The Whole Truth and Nothing but the Truth: Truth Commissions, Impunity, and the Inter-American Human Rights System." *Boston University International Law Journal* 12 (1994): 321.

Pion-Berlin, David. "To Prosecute or to Pardon? Human Rights Decisions in the Latin American Southern Cone." *Human Rights Quarterly* 16 (1994): 105.

Popkin, Margaret. "Guatemala's National Reconciliation Law: Combating Impunity or Continuing It?" *Revista IIDH* 24 (1996).

Popkin, Margaret, and Nehal Bhuta. "Latin American Amnesties in Comparative Perspective: Can the Past Be Buried?" *Ethics and International Affairs* 13 (1999).

Popkin, Margaret, and Naomi Roht-Arriaza. "Truth as Justice: Investigatory Commissions in Latin America." *Journal of Law and Social Inquiry* 20 (1995): 79.

Posner, Michael, and Scott Greathead. "Justice in El Salvador: A Report of the Lawyers Committee for International Human Rights on the Investigation into the Killing of Four U.S. Churchwomen." *Columbia Human Rights Law Review* 14 (1983).

Quinn, Robert. "Will the Rule of Law End? Challenging Grants of Amnesty for the Human Rights Violations of a Prior Regime: Chile's New Model." *Fordham Law Review* 62 (1994): 905.

Ratner, Steven R., and Jason S. Abrams. *Accountability for Human Rights and Atrocities in International Law: Beyond the Nuremberg Legacy.* Oxford: Clarendon Press, 1997.

Report of the Chilean National Commission on Truth and Reconciliation. Trans. Philip Berryman. Notre Dame: University of Notre Dame Press, 1993.

Richard, Hillary. "The Salvadoran Amnesty Bill." *Human Rights Internet Reporter* 12 (Winter 1988): 71.

Rivera, Sneider, *La Nueva Justicia Penal Juvenil, La Experiencia de El Salvador.* San Salvador: Corte Suprema de Justicia, FESPAD, UNICEF et al., 1998.

Rogers, George C. "Argentina's Obligation to Prosecute Military Officials for Torture." *Columbia Human Rights Law Review* 20 (1989): 259.

Roht-Arriaza, Naomi. *Impunity and Human Rights in International Law.* New York: Oxford University Press, 1995.

——. "State Responsibility to Investigate and Prosecute Grave Human Rights Violations in International Law." *California Law Review* 78 (1990): 451.

Roht-Arriaza, Naomi, and Lauren Gibson. "The Developing Jurisprudence on Amnesty." *Human Rights Quarterly* 20 (1998).

Rosenberg, Tina. "What Did You Do in the War, Mama?" *New York Times Magazine,* February 7, 1999, 52.

Rosenn, Keith S. "The Protection of Judicial Independence in Latin America." *Inter-American Law Review* 19 (1987).

———. "The Success of Constitutionalism in the United States and Its Failure in Latin America: An Explanation." *Inter-American Law Review* 22 (1990).

Salas, Luis, and José María Rico. *Administration of Justice in Latin America: A Primer on the Criminal Justice System.* Miami: Florida International University, Center for the Administration of Justice, 1993.

Sancinetti, Marcelo A. *Derechos Humanos en la Argentina Post Dictatorial.* Buenos Aires: Lerner Editores Asociados, 1988.

Shihata, Ibrahim. "The World Bank." In *Justice Delayed: Judicial Reform in Latin America,* ed. Edmundo Jarquín and Fernando Carrillo. Washington, D.C.: Inter-American Development Bank, 1998.

Stanley, William. *The Protection Racket State: Elite Politics, Military Extortion, and Civil War in El Salvador.* Philadelphia: Temple University Press, 1996.

Stanley, William, and Charles T. Call. "Building a New Civilian Police Force in El Salvador." In *Rebuilding Societies After Civil War: Critical Roles for International Assistance,* ed. Krishna Kumar. Boulder and London: Lynne Rienner Publishers, 1997.

Stephens, Beth, and Michael Ratner. *International Human Rights Litigation in U.S. Courts.* Ardsley: Transnational Publishers, 1996.

Stotzky, Irwin P., ed. *Transition to Democracy in Latin America: The Role of the Judiciary.* Boulder: Westview Press, 1993.

The United Nations and El Salvador 1990–1995. New York: UN Blue Book Series, 1995.

Valladares, Leo. *The Facts Speak for Themselves: Preliminary Report of the Commissioner for Human Rights in Honduras* (trans.). Washington, D.C.: Center for Justice and International Law and Human Rights Watch/Americas, 1994.

Van Dyke, Jon M., and Gerald W. Berkeley. "Redressing Human Rights Abuses." *Denver Journal of International Law and Policy* 2 (1992).

Verbitsky, Horacio. *The Flight: Confessions of an Argentine Dirty Warrior.* New York: New Press, 1996.

Vickers, George. "El Salvador: A Negotiated Revolution." *NACLA Report on the Americas* 25, no. 5 (May 1992).

———. "The Political Reality After Eleven Years of War." In *Is There a Transition to Democracy in El Salvador?* ed. Joseph S. Tulchin and Gary Bland. Woodrow Wilson Center Current Studies on Latin America. Boulder: Lynne Rienner Publishers, 1992.

Weissbrodt, David, and Paul Fraser. "The Report of the Chilean National Commission on Truth and Reconciliation." *Human Rights Quarterly* 14 (1992): 601.

Weschler, Lawrence. *A Miracle, A Universe: Settling Accounts with Torturers.* New York: Pantheon Books, 1990.

Whitfield, Teresa. *Paying the Price.* Philadelphia: Temple University Press, 1994.

———. "Staying the Course in El Salvador." In *Honoring Human Rights: From Peace to Justice—Recommendations to the International Community,* ed. Alice H. Henkin. Washington, D.C.: Aspen Institute, 1998.

Zabel, W. D., D. Orentlicher, and D. E. Nachman. "Human Rights and the Administration of Justice in Chile." *Recordings of the Association of the Bar of the City of New York* 42 (1987).
Zaffaroni, Eugenio Raúl. "Dimensión política de un poder judicial democrático." Comisión Andina de Juristas, Boletín no. 37, June 1993.
———. *Sistemas penales y derechos humanos en América Latina.* San José, Costa Rica: Inter-American Institute for Human Rights, 1986.
Zalaquett, José. "Balancing Ethical Imperatives and Political Constraints: The Dilemma of New Democracies Confronting Past Human Rights Violations." *Hastings Law Journal* 43 (1992): 425.
———. "Confronting Human Rights Violations Committed by Former Governments: Principles Applicable and Political Constraints." In *State Crimes: Punishment or Pardon.* Washington, D.C.: Aspen Institute, 1989.

Reports and Documents

Agency for International Development, Bureau of Latin America and the Caribbean. "Action Plan for Administration of Justice and Democratic Development" (1986).
Americas Watch. *Draining the Sea: Sixth Supplement to the Report on Human Rights in El Salvador.* New York: March 1985.
———. *The Continuing Terror: Seventh Supplement to the Report on Human Rights in El Salvador.* New York: September 1985.
———. *Settling into Routine: Human Rights Abuses in Duarte's Second Year: Eighth Supplement to the Report on Human Rights in El Salvador.* New York: May 1986.
———. *Nightmare Revisited, 1987–88: Tenth Supplement to the Report on Human Rights in El Salvador.* New York: September 1988.
———. *Challenging Impunity: The Ley de Caducidad and the Referendum Campaign in Uruguay,* 1989.
———. *A Year of Reckoning: El Salvador a Decade After the Assassination of Archbishop Romero.* New York: March 1990.
———. *Violation of Fair Trial Guarantees by the FMLN's Ad Hoc Courts.* New York: Human Rights Watch, 1990.
———. *Criminal Injustice: Violence Against Women in Brazil.* New York: Human Rights Watch, 1991.
———. *Chile: The Struggle for Truth and Justice for Past Human Rights Violations.* New York and Washington, D.C.: Human Rights Watch, July 1992.
———. *El Salvador—Peace and Human Rights: Successes and Shortcomings of the United Nations Observer Mission in El Salvador (ONUSAL).* Washington, D.C.: Human Rights Watch, 1992.
———. *El Salvador: Accountability and Human Rights: The Report of the United Nations Commission on the Truth for El Salvador.* Washington, D.C.: Americas Watch—News from the Americas, August 10, 1993.
Americas Watch and American Civil Liberties Union. *Report on Human Rights in El Salvador.* New York: January 26, 1982.
———. *Supplement to the Report on Human Rights in El Salvador.* New York: July 20, 1982.

——. *Third Supplement to the Report on Human Rights in El Salvador.* New York: July 19, 1983.

——. *As Bad as Ever: A Report on Human Rights in El Salvador, Fourth Supplement.* New York: January 31, 1984.

Americas Watch and Lawyers Committee for Human Rights. *Free Fire: A Report on Human Rights in El Salvador, Fifth Supplement.* August 1984.

Amnesty International. "El Salvador Army Officers Sentenced to 30 Years for Killing Jesuit Priests." AMR 37/WU 01/92a5 (February 7, 1992).

Asociación Americana de Juristas. *El Proceso por el Asesinato de los Sacerdotes Jesuitas en El Salvador, Informe del Observador Eduardo Luis Duhalde.* Buenos Aires: November 15, 1991.

Ballasteros Bernales, Enrique, and Roberto Garreton. *Aplicación de las Normas Internacionales de Derechos Humanos.* San Salvador: ONUSAL-PDDH, 1994.

Blair, Harry, and Gary Hansen. *Weighing In on the Scales of Justice: Strategic Approaches for Donor Supported Rule of Law Programs.* Washington, D.C.: USAID, 1994.

Bland, Gary. Conference Report: *El Salvador: Sustaining Peace, Nourishing Democracy.* Washington, D.C.: Woodrow Wilson Center Latin American Program, Washington Office on Latin America, 1993.

Boyce, James K. "Movilización de recursos externos." In *Ajuste Hacia la Paz: La política económica y la reconstrucción de posguerra en El Salvador,* James K. Boyce, coordinator. San Salvador: United Nations Development Program, 1995.

Call, Charles. "El Salvador Peace Plan Update #3: Recent Setbacks in the Police Transition." Washington Office on Latin America, February 1994.

Center for Democracy and Governance, Bureau for Global Programs, Field Support, and Research, U.S. Agency for International Development. *Handbook of Democracy and Government Program Indicators.* Washington, D.C.: Management Systems International, 1998.

Chipoco, Carlos. "El Derecho a la Verdad, un Análisis Comparativo." Paper presented at the 18th LASA International Congress, Atlanta, Georgia, March 1994.

Comisión Andina de Juristas. *Chile: Sistema Judicial y Derechos Humanos.* May 1995.

Comisión de Fortalecimiento de la Justicia. *Una Nueva Justicia para la Paz: Resumen Ejecutivo del Informe Final de la Comisión de Fortalecimiento de la Justicia.* Guatemala, April 1998.

CORELESAL. *Consejo Nacional de la Judicatura.* San Salvador, June 1988.

——. *Problematica de la Administración de la Justicia en El Salvador.* San Salvador, December 1990.

——. *Reformas Inmediatas al Código Procesal Penal.* San Salvador, July 1987.

——. *Terminación de Labores e Información del Trabajo Realizado por la Comisión Revisora de la Legislación Salvadoreña.* San Salvador, October 31, 1991.

Doggett, Martha. "The Assassination of the Jesuits: What the United States Knew." Paper presented at Latin American Studies Association meetings, Atlanta, Georgia, March 10, 1994.

Elusive Justice: The U.S. Administration of Justice Program in Latin America. Report on a workshop sponsored by the American University School of International Service and the Washington Office on Latin America. May 1990.

From Madness to Hope: The 12-Year War in El Salvador. Report of the Truth Commission for El Salvador. Appendix to UN Doc. S/25500, April 1, 1993. San Salvador and New York: United Nations, 1993.

Guatemala: Memory of Silence. Report of the Commission for Historical Clarification, Conclusions and Recommendations. Guatemala City, 1999.

Hammergren, Linn. "El Salvador's National Judicial Council." Paper presented at First Global Rule of Law Conference sponsored by the National Center for State Courts and the U.S. Agency for International Development, Washington, D.C., July 13–15, 1994.

———. "Fifteen Years of Judicial Reform in Latin America: Where We Are and Why We Haven't Made More Progress." http://darkwing.uoregon.edu/~caguirre/hammergren.htm.

Human Rights Watch/Americas. *Chile: Unsettled Business, Human Rights in Chile at the Start of the Frei Presidency.* New York: Human Rights Watch, 1994.

Inter-American Commission on Human Rights. *Report on the Situation of Human Rights in El Salvador.* OEA/Ser.L/V/II.46, doc. 23 rev. 1 (November 17, 1978).

———. *Report on the Situation of Human Rights in El Salvador.* OEA/Ser.L/V/II.85, doc. 23 rev. (February 11, 1994).

International Commission of Jurists. *A Breach of Impunity: The Trial for the Murder of Jesuits in El Salvador. Report of the Observer for the International Commission of Jurists.* Geneva, 1992.

Lawyers Committee for Human Rights. *El Salvador Certification: Summary of the Cases of Ten U.S. Citizens Killed Since 1980.* New York, 1984.

———. *Justice Denied: A Report on Twelve Unresolved Human Rights Cases in El Salvador.* New York: Lawyers Committee for Human Rights, 1985.

———. *El Salvador: Human Rights Dismissed. A Report on Sixteen Unresolved Cases.* New York: Lawyers Committee for Human Rights, 1986.

———. *From the Ashes: A Report on Justice in El Salvador.* New York: Lawyers Committee for Human Rights, 1987.

Lawyers Committee for International Human Rights. *Update: The Case of Four U.S. Churchwomen Murdered in El Salvador in December 1980.* New York, 1984.

Ministerio de Justicia, Dirección General de Asistencia Técnico Jurídica. *La Confesión Extra-judicial.* San Salvador: Ministerio de Justicia, 1993.

Mudge, Arthur, et al. *Evaluation of the Judicial Reform Project No. 519–0296, USAID/El Salvador* (1987).

———. *Reforma Judicial II Evaluación, Informe Final, Reforma Judicial II, Project No. 519–0376.* Washington, D.C.: Management Systems International, January 1997.

Murray, Kevin, et al. *Rescuing Reconstruction: The Debate on Post-War Economic Recovery in El Salvador.* Cambridge, Mass., and San Salvador: Hemisphere Initiatives, May 1994.

Obando, Jorge. "Reform of the Justice Sector." In *Governance and Democratic Development in Latin America and the Caribbean.* New York: United Nations Development Program, 1997.

ONUSAL. "El Habeas Corpus en El Salvador: Aproximación a la Actual Ineficacia." San Salvador, 1993.

Popkin, Margaret. *Waiting for Justice: Treatment of Political Prisoners Under El Salvador's Decree 50.* Washington, D.C.: International Human Rights Law Group, 1987.

———. *El Salvador's Negotiated Revolution: Prospects for Legal Reform.* New York: Lawyers Committee for Human Rights, 1993.

Popkin, Margaret, et al. *Justice Delayed: The Slow Pace of Judicial Reform in El Salvador.* Washington, D.C., and Cambridge, Mass.: Washington Office on Latin America and Hemisphere Initiatives, 1994.

———. *Justice Impugned: The Salvadoran Peace Accords and the Problem of Impunity.* Cambridge, Mass.: Hemisphere Initiatives, 1993.

Sancinetti, Marcelo, Jorge A. Bacqué, and Marco A. Castro Alvarado. *Programa para una estrategia de reforma judicial de US AID.* San Salvador: Checchi and Company Consulting, Inc., March 10, 1991.

Spence, Jack, and David Dye et al. *Chapúltepec: Five Years Later, El Salvador's Political Reality and Uncertain Future.* Cambridge, Mass.: Hemisphere Initiatives, 1997.

Spence, Jack, David R. Dye, and George Vickers, *El Salvador: Elections of the Century.* Cambridge, Mass., and San Salvador: Hemisphere Initiatives, 1994.

Spence, Jack, and George Vickers et al. *A Negotiated Revolution? A Two Year Progress Report on the Salvadoran Peace Accords.* Cambridge, Mass.: Hemisphere Initiatives, 1994.

Spence, Jack, George Vickers, and David Dye. *The Salvadoran Peace Accords and Democratization: A Three Year Progress Report and Recommendations.* Cambridge, Mass., and San Salvador: Hemisphere Initiatives, 1995.

Stanley, William, *Protectors or Perpetrators? The Institutional Crisis of the Salvadoran Civilian Police.* Washington, D.C., and Cambridge, Mass.: Washington Office on Latin America and Hemisphere Initiatives, 1996.

———. *Risking Failure: The Problems and Promise of the New Civilian Police in El Salvador.* Cambridge, Mass.: Hemisphere Initiatives, 1993.

Tamarit, José María. *Informe sobre el proceso judicial por los asesinatos de seis Jesuitas y dos Colaboradoras en El Salvador.* Prepared for Spanish Ministry of Foreign Affairs, 1991.

U.S. AID. *El Salvador Project Paper—Judicial Reform.* AID/LAC/P-175, Project no. 519-0296.

U.S. General Accounting Office. *Foreign Aid: Efforts to Improve the Judicial System in El Salvador.* Report to the Chairman, Subcommittee on Western Hemisphere Affairs, Committee on Foreign Affairs, House of Representatives. GAO/NSIAD–90–81 (May 1990).

———. *Foreign Assistance: Promoting Judicial Reform to Strengthen Democracies.* GAO/NSIAD–93–149 (September 1993).

———. *Foreign Assistance: Rule of Law Funding Worldwide for Fiscal Years 1993–98.* GAO/NSIAD–99–158 (June 1999).

Vickers, George, and Jack Spence et al. *Endgame: A Progress Report on Implementation of the Salvadoran Peace Accords.* Cambridge, Mass.: Hemisphere Initiatives, 1992.

Walker, William Graham. *Justice and Development: A Study.* Washington, D.C: USAID, January 1995.

Weiner, Robert. *A Decade of Failed Promises: The Investigation of Archbishop Romero's Murder.* New York: Lawyers Committee for Human Rights, 1990.

Williams, Jaime, Marco Augusto Sarmiento, and Leopoldo Schiffrin. "Análisis de Identificación de Areas de Reforma Legal y Constitucional." San Salvador: Checchi and Company Consulting, Inc. Presented to USAID El Salvador, June 1991.

Index